Brabham + Ralt + Honda

BRABHAM
RALT
HONDA
The Ron Tauranac Story

Until now, the man whose racing cars have won more victories than anyone else's, and whose design skills have brought fame to hundreds of drivers and made champions of a good many of them, has remained in the background.

Ron Tauranac – British-born, but brought up in Australia – always preferred to let his cars sing his praises where it really mattered – on the race tracks of the world. They have never been known as Tauranacs, but the names Brabham and Ralt will be very familiar to anyone who has followed motor racing since the Sixties. And so, of course, is Honda, the company which supplied the engines for some of Tauranac's most successful Brabham and Ralt racing cars and with which he still retains close links as a design consultant, working behind the scenes on several of their motor racing activities.

Author Mike Lawrence was one of a growing number of people who felt that Ron Tauranac's significant contribution to modern motor racing should be shielded from public view no longer, for there was a fascinating story to be told. It is one which weaves the familiar motor racing fabric of brilliant success laced with occasional bitter disappointment, and it has at its centre a man who throughout his life has never walked when he could run, has at times been insufferably demanding and a pain to work for, but whose skills, dedication to hard work, honesty and integrity have been such that those who have suffered the most from his tongue remain amongst his most fervent admirers.

Sir Jack Brabham, in his foreword to this long overdue biography, pays generous tribute to his former business partner into whose hands he entrusted the design and construction of all his own racing cars from 1962 until his retirement from driving in 1970, plus all the production Brabhams which brought so much success to many other top drivers during their formative years.

Sir Jack himself and his team-mate Denny Hulme both became Formula One World Champions in Tauranac-designed cars, many other drivers have won National and International championships in them, and nearly everyone who sits on a Grand Prix starting grid today has previously been a Ralt driver, along with former stars like Ayrton Senna, Nelson Piquet, Nigel Mansell, Derek Warwick and Martin Brundle.

Many of Ron Tauranac's former colleagues and customers – amongst them the most powerful people in motor racing today – speak candidly about the man they have known and worked with, someone who has never courted popularity, but whose talents have been such that his contribution to the motor racing scene is possibly beyond measure. Anyone who is either involved in the sport or fascinated by it will be delighted that through this book The Ron Tauranac Story has finally been told.

BRABHAM
RALT
HONDA
The Ron Tauranac Story

Mike Lawrence

Foreword by Sir Jack Brabham OBE

Ron Tauranacs contribution to Motor Sport was recognised by the Australian Governor-General in 2001 when he was awarded the prestigious Order of Australia

BROOKLANDS BOOKS LTD
PO BOX 146, Cobham Surrey, KT11 1LG, UK
www.brooklands-books.com

First published 1999 by Motor Racing Publications Ltd.

Copyright © 2010 Brooklands Books Ltd.

All rights reserved. No part of this publication may be reproduced, stored in a retrieval system, or transmitted, in any form or by any means, electronic, mechanical, photocopying, recording or otherwise, without the prior permission of Brooklands Books Ltd.

This edition published jointly by Brooklands Books Ltd and www.VelocePress.com, San Antonio, Texas U.S.A.

British Library Cataloguing in Publication Data

Lawrence, Mike, 1942-
   Brabham+Ralt+Honda : the Ron Tauranac story
    1. Tauranac, Ron 2. Automobiles, Racing 3. Designers – Great Britain –
     Biography
   I. Title
   629.2'28'092 (Original ISBN 1899870 350)

Brooklands Books Ltd ISBN 9781855209237

Typesetting and origination by Jack Andrews Design, Croydon, Surrey

www.brooklands-books.com

WWW.VelocePress.com

Contents

Foreword by Sir Jack Brabham OBE		6
Preface		7
Chapter 1	One-way ticket	9
Chapter 2	Roots and Ralts	14
Chapter 3	Starting a revolution	24
Chapter 4	Emerging from the shadows	32
Chapter 5	Joining the establishment	42
Chapter 6	The Repco connection – 1	51
Chapter 7	So near, so far	54
Chapter 8	The Honda connection – 1	63
Chapter 9	Holding steady	67
Chapter 10	The golden year	76
Chapter 11	The Repco connection – 2	86
Chapter 12	Double World Champions	90
Chapter 13	To finish first ...	97
Chapter 14	Towards the evening	103
Chapter 15	The last days	109
Chapter 16	Interlude	120
Chapter 17	Ralt revived	126
Chapter 18	Treading water	134
Chapter 19	The Honda connection – 2	137
Chapter 20	Formula Ralt	140
Chapter 21	Champions!	151
Chapter 22	Changing times	164
Chapter 23	Decline and fall	172
Chapter 24	Mad March days	179
Chapter 25	Free agent	188
Appendix A	Ron Tauranac's design philosophy for production racing cars	191
Appendix B	The first Ralts	196
Appendix C	The MRD/Brabhams	198
Appendix D	MRD/Brabham racing record, 1962-72	208
Appendix E	Freelance Tauranac designs, 1973-78	238
Appendix F	The later Ralts	239
Appendix G	MRD/Ralt racing record, 1975-97	244
Appendix H	The post-Ralt Tauranac cars	256

Foreword

Ron Tauranac and I go back a long way – about half a century in fact – to when we competed in hillclimbs in New South Wales. Not many people know that Ron's earliest successes in motorsport were as a driver, or perhaps I should say driver-constructor, because like a lot of people at that time, he competed in a car he had built himself. He called it a Ralt – a combination of his own and his brother's initials.

Although we were formidable competitors on the tarmac, we quickly became friends away from it and developed a healthy mutual regard, as much for each other's down-to-earth engineering approach as for our competitive instincts. In particular I was impressed with the breadth of Ron's practical knowledge and skills, also with his often innovative design ideas.

When my own racing career broadened internationally and, thanks to John Cooper, I was able to join the Cooper team in England, I kept in close contact with Ron with a regular flow of correspondence.

But I felt that Ron also needed to be back in England – where he had been born – if his talents were to be exploited to the full, and in 1960, when I decided the time had come for me to build, race and sell my own cars, I finally persuaded him to come over and join me in a formal partnership.

As a result, he is inevitably best known to many people as the designer and constructor of a long series of Brabham BT racing cars, but this was just an episode – admittedly an important one, especially for me! – in Ron's long and still active career in motorsport, where his versatility and experience are still much in demand.

Over the years he has never sought the limelight, so I am glad that he has finally agreed for his biography to be written and published. He has deserved far more credit than he has received for his many race-winning cars. The trouble is, Ron never shouted about what he had done or was capable of doing; he preferred to just put his head down and do it. This book will help to put the record straight.

Many racing drivers have good reason to thank him for giving them the cars with which to progress their careers. But so have the people who have passed through his hands and gone on to become racecar designers and engineers in their own right. He was a demanding employer, and at times he operated with a short fuse, but he provided a magnificent training ground because he understood the practical side of motor racing better than anyone else, and this, combined with his engineering knowledge and plain commonsense, has made him the world's most successful designer of production racing cars. The history of the cars reflect the man.

So I am more than pleased to be paying this tribute to my longtime friend and former business partner, and delighted that the size of his contribution, not just to my own racing career, but to that of hundreds of others, has finally been put on record.

SIR JACK BRABHAM, OBE

Preface

In the early 1980s a distinguished former racing driver sat on the awards committee of the Ferodo Trophy, which was presented annually for the most important technical contribution to the sport, and he'd canvass opinion from some of his friends. Every year I would say that Ron Tauranac should get the trophy, and every year he would say: 'But it's not Formula One, is it?'

Each year I would patiently explain that Formula One is not the be-all and end-all of motor racing and that a guy whose cars had just won every Formula Three race in Britain, and most of those abroad, should be in the frame because building customer cars that are consistent winners is one of the hardest jobs in the world. You can survive for 20 years in Formula One without winning a race (ask Arrows) yet to survive as a production car maker means you have to win week-in, week-out.

Further, each year I would say that Ron had been doing it longer and better than anyone else, and let's also not forget that his cars have won Formula One World Championships.

Ron never did get the Ferodo Trophy, but I lobbied for him three years straight. And Ron continued to do the business better than anyone else long after I made my last pitch for him.

Ron Tauranac is an unglamorous figure. You do not hear stories of how he pulled off this stroke or that scam, how he went bankrupt and bounced back with a different letterhead. In fact, there has never been a whiff of scandal around him. He has never been one to court the press, and therefore he has never impinged on the motor racing public as a personality.

He is a deeply honourable man, one could almost call him ascetic. Had he been a mediaeval monk (and if Ron had been born in the 14th Century he would surely have been a monk) one could imagine him badgering the Prior to replace the straw in the palliasses with rock and suggesting that prayer is more meaningful at three in the morning rather than idling in bed until four.

You hear stories about how he is difficult to work with, how he is a workaholic, how he doesn't suffer fools gladly. One of his friends said: 'I've seen people get on his wrong side and he's swallowed them whole and spat them out before they've known what's happening to them.'

Since Ron used to do most of his testing at Goodwood, which is on my doorstep, I saw a great many of his test sessions in the late 1970s and early 1980s. I spoke to Ron just once. I asked him a question, he snapped back a answer and I didn't speak to him again for 10 years, and even then it was an uneasy meeting. I was writing a book on March, and as Ron's company had been taken over by March, he had been coerced into giving me half an hour.

Another eight years went by before I spoke to him for a third time. A mutual friend, Tony McCaffrey, had seen my book on March, had presumably liked it, and after working on him for about a year had finally persuaded Ron that it was time that his story was told. This was how one day I came to hear Ron's voice on the end of my telephone. We agreed to meet, and I found a very different man to the one I had expected.

Ron is a shy man, which partly explains his persona, but he has a dry sense of humour. He is also very thoughtful and inherently kind. One thing which few people know is just how bright he is. I move in academic circles, and when I wear my mortar board I come into contact with world-class scholars, but I have never encountered a mind which is sharper than Ron's. He slices to the core of problems.

He once told me that his main difficulty when undertaking evening classes was writing reports because his were always deemed to be too brief. I have read some of them and all I can say is that they are exemplars of succinct prose. There is not a wasted word and they all read well. I am not an engineer. If WD-40 doesn't fix a problem with my car, then it's a call to the AA. Like all good engineers, however, Ron has the ability to explain complex ideas in a simple way.

I have always admired the man, but when I started this project I did not realize quite how remarkable his achievement has been. He has a reputation for being an arch-conservative, but he is nothing of the sort. Let's not forget that it was Ron Tauranac, not Colin Chapman, who first ran a Formula One car with wings at a Grand Prix meeting.

Ron is the most successful designer of racing cars in history – and even in 1998 about half the drivers who lined up on the Formula One grids had driven Ron's cars at some stage in their careers.

The two biggest problems when writing this book have been deciding what to leave out and knowing how to end it, because it is an on-going story.

Mike Lawrence
Chichester
1998

Thank you all

Ron Tauranac joins the author and publisher in thanking all his friends, former and current colleagues, customers and motor racing associates for their verbal, written and photographic contributions to this book, even those who have felt that a touch of tongue-lashing by way of retribution was perhaps in order. Ron also wishes to acknowledge the many hundreds of drivers and team owners who were his loyal customers over so many years and whose skill with his cars has contributed so much to this story.

1

One-way ticket

In April 1960, Ron Tauranac flew into Heathrow airport from Australia. He was 35 years old and had a wife and young daughter to support. He had reached an age when most people are considering their promotion prospects at work and perhaps thinking of moving to a bigger house or buying a better car. He had all that for the taking, but he chose instead to uproot and move to England to become a racing car designer.

These days that would be seen as a positive move bearing in mind that the best racing car designers can command salaries the size of the GNP of a Third World country, but go back to 1960 – who, then, designed racing cars? Apart from in a few mainstream companies which operated competition departments – though usually on an occasional basis – most designers were people like John Cooper and Colin Chapman, who had evolved from building specials.

Cooper and Lotus both employed draughtsmen, but they were just that – draughtsmen, not designers. The idea of setting out to be a designer from scratch was, to say the least, novel. So Ron was taking a step into the unknown at a time when motor racing had yet to establish its own industry.

Today, bright graduates can move straight from university to companies like Reynard or Lola or even one of the Formula One teams. In 1960 the sport was supported by a few pockets of activity, but they did not add up to an industry. If you wanted alloy wheels, you designed them yourself and arranged to have them cast. If you wanted a gearbox, you adapted a road car unit.

However, a few little firms were just setting up: here you could get a fuel tank made, there you could get gears cut. The embryo industry largely consisted of one-man outfits which were long on skill, but short on tooling, and operated from lock-ups and the arches under railway bridges. High-profile it was not. Also, you had to be in the swim because there were no trade directories to guide you, and Ron was a stranger in England. Furthermore, because he was arriving as Jack Brabham's secret weapon, he was discouraged from making himself known.

Back home, Ron had a reputation both as a racing driver and as an ingenious engineer, but Australian motor racing was primitive by European standards – it was a place where obsolete cars were sent to enjoy a new lease of life. So there was no way of knowing whether he could make a mark in a different environment, where he would have to measure up to the likes of Ferrari, BRM, Lotus, Cooper, Porsche, Elva, Lola, and dozens of other well-established competitors.

Ron stepped on to the tarmac at Heathrow with a simple brief – he had to be better than all these companies, plus Jaguar, and Aston Martin and all the others. It is a thought which should be savoured. Like a story from *Boys' Own Paper* – the kid from nowhere who runs the sub-three-minute mile and then swims the Atlantic before climbing Everest the hard way – backwards.

Australia was then a place you could emigrate to for £10 on an assisted passage – provided you were white and British. Apart from a few tennis players, a couple of kids' TV shows and Chips Rafferty, the all-purpose Aussie actor, nothing much had come from Australia apart from frozen mutton. In 1960, Earls Court was just a run-down part of West London. It was not yet Sydney-across-the-ocean and the spiritual home of the secondhand VW Caravanette with *Afghanistan or Bust!* writ large on the side.

Unlike most people who came to look for a place on the British motor racing scene, however, Ron did have one big asset, he had flown into Heathrow with Jack Brabham, the reigning World Champion. Jack had been racing a Cooper Monaco sports car in the United States and Ron had broken his journey there to help him with it. The two friends flew the final leg together and Jack put Ron up until he could find a place of his own.

Jack, indeed, had sent him the return air fare so, if things didn't work out, Ron could at least go home and pick up the threads of his former life. Not wishing to be parted from his family, however, Ron had bought a single air ticket and booked passages on a ship for his wife, Norma, and his daughter, Jann. When you're offered a return fare for yourself, but you choose a single and bring the family, you must have made up your mind.

Jack says: 'I wasn't happy with the way things were going at Cooper. It didn't seem to me that they were going forwards, but I knew Ron and I trusted him. I wouldn't have set up with anyone else.'

In retrospect, it might seem that Ron could not go far wrong. When a World Champion buys you a ticket, you go. If a World Champion offers you a partnership, you accept. Of course you accept. At the beginning of 1960, however, things were not that clear-cut. Jack may have been the World Champion, but being World Formula One Champion was no big deal at the time. Motor racing was a sub-sport.

To put it into perspective, the main media coverage of sport in 1959 was *Sports Report* on the BBC Light Programme – 5.00 to 5.58pm on a Saturday. That's when there was a hush in the house as Father sweated over his football pool predictions. We're talking about radio, of course.

The World Championship was then so unimportant that, when Jack Brabham pushed his car over the line to take the 1959 title, the report from America (the last item in *Sports Report*) was interrupted to bring us the final score in a Third Division soccer match.

Apart from the fact that motor racing was less important than Accrington Stanley in the wider world, within the sport itself, many people thought that Brabham had been lucky to win the title. He'd been with Cooper, the pundits said, and he wasn't half the driver that Moss or Brooks was, not to mention the new guys: McLaren, Surtees and Clark.

Certainly Jack had been lucky in so far as he had been in the right place at the right time. Cooper had shown that a mid-engined car was superior, but Cooper had itself lucked-in to the concept. John Cooper says that if the V8 Coventry Climax FPE Godiva engine had been made available in 1954 he would have built a Formula One car then and it would have been front-engined.

The mid-engined revolution had begun when the 1,098cc Coventry Climax FWA engine became available and Cooper had built a sports car to use it. John Cooper knew that it needed an efficient body and a friend of his worked for the Hawker Aircraft Company. This chap suggested that the body which had been designed for a 500cc Cooper record-breaker would do the trick if the tail was chopped.

Being of the 'suck it and see' school of engineering, Cooper built a chassis to fit beneath the body, and since the body was curved, so was the multi-tubular chassis – it was not a proper spaceframe. The little car worked, despite its crude engineering, but it is unlikely that anyone at Cooper knew precisely why it worked.

Jack, however, did understand why the Cooper worked, which is why he wrote to Ron enclosing some crude drawings, outlining some ideas for an improved rear suspension, whereupon Ron responded with solutions. The Tauranac contribution to the Cooper story has never before been documented.

When the 1½-litre Formula Two arrived in 1957, Cooper took one of its central-seat sports cars, narrowed the frame and converted it into an open-wheeled monoposto. A lot of people thought it should never have worked – Colin Chapman called Charlie and John Cooper 'blacksmiths' – but work it did. And when it received bigger and more powerful engines it proved good enough to win Grands Prix.

But this was while everyone else – including Lotus – was running front-engined cars, and by the beginning of 1960, Lotus had shown what could be done with a mid-engined car designed with a modicum of science. Even as Ron was stepping off the plane, it looked as though the days of Cooper's success were numbered, and as Cooper's fortunes declined so, surely, Jack's would decline with them.

What few people appreciated, however, was just how good Jack Brabham really was. Much of his success had been down as much to his ability as an engineer as to his sheer speed behind the wheel. At a time when mechanics would set up a car by pushing down hard on the tail and seeing how many times it bounced on its springs, Jack applied engineering to his set-ups.

If you want to know how versatile Jack was, as well as how quick he was, then consider this: whenever Formula Two is mentioned, Jochen Rindt's name inevitably crops up, along with the phrase, 'The Uncrowned King of Formula Two'. Jochen was magic in Formula Two, which was where he proved himself, racing on equal terms with his greatest rivals. Altogether he won 31 F2 races, to the 13 of Jim Clark – and the 27 of Jack Brabham. Pound to a penny, that fact surprised you. Most of Rindt's wins were in a Brabham; Jack never raced a Rindt!

At the opening round of the 1960 World Championship, in Argentina, Innes Ireland demonstrated the speed of the Lotus 18, and it shook everyone to the core. When the Cooper team returned to Surbiton, Jack got together with his team-mate, Bruce McLaren and, with John Cooper and Cooper's draughtsman, Owen Maddock, designed a new car. They put a seat on the workshop floor, took tubes from a rack and laid out the concept with chalk marks. Then Owen Maddock went away to draw it.

Nobody outside that tight circle knew that Jack was corresponding with Ron who had sent guidelines for the wishbone suspension, just as he had quietly produced other systems for Jack to use at Cooper. John Cooper knew all about Ron long before Ron rented a flat a few hundred yards from the Cooper factory!

The result of the factory floor exercise was the 'Lowline' Cooper T53 which took Brabham and Cooper to their respective World Championships in 1960, a feat which included winning five races in succession, something which no driver/car combination had done since Alberto Ascari with Ferrari in 1952.

In 1961, when Britain ran an Intercontinental Championship for 3-litre cars and Stirling Moss had the choice of a Cooper or a Lotus, he chose the Cooper. Brabham won two of the races and Moss the other three, but it was Jack and Ron's car which won all five.

Stirling chose to drive the Lotus in Formula One because it better suited the 1½-litre formula, but with the big engine, the Cooper was clearly the superior car. Not only was it more comfortable to drive, but there was also a small power advantage because unlike Cooper, Lotus had chosen to cant the engine over to reduce its height and had suffered a power loss through inadequate oil scavenging arrangements. You might say that this was the first time that Ron Tauranac defeated Colin Chapman, although it would not be the last.

Back home in Australia, any car which came from Europe was regarded as exotic. When Jack arrived in England in 1955, however, he could see the true picture. Cooper was a fairly basic operation, but it was a paragon compared to some of the cars which were running in the 1950s. Names like Lister, Kieft, HWM and Tojeiro have resonated down the years, but they were little more than special builders whose reputations were boosted by uncritical articles which appeared in the British motoring press.

Jack had seen Cooper from the inside and knew that he could do better. Racing drivers are not noted for being loose with money, and Jack was considered tight even by other racing drivers, but he knew a good deal when he saw one This is why he sent Ron the money for his air fare, offered him a partnership in a company they would jointly establish and, in the meantime, guaranteed to pay him £30 a week for other work.

Thirty pounds was a good wage for the day, it was what Ron had been earning as a works manager in Australia, and was twice the average wage in Britain at the time. So if coming to England was an act of faith on the part of Ron and Norma Tauranac, making it possible was equally an act of faith on the part of Jack Brabham. He was prepared to put his future in the hands of a man who had designed a few specials, mainly for 500cc racing, a category which had been virtually defunct in Britain for four years. Today, you might liken it to Schumacher, Prost, Hill or Villeneuve setting up a new team having plucked a designer from Formula Ford. It would only work if it was the right designer and we're talking long odds. Hundreds of people have designed or helped to design a racing car, but only a tiny handful have made a difference.

Until Jack brought in Ron via his letters, every Cooper had been a development of the one before and, as late as the customer cars of 1960, there was still evidence of the very first special, the car which came about when Charles and John had taken the front suspension from two scrap Fiat Topolini and built a frame to keep them apart and to hang bits on.

Tauranac, however, was different. He was perhaps the first postwar designer to have investigated the principles of car design and behaviour before sitting down to design his first car. Colin Chapman had a reputation for originality, but even his cars evolved and, in the early days, he was surrounded by brilliant volunteers who had been drawn in by the Chapman charisma, but whose very real contributions were to be largely unsung.

Ron, however, had worked alone and always from first principles. He designed his first car in 1949 for 500cc racing and, with its driver located far to the front and its swing-axle rear suspension, it predated the layout of designs which later would threaten Cooper's pre-eminence in Formula Three.

Tauranac has acquired a reputation for conservatism when, in fact, it is pragmatism. Long before he sat down to draw his car, he had studied the whole area of automotive design. He read voraciously, and he still recalls his delight at seeing the HMSO document on the prewar Mercedes-Benz and Auto Union cars. Then he learned the hard way, by driving his cars, crashing them, rebuilding them and developing them. He enjoyed what he was doing, but little did he know that he would design more race-winning cars over a longer period than anyone else in history. And why not? After all, he had prepared himself for the task in a way that nobody else had done before.

Nevertheless, as he stepped off the plane at Heathrow, Ron Tauranac knew he was stepping into the unknown.

2

Roots and Ralts

Tauranac is a French name and one of Ron's distant ancestors was a Huguenot who had fled murder at the hands of Roman Catholics in 16th century France. A Tauranac who meets another Tauranac anywhere in the world is likely to be a distant cousin.

Ronald Sidney Tauranac was born in England in 1925 in Gillingham, Kent, but when he was three, his father, who had been a boilermaker in the naval dockyard at Chatham, took his family to Australia in search of work and a better life. Yet Ron has spent more of his life in England than in Australia. He has two passports, British and Australian, and caught off-guard he will say he is English. But he'll also say: 'It depends on which is the most convenient at the time.' And on other occasions he'll say: 'You think of your home as the place where you grew up.' And again: 'I pay my taxes in Britain, so I must be British.' Ron's accent, however, is definitely not from modern England because those 40 years back in his home country have not erased the Aussie twang.

Tauranac Senior had a sister who had married an Australian serviceman during the First World War and settled in Melbourne, so that's where the family headed, but economic recession was spreading worldwide and would soon catch up with the Tauranacs.

Life was not easy in those early days and, to chase work, the family moved from Melbourne to Newcastle, then to Fassifern, 80 miles north of Sydney. There was a period when Ron's father had to work away from home, down in Tasmania. Some of the family's bright hopes for a new future took a battering and the hardships they endured have shaped Ron's attitude to money ever since.

By the time Ron was five he was attending a little two-room school house (there were just two teachers to cover the six classes) where the pupils might arrive on foot, or bicycle, or even on horseback. Money was short, but it was an ideal place to spend your childhood. 'There was the bush to play in, and creeks to swim in,' Ron recalls, ' . . . I didn't wear shoes until I was 12, except on an occasional trip to Sunday school.'

Ron was an enterprising youngster. He made model aeroplanes and sold them through a shop. He made a canoe by hammering out corrugated iron sheets, then he made some decking from old boxes, added some sails and turned it into a dinghy. He started a little business by selling these boats to his friends, who bought them on credit, paying a few pennies a week.

School was OK, there were no problems and it seems he passed all his exams without making any particular effort, or being particularly stimulated by school. By the time he was 12, family prospects were looking up. They'd moved yet again, this time to Woollongong, 50 miles south of Sydney. At his new school, Ron was able to enrol in a pre-apprenticeship class, which taught woodwork, metalwork and drawing. When he left school, aged 14, he drifted through a few jobs and then was told that his application to be a junior draughtsman with the Commonwealth Aircraft Corporation in Sydney had been accepted. To support him, the whole family moved to the city. By then the war had started and there was no shortage of work.

Commonwealth Aircraft made Pratt & Witney engines under licence, so by day Ron drew jigs and tooling, and in the evenings he continued his studies at a technical college, successfully completing diplomas.

A friend lent him a book on communism and, for a time, he was attracted by it. But these days he is a man who is more likely to consider issues individually rather than accept any particular party platform, although he is interested in politics generally and in the ways of the world. Similarly, his inquiring mind has not encouraged him to follow any particular form of religion. With faultless logic he says: 'If you want to be religious, how do you know which religion to choose?'

Typical of his approach to the concerns of society is: 'We are told there is a water shortage and yet we're losing masses of water through our 100-year-old mains system. So why not do something really simple, like pass a law which says that every new lavatory should have a short flush, for when you take a leak, as well as a long flush? I moved into my present apartment at the end of 1996. It was brand new and it has every mod con, yet it doesn't have this simple device which, fitted to every new lavatory, could save millions of gallons of water every day.'

As well as Ron's attendance at academic evening classes, he also learned ballroom dancing, which was unusually difficult for him because he has no ear for music and he dances more or less by rote. According to one eye-witness – former Grand Prix driver John Watson – Ron is a very good dancer. Norma Tauranac says: 'He did it by numbers. I think Ron has done a lot of things by numbers, like when he learned to ski and when he took up golf. He's a good ballroom dancer, but I still have to tell him whether it's a foxtrot or a jazz waltz!'

Learning how to dance, however, was part of Ron's intention to improve himself. A man who has always believed in filling every hour, Ron also enjoyed sport – he was a useful middle-distance runner – and he is still spare of frame, probably because he diets carefully and swims every day when he is at home.

As a teenager Ron joined the air cadets, which filled weekends and sometimes evenings. It also meant that, although he was in a protected wartime occupation, he was able to argue his way into joining the Royal Australian Air Force, where he was accepted for training as a fighter pilot.

But the longer the war went on, and the more successful the Allies became, the less urgent became the need for new pilots, so Ron spent a great deal of time being trained, mainly on Harvards and Wirraways, an Australian fighter. His training was continually extended so he never did see action, and he was allowed to apply for an early discharge. That was a stroke of luck because he was able to start a new job in Civvy Street on VJ Day instead of kicking his heels in a camp for months waiting to be demobbed.

Ron left the RAAF as a Flight Sergeant – there had been too many skirmishes with authority for him to be commissioned. There was the time, during training on Harvards in Canada, when he had indulged in some low-level aerobatics, which got him banged up in the guardhouse for two weeks. Then there was the time when his leave was cancelled, he thought unfairly, so he took it anyway. That led to a second Court Martial.

He applied to be a commercial pilot, but of course at that time there was a glut of pilots. Ron had more than 400 flying hours to his credit on single-engined planes, much of it at a very advanced level, but nobody got a look in unless they had at least 4,000 hours on four-engined planes. He has not flown an aircraft since.

Like many an ex-serviceman returning to civilian life, he found that those who had remained in their protected occupations now held a decisive advantage in career prospects, so he enrolled for some evening courses in business management and psychology at the Sydney Technical School. These served him well not only for finding himself a better job but, later on, when he began to run his own companies.

His first job in the new phase of his life was as a draughtsman with the Eagle and Globe Steel Company, which imported metal from Britain. It is an important piece in the jigsaw because it gave him a grasp of metallurgy. Then he moved on to a small machining company where he was an estimator, commissioning work from subcontractors. This meant he got out and about and, when he was 24, he even got his first car, an Austin Seven.

One Sunday he was out in his Austin when he heard an interesting noise. He investigated and found a handful of enthusiasts running impromptu races on the Marsden Park airstrip. Ron watched them for hours and became hooked. He made some inquiries and this led to him meeting the Hooper brothers, Jack and William, who were motorcycle dealers and engine tuners in Sydney and had just built a car for the new 500cc racing category. Ron and the Hoopers became friends.

He also discovered that there was a 500 Car Club so, fired up, he attended its next meeting. He found that while there was a lot of talk about building 500cc cars, nobody appeared to be doing much building. Given Ron's temperament, this was a spur.

During the War a number of enthusiasts in Britain had been discussing what form postwar motor racing should take. Correspondence in *Motor Sport* had thrown up the idea of building cars using 500cc motorcycle engines – they'd be cheap, yet should be capable of the magic 'ton'. More than that, they could provide motor racing for the man in the street, not just for the well-heeled.

Ron set out to join in the fun, but first he haunted the Mitchell Library in Sydney during his lunch breaks, mugging up on anything to do with car design. He also bought, examined and sold a number of road cars in order to learn from them. He traded the Austin Seven for a 1928 Lea-Francis, and with his younger brother, Austin Lewis Tauranac, who was running a one-man garage business at the time, he took it apart to see what made it tick. They then reassembled it, made it into a going concern and sold it on at a profit. The money helped finance the first Ralts.

Ron recalls: 'I went through several cars, including a Morris Minor. It had an engine with an overhead camshaft and you'd think that an overhead camshaft should be better than side valves. I can tell you it wasn't. There wasn't anything clever about any of the cars I bought.

'I went back to papers and articles written from the 1920s onwards and found that most of the important discoveries had been made prewar. During these years, the designers had experimented for the first time with ideas which were radically different from the notions which sprang up with the early days of the car industry.'

When he had absorbed all that the library could offer, Ron sat down and designed and built his car. It had a chassis-frame made from 2-inch tubing, double-wishbone front suspension, and short swing-axles at the rear with an underslung transverse leaf spring. At first the car was fitted with 19-inch wire wheels from an old Morris.

The first Ralt (Ron and Austin Lewis Tauranac) Special was built in a rented lock-up with no more than the tools you'll find in most people's sheds. Even so, virtually every part of the car, with the exception of items like universal joints, was made by Ron from scratch. Austin helped in areas like the electrics and setting the carburettors, which were his speciality. He recalls that he and Ron, who were still living at home at the time, assembled the components in the bedroom they shared and then they were all brought together when they could obtain the lock-up.

Ron recalls: 'I made two fundamental mistakes on that car. One was that I put the seating position too far forward, and the other was that I used swinging half-axles at the rear. The seating position gave me a theoretically correct weight distribution, but it also made the car much harder to drive because you just didn't get enough warning when the back end broke away.

'The engine was virtually home-made. It was based on a 1937 Norton ES2 pushrod unit. I found that fitting the camshafts from a Norton WD side-valve engine gave me the valve timing I wanted. Over time, we made a new crankcase, fitted a locally made piston, which gave a 14:1 compression ratio, and ran it on methanol with an Amal carburettor. Originally it had a cast-iron flywheel, but I made a steel one, which Jack Brabham machined for me, and then we played around with new barrels and, eventually, it was enlarged from 500cc to 600cc. I learned about engines from that.'

The Ralt Special made its competition debut on November 20, 1950 in the Hawkesbury hillclimb, and it was very nearly both the beginning and the end of Ron's motor racing career. He'd had to count every penny, so although the car had taken the best part of two years to build, it still wasn't quite complete because it was still lacking its shock absorbers; Ron's decision to run it without shockers nearly cost him his life. The novice racing driver, whose driving experience until then had been confined to prewar saloons, found that handling a purpose-built single-seater was rather different. On his first run, the Ralt, which had already given him a few frights in the first corners, ran wide, hit a drainage gully and flipped. Ron was thrown out and was taken to hospital to be stitched together.

Meanwhile, Austin had been building a Ford E93A-engined Ralt 1100, which later caused such a favourable impression that the magazine *Australian Motor Sports* featured it in a two-page spread. The article said: 'The frame and suspension were designed from first principles by Ron Tauranac, who is a draftsman (sic) by trade and an automobile engineer by inclination.'

The Ralt 1100 (see Appendix One for details) was a deceptively simple cycle-winged sports car and Austin had carpeted the floor, trimmed the interior in leather and even had 'Ralt' engraved on the steering wheel boss. It was this attention to detail and pursuit of excellence which would see Austin progress from his one-man garage business ultimately to become head of Saab in Australia.

The article commented on the 'hairsbreadth' accuracy of its steering and said that 'main road corners just don't exist,' while the fuel consumption for a normal trip by road was 'in the vicinity of 60mpg.' The Ralt 1100 was used by Austin as a road car, but it was well prepared and tuned and when it appeared in club competitions it could see off MG TCs, which were then considered to be exotica by Australian standards. In one sprint event it even returned a time identical to Ron's single-seater.

It was an excellent car, but the problem for the Tauranac brothers was lack of money. They were still making their way in life and everything had to be paid for from their modest wages. Then in late 1950 Austin married, and soon afterwards the Ralt 1100 was sold.

When Ron had recovered from his crash at Hawkesbury, he repaired his car, fitted shock absorbers, stiffened the rear springs, and took it back to the hill. He set some impressive times during practice, but on his first competitive run, one of the back wheels tucked in under the car and again the Ralt flipped. For the second time, Ron might have been killed, but fortunately the tail finished up on a guardrail, just beyond which was a sheer drop off the side of a mountain . . .

So Ron had been lucky once again and this time he came away from his brush with eternity with nothing worse than abrasions and a broken bone in his right hand. He says: 'Until then, fast driving had looked to me to be a piece of cake, but after two prangs from two starts I was not so sure!' One of Ron's friend's says: 'If you'd been there on Ron's first two runs, you would not have said, "Yes! That man is the next Ettore Bugatti!"'

A shackle on the rear spring had broken and caused the wheel to fold under the car since the spring was the main location medium. With his hand in plaster, Ron went back to the drawing board and worked away on improving the suspension of his car. After two big accidents, he had plenty of incentive to do so.

Although he'd mugged up on the theory of design, the actuality was another matter. It was the combination of lessons learned in the library and those learned on the track that moulded Ron into a designer. It also shaped his philosophy as a builder because none of his future production cars could ever be described as fragile. In fact, they became a by-word for dependability.

Ron says of that first Ralt: 'I raced it in quarter-mile sprints and I got the Australian record for the standing-quarter in it, I drove it in hillclimbs and, once a month, we raced on an airstrip at Mount Druitt on a course which used the runways and a wiggly bit up a hill. There weren't many factory-built cars, apart from prewar machinery, but there were a lot of Ford V8 specials.

'Usually we ran in handicaps, which was a bit unfortunate for me because I was among the quickest qualifiers, so I used to have to start from the back. There was no way I could pass the V8 cars along the straights and you couldn't pass anyone on the twisty bits.

'In 1951, Jack Brabham put a *For Sale* advertisement in a local paper for a Velocette motorcycle engine and I went to see it. I saw he had a nice little machine shop so I asked him if he'd do some machining for me. He said "No," because he thought I meant machining on racing cars, but this was not what I had in mind. I meant him doing some subcontracting for the company I was working for, and of course that was different. I put work his way and our relationship grew from that.'

John Arthur Brabham was a skilled mechanic who had also served in the RAAF. Afterwards he had dealt in secondhand motorcycles and made enough money to open his own small engineering business. By the time Ron met him, Jack had won State, Regional and National Championships in midget racing cars and was already something of a celebrity. The driving style he developed on the speedway tracks – hunched over the wheel with the tail hung out – would remain with him throughout his career. Critics in England, when they saw it, labelled it 'the blacksmith style of driving', but none of them would win three World Championships.

Ron continues: 'My job meant that I had flexible hours, so I could time my trips to arrive at Jack's workshop at lunchtime, then he'd allow me the use of his equipment to machine bits.

'By then I was working for CSR Chemicals, which was a subsidiary of Colonial Sugar Refining, one of the three biggest companies in Australia, and they were building a new plant to make plastics. I was one of about 50 draughtsmen employed on the job, and when we'd done the drawings they selected four of us to go out and subcontract people to build the plant. It was new work to Australia because it was all in stainless steel, and one of the things that we required was stainless steel castings for things like the valves.

'I was subcontracting work to a company called Quality Castings, but they were on a learning curve. That led to me taking an interest in casting and I developed systems to produce accurate castings to a consistent standard. That did me no harm with the company and later it also stood me in good stead with my business in motor racing.

'When interviewing job candidates I'll often ask them how they would cast something. Not many designers have much experience of casting, but it is important if you are going to be cost effective. From casting it's a short leap to body moulds because there too you have to consider practical things like split lines and you also have to consider what it will cost to make. Maybe it doesn't matter in Formula One, but you have to do it down to a price in production racing cars.

'By the time I was subcontracting work to Quality Castings, I was already making and selling my own cast alloy wheels. The only sort you could buy otherwise were skinny motorcycle wheels or very heavy car wheels, and we needed a 13-inch wheel which would take as wide a tyre as we could get. I had the rims spun in steel in two halves, which were then welded together and bolted to an aluminium alloy centre-section.'

Jack says: 'I think it was the wheels which made me realize that Ron was out of the ordinary. Midget racing was pretty rough, but if I bent a wheel which Ron had made it was only the steel outer section and that was easily replaced. The centre-section was made of a heat-treated aluminium alloy and it never ever broke. People used Ron's wheels for years.' More than 45 years later, Jack not only remembers the wheels, but the precise alloy from which they were made – AA226, or LM11 in Europe.

Ron continues: 'In 1953, when the chemical plant was finished, I was offered a job as a shift superintendent with CSR, which was fine for a while because it enabled me to work at night and spend time during the day on my racing cars.

'The war had interrupted my studies, but CSR had taken me on as a draughtsman and had given me a load of opportunities – from designing the plant to building it. That was good because I could see how a business was run from the ground up. People liked working for CSR, it was a good company, which paid its bills on time, and everyone was approachable. Just by being there you could pick up a lot of things, like the way books were kept, and that gave me a sound grounding in running a business.'

Paying your bills on time is central to Ron's philosophy. Say to him: 'What about so-and-so?' and he might reply: 'He's good company, but I hear that he doesn't pay his bills.' You say: 'I hear that Charlie Whippingtop is doing well,' and he'll say: 'Now he'll be able to pay his bills.'

One reason why Ron did so well in business is that he paid his subcontractors on the dot, to the penny, which is why Brabham, and later Ralt, invariably got priority over everyone else. Lotus used to spend as much creative energy in thinking up excuses for non-payment as went into the engineering of their cars.

It would be easy to say that this attitude to always paying his way was a result of the privations his family had suffered when he was young. No doubt that had an influence, but it goes much deeper than that. It is all a matter of integrity, something for which in engineering terms his cars have always been admired. In this respect they have been expressions of Ron's own personality.

He continues: 'The shift work at the chemical plant eventually caused me to leave CSR because I'd just got married and my wife, Norma, wasn't too happy with the arrangement.' Ron had thought he'd always be a bachelor, but he met Norma Dixon at a dance in 1952, proposed six months later, and they were married in June 1953. They are still married.

Norma says: 'The first thing that impressed me about Ron was his dancing, then we got to like each other. Then Ron took me home to meet his mother. I think she'd accepted that he was destined to be a bachelor. He had taken girls home before, but I believe I was the first one his mother approved of, and I think that counted with him.'

Meanwhile, Ron adjusted to his new situation, and that included a change of lifestyle. 'I'd been burning the candle at both ends. During our courtship I'd only been able to see Norma on a Saturday night, and things really came to a head when Jack and I did the first Redex Trial in 1953.

'This was an endurance event across the outback. We had a specially prepared Holden and Jack did most of the driving, with me navigating. I'd take over the wheel on the easier sections, and Jack would just fall asleep. He's got this gift of being able to sleep anywhere – I've known him be able to sleep all the way from Australia to England.

'Anyway, we finished the Trial with a clean sheet, but so did seven other crews, so a tie-break section was arranged. We went out with transmission trouble, but the main point is that I was pretty emaciated beforehand and I lost a further stone on the Trial.

'Things had to change, so I joined a company called F G Spurway, which made bolts, screws and all types of fasteners. That was also new to me at the time, but again it came in handy later. I started off again as a draughtsman, but I was soon made the assistant works engineer.

'Then Quality Castings heard that I'd left CSR and they headhunted me. They made me works manager and I stayed with them until Jack persuaded me to come to England in 1960.'

That was Ron's life away from motor racing, and it helps to explain why he became successful not just as a designer, but as a builder of practical racing cars, as a factory owner and as a businessman.

Returning to that first Ralt, he had added long-arm, low-pivot rear swing-axles in late 1951. By lengthening the swing-axles and adding universal joints he was able to lower the roll-centre of his car by 6 inches. When Mercedes-Benz unveiled its W196 Grand Prix car in 1954, which had a similar rear suspension layout, the Aussie press was quick to point out that one of their own had done it first, three years before!

The next single-seater, the Ralt Mk III, began life as the Hooper Special and was built for Austin Tauranac. It started out with prewar wire wheels because at first the brothers could not afford to fit Ron's special wheels, but when they did the handling was transformed. Ron redesigned the chassis within the constraints of the existing components, fitted a body and swapped the existing JAP engine for a single-overhead-cam Norton.

Ron says: 'We were still affected by handicapping, so the name of the game was to keep one step ahead of the handicapper, just like at Brooklands. We'd put on the entry form that it had a 10:1 compression ratio when it was running at 7.5:1, and when the handicapper saw that it was slower than it should have been, we got a better handicap. Then we raised the compression ratio to 8:1, and so on.'

Austin won a race at every meeting he entered at Mount Druitt for the best part of 18 months. He raced for the thrill of it, and was good, whereas Ron raced as an extension of his desire to build a good car. Austin's wife was not entirely happy about him racing, and when their daughter was born, Austin agreed to give in to her misgivings and the car was sold.

Ron recalls: 'Once we had built the Mk III, the specification was set except for the engine, which as I said we developed gradually. That way it was reliable, and Austin had a successful career with it. He was actually more successful than I was because I kept changing my car. I kept trying new things and sometimes they didn't work, but that's how you learn.'

In September 1954 Ron took his original Ralt to the Newcastle hillclimb where the New South Wales Championship was being staged. There he shattered the course record and, among the other drivers he beat was Jack Brabham, who had a Cooper-Bristol at the time. 'First prize was a canteen of cutlery, and Jack had set his heart on winning it. He's never forgotten or forgiven me for that!'

Not long afterwards, in 1955, the Ralt was sold to finance Ron's next car. The Ralt Mk IV had a 1,000cc Vincent engine and featured a spaceframe chassis, a glassfibre body, cast aluminium wheels and a de Dion rear axle with a transverse twin-leaf spring. As usual, money was tight and it took a couple of years to finish the car.

Ron and Norma remember it for different reasons. Norma recalls: 'When we were first married we shared a house with another couple. We had our own kitchen, bedroom and lounge/dining room and a shared bathroom. I couldn't stand the other woman and I believe she had keys to our part of the house. I used to work three days a week simply to get out of the house.

'At weekends we'd stay with Ron's parents – his mother was a keen golfer so she'd go off to play golf and I'd do the cooking. Eventually we got our own place and Ron built the chassis of this car in the spare room. That was bad enough, but when he came to take it out, he just did it. He knocked the paintings off the walls, then knocked over and broke all my ornaments, including wedding presents. I was furious!' (Forty years later, Ron looks suitably sheepish when reminded of the incident – and not many people in motor racing have seen Ron look sheepish.)

As for the car itself, he says: 'Everyone said that you had to have a de Dion rear axle, but I soon found that you didn't. The problem was that the splines on the drive-shafts used to stick – perhaps it was because the car was so light. I used it a couple of times, then someone insisted they had to have it, so I sold it on and used the money to lay down a little production line of five cars.'

These had multi-tubular frames rather than properly triangulated speceframes, but then the engine/gearbox unit played its part in the overall stiffness of the frame. Sophisticated it was not. To keep the record tidy, a Ralt Mk V was designed for Austin, but was sold before it was completed – details are in the Appendices.

To go back in time, in early 1955 Jack Brabham, having become Australia's leading driver, caught a boat to England and more or less charmed his way into the Cooper works. John Cooper recognized a kindred spirit and Jack soon became part of the Cooper set-up. It was Jack, for example, who visited the French firm ERSA, and brought back the Citroën-based gearbox which Cooper then adopted. Incidentally, like Ron, Jack is a man of simple tastes, so when he journeyed to the gourmet capital of the world, he took a packed lunch...

When Jack had an idea for lowering the Coventry Climax engine in the frame of the 'Manx Tail' Cooper sports car by 3 inches, he took a ballpoint pen and drew over a diagram of the Cooper's rear end which had been published in *The Autocar* and sent it to Ron with a covering letter asking for his comments. Ron designed a bellhousing enclosing a step-gear cluster and had it made, which Jack later collected during the first of what became annual visits to Australia, and he brought it back to England as part of his luggage. Cooper used Ron's gear cluster for years, but probably only about half a dozen people in the world knew about the Tauranac connection with it. Later, when Jack wanted to improve the suspension layout for the 'Lowline' Cooper, he again consulted his old friend. Ron wrote back, not with drawings this time, but with practical advice about the correct geometry and wishbone lengths.

The longer Jack was associated with Cooper, the more he thought he could do better, either by buying the company, which he and his team-mate, Roy Salvadori, had once tried to do, or more likely by setting out on his own. In particular, Cooper's unconventional approach to production priorities must have bemused him at times. For example, Tony Marsh, the champion hillclimber and Formula One and Two privateer, was a regular customer, who made sure that he never had to wait too long for his car to be completed.

Tony's business was concerned with pork products, and Charlie Cooper just loved York ham, which was then hard to obtain. So Tony would arrive at the Cooper works, show Charlie a large ham, and tell him he would be camping in his van outside the works until his car was completed. He would be living off the ham, but when the car was ready, he would leave Charlie with whatever remained of it! Tony never had to wait long for his car.

Jack felt that Charlie Cooper was at the root of a lot of Cooper's problems because even in those days if you wanted to stay on top in motor racing you had to be prepared to spend money, and this was something that the Old Man was often reluctant to do. Jack says, 'I was always getting John to spend money that Charlie never knew about.'

Gradually, the idea of setting up his own team took shape in Jack's mind and from time to time he would discuss the idea in general terms with Ron. By the time he had clinched his first World Championship he already had his own garage in Chessington, so when the time came he was sufficiently secure financially to be able to offer Ron the opportunity to return to England and become part of the fledgling motor racing.

The offer came at the time Ron had laid down the line of five cars to sell. They had originally been designed for 500cc racing, but even in Australia that class had faded. Ron says: 'The cars worked quite well. They'd got wishbone suspension because I'd finally got swing-axles out of my system. The first one I made went to someone who fitted two Triumph motorcycles engines, and he was quite successful with it.'

Then, when Jack's proposal came, Ron swallowed hard and sold the bits he'd made, plus the drawings and the patterns for the alloy wheels, to a company called Lynx Engineering. By the time Lynx got round to finishing the cars, Formula Junior had arrived, so most of the last batch from the first generation of Ralts were converted for the new category. They were successful for a while in Australia, but by then Ron was no longer involved with them.

In theory, Ron was coming to Britain for six months, so Quality Castings kept his job open for him. But five years would pass before he returned home, and then it would only be for a week's holiday.

3

Starting a revolution

Ron moved in with Jack and Betty Brabham, and when Norma and Jann arrived they camped there as well. Norma had no connections with England that she knew of, so as a young mother the move was an act of faith on her part as well. She came from a tight-knit family and it was a wrench. 'I still don't know why I wanted to come, I guess it must have been a spirit of adventure. The arrangement was that we'd come over on a six-month trial, but it was 12 years before I paid a visit home.'

On Easter Monday, 1960, Ron and Norma went to the motor race meeting at Goodwood. Jack wasn't there because he was busy winning the Formula Two race at Pau, so there was no special influence and Norma and Ron had to pay to go in and stand with the hoi polloi. But Ron felt that he was coming home, so during their first six months, the Tauranacs spent their weekends visiting Ron's many relations. In most cases, it was just the one call.

They rented a flat over a shop in Surbiton, about half a mile from the Cooper works. Ron does not recall ever dropping in on Cooper, although John Cooper remembers Ron from those early days. However, there was a need for discretion because Jack was still under contract to Cooper, and his plans with Ron were long-term. Although John was in on the secret, his father Charlie was not, and it would be two and a half years from the time Ron stepped off the plane at Heathrow before the first Brabham Formula One car would race. Things were on a slow fuse.

Ron had come to England with the idea of doing some racing himself, but he soon shelved the idea. 'There was too much work for one thing. Then I figured it would be unfair to risk injury with a wife and daughter to look after. You can tell from that I wasn't a true racing driver. If I'd been a real racing driver I wouldn't have worried about them – I'd have sold them if they'd got in the way.'

Ron's first job for Jack was converting road cars. One project was a twin-Weber tuning kit for the Sunbeam Rapier, and another was to modify the Triumph Herald, which was then a new model, to take a Coventry Climax engine. After some mods to the brakes and suspension, the Herald-Climax was quite a little road-burner and would cover the 0-60mph sprint in 11.5 seconds. That's not much these days, but back then it was roughly the same as an

Austin-Healey 3000. Unfortunately, it also cost about the same as the Big Healey. Also, the limitations of its swing-axle rear suspension restricted its potential. Nevertheless, about 100 Herald-Climaxes were turned out by Jack Brabham Motors.

By day, Ron worked on the Brabham garage projects, then by night he would work at the drawing board in his bedroom designing Motor Racing Developments' first car, the MRD-1, or as it would subsequently be known, the BT1.

It was not an easy time for Norma, with a young child to look after. The district in which the Tauranacs lived was not the sort of place where you find Residents' Associations. Norma had been used to having friends and family around her, and being in constant touch with her mother. Now she was lonely – desperately lonely – but she kept faith. She was the homemaker, the woman who gave her man something to come home to.

She seldom went to races and she was certainly not inclined to sit on a pit counter with two stopwatches and a clipboard along with the pit popsies. There are people who call her Saint Norma. She says: 'When we were in Surbiton, I used to take Jann to school, but none of the other mothers seemed inclined to talk to me. The only people I spoke to were shopkeepers.

'Then things got better in 1962 when we moved to Pyrford, near Woking. There I could join in with things like coffee mornings, but Ron worked a seven-day week so we had no joint social life. I was still finding it difficult to come to terms with England. At first, our new house had only partial central heating, and in winter I found it so cold I had to put on gloves before I went upstairs to make the beds.

'I have never believed in passing over my own children to other people, so I never had babysitters. That meant that I had very little to do with motor racing and therefore never became part of the social scene.

'It was different with Jack. We'd grown up with him and Betty, so we were always on a different basis. Then when Graham Hill drove for us, I started to go to the races, and Bette Hill, who was expert at timing laps and keeping lap charts, tried to teach me to do the same, but I was terrified that I'd make a mistake. These days, I watch Formula One on television, but I'm usually asleep before the end of the race.

'I may have made a mistake early on. Both our girls, when they were babies, had trouble sleeping at night, but I took the view that since Ron worked hard all day, they were my job. So Ron never changed a nappy or fed them a bottle, in fact I can't even remember that he ever picked them up and gave them a cuddle.'

Jann recalls: 'It's true that Dad wasn't around much, especially when I was young. Even our family holidays were taken at the race track at Zandvoort. But as I got older he always seemed to be there at the critical points in my life. I remember him pushing me at exam times to do just that bit better, and he taught me to drive – and I was lucky to get away with just a few of his racing manoeuvres! When it was time for University I thought I would go to a Uni near home, but Dad thought it would be a good time for me to leave home and become independent, which I did, and I have never regretted it.'

Looking back to those early years in England, Ron concedes: 'Yes, this was a tough time for Norma, and although I had my own problems as well, at least they were confined to my work, with which I was completely preoccupied.

And believe me, it really was hard work at that time. Because of Jack's insistence on secrecy I wasn't allowed to make myself known to a lot of the people I needed to be talking to on the supply side – the sort of people anyone who was building a car might go to for bits and pieces. As far as Jack was concerned, the fewer people who knew I was even in the country the better, and even those who did had to be convinced that I was just here giving Jack a hand with his road car conversions.

The MRD-1 that Ron drew was built for Formula Junior, but it didn't have a designation at all at the time. In fact MRD had made many different cars before they got around to giving them type numbers, so the first one was only retrospectively called the BT1, BT standing for Brabham and Tauranac. Until then the car had been referred to simply as the MRD, not even MRD-1.

Formula Junior was a logical choice for the first car because, as Jack says: 'It was cheap and at the time it was the nearest thing to Formula One.' Formula Junior had been conceived in Italy by Count 'Johnny' Lurani as a single-seater class, and as its name implied it was designed to encourage up-and-coming driving talent. For that reason, it was governed by relatively simple rules, the most important being that the engine had to come from a production car, be restricted to no more than four cylinders and overhead camshafts were not allowed.

Formula Junior had been given International status by the FIA and had become an extremely popular and successful class of racing. By 1960 at least 159 different makers of Formula Junior cars had been listed and every conceivable layout had been tried. There were cars with the engine in front of the driver and some even had the engine ahead of the front axle. There were mid-engined cars, rear-engined cars and cars with the engine alongside the driver. Every one of them had been someone's best hope for glory, but by the end of 1960, Lotus and Cooper had wiped most of them out, and with them had gone much of the fledgling racing car industry in other parts of the world. Producers of racing cars, who previously had been concerned only with building cars for local national classes, had for the first time to compete with rivals from other countries building cars to the same rules, and the 1960 Formula Junior season had found most of them to be sadly wanting.

It had become abundantly clear that the best FJ cars were being made in Britain, and when drivers bought British cars, not only were producers of cars in other countries suffering, but so were the subcontractors who had previously serviced their own products. A potentially bright young designer in, say, France or Germany, if he could not see a future in motor racing, was just as likely to go off and design furniture instead. The only small companies which survived the 1960 shake-out tended to be those who copied the British cars (and during the next decade, most would copy Ron's designs) and, since they were copying, they didn't need true designers, only draughtsmen.

But even in Britaln, there was still not much of a motor racing industry when Ron designed the BT1. He couldn't, for example, open a catalogue and have his pick of wheels; first he had to design his own and then arrange to have them cast. Also, at the time Ron knew of no-one who was making transmissions for mid-engined racing cars, so he solved that problem by getting in touch with Volkswagen, who allowed him to attend a training day for garage mechanics. Then, having learned what made the Beetle transmission work, and satisfied himself that the casing and selectors could be used in a single-seater, he contacted the gears specialist Jack Knight and asked him to cut some new gears to give him the ratios he needed. Meanwhile, Mike Hewland was doing something along similar lines for Lola, and in the years ahead Hewland gearboxes would be used widely in Ron's and most other people's racing cars.

Ron was already in touch with Jack Knight Engineering because they were doing a steering rack for him. 'I had made our first steering box in Australia, using a Morris Oxford pinion with a specially cut rack. I had a casting made and brought the pattern to England with me, then I went to Jack Knight's place, told them what pinions to use, gave them the drawings and the patterns and they started to make them for us.

'Eventually they were made available to everyone because my thing became the first Jack Knight steering rack. Then the Morris Oxford pinions went through a bad patch with the teeth coming out eccentric to the shaft. You could just about live with it on a road car, but definitely not on a racing car, so they had to start making their own pinions.' Today, Jack Knight steering boxes are virtually standard wear on racing cars – but there are probably very few if any people in the country who know that it was Ron Tauranac who set them off on this line of business.

'The BT1 was not only the first water-cooled racing car I'd designed and of course my first Formula Junior car, it was also my first to have a laydown seating position – something that Cooper had introduced on their 'Lowline' car while I was on my way to England. Although I drew the car on the drawing board in the bedroom, there was no question of history repeating itself and the car taking shape up there as well, just like that early Ralt! At first, we rented a lock-up in Wimbledon, but this was not very convenient, so after a while we found a room at the back of a garage on the Esher bypass, which was easier to work in and much closer to where both Jack and I were based. I bought myself a set of gas bottles and taught myself to weld, with the idea that I might be able to build up the frame myself, bearing in mind there was no question of putting the work out to one of the recognized chassis-builders.

'But bearing in mind this was my first crack at welding, it was obviously going to take too long, so it was fortunate that I came across Buckler Cars, at Crowthorne, Berkshire. Derek Buckler was a pioneer in the construction of kit cars and of spaceframes, and his standards were high, so to speed things up and make sure the job was done properly we gave them the job of producing the first frame. It was a good arrangement, especially as in motor racing terms Buckler was a bit off the beaten track,' (Buckler's son, Malcolm, still recalls that the frame was made under conditions of the utmost secrecy) 'and it also gave me the chance to work with the fabricator to put in an extra tube here or there as I thought it was needed.'

The BT1's aluminium body was made by a firm Ron tracked down close to his flat, while the wheels were a simple compromise which would be unique to the BT1. The distinctive 'four-lug' cast alloy wheels which feature on most Brabhams would not be ready until production was under way for the 1962 season.

Ron reckons that even with a certain amount of input from subcontractors, that first car took about twice as long to build as it would have done if he had been able to work openly and have access to all the established suppliers. 'Even getting the right nuts and bolts is difficult when you don't know where to go for them!' But eventually the job was done and the car was virtually finished before Ron had engaged his first employee. He was Keith Lavery, from Sydney, the first of a long line of Aussies and Kiwis who in the years ahead would knock on Ron's door asking for a job, many of whom would make a considerable mark for themselves in the sport in various ways.

It was while Ron was building the BT1 that he suddenly found himself involved in an interesting little exercise after Jack had received a request from Vanwall and passed it on to his partner. Although in 1957 a Vanwall had been the first British car ever to win a World Championship Formula One race and in 1958 the team had won the inaugural Constructors' Cup, at the end of that season Tony Vandervell had withdrawn his team from the Grand Prix scene, although a small racing shop had remained in operation and occasionally a car would be entered in other races.

Although their major successes had been achieved during the front-engined era, Vanwall had since built a mid-engined car and had entered it for the 1961 International Trophy race at Silverstone, which took place on a miserably wet day. John Surtees had driven it, but although he was brilliant in the wet, and had the most powerful engine in the field, even he had finished three laps down. Clearly, something was seriously wrong with the car.

Vanwall also owned a Lotus 18 at the time, which it had bought for evaluation purposes, and Jack had been asked to arrange a torsional stiffness test on both the Vanwall chassis and that of the Lotus, which is where Ron entered the story.

Ever practical, he took each frame in turn and secured the top of it to a wall, then, after supporting it underneath, he took a long iron bar, which he measured carefully and attached to the frame so that it extended at right-angles to the wall. Then, having confirmed his own weight, he stood on the end of the bar so as to measure the amount of deflection, which he could then convert into pounds/foot per degree.

As he explained, it was a simple yet effective exercise. 'If you stand still on the bar you can take your measurement, then if you jump up and down you can watch where the frame actually flexes, and then you can do something about it.' In the event, the Lotus 18 frame was measured at 1,400lb.ft per degree and the Vanwall frame at a mere 660lb.ft/deg, which implied that the Vanwall's torsional stiffness was somewhat akin to that of a Swiss roll. It also explains why the car was raced only once. It seems remarkable that a company that so recently had been at the top of the motor racing tree had been unable to carry out a straight-forward torsional stiffness test themselves. Presumably, they hadn't troubled. Ron's own cars would work because he always took trouble.

It was not until the middle of 1961 that the BT1 was ready to make its debut. Ron recalls: 'Jack had just got his pilot's licence and he flew a group of us to the Isle of Man to watch the TT motorcycle races. On the trip was a mate of his, Gavin Youl, from Tasmania. He'd raced a Porsche 90 in Australia and done pretty well with it, and his brother John had a Formula Junior Cooper. I sold Gavin our first car on that flight.'

Youl had never before driven a single-seater and Formula Junior was a hard school. He began with a 1,000cc Ford engine (the original Formula Junior operated on a capacity/weight basis) and he scored a couple of second places in a club meeting at Mallory Park. He also ran in the Commander Yorke 100-mile race at Silverstone and finished sixth there despite having to make a late stop for fuel, and then he entered the Bank Holiday meeting at Goodwood on August 25, 1961.

Nobody had taken much notice of the car on its early outings because club meetings got little coverage, there were plenty of specials around in Formula Junior, and so far nobody had made the connection with Jack. Goodwood, however, was different because the Formula Junior event was the main support race to the Tourist Trophy, which meant that the circuit was packed with press, Formula One stars, constructors, everyone who was anyone.

It was the first time that Gavin had driven at Goodwood, but by then he had a new 1,100cc Ford engine developed by Holbay and he caused a sensation during Saturday practice by setting pole position for his heat, 0.8 second under the lap record. Ron recalls: 'Some Lotus drivers made frantic calls to Cosworth and rushed off to get new engines.'

Things were looking good, but then the car caught fire and it began to look like it was a write-off. But it was loaded onto a trailer, driven back to Surbiton, where Ron rebuilt it, then rushed it back to the circuit in time for the race on the Bank Holiday Monday.

Gavin Youl managed to finish fourth in his heat, and it might have been higher, but he over-cooked it on a corner, the car still not feeling quite right after its hasty repair. In the final, however, he stayed out of trouble and finished second to Alan Rees' Lotus. Rees was very much a rising star, whereas Youl was considered a novice, so people took notice – not so much of the driver as of the car. One journalist wrote that it had been the first time that the supremacy of Lotus in Formula Junior had been challenged.

The paddock buzzed with speculation and some people were adding two and two to make four. Jack was still seeing out his contract with Cooper so *The Autocar* captioned a photograph of the BT1 with: 'The full importance of this new car will be appreciated when it is revealed who is behind it, and the plans they are likely to have for it.'

At this time Jack had a column in the monthly magazine *Motor Racing*, and his copy was noncommittal. He wrote: 'The MRD is a little project on which Ron Tauranac, an old friend of mine from Australia, has been working. Ron and I have enjoyed playing motor cars for several years and I felt that his talent was being wasted in Australia. So I was delighted when he decided to come to Britain to work for us. His particular flair is in the suspension department.

'The MRD is pretty conventional by today's standards, but I think that some of the detail work is not too bad.' That was an understatement because the MRD-1 was the first racing car to have adjustable roll bars – an interesting fact bearing in mind that the popular perception of Ron in the years ahead would be as an arch-conservative rather than a pioneer.

Jack continued: 'We will be making a few models in kit form for a firm in Australia, and I suppose that if there is a demand we might consider making some for the British market at a later stage. Anyway, the car has had an encouraging start, and I must say that it is very pleasant to have toys of your own to play with.'

That was hardly a fanfare of trumpets. In truth, Jack had been beavering away in the background to ensure that the BT1 would be launched properly, because by now a select few people had already been taken into his confidence. It also looked as though Motor Racing Developments, the existence of which was now in the public domain, had more than the production of some Formula

Junior cars to think about.

That May, Jack had been to the Indianapolis 500, where he had raced a modified 'Lowline' Cooper powered by a Coventry Climax Formula One engine 'stretched' to 2.7 litres. Despite giving away 1,500cc to the Offenhauser opposition, he had finished ninth and could have been higher had his inexperienced crew chosen a better fuelling strategy.

The Cooper had caused a stir at Indy, where everyone else was running front-engined roadsters, and Jack spoke to a firm called Paxton Products, a company which made superchargers. Paxton was a subsidiary of Studebaker-Packard and an adventurous Indy sponsor.

A deal was hammered out for MRD to build a car for the 1962 Indy 500, for Jack to drive. A draft contract was drawn up, which laid out the car's broad specification – mid-engined, all-independent suspension, etc. Paxton would pay $12,500 for the prototype, rather less for production cars, and would act as MRD's agent in the States. It guaranteed a minimum order each year, six cars for 1962 and 10 in subsequent years. It was an imaginative and bold offer, but nothing came of it, for reasons which neither Jack nor Ron can remember. In fact Ron did not believe the story until he was shown the contract which had been drawn up by Paxton.

Meanwhile, Gavin Youl ran the MRD a couple more times in England, but was sidelined by engine problems, then he took the car back to Australia, where it was welcomed as the very first Australian racing car to have run in Europe. The Australian press burst with pride – one of their own had shown up the Pommies!

In March 1962, Gavin and the MRD won the Australian National Formula Junior Championship on the Catalina Park circuit in New South Wales. It was both the first victory and the first championship to fall to the new marque.

While Gavin Youl covered himself in glory in New South Wales, in Britain there was considerable interest in the follow-up car. It was a relief to both Ron and Jack to know that they were on the right track, but of course, the cat was now out of the bag so far as Jack's own plans were concerned.

Charlie Cooper was offended. 'After all that we've done for him,' he spluttered, but John understood Jack's ambitions, and after all he had known about them from early in 1961. It is the nature of motor racing, however, that the success of one car manufacturing team can cause the demise of another, and MRD was to help to bury Cooper.

Among the first people from outside to become associated with the new marque was the Paris-based Swiss journalist, Gérard 'Jabby' Crombac. Jabby was an adviser to a number of people and organizations in motor racing. He recalls: 'The hot young prospect in French racing at the time was Jo Schlesser, whose team-mate was picking up the tab. I got Jo to the 1962 Racing Car Show in London and he was very impressed with Ron's car because it was so clean and straight-forward. He wanted one, so then his team-mate (really his patron) wanted another, so we told Ron that we'd have two, but we had one reservation, which was the car's name.'

Jack and Ron had agreed not to use their names in the venture, but Jabby Crombac pointed out to Jack that MRD was pronounced merde in French and they would stand a better chance of selling cars in France if the name didn't sound like the French word for shit!

Jabby suggested there was nothing wrong with the name 'Brabham', after all, Jack was a double World Champion. Ron says: 'Jack phoned me up out of the blue and told me this. I was put on the spot when he suggested we should call the cars 'Brabhams', but somewhat reluctantly I agreed.' The thought still rankles with him, even though he and Jack have remained close friends. 'For a while, even the name of the company was changed to Brabham Racing Developments (it later reverted to Motor Racing Developments), but what people didn't realize was that during 1962-65, the Brabham Formula One cars were actually MRD customer cars, which we sold to the Brabham Racing Organisation, a separate outfit through which Jack did all his racing negotiations and which was wholly owned by him.

The basis of Motor Racing Developments Ltd had originally been a 50/50 partnership, but then Jack said that as he had been the one who had put up the capital (a relatively modest sum of £2,000) he thought that it would be more appropriate if MRD became a 60/40 partnership in his favour.

Originally Formula One was to be part of the shared business (after all it was the reason for Ron's decision to come to England), but after the first year with the BT3 Jack decided that BRO (his company) would purchase and run the F1 works cars. One effect of this decision was that it lost Ron's development input throughout each season.

'In fact as far as MRD was concerned, the Formula One cars were really afterthoughts, something to be involved in after we'd made our Formula Junior customer cars. During that period, Jack bought his cars and looked after them separately. I had nothing much to do with them except perhaps when he desperately needed a spare part and thought, "Who can we get to bring one over to us? I know, we'll give Ron a call." We supplied BRO with new bits, of course, but we probably made a loss on the deal.'

That arrangement also still rankles with Ron. Admittedly, the cars were designated BT (Brabham-Tauranac) and Jack has said he would not have gone into partnership with anyone else. On the other hand, as the story unfolds it will emerge that Jack was one of the shrewdest operators there has ever been in the motor racing business.

4

Emerging from the shadows

The Australian spare parts business Repco (a shortened version of Replacement Parts Company) had a UK facility in Victoria Road, Surbiton, about a mile from Cooper Cars. Jack had been dealing in Repco parts and equipment for some years – in fact he had become the identifiable face of Repco in Britain – and they agreed that MRD could take over part of their space for the assembly of cars. It was only to be a short-term arrangement, but while it lasted the cars were called Repco Brabhams, which in the light of subsequent events has caused some confusion.

Meanwhile, Jack had also based the Brabham Racing Organisation in Victoria Road. BRO had been in existence for some time, but its function was primarily the preparation of Jack's own cars, in particular those which he took Down Under at the end of each year to race. It also looked after his personal deals, and he was probably the first star works driver in Europe to run such an operation on the side.

By the spring of 1962, when the BT2 was announced under headlines like *The First Brabham!*, Jack had left Cooper and through BRO had bought a Formula One Lotus for him to race. Of course, by now everyone was expecting to see a Brabham Formula One car at any time, but there was to be no official comment about this until well into 1962.

Early in the year, Jack shook down the BT2 at Goodwood. The official Formula Junior lap record stood at 1m 33.6s, although winter testing had produced a new target time of 1m 29.0s. Then Jack went out and set a new mark – 1m 26.8s, which was under the official 1½-litre Formula One lap record.

By now, of course, Jack and Ron's association was out in the open, and they didn't mind a bit if people got the impression that here were just a couple of simple guys quietly getting on and doing their own thing. To an extent this was true because they certainly didn't trumpet each new development, nor did they issue many press releases.

Yet, on the other hand, Jack knew all about the value of publicity. At that time he was the only driver to have his own column in a motor racing journal. He also had a column in a national newspaper, and the Rootes Group had built an entire advertising campaign for Sunbeam cars around Jack's endorsement. When Jack opened his garage at Chessington, the stars of the sport were all there and photographs of Stirling Moss cutting a ribbon appeared in the national press, not just the motor racing press. Jack, in fact, was a very shrewd operator, much more so than he has been given credit for, and he has remained that way ever since.

A man of few words he may have been, but he knew how to generate publicity and use it to his advantage. When it was time to launch the BT2, a few journalists, all of whom had international outlets, were not only given exclusives, but one of them even got to drive the BT2 during that first test session at Goodwood, which was almost without precedent.

Ron, though, had been dead against the idea, and as far as he was concerned it would be the last time a journalist would be let loose in a Brabham. The journalist in question was John Blunsden, now the publisher of this book, but at that time writing track test reports for *Motor Racing* magazine, *Sports Car Graphic* and other outlets.

He remembers: 'After Jack had finished driving the BT2 he left pretty smartly because the weather was closing in and he had to fly back to Fairoaks – he landed there later in a snowstorm! This left me with Frank Gardner, who was due to drive the works car that season, and Ron, whose stoney expression left me in no doubt that he thought this was not only a very bad idea, but also a complete waste of time!

'It didn't snow at Goodwood, but there was a deluge of rain just before I went out on the track, which had already been liberally coated with someone's oil all the way through Fordwater. So with a last look at Ron, whose expression said "Bring it back with so much as a dent in it and you're dead!", I set off cautiously, then after a lap or two to find out where the puddles and oil slick were, I gradually worked up to a pace at which I could at least see what the car was trying to do.

'Conditions like that tend to concentrate the mind, and I managed to keep out of trouble until it was time to come back in. Down the straight for the last time, and beginning to think about what I was going to write, through the double apex at Woodcote and suddenly the tail is away, and round we go on to the grass before the chicane. I'd committed the cardinal sin of relaxing my concentration before I was back in the pits. Fortunately, no harm was done, and I drove back to meet the 'reception committee'. Frank Gardner was in stitches, and was obviously loving every minute of it, but Ron? He didn't say a lot, but his look – a peculiar mixture of anger and relief – said it all.'

Ron recalls: 'The way I saw it, there didn't seem any point in the exercise. The guy couldn't tell if the car was any good, so it was just giving him a joy ride.' Jack, though, saw it all rather differently, at least he did when all that free publicity came out in print in the weeks ahead!

Although the customer Formula Junior cars were broadly similar to the prototype, there was a mass of detail revision, the main points of which are listed in Appendix C, along with specification details of every other Brabham. Various outside suppliers had been geared up to a production run, although at that stage, of course, the size of the run was still unknown. By this time Mike Hewland was in a position to supply a five-speed transmission using the casing from a Volkswagen Beetle, Progress Chassis (a company formed by ex-Lotus personnel) were to make the frames, and Specialised Mouldings were given the contract to make the glassfibre bodies after Ron had produced the first one and the mould, having decided on the split lines and designed the fastenings.

Meanwhile, since Jack's Formula One car was taking second place to the customer Formula Juniors and would not be ready for some time, he had ordered a new Lotus 24, into which went one of the latest V8 Coventry Climax engines (his Lotus 21 had been powered by the earlier four-cylinder Climax). In the 1961 German Grand Prix, when Jack was still driving for Cooper, he had been the first person to race the Climax V8 – of which only 33 were to be made in total.

His 1962 season was supposed to have got under way with the Lombank Trophy race at Snetterton in April, but a fire in the workshop had damaged his car, and in the end Jack raced the Lotus 21 only twice – in the Aintree 200 and the non-championship Pau Grand Prix – and covered just nine laps before retiring from both races. Then he took delivery of the V8 car just in time for the International Trophy at Silverstone, where he could finish no higher than sixth after being lapped.

As the season wore on it began to look as though he might have made a mistake in leaving Cooper. His performances appeared to be lacklustre – he was 15th on the grid for the Belgian Grand Prix and 11 seconds off the pace, for example – and he was far from happy with the way the Lotus handled. Its tendency to wander on the fast Spa-Francorchamps circuit was particularly disconcerting, and he counted himself very fortunate to pick up a point for sixth place after finishing two laps down. Then he finished second to John Surtees' Lola in the 2000 Guineas race at Mallory Park, and followed up with fifth place in the British Grand Prix at Aintree. These were not the sort of results expected of a double World Champion, and many people seemed to be ready to write him off.

Meanwhile, Cooper had won the Monaco Grand Prix and the non-championship race at Reims and had taken second place in Belgium and third in the British Grand Prix. Overall, the season had turned into a fight between Jim Clark (Lotus-Climax) and Graham Hill (BRM), but young Bruce McLaren, Jack's successor as Cooper team leader, was now the best of the rest.

The problem with Jack's Lotus 24 was that its aerodynamics were suspect. At high speed, the car was so inept that Jack couldn't even keep it in a straight line as it blasted through the grandstand complex at Reims. Ron says: 'We didn't understand a great deal about aerodynamics at the time, but my guess is that the root of the Lotus' trouble was its high nose. I had always been an advocate of a low nose, so as to allow the air to bear down on the front of the car and give it some stability. With the Lotus, due to its high nose, the air was getting underneath the nose and tending to lift the car, which of course was the last thing you wanted.'

But while Jack's personal reputation was taking something of a beating, the Formula Junior cars that bore his name were doing well. The Brabhams soon had a deserved reputation for being an ideal customer car – safe, straightforward, easy to work on and to set up, and forgiving to their drivers. They were also very adaptable – you could set them up for oversteer if you wanted to, or for understeer if that was your preference. Ron says: 'I don't think any of us were clever enough to do this consciously, so it was just lucky that all my cars were easy to drive.'

Not that the Brabhams didn't meet tough opposition in some markets. For example, in the early 1960s, Elva, who were based on the south coast of

England, were very successful in America, whereas their cars were relative also-rans in Europe. Keith Marsden, Elva's designer, says: 'We did well in America because I designed cars which oversteered. The Americans were a bit 'Cooperish' in that they showed the car a corner, hung the back out, maybe changed gear in the middle of the corner, or went through with the brakes part on – they were unbelievably amateurish – and then they applied the power. Driveability was the main thing to give an American racer at that time.

'The Lola Mk1, with which we couldn't live in Europe, wasn't that easy to drive, and few drivers could get the best out of it. They tended to understeer, so you had to be pretty skilled, and courageous, to drive one to the limit since you had to commit yourself to a corner a long way ahead. You can always predetermine when a car is going to break away, and I could have given our customers the ultimate cornering power of the Lola. But if you do that, when the car starts to go it's difficult to catch, so we set our mark lower, gave the driver a bigger margin, and they liked that.'

It's a familiar story. When you're making production racing cars in quantity you have to make compromises, and you have to bear in mind that the customer is perhaps preparing his car by himself, so you can't make things too sophisticated. Ron's genius was to build cars which were readily adaptable, so that they could be tailored to a wide range of customer needs. Elva did well in America, Lola did well in Europe, but Brabhams worked anywhere. If there was a secret to the BT2 and all later Brabhams it was the rigidity of their chassis. This provided the firm base from which the car could be set up.

But the reputation for reliability and safety which the Brabhams soon earned was not won without incident. Ron recalls: 'One of our first cars went to Briggs Cunningham and the steering column sheared. Can you imagine? I almost killed Briggs Cunningham! What had happened was that one of the mechanics had fitted the wheel to the column and had taken a file to the weld to make it look neat. That had weakened the weld and the steering column sheared. After that, I personally checked every car that we built. I became obsessive about safety.' Ron acquired a reputation as a 'worrier', and it has often been told against him. But if you were to commit yourself to a flat-out, top-gear corner, would you prefer your steering wheel to be have been fitted by a 'worrier' or some laid-back guy who likes welds to look neat?

During 1962, BRO and MRD moved out of the Repco facility and found their own premises at New Haw, near Byfleet, but before long, BRO would have its own workshop in Guildford. Ron recalls those days: 'I used to get to the works at about eight in the morning, but I always insisted on going home for lunch. Norma thought that this was a bit unfair because it meant she had to be at home to cook for me, but I needed the break. I'd come home again for supper and then go back to the works until about 10.30pm.

'When we came to build the first Formula One car, there were many times when I'd go back to the works after supper and then return home for breakfast the following day. After breakfast I used to help Norma with the washing-up because if I'd stayed seated I'd have fallen asleep.

'It was during that time that I came the closest I've ever been to falling out with Jack. I'd mapped out where all the components on the Formula One car were going to go, and once, when I'd gone home to eat, he changed the position of one of them. We were all tired and I lost my temper. I made it very clear to him that I was in charge of design and build, and that what I said, went! It needed saying so that we defined our roles – I reckon there's only room for one boss. We never had a problem again.' Jack says: 'Ron fell out with everyone at one time or another. We continued to have the odd disagreement and the really annoying thing was that Ron was always right!'

Even as the first car was being readied, more people were being taken on. Among the first of Ron's employees had been Michael Scarlett, later to be Technical Editor of *Autocar*. Michael recalls: I'd trained at Hawker, the aircraft manufacturer, but projects were being cancelled, morale took a dive and, along with the rest of my generation, I left.

'I managed to get a job at Cooper. I'd applied to be an assistant designer, but was taken on as a shop floor worker until a job became vacant. A little while before the first photographs appeared of Jack and Gavin testing the new car at Brands Hatch, the buzz went round the works that Jack was setting up his own team. I wrote to Ron asking if there was a job as an assistant and I was taken on.

'The trouble I had was that Ron would set me to do something, then he'd change his mind without telling me and it would all finish up being my fault. I eventually got as close as I've ever been to having a nervous breakdown!'

When the company moved to the new premises another person to be taken on was David Mills, now the proprietor of Grand Prix Sportique. David says: 'I had just left the RAF and had taken my Sunbeam Rapier to Jack's garage to be fitted with a tuning kit. Jack and Ron suggested I should join them, manning the office, so I answered the phone, ordered spare parts and so on until the end of 1966.

'When I say "answer the phone", that was if Ron didn't get there first because if he hears a phone ring, no matter what else he's doing, he has to pick it up. He would die rather than let a phone ring.'

Although Peter Arundell in his works Team Lotus 22 dominated the 1962 Formula Junior season in the UK, Brabhams were usually the most successful cars amongst the private entrants. On the Continent, meanwhile, Jo Schlesser won a number of important races with his BT2 and he finished the year as the French Formula Junior Champion.

That may seem a flat statement, but it should be remembered that since there was no Formula Two at the time, from 1961-63 Formula Junior was the single-seater racing category immediately below Formula One. Participants ranged from no-hopers with home-made cars to works teams from top outfits like Lotus.

The top runners tended to appear only at the important meetings, such as in the support races to Grands Prix, but the also-rans in those events were the regulars in the national championships. Furthermore, most club meetings had a Formula Junior race as a highlight of the day's programme, so the scene was not as clear-cut as, say, Formula Three today.

The really quick guys were often well down on or absent from the championship points listings because their racing appearances would be confined to wherever the starting and prize money was best. Peter Arundell, a highly talented driver who became known as the 'King of Formula Junior', did not win a championship in 1962.

Ironically, a Brabham driver's first national championship victory in Britain did not come until 1966, by which time the marque had won Grands Prix, World Championships for drivers and constructors, as well as IndyCar, Tasman Championship and Formula Two races. Brabham had also built more than 200 cars and was top of the heap so far as customer racing cars was concerned. The first Briton to win a championship for Brabham was Harry Stiller, a jeweller from Bournemouth, who gave up racing after visiting a clairvoyant who told him that unless he gave it up he would be killed!

In assessing the performance of Brabham as a car maker in Formula Junior it is important to be aware of the status of each individual race and whether or not Team Lotus was present. There is no doubt that the successes of Team Lotus' own cars helped to sell cars to customers, although everyone knew that a works Lotus was built to a different standard to the customer cars. One of Ron's great achievements was to provide customers with as good a car as the factory ran. Indeed, there were occasions when customers took delivery of the latest Formula One machines even before BRO did. Entering a market in which Lotus, Cooper, Lola and Elva were already well-established, MRD did well to build 15 Brabhams in 1962.

Fellow Australians Gavin Youl and Frank Gardner were the Brabham works drivers that year, but this meant little more than that they were allowed to operate from the factory. Correction – it did mean they could negotiate better starting money from race organizers! Gavin was a gentleman amateur who, having decided he had reached his ceiling, did not see out the season. Frank, on the other hand, was a brilliant all-round sportsman who ironically might have achieved more in motor racing had he been less gifted. That may seem an odd thing to say, but everything came so easily to him, whether it was boxing, swimming, motorcycle racing, car racing or surfing, that he was not truly focused.

As the company had geared up for production, MRD became a hectic hive of activity over the winter of 1961/2: Ron was everywhere, looking over people's shoulders. The one employee had soon become two, then three, then four, and Ron was not merely employing them, he was training them in his way of doing things, and apart from everything else, that meant keeping busy. One of his earlier employees recalls: 'You'd see guys hopping about on one leg wondering whether they would be allowed to take a leak! Yes, there was a lot of pressure, but then every now and then someone would arrive to place an order, and everyone's spirits would be lifted.'

One of the problems of working at MRD – and in years to come it would be the same at Ralt – was that you were working for a hands-on boss, and whatever you were engaged on the chances were that your boss could do the job at least as well – and probably better – than you could.

Jumping forward briefly to the 1980s, one of Ron's employees was someone who today is well-known and has a good reputation as a designer. But while he was at Ralt, Ron put him to work to draw up a rear suspension. The poor guy toiled away for about 12 weeks on this, with Ron looking over his shoulder all the time, watching what he was doing. Clearly, he was struggling, and his self-esteem had dropped to zero. Then, one Friday, Ron said: 'Give it to me, I'll give it a go.' So Ron took the drawings away that night and came in on the Monday morning with everything finalized. It destroyed the guy, and he skulked off to the relative calm of Formula One.

Michael Hillman, who was in the drawing office at Brabham for seven years, says: 'Ron was always looking over your shoulder and making comments, and it could be very infuriating, but almost always he was right.

'I never did know what time he used to get into work because he was always there before me and he had his finger on everything. He knew the price of everything and I reckon he knew to the last five bob what a car cost to make. We used Standard-Triumph front uprights and stub-axles with Vitesse hubs, and fitted extensions to the bottom of the uprights for the Formula One cars. The track rod ends were Renault. A lot of parts were straight from a catalogue.

'I bet he got discounts on everything, as well, because he could be brutal with suppliers and subcontractors. He would play merry hell with them until they produced exactly what he wanted. At first they didn't know what hit them and would grumble, but he stuck to his guns.

'Then they would find that he paid them on the dot – he was always strict about that – and when that happened they couldn't do enough for him. There were times when a subcontractor would be going through a bad patch, but if Ron trusted the guy, he'd pay for things in advance. As a result we used to get everyone's best effort.'

Ron never changed, and Richard Barnes of SPA Fabrications recalls the first time that Ron contacted him in 1985, in the Ralt days: 'He wanted supports for the rear wings of a car and he wanted them made from aluminium honeycomb. Even in 1985 we're talking £500 for a sheet of honeycomb. We're not talking crepe paper.

'Ron phones through the coordinates, we want the business, so we get stuck straight in. We complete it and the phone goes. It's Ron, who has decided to change the location of one of the holes through which the bolts will go. OK, we want the business so we do a second one. Then the phone goes again. It's Ron, and he wants one of the holes drilled somewhere else.

'So we do it. The phone goes, it's Ron again, and – you've guessed. We junk three sheets of honeycomb at £500 a sheet and finally we complete one without the phone ringing 10 minutes later. We know somebody who's going to the Ralt works and he takes the two supports down with him the same day – we are talking rapid service here.

'The following day we wait anxiously and then the phone goes. Ron is on the other end and he is unbelievably rude. Apparently we're 10 thousandths of an inch out on one of the holes. So far as he's concerned it's junk. I am well cheesed off by this time, and I stand up to him, asking him how he took his measurements and so on. We had words, then one of us slammed down the phone. Later that day he phones again, sweet as pie, and orders 10 sets. We became a regular subcontractor.

'He's an amazing guy, I've seen people cross him and he has swallowed them whole and spat out the bits, but an hour later he's perfectly at ease with them – then was then, now is now. He can be the most infuriating man on earth, but he inspires the most incredible loyalty. Get to know him, which is not easy, and you finish up loving him. There are a lot of dodgy people in motor racing, but I have never even heard a rumour of a whisper of Ron breaking his word or failing to settle a bill on time, and in full. There are not many people in motor racing you can say that about.'

While Brabham established itself as a leading marque in just a matter of months, Cooper began to struggle in Formula Junior. In 1963, production of Cooper Formula Junior cars would be half the 1962 figure, while that of Brabhams would almost double; Jack had not merely left Cooper, it looked as though he was in the process of destroying it.

But his own reputation was also taking a battering because by mid-1962 he had scored only three World Championship points driving his Lotus, even though, thanks to his connections, Jack had been able to secure one of the latest Coventry Climax V8 engines for it. Nor did things improve very much when the BT3, the first Brabham Formula One car, made its debut in the German Grand Prix. Unfortunately, Jack blew an engine early in practice and had to cobble together another, which meant he could only qualify near the back of the grid, 24th of the 26 starters. It was atrociously wet for the race, but despite the conditions Jack managed to pass car after car on the first lap and ran in mid-field before retiring with a deranged throttle linkage after 10 of the 15 laps. But after that disappointing start, he seemed to get his old sparkle back and better results were to come.

That first car had been built with a Colotti six-speed gearbox, but by this time Mike Hewland was up and running with his own transmissions and would supply all subsequent Tauranac-era Brabhams except for some Indy cars, which used Weismann 'boxes. The big attraction of the Hewland gearbox was that the entire innards could be withdrawn in a piece to be worked on.

Ron recalls: 'We needed a beefed-up gearbox, so one Sunday, Jack and I went over with Norma and Betty to where Mike Hewland and his wife lived, and while the girls spent the afternoon together, Mike, Jack and I designed what became the Hewland Mk V gearbox. Mike listened to what we said and then he went away and drew it. It worked OK except that the oil got too hot. We knew this because we ran it on the rolling-road at MIRA and measured the power loss. It would probably have been better had we dry-sumped it.'

Jack's next outing in the BT3 was in the International Gold Cup at Oulton Park, in August, where he finished third despite a troubled run. Then he missed the Italian Grand Prix because he could not reach agreement with the race organizers over starting money. This, remember, was long before the formation of the Formula One Constructors Association (FOCA), when individual entrants had to make their own deals with the organizers.

So Jack next appeared in the United States Grand Prix, at Watkins Glen, where he ran with new, heavier duty front brake calipers, qualified fifth and finished a fine fourth. He followed that with second place in the Mexican Grand Prix, having led for much of the way until slowed with falling oil pressure. Unfortunately, though, this was not a Championship race in 1962. Then Jack finished the season by taking fourth place in the South African Grand Prix, just behind the Coopers of McLaren and Maggs. Ron says: 'Had Jack still been with Cooper he would have probably won the Championship. Bruce McLaren should have won it, but he was let down by unreliability, and that would not have happened had Jack still been in the team.'

At the end of 1962, the first year that Brabham single-seaters had been built and sold, a fair assessment of Ron's cars would be that they were unusually promising. They were not yet world-beaters, but they had already made a mark, had won races, and – most importantly – customers liked them. A good story was spreading about them.

Over the European winter, Frank Gardner took his Brabham BT2 to Australia and won everything that he entered. He could have had a permanent berth at Brabham, but now he was a man in demand, and Ian Walker made him a better offer to drive for his team. This, together with the fact that Gavin Youl had retired from the sport, opened the door for Denny Hulme.

In 1960, together with George Lawton, Denny had been chosen by the New

Zealand International Grand Prix Association to follow Bruce McLaren on their 'Driver to Europe' scholarship scheme. But sadly, George, who tended to be the quicker of the two, was killed in the Danish Grand Prix, a Formula Two race, and Denny nearly quit at that point.

However, he decided to persevere, and he stuck it out in Europe. Jack offered him a job as a mechanic, with the promise of some driving, and Ken Tyrrell, too, entered him in some FJ races. It was while working as a mechanic at Jack's garage that Denny became close friends with Phil Kerr, a fellow-Kiwi, who began to promote his career. While some racing drivers liked to live up to the image and raise hell, Denny was a man with simple values who preferred to spend his evenings doing DIY jobs around the house.

But he soon proved that he was no mean driver. After Gavin Youl had retired from racing, Denny drove his BT2 at Crystal Palace, set pole and finished fourth. Then, in a second outing at Brands Hatch, he won his race and set a new lap record. When Frank Gardner left to drive for Ian Walker, Denny inherited his seat.

Ron says: 'We loaned Denny a car and he and his wife, Greta, trailed it all over Europe. There was just the two of them, no mechanic. Then, in the winter, Denny would come and work for us. Most of our employees were people who came over from Australia or New Zealand, knocked on the door and asked for a job.' An Englishman who was at MRD at the time says: 'If you knocked on the door and you spoke through your nose, you arrived with a yard of credibility.'

After a full season, with feed-back from a dozen customers, to say nothing of Jack's contribution, Ron had a solid basis on which to go forward. Orders were rolling in and 27 cars would be made in 1963. The little company had established itself as part of the motor racing scene in fewer than 18 months. The gamble by both Jack and Ron had paid off and, further, the Brabham Racing Organisation was to be joined by Californian Dan Gurney, one of the quickest drivers of that or any other day.

At the end of the year, just before Christmas, Ron and Norma celebrated the birth of their second daughter, Julie. Ron had to drive Norma to the hospital through a fog so thick that Jann, who was then just six and a half years old, had to walk in front of the car to guide them.

A generation on, Julie adds further insight into how Ron pursued the often conflicting roles of busy businessman and father: 'My initial thought was that Dad couldn't have had much influence on me as I was growing up because he was never there. Yes, he would come home for dinner at 7pm, but then he would go back to the factory afterwards, except at weekends, when he would often fall asleep in front of the telly! Yet the strength of his character must have come through.

'I used to think we were poor because he always drove around in an old Ford Escort van, wearing an anorak that had definitely seen better days. Any purchase seemed to have to satisfy a full cost-benefit analysis, which was probably not a bad philosophy at all – even now I find it hard to go on a spending spree, and I always shop around for a good deal.

'He would push me to do well at school, trying to drive the competitiveness in me, but even when I scored 98% he would ask me what had happened to the other 2%. Of course, it was all meant as a joke, but I probably took it to heart too much. Like the time I walked into the living room one evening before going out wearing the latest fashion – cropped trousers. I asked if I looked OK, but was somewhat disappointed when Dad asked if I couldn't afford the rest of the trousers!

'But it's thanks to Dad that I passed both my car and motorbike tests within a few months of being 17. I had been mad on horses, but he'd steered me towards motorized things by getting me interested in a monkey bike he had bought for use at the race circuits – so much so that I wore out the back garden with it and ended up driving it 20 miles a day to college and back. Then one day, disappointed to hear that I'd been overtaken going down hill by a milk float, Dad got Roberto Moreno to tweak the engine – which was great until it seized. A neat way of getting a proper bike, though!

'Yes, I was definitely becoming a tom-boy, and was kicking myself for not having got interested in competition driving earlier, but the more interested I became, the more Dad cooled down on the whole thing.' 'At one stage Julie wanted to work in the business,' Ron says, 'but I didn't think there was enough future for her there.'

'After University, Dad's outlook seemed to change. All along I'd been led to believe that I had to stand on my own two feet, make my own way and, after education, earn a living. But suddenly he was offering me the chance to take a year off before starting work to be a ski guide. Looking back, maybe I should have taken the opportunity, but the way I had been brought up, I just couldn't come to terms with having to rely on him for income.'

All that, of course, was in the future, and as Ron and Norma were guided on their way to hospital on that foggy night by Jann, they were preoccupied with the more immediate problems of parenthood.

By the time Julie was born, the family had settled into a comfortable home on the outskirts of Woking. Each morning Ron would drive to work, come home for lunch, then it would be back to the factory until at least seven at night. The neighbours, mainly bank managers and the like, had no idea that the quiet man in their midst was creating his own little industrial revolution.

5

Joining the establishment

To cope with the increase in work, Ron took on Michael Hillman as an assistant designer. Michael, who as I write is a Director and Vice-President of Harley-Davidson, the motorcycle manufacturer, recalls: 'I had graduated through the Rolls-Royce training programme and come top of my class, winning a prize. I had been hired at £3 5s (£3.25) a week and there was no sign of an increase. When I broached the matter, modestly pointing out that I had been the star pupil on the programme, I was told about the honour of working for Rolls-Royce . . . I left.

'A little later I was walking down Dover Street, in London, when I passed an employment agency. I went in and said that I was a car designer looking for a job. They said: "That's funny, we had Jack Brabham in here this morning and he's looking for a designer." Apart from anything else I was a motor racing enthusiast and I imagined that there'd be a queue around the block for a job like that. So I phoned the works at once, Ron told me to come down and I caught the next train.

'The first thing he did was to point at the phone on his desk and say: "How would you cast that?" "You don't cast it," I said, "it's injection moulded." "But if you had to cast it," Ron said, "how would you do it?"

'We talked for about 10 minutes and I must have said a few things that made sense because he said: "Come with me." We went into the workshop and there was Jack leaning against a wall. You never saw Jack stand if there was a wall to lean against. I never even heard of him doing any exercise. I reckon the most strenuous thing he ever did was to get up from leaning against his wall. He was amazing!

'I remember him once testing a Formula One car at Goodwood and he was going balls-out. He came in and told me that the front suspension was flexing. He was right on the limit and he still had time to watch the front suspension.' (Professor Sid Watkins, Formula One's medical chief, records in his book *Life At The Limit* that Jack's blood pressure and pulse-rate actually went down when he sat in a racing car whereas that of every other driver he has known has gone up.)

Michael Hillman continues: 'We were at one race, at Zandvoort, and we had a problem with the oil tanks. We had to make them there in the pits between practice and the race. Jack got into his plane, flew back to England, picked up the kit to weld aluminium and flew back, landing at two o'clock in the morning of race-day. I think that was the year he finished second in the race.

'That was the thing about Brabham the company, and Brabham the man. Jack and Ron were there for everyone. Can you imagine a modern equivalent? You'd occasionally get some punter who complained about his car, so Jack would turn up at a track and show the guy how fast it could be driven. You can't argue with lap times.

'Anyway, after my 10-minute interview, I'm following Ron through to where we come across Jack leaning against this wall. Ron goes up to him and I hear this stream of noise. It was Ron speaking in Strine – English as spoken by Australians. I'd never heard anything like it. It was incomprehensible to me, because in the early 1960s most of us in England had never heard Strine spoken in full flow. Then Jack grunted, and that meant I was hired.

'Ron said: "The pay's £18 a week, can you start this afternoon?" Not next Monday, or next month, but right after lunch. I had to tell him that I didn't have my drawing instruments with me, so I started work next morning.

'I went there with Rolls-Royce training and a prize, but I was green. On the other hand, I got the best possible training imaginable. It was spectacular. For a start I had to go from text books to immediacy – you don't win races by turning up a day late.

'For seven years I was Ron's pencil, and during that time I worked on 60 or 70 different types of car – you've got to remember all the variants, the hillclimb cars and so on. Can you imagine that, 70 cars in seven years?

'You've also got to remember that we went through the most radical period of change that there has been in motor racing, from 1½ to 3 litres, from spaceframes to monocoques, then there was the arrival of wings. The best way I can put it is to say that my first job was to draw a wheel which was 15 inches in diameter and 6 inches wide. At the end I was drawing wheels which were 13 inches in diameter and 18 inches wide.

'I only wish that we had a racing programme at Harley-Davidson so that our young engineers could go through the same experience. When I first joined Harley in 1975 I could not believe how long product development took, it was five or six years. OK, we have to take account of a lot of laws, rules and regulations that motor racing doesn't have to consider, but my training at Brabham helped me to reduce the lead time.'

Although the most public face of Brabham would be the Formula One cars, Ron was actually to have very little to do with the running of them until 1966. In fact, MRD made a loss on the cars it sold to BRO, and that became a source of irritation.

On the other hand, Jack was not a sleeping partner in the core business. He was frequently at the factory and it was only through his network of connections that Ron was able to use the full-scale wind-tunnel at the Motor Industry Research Association (MIRA). Normally this was reserved for the car industry, but first Jaguar, and later the Rootes Group, booked time in the tunnel and passed it over to MRD. Ron was using the facility from early 1963 and at that time Brabham was the only racing car company to do wind-tunnel testing.

Lotus had introduced inboard suspension, to get the springs out of the airflow, and since Jim Clark and the Lotus 25 were the class act in Formula One, it became the fashion to have inboard suspension. But Ron decided not to follow the fashion and some commentators thought he was being conservative. Not a bit of it, he had done wind-tunnel testing to find out precisely what the reduction in drag was by mounting the springs inboard and it turned out to be less than 2 per cent.

Since most of Ron's customers had only one mechanic, and that included Formula One customers, the slight advantage which was gained by taking the springs out of the airflow was negated by a more complicated design which would take longer to set up. Ron's guiding principle was: 'No matter how good he is, a tired mechanic makes mistakes', and he stuck with the simple solution. Because customers could work on their cars more easily, and make adjustments more quickly in the limited time available to them, they were better able to get the most out of their cars. Simple, when you think about it, and Ron had thought about it.

Besides, as he points out: 'Inboard suspension took up room at the front where the car is narrow and where the driver's feet have to go.' Since he didn't jump up and down and shout about it, people assumed that it was just conservatism, but if you know, positively know, that the latest tweak which has the opposition in a tizz doesn't actually work, you'd be dumb to tell them.

Much the same happened a few years later when everyone in Formula One got excited by four-wheel drive. BRM had built a 4WD car in 1964, tested it, then put it aside. Three years later, Lotus, Matra, Cosworth and McLaren were all building 4WD cars, but not Ron. He says: 'I did a design study on four-wheel drive, which we called the BT27, but it was only a study. It was never designed, let alone did we cut metal.

'For a start, a 4WD system would have added 80lb to the car, and I couldn't see how we could get it down to the minimum weight limit. Then there was the matter of power loss through friction. Then you had to run a drive-shaft alongside the driver, which would have meant a wider car. Finally you had to allow extra space at the front to accommodate another differential. You had to finish up with a car that was heavier, wider, longer and less powerful, and I could see no advantage in that.'

Leading Formula One teams did not go through the same mental process and they wasted a lot of time, effort and money. What Ron did instead was to introduce wings to Formula One. To be accurate Brabham and Ferrari dead-heated on this, but everyone else soon realized that aerodynamics could provide the grip they had been seeking.

Ron's reputation for being an arch-conservative came about principally because he stuck with spaceframes longer than anyone else, but the fact is that he was the first to use adjustable anti-roll bars, doughnuts instead of splines for plunge (length change) in the final-drive, and aerofoils. Standard-Triumph uprights were commonly used by most constructors, fitted with their trunion at the bottom which meant the wishbone had to be inclined at the castor angle. By machining the bottom of the upright to fit a spherical bearing Ron was able to mount the wishbone with its axis horizontal, which made chassis-frame manufacture simpler and at the same time gave a measure of anti-dive.

As for the accusation that he was tardy in switching to monocoques, he says: 'A good monocoque is stiffer torsionally, but that is not the only stiffness you need. We had tubes running directly from one load point to another so the suspension loads from the spring units were fed into the tubes and across the car.

'Since the cars were then comparatively softly sprung, torsional stiffness was not nearly as important as in today's cars which are sprung so stiffly. With a spaceframe you can allow for the deflection made by the right front wheel, and let the front left absorb the stresses, so our frames didn't suffer breakages and yet were stiff in the way I thought was important.

'Anyway, our customers preferred spaceframes. They were easier to service and maintain, and the Formula Two and Three circuses travelling around the Continent had to earn their starting money in order to live. If they had a mild shunt they could straighten a spaceframe relatively easily, but even an exchange monocoque meant days rebuilding the car.

'One of the main things that the monocoque did was to clean up the outside of the car, but I don't think that anyone took advantage of that for some time. We could get the same effect by shaping our fuel tanks because they were made of aluminium, were not load-bearing and were hung on the frame.

'When I was in Australia I experimented with design, and it was a hobby, but when I came to England it became my livelihood, and I suppose you could say that I became a commercial engineer rather than an innovator. I had to earn a living and establish a business producing racing cars. That fact was a stabilizing influence on the cars I designed. In this business you can't afford to produce a loser, and so long as you produce successful cars you don't want to produce cars which are too far ahead of their time, because this will immediately show your innovations to the opposition, and it's quite simple for people to produce replicas.'

For 1963 MRD offered four models, the most popular of which was the BT6 Formula Junior car, a revision of the BT2. Ron says: 'If you have to make a new car each year, unless there's a change in the regs, it's an admission that you cocked-up on last year's car. In that respect my philosophy was different to Lotus, but part of that I think was that Lotus employed designers, and the designers felt they had to come up with new cars all the time. I just did development when I could because I was doing everything myself.

'It also meant that, because the cars were developments of the previous model, when someone came to buy a new one he had a good market for his old car. If we had adopted the Lotus philosophy, this would not have been so. Long-term, my philosophy proved to be the right one, which is why we were more successful than other people at selling production cars.'

The 1963 season also saw the arrival of the first Brabham sports car, the BT5. Ron recalls: 'The Rootes Group ran a quarter-scale model in a wind-tunnel for us. You couldn't call it serious wind-tunnel testing as we know it today because nobody knew very much about that at the time. For example, we had no idea of the influence of the road on the aerodynamic performance of the car because there was no rolling-road facility in tunnels in those days. But by putting the model in the tunnel at least we were able to get a drag figure for the body shape we intended to use, even if we didn't know enough at the time to make much use of it.

'What we didn't realize at first, when we completed the BT5 and started testing it, was that the back end was lifting, causing the car to oversteer severely on fast corners, which we found we were unable to correct by making the usual suspension adjustments. We only found out the cause the following year with the BT8, which had basically the same body. We took it to Goodwood, and while Jack drove I knelt in the passenger seat with my head under the engine cover – no helmet, no harness, just me hanging on the best I could, looking at what the back end of the car was doing at high speed. Jack didn't hang about, either, or we'd have learned nothing. That's how we discovered that the back end was lifting. We were able to fix it by adding a flat sheet across the back of the body and adjusting it up and down as necessary. You'd call it a spoiler now, but I called it the "duck tail". One of the BT5s was bought by a Canadian driver and he went over the top of the banking at Monza in it, and I often wonder whether it was because the back end became light.'

In very broad terms, the BT5 was a two-seat version of the Formula Junior car, but with a Ford-Lotus Twin Cam engine in the back. 'I didn't really like sports cars,' says Ron. 'You have to worry about things like doors and you've got all those extra panels to fasten to the chassis. Besides, we were going through a lot of changes, both with tyres and the regulations, and it's so much easier to respond to changes on open-wheeled cars. The BT8, for instance, was designed for 15-inch wheels, and then Dunlop introduced these fat little 13-inch wheels, and at the same time there was a new rule laying down a minimum ground clearance, so we had to jack the whole thing up.'

Two BT5s were built and Ian Walker bought the other one and ran it for Frank Gardner and Paul Hawkins, another Aussie. Sometimes they raced it with a Ford 1,100cc Formula Junior engine, but it was never a great success. The Lotus 23, which was the BT5's main rival, already had more than a year of development behind it, there were a lot of them around, and some pretty good drivers were racing them. Against that, Ron needed a fifth ace up his sleeve, and he didn't have one.

His next Formula One car was the BT7, which had a longer wheelbase, a different body profile and revised rear suspension. 'That was the story of my cars,' Ron says. 'We'd begin with a wheelbase which was the current standard at the time, and as we increased it, so the car got better.'

The BT7A was the 'International' car. Most of these went to customers in Australia and New Zealand, where the Tasman series was run to a 2½-litre formula, which enabled people to run old Formula One cars, including front-engined ones. Usually the BT7As were fitted with a four-cylinder Coventry Climax FPF engine.

Altogether, 27 cars were built and sold in 1963, and although BRO was only a customer, with which Ron had little daily contact, the fact remains that Formula One was the ultimate test for his design ability, especially since his cars shared Coventry Climax V8 engines with Cooper and Lotus, enabling direct comparisons to be made.

Dan Gurney signed for BRO, but he did not begin his season until the Monaco Grand Prix in May. Jack says: 'Neither Dan nor I were actually paid by the Brabham team. BRO provided the cars, but our earnings came from prize money, which wasn't that much, and by contracts with trade suppliers.'

Jack had run the earlier BT3 in the British curtain-raisers and had looked as though he would at least take second place in the Glover Trophy at Goodwood until he was delayed by a loose wire. Then he qualified second fastest for the Aintree 200, but a piston broke on race morning, so he became a non-starter, while in the International Trophy at Silverstone he was hampered by his engine cutting out. This race was won by Jim Clark and his Lotus 25 – and that was to be the story of 1963.

Jack says: 'Coventry Climax didn't have the resources to give all of its customers proper service, and their best efforts went to Lotus and Jimmy Clark. Then there was the problem with the supply of gearboxes until Mike Hewland got on top of things. Colin had got his own gearbox and he was also pretty good at installing engines in cars.'

At Silverstone, Jack had a new Hewland five-speed gearbox. It was a development of the transmission already used on the Brabham Formula Junior car and MRD did more than any other make to put Hewland on the map.

The troubles the team had in the non-Championship races continued in the first Championship round at Monaco, where both Brabham and Gurney had engines blow in practice. Colin Chapman then lent Jack a spare Lotus 25 so he could make the start, but he was all at sea in the car.

Gurney had a new BT7 for this race. Right from the start, Jack had agreed to take second place in the team so, while the new car was handed to Gurney, he waited patiently in line behind other MRD customers for the second BT7 chassis to be built. After some wind-tunnel work – serious work this time, with the whole car in the MIRA tunnel – Ron had remodelled the nose to prevent under-car air turbulence. It was still probably the only Formula One car of the day to have had the benefit of serious wind-tunnel testing.

Gurney retired at Monaco, but at Spa he qualified second fastest and looked like finishing second in the race until the heavens opened and, no lover of Spa in the wet, Dan eased off to finish third. At a time when cars were tending to get smaller, the size of drivers was becoming increasingly important. Jack himself was only a touch under 6ft, but Dan was a giant by comparison and he weighed more than any of his rivals. In a formula where engines were producing only about 180bhp, his extra weight and the drag caused by his height meant that Gurney must have lost about 5 per cent of his available engine power in comparison with a slightly built driver like Clark. Perhaps this meant he was having to drive that much harder, which would partly explain the woeful lack of reliability his cars suffered. Dan Gurney should have won far more than four of the 86 Grands Prix in which he took part.

It was around the time of the Monaco Grand Prix that Ron went down with mumps. Michael Scarlett recalls: 'I was called to Ron's bedside at his home for a conference. I was absolutely terrified because I was not only in fear of Ron at the best of times, but I was also afraid of catching mumps. It's highly contagious and very nasty if you catch it as an adult. Ron was particularly tetchy that day because he was inactive, and soon after, when Mike Hewland made me an offer, I took it. Mike was demanding, but he was not like Ron.

'At lunch time a group of us – David Mills, Michael Hillman, Tony Southgate, Frank Gardner and myself – would drive off to a local pub, and there was always a point when someone would say: "Right. One-two-three..." and on "three" we would shout "Bollocks to Tauranac"!

'We called ourselves the Dustbin Club because we all felt we'd been rubbished by Ron. We even got as far as discussing a club tie – it would have been in dark green with a roundel in the middle, and in the roundel would have been a dustbin. Of course, we never actually got around to doing it.'

As the season progressed, so BRO improved. Gurney came second in the Dutch Grand Prix despite a pit stop when a chassis member broke. He had one of the new flat-crank Coventry Climax FWMV units and the engine bay had been modified to accept it. The tube which broke had a fuel pipe on it, so it had to be taped up. Brabham, who was driving his new BT7 for the first time, held

47

second until a throttle spring broke . . . again.
   Ron says: 'Jack ran a tight ship, so there was only one mechanic on each car. I think that one extra mechanic on the team might have made the difference; it would have been a case of laying out a little more and gaining a bigger return.
   'The Formula One cars had a lot of problems with their throttle linkages. This is only a guess, but I reckon it was due to the drivers insisting on a 100 per cent throttle opening, whereas you don't actually need a completely open throttle in order to gain maximum power – you need a little bit of play in the cable. Like everyone else, we used Bowden cables, but BRO had more breakages because when the accelerator pedal was pressed against the stop there was a slight stretching of the cable and that was causing the problem.'
   Both drivers qualified in the top five at Reims for the French Grand Prix, where Jack finished fourth and Dan fifth, and both were on the front row at Silverstone, where they led the opening laps until the inevitable Clark spoiled their fun. In any case, both Jack and Dan later retired with engine problems.
   Jack took a single car to Solitude for a non-Championship race, and won it. This meant that Brabham had scored its first victory in Formula One before its first anniversary, a remarkable feat. Even though it had not been a Championship event, Jack had beaten a strong field.
   But there was a less happy time at the Nürburgring for the German Grand Prix when Jack's transistor box failed on the line; he did well to claw his way back from dead last to seventh, while Dan retired with gearbox failure.
   At the Kanonloppet, another non-Championship race run in heats at Karlskoga, Sweden, the BT3 was entered for Brabham's protégé, Denny Hulme, who finished fourth overall. Meanwhile, Jack had the pleasure of heading Jim Clark and Trevor Taylor in the works Lotuses in the first heat, only to have his engine cut out, but he got going again and finished third. Then the rain came, and this led to a ploy by Lotus which was classic gamesmanship.
   The overall result was decided on a points basis with the aggregate time of the two heats being the tie-breaker. In the second heat, when it rained heavily Lotus went for a secure finish and simply followed Jack at a safe distance. At the end of two heats all three had scored equal points. Clark and Brabham each had a first and a third (1+3=4) while Taylor had two seconds (2+2=4), but when the times were taken into account, Clark, who had won the faster heat, was the overall winner with Taylor second and Brabham third.
   In the Mediterranean Grand Prix at Pergusa, one of a host of non-Championship Formula One races that year which attracted a field of privateers graced with a sprinkling of stars, Brabham retired, but he won the non- Championship Austrian Grand Prix. Like the earlier race at Solitude, the entry was a strong one and included Clark in his works Lotus. It turned out to be a race of attrition and at the end only three drivers were classified as finishers. Jack won by five laps, which is a record for a Formula One race.
   Gurney led the Italian Grand Prix, swapping the lead with Clark, but he retired with a fuel feed problem, while Brabham was on course for third until he had to make a late stop for fuel, which dropped him to fifth. Neither driver was too happy in the Oulton Park Gold Cup, although Jack took fourth place, and he was fourth again in the US Grand Prix, while Dan, who had been battling for second place, retired with a broken chassis-frame.
   Gurney held second in the Mexican Grand Prix (which was a Championship race in 1963) until he untaped a fuel tap to change over to another tank and fuel

flooded the cockpit. That necessitated a pit stop, which dropped him to sixth, but the Guv'nor inherited Dan's spot and came home second. Dan then made amends by taking second in South Africa, while Jack spun off. For a first full season it had been a good showing, with Gurney finishing fifth in the Drivers' World Championship and Brabham third in the Constructors' Cup.

Cooper, however, continued to slide. After Jack had left, the Coopers kept Bruce McLaren at arm's length on the technical side. John Cooper has said that they didn't want to become too reliant on a driver who might leave at any time. But this was a fundamental error because Bruce had a lot to offer, and since Cooper was not utilizing his talent, it meant that he had a progressively less competitive car to drive, and that, in turn, made him the more likely to leave.

Like Jack, Bruce had established his own racing team to look after the cars he raced privately. When Owen Maddock left Cooper at the end of 1963 his first job was to design the McLaren M1 Group 7 sports car. Then early in 1964 Bruce announced a tie-up with Elva to manufacture this car, which would lead the way to him establishing his own Formula One team.

As well as Brabham's promising showing in Formula One, MRD had done well with its other customer cars, and of the 16 most important Formula Junior races this year in Europe, nine had fallen to Brabham BT6s. The most successful Brabham driver was Denny Hulme, who won six of his 14 starts with the works car and he also broke five lap records.

Denny would become an integral part of the Brabham story for several years, although not yet in Formula One. Jack was still enjoying his racing, and in Gurney he had a driver so quick that Jim Clark would say that Dan was the only rival he feared. Dan was also interested in engineering, although Len Terry, who later designed cars for him, says that he was prone to tinker with his machines when they were best left alone. Ron concurs: 'Jack was always changing things, but that's different from being a fiddler. Dan reckoned he could tell a eighth of an inch difference in the adjustment of a roll bar, but I reckon that you'd have to go to half an inch before he, or anyone, would have noticed.

'The trick with Dan was to engineer his brain. He'd ask for adjustments, and all you had to do was disappear around the back of the car, pretend to do things and then tell him everything was OK. Then, once his mind was at ease, he would go out and be as quick as anyone.'

There was one other notable Brabham driver in Formula Junior in 1963 – Roy James. Roy had turned up at the works over the winter and had bought a new BT6 for cash. He was a bit on the wild side, but he was quick. In fact, in British national racing in 1963 he was the most successful driver until late August, and trailing him was a young Scot called Jackie Stewart.

Then, at the August Bank Holiday meeting at Goodwood, Roy set pole position during the Saturday practice session, but on race day, Monday, he was nowhere to be seen. Instead, dozens of coppers were at the circuit, all wanting to finger Roy's collar. The race went ahead without him. The meeting was taking place just a few weeks after the Great Train Robbery, and in due course Roy received a 30-year gaol sentence for his part in it. For months afterwards, people were spotted at night at Goodwood with torches and spades . . .

At the end of the year, Jack and Denny took a couple of BT7As Down Under for the Tasman series. Denny won one race, Jack won three, but Bruce McLaren and his Cooper won four and the series. A nice feature of this year's series was that Bruce won the New Zealand Grand Prix and Jack won the Australian Grand Prix.

The Tasman series was a pretty satisfactory arrangement for all concerned. The stars could command good starting money and expect to come away with the lion's share of the prize money, while the local drivers were thrilled to meet and be able to pit themselves against the stars. Also, the social life was pretty good.

One of the locals attracted to the series just a little later was a New Zealander called Bill Stone. Bill would come to Europe to race in the late 1960s and would play his own part in the story of the British racing car industry. In 1969 he would become the very first employee of March Engineering and, four years later, he would co-found with Adrian Reynard a company called Sabre Automotive, which would evolve into Reynard Racing Cars.

Bill recalls: 'I used to work half the year and race the other half, ultimately with a Brabham fitted with a Ford Twin-Cam engine. This meant I got to race against and socialize with the likes of Clark, Hill, Brabham, McLaren and Surtees. In all, I drove in four New Zealand Grands Prix and the record books say that I was a Grand Prix driver! I raced Brabhams back home and then raced one when I came to Europe – Frank Williams sold it to me. The great thing about them was that they didn't need setting up, you just drove them. That led me to think that I was pretty good at setting up my cars. Then I bought a McLaren M4A, and it quickly taught me that I knew nothing.'

Many of the visiting drivers from Europe brought over their own cars and at the end of the series, which usually lasted from the beginning of January to the beginning of March, the cars would be sold on to local drivers. All in all, it was a lucrative and enjoyable way of either paying a visit home or having a holiday in the sun. That was one of Jack's perks, while Ron was stuck at home minding the shop. It was beginning to irritate him just a little.

6

The Repco connection – 1

Repco is an important thread in the MRD story because not only did the company allow MRD the use of a factory when it was starting up but, most famously, it provided the engines which won two Formula One World Championships. In recent years we have become used to many good things coming out of Australia, but until the 1960s Australia tended to be a place people went to rather than came from. So Repco played its part in defining a new Australia, one that could take on Europe at anything and do its share of winning.

Ron takes up the story: 'Coventry Climax had been taken over by Jaguar in 1963 and Jaguar supported motor racing only when they could see a profit in it, or when it helped them to sell more cars. Immediately following the takeover there was talk about Climax withdrawing from motor racing – I don't know what pressure was put on them to stay, but they did agree to stay for the time being. Even so, Climax stopped building its four-cylinder engines and they had a batch of them on their hands. Jack did a deal, we got the engines cheap, and we built the BT8 sports car to use them.

'The Climax FPF had been virtually the only engine used in the Tasman series and Repco had an arrangement to service and make parts for them, so there was never going to be any problem with spares for our batch of cars. Repco had also modified some of the engines we'd used in the Tasman series. But with the production of the FPF coming to an end, a replacement unit would be needed for the Tasman series.'

The number of new cars taking part in the Tasman races was not great, the 'pool' of cars tending to increase by only about five or six each year. However, as most of them used the Climax FPF engine, by buying all the remaining stock, Jack advanced the time, by perhaps as much as two or three years, when a replacement would be needed.

Ron continues: 'Jack began to suggest to Repco that a light, simple, V8 engine would be an ideal replacement for the Climax FPF. Frank Hallam, who was Repco's General Manager, was responsive to the suggestion – he was a motor racing enthusiast. So Jack began to work away on him, knowing that a 2½-litre Tasman engine could provide the basis for a 3-litre engine for the new Formula One which was coming in 1966.

51

'Jack knew that he couldn't ask Repco to undertake the design and build of a ground-up new racing engine (although Ford would soon finance Cosworth Engineering to produce the DFV, Repco were not in that league). Therefore he had to sell the idea gently, and he began by looking around for a suitable block.

'Buick and Oldsmobile each had a lightweight unit of the right size – they were virtually identical, but the Olds had more studs in the cylinder head, which made it the first choice. When negotiations with Repco had progressed a little further, Jack produced an Oldsmobile block and also some pilot layout drawings.

'He demonstrated to Repco that it would be possible to make an all-Australian racing engine at a fairly low cost using an existing block and some other proprietary parts. He sold it on the basis that it should be reliable, could be capable of finishing in the points, and would be a new product for Repco to sell. It would also beat the drum for Australian engineering.'

Jack had prepared his case well, and it helped, of course, that he was already a double World Champion – there were not many international celebrities from Oz at that time. The real point about the proposal, however, was that it reflected the approach that Jack and Ron adopted in their own business, in which they had been demonstrably successful.

During 1963, Repco made its preparations and appointed an engineer called Phil Irving to work with Jack and Ron. Irving was an Australian who had spent some time in England where he had worked on Velocette and Vincent motorcycle engines. He had also created a special cylinder head, which Repco were making for Holden engines. Irving had a reputation for being difficult, even eccentric, but he also had a devoted following since he had written a number of books on engines. He claimed not to be interested in self-publicity, yet his autobiography runs to more than 560 pages.

An initial budget of £10,000 was earmarked for the project (which had to include Irving's salary), and in March 1964 he set up his drawing board in a rented flat in London. Irving needed to be in England in order to have close liaison with Jack and to be able to speak directly to suppliers of ancillary equipment such as fuel injection kits.This meant he was 12,000 miles from the Repco works, and the main method of communication was by airmail letter.

Irving's principal task was to design a new cylinder head, but the head which was delivered to Repco was not quite the one which they had been expecting. The official excuse was that communication had broken down because of a long postal strike in the UK, but the real reason was that Irving had departed from the original brief. The strike was only in Britain and as Jack was racing on the Continent most weekends there was no difficulty in posting letters out, while letters from Repco could have been sent to someone like Jabby Crombac, who lived in Paris and was at most of the races.

Anyway, there were variations from the original plan, and Frank Hallam, who was himself a fine engineer as well as a crusty individual, was not happy with them. He was also not impressed by Irving filling parts of the block with Araldite, although the engines used to win the 1966 World Championship had Araldite in them. Araldite was then a new substance, and Irving mixed it with aluminium dust to form a material which could be applied to the block and, when set, machined.

Neither man being easy-going, a clash was inevitable – and it would come in 1966 – but by the end of 1964 a solid basis for progress had been established.

The Repco connection – 1

Ron recalls: 'Jack worked with Phil Irving, not in designing the engine, but keeping Phil supplied with parts and putting him in touch with people who could do work for us at the English end. Jack and I both took the view that it is better to use components which you can readily buy, and which have been developed, so the Repco unit had an Oldsmobile block, Daimler conrods and Alfa Romeo cam followers. That way we had ready access to spares and it speeded up the design and build processes. If you design everything from scratch it can take forever, and it can cost too much.

'Jack also arranged for some of the machining to be done at HRG. They had once made sports cars and their works were close to his garage at Chessington. I vetted everything to make sure that it would fit into the frame. The engines were assembled in Melbourne by a company called Repco-Brabham Engines Pty, who dyno-tested them and then shipped them back to Britain where they were maintained and developed.'

Phil Irving had an assistant, John Judd, who went on to become one of the top engine designers in motor racing. When it became clear that Coventry Climax was withdrawing from racing, Jack approached Harry Spears, who was in charge of the Climax engine build shop, with an offer to take charge of the engine shop Jack intended to set up at BRO. Harry accepted the offer, and John Judd, who was his junior, said that he would like to follow him. Then Harry's wife objected to the move from Coventry to Surrey, whereupon Harry suggested that Jack should employ Judd instead. So John Judd was employed by BRO, but was then loaned to Repco to work with Irving in London, although he also spent two spells in Australia.

Perhaps it is appropriate at this point to dispel a popular misconception: the Repco 640 unit was not based on the Buick V8 engine which was sold to Rover. It was derived from that engine's twin, although even that link was limited because the amount of Oldsmobile in the finished Repco product was confined to the cylinder block. Nothing that moved was Oldsmobile.

The prime objective of the Repco V8 was to be a credible successor to the four-cylinder Coventry Climax FPF engine as the next-generation Tasman engine, mainly for use by amateur drivers. But Frank Hallam was able to sell the project to the Repco board because of the revenue which was expected to come not only from the Tasman engine, but also from a planned 4.3-litre sports car unit. By this time Repco had developed ambitions to become a major engine manufacturer, attracted by opportunities which were opening up all around them as 'big-banger' sports-car racing began to take off throughout the world.

Repco seemed to be in the right place at the right time, and exactly 51 weeks after Phil Irving had bought a drawing board in London, the first engine, a 2½-litre Tasman unit, was fired up. But it might as well have stayed in its box. It was a failure as a Tasman unit because Jack had no interest in it. Repco engines only worked in Formula One because those engines had a BRO input.

John Judd says: 'I think that Jack did a switch on Repco.' Be that as it may, the fact remains that the only Repco engines which were successful either on the track or in the marketplace were those with which Jack was intimately associated.

7

So near, so far

The 1964 season began with the prospect of up to seven Brabham cars appearing in a Grand Prix field because, after only one full season, the marque had replaced Cooper and Lotus as the first port of call for the Formula One privateer. Like so many landmarks in the Tauranac story, it is something which can be recorded in a sentence, but it takes longer to weigh and digest.

The BT3 was sold to Ian Raby, a car dealer from Brighton who, then 40 years old, had been described as 'one of motor racing's most professional of amateurs'. By concentrating mainly on non-Championship Formula One races, he managed to make a small profit from his racing while enjoying himself. He fitted a BRM V8 engine to his car which, by then, had been equipped with a Hewland gearbox.

A new Climax-powered BT11 was sold to Bob Anderson, a former motorcycle racer who had turned to cars comparatively late in his career. Bob was capable of fine performances while traipsing from circuit to circuit, living off starting and prize money. Many observers thought that he deserved a works drive, but he never quite cracked the system.

Rob Walker, who had enjoyed great success with Coopers and Lotuses, and had been Stirling Moss' entrant, paid Ron the accolade of ordering two Formula One BT11s for his team, which by then enjoyed the same status as a works entry. His Brabhams were to be raced with BRM engines coupled to six-speed Colotti gearboxes. Walker's regular drivers were Jo Siffert, from Switzerland, popularly known as 'the last of the late brakers', and the Swiss-domiciled Swede Jo Bonnier, while Jochen Rindt, from Austria, and the American Hap Sharp were occasional drivers.

By the beginning of 1964 there was a new young face at MRD, Nick Goozée, later to become the Managing Director of Penske Cars, the branch of the Penske empire which builds the cars for Team Penske to race. Nick recalls: 'I was brought up in a military family, sent to a good public school, and was basically expected to become Prime Minister or, at least, a Major-General.

'Every week we used to write our letters home and I'd also write letters to my two heroes, Stirling Moss and Jack Brabham. I even got some replies from Jack, so he moved up in status and became special.

'Then my father was posted to a base in the Home Counties, and we moved to a house near Byfleet. When I came home during the summer holidays in 1963 I cycled up to Surbiton and looked in at Cooper. It was summer, the garage doors were open and you could just stand there and look at people like John Cooper and Bruce McLaren working on the cars.

'I was invited in to take a closer look and I said something about wanting to be in motor racing. John said they were looking for a boy to help out, and was I interested? Was I ever? I was on my bike, racing home at the speed of light, when I had a thought. If I could get an offer from Cooper, perhaps I could get one from Brabham. When I reached Byfleet I saw a postman and he told me where the factory was.

'I presented myself and I was taken on – it was supposed to be just a holiday job. It was £5 for a basic 60-hour week and I thought I was rich. Of course, I was given all the rotten jobs, like there'd be a sack of Triumph Herald uprights and I was given a file and instructions. The thing was that I didn't want to leave, I was there with my heroes and I was telling my parents that a racing mechanic could earn a basic £15 a week and, so far as I was concerned, that was almost beyond imagination.

'Of course, my parents wanted me to stay on at school and complete my studies, and Ron took their side and tried to persuade me against the move. Finally I did go back to school, but I didn't complete my final year and basically I had my apprenticeship at Brabham. Ron and Jack gave me my chance, but it was Denny Hulme who took me under his wing. By turns, I became a fabricator and then factory manager, until I left to work for Penske in 1974.'

Sports car racing was enjoying a revival in 1964 and MRD was to make 12 BT8A sports-racers. Although the car was always known as the BT8, it was actually the BT8A; it had started out as the BT8 on skinny 15-inch tyres, but was adapted to the new and wider 13-inch wheels. What had started out as a problematic design was converted into a race-winner.

Although designed to use up Climax engines, the first BT8A had a 2-litre V8 BRM unit, and Jack won his class with that car at the Easter Monday Goodwood meeting, even though the engine was 'all revs and no power'. The BT8A was fundamentally similar to the BT5, but it had a 3-inch longer wheelbase and revised weight distribution. It also had the benefit of a year's experience with the BT5.

Although the BT8A is now barely remembered, it was a very successful car at national level. It flowered in the transitional period between the 1,500cc Lotus 23, which had embarrassed cars with twice the engine size, and the advent of the 'big banger' V8-engined sports-racers which would find their apotheosis in CanAm racing. It was light and nimble, which was beneficial, and it was also much more reliable than the early British-built cars with American V8 engines. Although the Yanks had engine reliability well under control, problems tended to arise when their engines were installed into British chassis.

Roger Nathan, a prominent club racer of the day, had a hugely successful season in his 2-litre BT8A; Stirling Moss bought a 2½-litre version for his SMART team; and Sid Taylor entered a BT8A for Denny Hulme. There were not many top-class sports car races in Britain, but Denny tended to win his class at the few that were staged, and in 1965 he would win outright the Tourist Trophy (which had no upper capacity limit) in his 2-litre BT8A.

During 1964 and 1965 the BT8A was the best sports-racer in the class immediately below the big V8s, and they continued to win in lesser events for a couple more years after that. One was even raced with a glassfibre top, pretending to be a GT car.

Alain Fenn recalls that when he was at Willments, Frank Gardner, who was their test driver, was asked to check out the Lotus 23c sports car that Paul Hawkins drove for them. He said 'it doesn't point', and suggested they fit a Brabham steering rack in place of the Triumph Herald one used originally. It did the job.

Meanwhile, Formula Junior having become a little too sophisticated to meet its original purpose as a single-seater 'primer', its replacement, Formula Three, was restricted to 1-litre production-based engines with a single carburettor and with a total minimum car weight of 400 kilograms. To spectators they looked little different from Formula Junior cars, although the '1-litre screamers' would produce some of the closest and most exciting racing ever seen. The cars were very closely matched in performance, and as there were still plenty of high-speed circuits available, some astonishing slipstream battles would take place. Some people continued to run their BT6s in Formula Three, while others converted theirs to the new Formula Two.

Like Formula Three, Formula Two was restricted to four-cylinder engines of no more than 1,000cc, but these could be bespoke racing engines provided they used a cylinder block from a production engine. Overhead camshafts were permitted, and the only real restriction was that they had to run on pump fuel. Cosworth Engineering took a significant step in the company's development by producing the SCA engine (Single Camshaft, Series A) in which the Cosworth cylinder head was mounted on a Ford 116E block.

The introduction of Formula Two helped MRD virtually to double its annual production once again, but the total of 50 cars built for the 1964 season included the BT12, an Offenhauser-engined car for Indianapolis. In its third full season, therefore, MRD's cars were competing in F1, F2, F3, sports car racing and at Indianapolis. Only Lotus had as wide a spread of activity and it had taken Colin Chapman rather longer than three years to achieve it.

The BT12 car for Indianapolis was ordered by John Zink, a leading IndyCar owner and a man with a record of innovation. He approached MRD after having consulted a number of people, including Dan Gurney, but he laid down some firm conditions. One was that Jack should drive the car, which in true Indianapolis style was to be entered as the John Zink Track Burner Special, and another was that it had to have Formula One spring rates, which was a big mistake.

Ron says: 'The customer had confused spring rates with wheel rates, and it was too softly sprung. I only went out to Indianapolis for the last few days before the race and I tried to get them to change the spring rates, but they knew best. I think they wanted what they saw as the magic of our Formula One car.'

Most of the work on the car was undertaken by Tony Southgate, who had been an apprentice at Dowty, in Coventry, and had built his own 750 special before landing a job as Eric Broadley's assistant at Lola, making him among the very first employed racing car designers in Britain. Then Ford bought Lola's undivided attention for a year to build what became the GT40. But when suits from Detroit descended upon the little factory in Slough, each eager to have a finger in the pie, Eric and Tony became thoroughly cheesed-off. Although Eric was under contract to Ford, Tony was not, and he voted with his feet. He joined

Ron and stayed at MRD for about 10 months. Then, when the guys in the suits left, he returned to Lola.

During his time with Ron, Tony had a hand in all of MRD's current projects, but was particularly involved in the BT12 IndyCar, which was essentially a modified BT11 Formula One car with a longer wheelbase and the Offenhauser engine. Tony does not remember his time at MRD with unbounded affection. 'At the time, Ron was not doing any drawing himself, but he'd give people a concept. If he didn't like it you'd hear this long nasal sound, "Noooo, noooo," – you've got to imagine the Australian accent. If you were at the receiving end, it was devastating. We used to have someone leave every week!

'I'd been used to working with Eric, who was an innovator. Look at his Lola Mk6 GT, that was awfully ambitious for a small company. I don't think that in those days Ron had sufficient confidence in himself to do anything original. He was much happier buying in parts, like stub-axles, and drilling a hole in them to make them work for his purpose.

'Against that, he provided the customers with what they wanted and the cars worked. Eric Broadley would have done anything to have avoided Ron's conservative approach, but that was the way that Ron worked, and what can you say? His cars won races. I can't say it was the best 10 months of my life, however.'

Recalling the race at Indianapolis, Ron says: 'We had to accommodate 59 gallons of fuel, and one advantage of a spaceframe is that there's always somewhere to hang a tank. However, one of the tanks split under the sheer weight. Jack came in for his first pit stop, I was running the pit, and we descended on him not realizing he was sitting in a bath of fuel. He was waving us away, but we got stuck in, refuelled it, and the fuel was dumped in the pit lane.'

It was not a great debut, but the car remained in the States and it was not unprofitably employed. Jim McElreath won three IndyCar Championship races with the BT12 in 1965 and finished third in the Championship. It was a remarkable feat for a driver who had been considered over the hill.

At the same time, an identical twin to the BT12 was doing well. During 1964 the BT12 had been crashed, and Clint Brawner, Mario Andretti's crew chief, offered to repair it provided he could make a copy. Zink agreed, and Mario Andretti won the 1965 Championship with his Brawner-Brabham, although it went under the name of Dean Van Lines Special. Mario was the first rookie to take the title in decades.

With a Ford engine fitted to the BT12, McElreath won the opening round of the 1966 series as well, and was runner-up in the Championship, while the car with which Andretti won his second title – still called a Dean Van Lines Special – was a further development of the Brabham-copy. Some designers would be quick to tell you all they could about something like that – justifiably proud of their achievement – but Ron had to be reminded of it. 'Yeah, I heard that's what happened,' he recalled.

Looking ahead for a moment, in 1966 Graham Hill (Lola) won the Indy 500 from Jim Clark's Lotus, but who was third, and catching them both after losing a minute in the pits because he'd stalled his engine? It was Jim McElreath in his two-year-old Brabham BT12, that's who!

Meanwhile, to return to Formula One, the 1964 car, the BT11, was a refinement of the BT7, with the same broad outline, but tidied up in detail and with modifications at the rear to accommodate the new breed of fatter Dunlop tyres. In line with MRD policy, the first BT11 went to a customer while the works drivers continued with adapted 1963 cars, which again had been modified to accept the wider tyres. Most constructors would only let the customer buy last year's technology, but MRD was a new breed of constructor and BRO was still only a customer.

Nevertheless, BRO's BT7s worked very well on the new Dunlops – as Ron points out, one of the most important design parameters is to make the tyres work – and in 1964 Brabham had a decided edge on the field. His season did not start too well when he spun and crashed in the very wet Lombank Trophy at Snetterton, but two weeks later he gave notice of his car's improvement by taking pole for the News of the World Trophy at Goodwood, then he disputed the lead with Clark and had second place in the bag until a broken wheel caused him to crash.

Jack then won the Aintree 200 after a battle with Clark which ended when Jimmy, in second place, tangled with some backmarkers and crashed. Although it was not a Championship event, everyone apart from Ferrari was present, so it was a good win. Then in the International Trophy at Silverstone, Gurney and Brabham took the first two places on the grid and Dan led until half-distance, but then retired with rear brake failure, whereupon Jack took the lead. Hill's BRM then moved up and the two men had an enormous dice for much of the second half of the race, which was only resolved on the last corner when Brabham went round the outside at Woodcote to win by about 2 feet, the timekeepers being unable to separate them.

Those early races demonstrated that the Brabham team had joined the very top rank. While others were busily copying the monocoque of the Lotus 25, and creating problems for themselves in the process, nobody thought to copy Brabham and stay with spaceframes, yet at the start of 1964 the BT7 was the class of the field.

The World Championship opened that year at Monaco, where Brabham shared the front row of the grid with Clark. Jimmy made his usual lightning start, but Brabham and Gurney lay second and fourth, with Hill's BRM in between. Both the BT7s, however, were to retire, Brabham's being the first to go, with a fuel injection problem, while Gurney dropped out with a broken gearbox.

Dan then put his car on pole for the Dutch Grand Prix and ran strongly until his steering wheel broke; unfortunately, the team had no spare in the pits. Jack, as previously noted, ran a tight ship and would never splash out on spares which were unlikely to be needed.

Dan took pole again in the Belgian Grand Prix and pulled out a huge lead in the race until, with two laps to go, he started to run out of fuel. He rushed into the pits, but teams were not then allowed to keep fuel in the garage, so rather than wait for the mechanic to fetch some from the paddock, Dan drove off again and ran dry. Then Hill's BRM, which had inherited the lead, did the same, which meant that Clark, who had been delayed by overheating, then took the flag, and promptly ran out of fuel on his slowing-down lap. Gurney's fine effort was scarcely rewarded by sixth place. So two races had been needlessly lost, and Dan is on record as saying: 'Jack was tighter than a horse's arse in summer', to which Ron comments: 'Dan should be the last man on earth to complain about someone else being tight!'

In the French Grand Prix at Rouen, Clark was on pole from Gurney, but when the Scot retired with a broken piston, Dan stroked home to win, with Brabham third. It was the American's first World Championship win for Brabham, and the first for the Brabham Racing Organisation, and both were long overdue.

In the British Grand Prix at Brands Hatch, both works cars were quick in practice but, more remarkably, there were no fewer than seven Brabhams in the field, this from a marque which had yet to celebrate its second birthday in Formula One. Apart from the two works cars and those of Raby and Anderson, Jo Bonnier had Rob Walker's BRM-powered BT11, Jo Siffert had a similar car, while Frank Gardner had a Formula Two BT10 fitted with a Ford Twin-Cam engine, which qualified faster than some pukka Formula One cars. However, this numerical show of strength produced nothing better than a fourth place for Jack Brabham and this after a couple of pit stops.

The following weekend, Bob Anderson finished third in a very wet Solitude Grand Prix, and in doing so he vividly demonstrated the validity of the Tauranac design philosophy because early in the race he had spun into a ditch, bent a chassis tube, but then been able to continue. Two weeks later he took the start in the German Grand Prix, having effected a simple and inexpensive repair.

At the Nürburgring the BRO cars were very competitive, and Gurney looked as though he was heading for a win when he took the lead on lap 4 and began to pull away. But then the Brabham luck struck, waste paper became caught in the nose of his car, causing the engine to overheat, and he finally finished 10th. When did anyone last see litter in Germany? Jack suffered a broken crownwheel and pinion, but Jo Siffert brought his Rob Walker car home fourth and established a claim to be noticed.

Siffert strengthened that claim in the Mediterranean Grand Prix at Enna, where he started from pole position and won. It was not a high-class field, but it included the Lotus team, and while Clark was only a tenth of a second behind at the flag, he was still behind, and Siffert had beaten him in a privately entered car.

The remaining races that year were all World Championship events apart from the Rand Grand Prix, which BRO did not enter. The cars qualified well at every circuit, with Gurney always in the top four, but in the races, although they ran at the sharp end of the field, every time bar one they either retired or were hampered by some fault – here a collapsed front suspension, there a flat battery. There was no pattern to the troubles, and it seemed as though luck had deserted the team.

The exception was the Mexican Grand Prix, where Jim Clark appeared to have the race, and the World Championship, in the bag when his engine blew on the last lap, allowing Gurney to slip by and win. But it was a victory which went almost unnoticed as Surtees had come home second in his Ferrari to clinch the title. It was tough on Clark and Lotus, but Gurney and Brabham had endured more than their share of bad luck during a year which had started so well for them.

Although he had taken two wins, Gurney finished only sixth in the Championship, one place lower than the previous year, when he had scored no wins at all. In fact, Gurney scored points in only three races, the two that he won and that sixth place at Spa, which should have been a win but for the cock-up over fuel. Dan should also have won the Dutch and German Grands Prix and gone on to take the World Championship. The Brabhams had the edge on the field in terms of performance, yet could not string the results together. Jack also only finished in the points three times.

It would be easy to say that there was something fundamentally wrong with his team, but Brabham was not the only team to misjudge the fuel situation at Spa, and who else has lost a Grand Prix through a broken steering wheel? Other people have suffered overheating through waste paper clogging the radiator, but in Germany? Gurney must have encountered the only scrap of litter in the country. The team suffered sheer bad luck, there's no other way of putting it.

Still, Brabham had won its first two World Championship races and MRD had replaced Lotus as the leading maker of production racing cars. This was something which nobody would have predicted only a year or so before since not only did Lotus have unmatched glamour, it also ran works cars in the lower formulae to help maintain its position.

The Formula Two BT10 was more or less a BT6 with sheet steel welded underneath, which both stiffened the frame and brought it above the minimum weight limit. It won nine of the 17 races, and since virtually everyone used the Cosworth SCA engine, the BT10 won on merit.

Denny Hulme partnered Jack in the official works Formula Two team, and each won races. There was no official European Formula Two Championship, so the French organized a championship built around five races held on French circuits and one at Avus, Berlin, and Jack won the title, with Denny second and Alan Rees in another BT10 third. In fourth place was Jim Clark. Jack has not always had his due credit for being a very quick driver, but during 1964 he beat both Clark and a newcomer, Jackie Stewart, both entered by the Ron Harris team, which looked after Lotus' interests in Formula Two.

Apart from the fact that Brabham cars were the class of the field in every single-seat formula, there were three other significant developments. One was that the veteran entrant John Coombs abandoned the Cooper he was running for Graham Hill and replaced it with a BT10. Coombs had enjoyed a long relationship with Cooper so it was quite a big step, and he would remain loyal to Brabham, always employing top drivers in his cars.

Ron says: 'I have always hated bartering. I have always taken the attitude there is the car, it costs so much – take it or leave it. But Coombs was a car dealer and he had to barter, it was his nature. When he arrived at the works, I'd warn David Mills, who really ran the place, and he would add 15 per cent to the price. Coombs would then haggle and he'd leave happy if he took 10 per cent off us.' John Coombs looked really pained when he was told about that in 1997.

Another significant fact was that Alan Rees was entered by Roy Winkelmann, and Roy Winkelmann Racing would eventually become the official works entrant for MRD; the Winkelmann outfit set new standards for the preparation of racing cars.

The third element was the arrival, at the wheel of a BT10, of a sensational new talent called Jochen Rindt. At Mallory Park, in May, in his first ever Formula Two race, Rindt sat on pole ahead of the works Lotuses of Jim Clark and Peter Arundell. It has to be remembered not only that Clark was the reigning World Champion, with a record seven wins during 1963, but that Arundell was considered by some to be potentially even quicker than Jimmy, so to set pole ahead of Clark and Arundell was an astonishing feat for any privateer, let alone a Formula Two debutant.

Attempting his first racing start in Formula Two, Jochen stalled on the line and was last away. Gritting his teeth, he hauled in the rest of the field, one by one, and finished just 8 seconds behind Clark and Arundell in a race of barely 40 miles. Two days later, at Crystal Palace, Rindt beat everyone, including Clark, Hill and Hulme. No other driver has arrived like a bolt from the blue in the way that Rindt did.

Since the coverage of motor racing in the mass media was then fairly skimpy, Rindt's achievement was, paradoxically, the more sensational. Many people only knew about it when they bought their copies of *Motoring News* and *Autosport*. The news hit you between the eyes.

Although Jochen was unable to sustain that form throughout 1964, that Whitsun weekend was enough to put him on the map. Later he would drive for Brabham in Formula One, and though that was to prove a disastrous season, the vast majority of Jochen's single-seater race wins would be in Formula Two Brabhams.

However, the 1964 Formula Three season was dominated by Jackie Stewart and Warwick Banks in Coopers. It was to be last successful season for Cooper in a formula in which the company had begun its life and in which it had ruled for so long. Their success was helped by the fact that the team was being run with great efficiency by Ken Tyrrell, that Stewart was maturing into one of the greatest of all drivers, that he had a special car which was lighter than customer cars, and it helped, too, that BMC supplied works engines which were at least as good as most of the Ford-based units. It took a little time for firms like Holbay to get the best from the Ford 105E engine under the new Formula Three tuning restrictions.

In numerical terms, Lotus had the upper hand, but won very little of consequence. Part of the problem was that Cosworth Engineering was so involved in Formula Two that its Formula Three engine lagged behind the Holbay unit. Although Lotus took its share of Formula Three wins in Britain, these were often at minor meetings; at the time, it was not unusual for even club meetings to include a Formula Three race in their programme.

Brabham was not as well represented as Lotus in Formula Three in Britain, although it figured strongly on the Continent, where there were also Brabhams under other names. For example, the new Formula Two and Formula Three cars from Alpine came about through a deal brokered by Jabby Crombac whereby MRD sold Alpine a car, some kits and the licence to make and develop the designs.

Being Alpines, they ran with Renault engines, and although they were outclassed by the Cosworth SCA unit in Formula Two, they did rather better in Formula Three, where Henri Grandsire won the French Championship. Jabby is of the opinion that they were probably slightly superior to the original car because, he thinks, the aerodynamics were a little better.

Less official a copy was the Italian De Sanctis, which was very successful in Italy. De Sanctis had been an early competitor in Formula Junior and when the Brits arrived and showed everyone how to build racing cars, De Sanctis copied the Brabham BT6. Imitation is the sincerest form of flattery, and Ron would be flattered by other outfits over the years. It is noticeable than when other firms were stuck for ideas, they invariably turned to Ron's cars to stimulate them;

you never saw copies of Lotus or Lola designs. Quite often, the copies were fairly successful, or in the case of the Brawner IndyCar, very successful.

It is fairly unusual for copies of racing cars to be as good as the original, but there were no secrets in a Brabham. So many parts came from catalogues that it was relatively simple to reproduce the design. What is extraordinary is that despite the simplicity of the cars, they were winners at every level. Their secret was harmony. Racing cars today are mainly about aerodynamics. Look at the car on pole and then look at the last car on a Grand Prix grid and their broad specifications will be the same. They'll both have carbonfibre monocoques, carbon brakes and so on. The backmarker will be produced to an astonishingly high standard and the main difference between it and the car on pole will not be engine power, but aerodynamics. A top Grand Prix team will have its own wind-tunnel and perhaps 20 people employed there. The ultimate sanction is the laws of physics.

Go back to the 1960s and designers could express their personalities through their designs. Colin Chapman was a charismatic but volatile man, and if you look at his portfolio you will find expressions of sheer genius and also some appalling designs which should never have left the drawing board. Look at Ron Tauranac's output and you will find the odd design which was not terribly successful, the odd car which needed working on, but there has been nothing which has been beyond redemption. His designs have always been harmonious and practical, in sharp contrast to some of the cars that Colin Chapman put his name to.

One person who worked closely with him for many years, however, says: 'Ron was mesmerized by Chapman. If Chapman came into a room at, say, a prizegiving, Ron's eyes never left him. I think that if Ron could reincarnate, he'd want to come back as Colin Chapman.'

8

The Honda connection - 1

Ron's relationship with Honda goes back to the early 1960s and it seems set to continue into the 21st century. It is one of the most remarkable, yet least remarked on, relationships in motor racing history, and it began through Jack.

As part of its long-term strategy, Honda bought a Formula One Cooper-Climax and they had difficulty in setting up the Weber carburettors. They asked for help and Jack Brabham broke one of his trips between Europe and Australia to show them how to do it. He made an indelible impression.

Everyone is vague about the year, but the best guess is 1961. The car was a Cooper T53 with a 1½-litre Coventry Climax FPF engine, and today it is in the Honda museum. Incidentally, 1961 was also the year when Honda won its very first motorcycle World Championship.

Only a couple of years earlier, the fact that a team of bikes and riders from Japan had entered the TT had attracted notice in the British national press; anything from Japan in those days was a novelty. However, when the three Hondas finished sixth, seventh and eighth in the 125cc race and won the team prize, it was not considered exciting enough to be given much prominence. But insiders noted it.

When Honda first appeared in competition, everyone looked to see who they had copied because for years Japan had been an imitator of European products. The cynics had a shock, however, because Honda's designs were not only original, the engineering was advanced.

Soichiro Honda had been a racing driver when a young man - most Japanese racing in the 1920s and 1930s had been on ovals - and he was acutely aware of the value of racing in developing ideas and promoting a company. In theory, a lot of companies have known that, but in practice not all have been able to use success to their best advantage. Honda has been unusual in that it has made participation in motor racing part of its corporate philosophy.

Tadashi Kume, with Kimio Shimmery, was set the job of designing the first motorcycle racing engines in 1957, and Kume recalls working in a small building with a leaking roof. 'As I was drafting drawings, I even had to put an umbrella over the drawing board.' That was the state of Honda when Soichiro Honda decided to go racing. He had visited the Isle of Man three years earlier and had determined that he would return to the island with his own team.

Fine, but at the time all Honda was making were engines you clipped on to bicycles and a small motorcycle with a top speed of 45mph. But Mr Honda was nothing if not ambitious and he went for it.

He was a volatile man, given to wearing colourful clothes at a time when most Japanese businessmen preferred dark-suited anonymity. If upset, he was as likely to express himself with a thrown spanner as a few angry words, but perhaps a more restrained person might have had a more restricted vision.

For one thing, he was a hands-on manager, who personally followed the progress of every new project on a daily basis and who fed his designers with his own ideas. Then – and this was most unusual in Japan – he did not groom his son to take over from him, but actually debarred his family from holding senior posts in the company. He realized that if a company is perceived to be a family dynasty it is unlikely to attract the best recruits from outside. Honda was striving for excellence in engineering, while running a Japanese company with a traditional hierarchical structure. This structure, with its emphasis on respect for seniority, was not conducive to tapping into the talent of young engineers in their most creative years.

One English designer of long experience who once worked for a Japanese company says: 'It's wonderful working for them. Back home I'm regarded as a Boring Old Fart who's over the hill. I go out to Japan and say: "I think we should have four wheels", and because I have age on my side they all bow and say: "Oldfart-san say four wheels. Good." Then I say: "An engine would be good." Then they all bow and say: "Oldfart-san say engine good. We have engine." We waste time holding meetings to agree that we need four wheels and an engine.'

It was that sort of attitude that Soichiro Honda wanted to break. A motor racing programme would allow his brightest engineers to experiment and compete, but within an alternative hierarchy. He recognized that while traditional Japanese practices had their strengths, there were lessons to be learned from the West – in particular, the ability to make decisions quickly.

The strategy worked. Tadashi Kume remembers: 'Jack-san and Ron-san constantly asked "Why?". That word drove me into a corner many times, but the word "Why?" became a valuable lesson in the later stages of my career.'

Nobuhiko Kawamoto says: 'When you are in a race, it does not matter whether or not you are a college graduate, or who you are. You feel that you are almost stripped to nothing. You are judged only on the basis of whether or not you can do your job.'

In a very short period of time, from 1958 to 1962, Honda went from being a leading player in the burgeoning Japanese market (which was anyway protected by trade tariffs) to being an international player and the world's largest producer of motorcycles.

Soichiro Honda, however, had always had one burning ambition, which was to produce cars bearing his name. He achieved this in 1962 with the S500, a baby sports car with a 531cc engine and twin chain drive - one to each rear wheel. Motorcycle thinking pervaded the car, which had such features as double overhead camshafts and one carburettor per cylinder, which otherwise you only got on racing engines.

As part of the company's excursion into cars, it was decided to go into Formula One. It was an incredible move. For a start there was then no major manufacturer in Formula One, nor had there been been since the brief

Ron the racer. Here he is at the wheel of his first Ralt in close company with Stan Jones' Maybach Special at Parramata Park, Sydney.

On the way to a new hillclimb record. Ron and his Ralt 500, now with low-pivot rear suspension and different wheels, climbed the 0.7-mile Newcastle course in 58.13sec to win the New South Wales Hillclimb Championship in September 1954, beating Jack Brabham.

The Tauranac brothers, Austin and Ron, with the Vincent V-twin-engined Ralt Mk IV, which was the last car Ron raced before coming to England.

One of a batch of five spaceframe chassis that ended up as Lynx Mk II Formula Junior cars after Ron had sold the drawings and parts to Lynx Engineering prior to leaving Australia for Europe.

Gavin Youl caused a sensation by claiming pole position with the original Formula Junior MRD at the 1961 August Bank Holiday meeting at Goodwood. The car was subsequently given the designation Brabham BT1.

The BT2 production version of the FJ Brabham was equipped with a Hewland Mk 5 gearbox and a glassfibre body by Specialised Mouldings, and was built for the 1962 season.

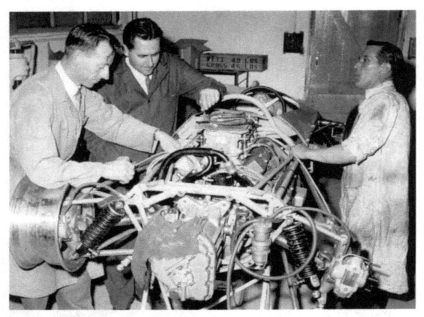

Ron and Jack join mechanic Stan Ellsworth in the MRD workshop as the BT3, their first F1 Brabham, nears completion.

The BT3 was subsequently sold to privateer Ian Raby, who replaced the original Coventry Climax engine with a BRM unit. Here he is leading Alan Rees' F2 Brabham-Cosworth at Brands Hatch.

The original Brabham sports car, the BT5, had been powered by a 1.6-litre Ford Twin Cam engine, but much the same body went over the BT8A, to which a duck tail was added to prevent the rear end lifting at speed. David Mills, who looked after the office for Ron and Jack, seems to be directing the photographer.

When Jack tested the BT8A for the first time at Goodwood it was fitted with a 2-litre BRM V8 engine, although the car was intended to use up a supply of surplus Coventry Climax engines.

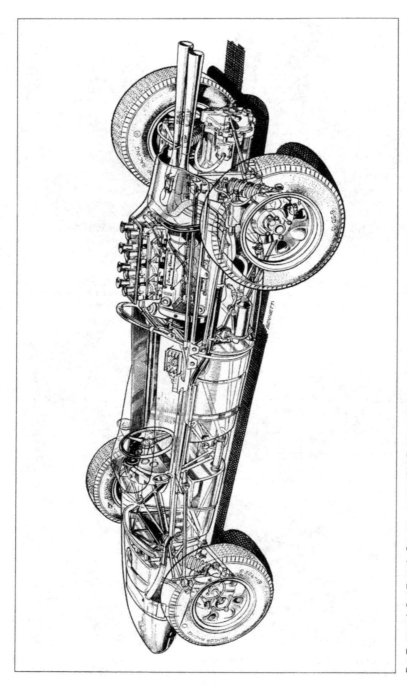

Ron Tauranac's first Formula One car was the 1962 Brabham BT3, powered by a Coventry Climax FWMV 1.5-litre V8 engine and fitted initially with a six-speed Colotti gearbox, although a Hewland five-speed unit would later replace it. Artist Bill Bennett's cutaway drawing for *Motoring News* reveals the spaceframe chassis, sidemounted fuel tanks, steeply inclined outboard suspension units and outboard-mounted Girling disc brakes.

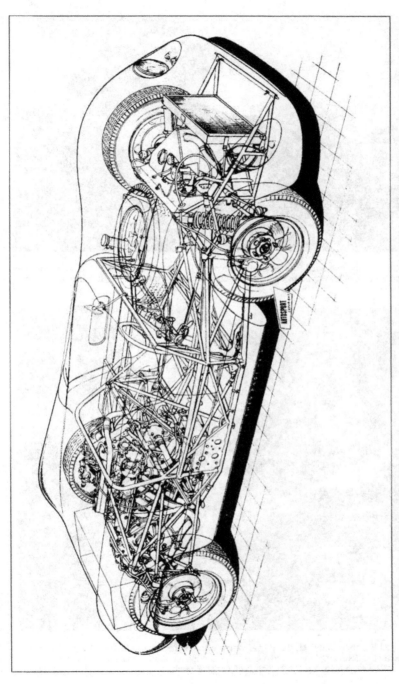

Although he much preferred single-seaters, Ron was prevailed upon to design a sports car in 1964, which in production form became the Brabham BT8A. Although intended primarily for the Coventry Climax FPF four-cylinder engine, the first car was tested with a 2-litre BRM V8, driving through a Hewland five-speed gearbox. The late Theo Page's drawing for *Autosport* highlights the absurdity of regulations which demanded space for a spare wheel and luggage.

Dan Gurney became Jack Brabham's first driving partner in his Formula One team and they worked well together from 1963 until 1965, after which Dan decided to build and race his own Eagles.

Ron's first Brabham IndyCar, the BT12, which was commissioned in 1964 by John Zink and entered as the John Zink Track Burner Special. Although it retired at Indianapolis, it subsequently won four Championship races in the hands of Jim McElreath.

appearance of Mercedes-Benz in the mid-1950s. There was the risk that Honda would fall flat on its face just as it was attempting to establish its reputation.

Still, a party of engineers under Yoshio Nakamura, Honda's director of motor sport, was sent to Europe to look at motor racing under the guidance of Jabby Crombac. Jabby says: 'I had put together a field of cars and drivers for a major race in Japan so I was known there. That was the point of contact, and when they came to Europe I took them to see Lotus, Brabham, Cooper, Lola, all the main teams.'

Tadashi Kume had designed a transverse V12 Formula One engine to be mounted amidships, which was bold because the only precedent in Formula One, the Bugatti 251 of 1956, had been an unmitigated disaster. The reason for the layout was that motorcycles had transverse engines, but it was typical of Honda's naivety that the engine was designed in isolation. A Formula One chassis engineer would have pointed out that while a transverse layout would allow a shorter wheelbase, it would inevitably increase frontal area.

Jabby says: 'In principle we agreed that Honda would ask Lotus to design a car for Formula One – they wanted Jim Clark in the car – and Brabham would be invited to undertake a Formula Two programme.'

Colin Chapman encouraged the approach and Honda dispatched the mock-up of an engine to Lotus. Chapman sat on it for some time and used it to wind up Coventry Climax, which had been threatening to withdraw from motor racing following the takeover by Jaguar. Chapman wanted to continue with Climax and he said that if Honda was coming into Formula One with a 12-cylinder engine, which he thought would make the Climax eight-cylinder engine obsolete, then he wanted a 16-cylinder engine.

Coventry Climax obliged, although the engine was never raced. There is a small irony in that the car Jack used to win the 1966 World Championship was designed for the Climax flat-16, and there is also an irony in that he won it using a simple eight-cylinder engine while Lotus struggled with a complicated 16-cylinder unit from BRM.

Having been left dangling by Chapman, Honda then approached MRD, but as Ron says: 'I had doubts about my ability to design a frame to take a transverse engine and, in any case, by the time we received the engine it was too late to design and build a new car.' The mock-up sat for a while in the garage of Ron's house in Woking while he considered the proposition. It never went into the factory.

Chapman's delaying tactics put back Honda's entry into Formula One, which meant that he had one less rival to contend with. It was typical Chapman gamesmanship, but it removed him from Honda's list of favourite people. On the other hand, the response made by Jack and Ron was correct, it was direct and honest, and it strengthened Honda's respect. Before very long Honda and MRD would be working together and it would be a long-term relationship.

Honda finally entered Formula One in 1964 with a chassis designed by Tadashi Kume. It made its debut at the German Grand Prix and soon afterwards Kume set to work on a Formula Two engine. It was based on a four-cylinder engine block earmarked for a GT car which was never actually built.

The block was from the S1300 engine designed by Nobuhiko Kawamoto, which is why he has sometimes been given credit for the Formula Two engine. In fact the racing version was designed by Tadashi Kume, with a Mr Tamai as his second-in-command, while the young Kawamoto was the junior member of the three-man team.

Today, Mr Kawamoto says: 'The engine was based on a production block and the stroke was too long. We did not really understand how to make a racing engine. For example, a racing engine should have a wide torque band, should be easy to maintain and should be able to produce its maximum potential consistently.

'We had become too accustomed to the very complicated motorcycle mechanisms and had based our car engines on them. While a motorcycle engine can be mounted on a chassis with only two bolts, a car engine is not only bigger, but it also has the transmission, propshaft and many other components attached to it. We did not consider all this complexity when we designed the initial Formula Two engine and that is why the 1965 engine had all the problems you can think of. Still, the experience taught us many lessons, which were valuable when designing subsequent racing and production engines.'

In 1964, Honda's total car output was just 5,210 units, and they were not high-value cars, yet the company was not only in Formula One, it was about to go into Formula Two as well. Further, Honda's first cars were not particularly well received. Output would rise to 30 cars a day in 1965, but then it slumped to 10 a day in 1966. People in the West did not realize how much of a gamble Honda was taking when it entered motor racing.

9

Holding steady

For the third year running MRD substantially increased its production and made 70 cars in 1965, all but two of them single-seaters. Meanwhile, Cooper made 29 single-seaters, Lotus made 28 and Lola just five. MRD production included 10 *'Formule Libre'* cars, which included machines for hillclimbing as well as cars for circuit racing. There was a sudden interest in fitting larger engines to cars, partly because tyre technology was increasing at such a pace that the rubber could handle the extra power.

For once, MRD production included no Formula One cars since the 1½-litre formula had only the current season to run, so most of the British teams stuck with what they already had. In most cases the chassis designers were tearing out their hair wondering how to handle the 3-litre Formula One which was due to start in 1966, their task being made all the more difficult by the lack of a suitable engine. A racing car without an engine is not a lot of use, but Jack had the situation well in hand, and the Repco engine was coming along nicely.

As before, the emphasis of the MRD range was on detail improvement rather than radical change, but MRD actually built two types of Formula Three car. There was the basic BT15 as well as the BT16A, which was based on the Formula Two BT16 and had a higher specification. The chassis and body were the same, but the BT16A had heavier-duty drive-shafts, larger brakes and other improvements.

However, it is a common mistake to believe that more is always better. For example, a racing car can have too much braking power, and in a category like Formula Three you need to be able to strike a balance because the primary consideration, as in every form of racing, is to keep the tyres happy. 'Overbrake' a Formula Three car and you can put too much heat into the tyres in too short a time and they can't cope. Since the tyres are the medium of communication between the brakes and the road, you have to keep them sweet. It is easy to finish up with less efficient braking than you would have achieved with smaller brakes. It comes back to the one word, *harmony*, and that is what Ron has achieved more consistently than any other designer.

Since customers could still win races with their BT10s, the Formula Three grids were awash with Brabhams. At Brands Hatch, in June, there was a race for a £500 prize so it attracted all the stars of Formula Three – the equivalent

67

today would be a prize of £10,000. It was won by Piers Courage with a BT10 from Roy Pike (BT16), Charles Chrichton-Stuart (BT10) and Tony Dean (BT15). You didn't need the latest Brabham in order to win races, and results along that line were repeated weekend after weekend.

During 1965 Brabhams of various types won 42 races in Formula Three, yet they were up against a considerable number of other makes including Lotus, Lola, Cooper and Merlyn in Britain, Alpine, René-Bonnet and Matra in France, at least nine Italian makers (some of them happily ripping off Ron's designs) and various other ventures such as the Swedish Svebe.

The Svebe was built by Ronnie Peterson's father for Ronnie to drive. Peterson Senior had made successful 500cc cars under the Svebe banner, and when reviving the name he made a copy of a Brabham, but as Ronnie said later, by the time it was finished it had cost more than buying a new Brabham would have done, and it didn't go as well!

In only its third full year of operation, MRD was in the process of wiping Cooper out of the market – the Surbiton company would make just seven Formula Three cars in 1966 and only two in 1967. MRD had also knocked Lotus off its perch – the monocoque Lotus 35 Formula Three car failed to score a single major victory. The other important player, Lola, was fast losing interest in being beaten all the time and would soon drop out of Formula Three altogether. This is one of the hazards of the motor racing industry: whereas no doubt someone today is making a handsome living by producing the world's 20th best washing machine, nobody wants to buy even the second best racing car.

As Ron says: 'The world's 20th best washing machine is a matter of opinion, but at the end of every race you have a finishing order and one car has come first. There's no debate about that. You also have a finite market because there are only so many people each year who want to buy a new Formula Three car. It's not like you're dealing with an expanding market as you are with washing machines where, each year, people buy their first one. It's a hard game because each sale you make is a sale someone else has lost. I used to tell Mike Hewland that he was the only winner in the game because he supplied everyone. If Lotus took a sale from me, Mike would still sell a gearbox.'

In 1965 both Lotus and Lola made monocoque cars for the lower formulae. Normally this would have had drivers queuing round the block because 'monocoque' was all the rage and drivers in the learning categories like their cars to be as close to Formula One as possible. They might as well not have bothered.

'Lola's car was not a true monocoque,' says Ron, 'it was stressed sheets over a tubular frame, like Ferrari's first monocoques. Every year Lola would produce a prototype at the end of the season which would give me cause for concern, but somehow the production cars would never quite live up to the prototype. Somewhere along the line from prototype to production car they lost it. They were close, but they never quite made it.'

Lotus was so rattled by being consistently beaten by Brabham that it dropped its monocoque design for 1966 and reverted to a spaceframe. Chapman would have died rather than admit it, but he made his 1966 Formula Three car on Brabham lines and that alone helped him to claw back some of his market.

In Formula Two, most of the winning went the way of Jim Clark in a Ron

Harris Lotus, although Rindt and Rees in Winkelmann Brabhams were always in contention. Ron Harris was a film distributor – mainly the sort of film which charted the leisure hours of Swedish nurses when they wished to be free of constraints such as clothing. He had a penchant for motor racing and his team became the official Lotus presence in Formula Two.

Roy Winkelmann was an American with connections to the intelligence services and his main business was security. He also owned a bowling alley in Slough and his team was based underneath it. Managed by Alan Rees, who also drove for the team, the Winkelmann Brabhams set the highest standards for preparation and turn-out. In 1965 Roy Winkelmann Racing was just another MRD customer, but it would become the Brabham Formula Two works team in all but name.

The Brabham Racing Organisation ran BT11s during the 1965 season, but while Gurney and Brabham were front-runners, they did not have the edge they'd enjoyed the previous year. Once again BRO suffered more than its fair share of retirements and once more there seemed to be no pattern to them. Perhaps the drivers made excessive demands on their cars. Perhaps, too, Jack was stretching himself too thinly, for apart from driving in Formula One, he was supervising his team and driving in Formula Two as well.

Eight Brabhams, including some Formula Two cars, were entered for the South African Grand Prix which started the 1965 season. Jack qualified third and ran third in the race until problems saw him slip to finish eighth, while Gurney was an early retirement with ignition trouble. But despite the disappointing results, history had been made in that race because Gurney's car was fitted with Goodyear tyres.

Goodyear traditionally had been the number two tyre supplier behind Firestone in the United States, but had decided to rectify that with the aid of a competition programme. The new tyres appeared to be competitive in the dry, but Goodyear still had something to learn about wet weather racing.

Ron says: 'Goodyear came in because of Gurney, but Jack flew over to Riverside and did a lot of their testing. Jack really impressed them because they tried to fool him by switching to old rubber without telling him. He would come into the pits and his comments about the tyres were identical to what he'd said the first time round. Goodyear was very impressed by this and we developed a good relationship with them.'

In the Race of Champions, at Brands Hatch, Gurney finished second to Clark in the first heat and led the second when Jimmy made an uncharacteristic mistake while trying to pass on the first lap. Dan then sailed into the distance until his engine went sick. It then looked as though Jack had the race sewn up until his engine lost its oil. The list of races which BRO should have won but didn't is a long one.

Jo Bonnier, driving Rob Walker's BT11-BRM, took fourth place in the Syracuse Grand Prix, but the sensation of the day was Jo Siffert, who led the works Ferraris – and the race – until, with only 10 laps to go, he happened to snatch fifth gear just as his car went over a bump, the revs soared sky high and the engine blew.

Jack was third in the *Sunday Mirror* Trophy at Goodwood, where Gurney had seemed set for a win until he lost oil pressure, then Brabham seemed about to win the International Trophy at Silverstone until his gearbox broke, causing his retirement. Gurney being busy qualifying at Indianapolis, Denny Hulme took over his car at Silverstone, but was an early retirement with an oil leak. Although these were all non-Championship races, they invariably attracted very strong fields. Ferrari were not at all of them, it is true, but having won the World Championship in 1964, the Italian team had entered one of its periodic troughs. So whether Ferrari appeared in these races or not was of little consequence.

Like Jim Clark, Dan Gurney missed the Monaco Grand Prix in order to race in the Indianapolis 500, and as at Silverstone his place in the Formula One team was taken by Denny Hulme. This was the year that Clark won at the 'Brickyard', and Mario Andretti, still in his rookie year, was third in his Brabham-copy.

At Monaco, Brabham had a four-valve Coventry Climax FWMV engine and he qualified second to Hill and his BRM, while Hulme did a workmanlike job to qualify eighth on his World Championship debut. Despite his front-row position Brabham was only fifth on the first lap, but after other drivers had run into trouble he was in the lead by one-third distance. But then his rev-counter broke and he over-revved his engine. Hulme finished eighth, driving his final laps slowly after two studs had sheared from a rear wheel hub.

The Belgian Grand Prix was run in very wet conditions, and Gurney, who had qualified fifth, had to struggle with both his dislike of Spa in the rain and an ill-handling car, for his Goodyears were not up to scratch. He finished 10th, two laps down, while Brabham came home fourth, a lap down on Clark and Stewart.

Since Denny Hulme knew Clermont-Ferrand well from Formula Two (he had beaten Stewart and Rindt in winning the 1964 race) Jack stood down from the French Grand Prix in favour of his protégé. Denny rewarded the boss' confidence by being quickest on the first day of practice and eventually finishing fourth in the race. Gurney had run third in the early stages, but he retired with engine trouble before half-distance.

Jack was now in his 40th year and beginning to consider retirement in order to concentrate on running his team. But he would only do this when he knew he had a star driver in at least one of his cars on a long-term basis. For the moment he had one in Dan Gurney, but he knew that Dan had other plans for the forthcoming 3-litre formula. However, when Gurney's four-valve engine broke during the warm-up lap for the British Grand Prix, Jack didn't hesitate to climb out of his own car and hand it to over to Dan. He could have told Denny Hulme to stand down instead, but he preferred to make the gesture himself. However, it brought a modest reward for Dan could only finish sixth in a car in which he did not fit comfortably, while Denny retired with a broken alternator belt.

Jack stood down in favour of Hulme at the Dutch Grand Prix, where both cars used two-valve engines. In an age when we venerate four-valves-per-cylinder we might remember that not until the Cosworth FVA and DFV arrived was the case for them proved. Gurney ran a close second to Clark until the bright young newcomer Jackie Stewart went by in his BRM and he had to be content with third place, with Hulme in fifth.

Jack was back in the cockpit for the German Grand Prix where he could qualify no higher than 14th, 22 seconds off Clark's pole time and 15 seconds slower than Gurney. Dan had another good race, finishing a strong third, and Brabham came home fifth, while Hulme retired with a fuel leak.

Hulme and Brabham then ran in the Mediterranean Grand Prix, and although they finished only fourth and sixth, it was a good day for Brabham cars. In third place was Frank Gardner, in the Willment car, but the winner, for the second year in succession, was Jo Siffert in Rob Walker's BT11-BRM. Once again Siffert had beaten Clark – this time by just three-tenths of a second.

For the Italian Grand Prix Brabham again stood down and the team ran Gurney, Hulme and Giancarlo Baghetti, who had one of the old BT7s. None of the cars was able to qualify in the top 10, and Gurney's engine was decidedly tired. Still, while Baghetti retired with a broken conrod and Hulme with front suspension trouble, Gurney managed to come home third.

Only two races, both in North America, remained of the 1½-litre formula and for both of them the driving team consisted of Gurney and Brabham. In the United States Grand Prix they came home second and third, respectively, and in the Mexican race, Gurney finished second, within 2 seconds of Ginther's winning Honda, while Brabham retired with an oil leak.

Thanks to his late-season performances, Gurney was placed fourth in the World Championship behind Clark, Hill and Stewart, while Brabham finished third in the Constructors' Cup behind Lotus and BRM, which between them had won every race that year except for the last one.

If only Jack had been prepared to spend a little more money, the results could have been so much better. That is said with hindsight, but the motor racing culture of the day was not as it is now. These days items like alternator belts – which caused Denny's retirement at Silverstone – are replaced on a set schedule. Every component has a designated life and every failure is investigated.

Before the end of the season, Gurney confirmed to Jack that he was going to form his own Grand Prix team and this caused Jack to postpone his retirement. The irony is that Dan's decision led to Jack winning 10 Formula Two races and the Formula One World Championship in 1966, while Dan would not win a single international race.

Jack gave up his chance of being competitive in Formula Two in 1965 to pursue a relationship with Honda. Ron says: 'The first engine was delivered to my home and Denny and I played around with it in my garage, to get the fitting right. It was all hush-hush and I wasn't even prepared to take it into the works.' Tadashi Kume came over with two engineers in 1965. Although he was a senior designer with a major company, he says: 'My job was to work as a mechanic, Ron-san was the engineer.

'We stayed at the Seven Hills Hotel. At the time the only English I had was "Yes", "No" and "Thank you", but the owner, Mr Runstham, and his staff looked after us very well. In fact, they made a big contribution to our overall success.

'I was a skinny and quite handsome young man until I discovered draught beer and fish and chips. I was never under 10 stone again. Later I considered importing English newspapers and opening a chain of fish and chip shops in Japan. You'd have to have English papers to get the genuine smell!'

Jack ran the Honda in practice for the opening race at Silverstone, but he was 9 seconds off the pace – and pole was set by an old BT10. In the event, the meeting was abandoned due to a deluge.

Things were not much better at Oulton Park a fortnight later. Denny, in a Cosworth-powered car, was on the front row (and he won) while Jack was on the back row. He was ready to withdraw his entry, but the organizers persuaded him that the crowd would like to see the car run. So he ran around near the back of the field, but retired before half-distance with a 'broken sparking plug'. Jack's retirement was almost certainly not caused by that, but it was his practice to cover up any problems with an engine which had been provided to the team if it was at all possible.

After its first two outings, the Honda engine was not looking very clever – you'd certainly not have predicted utter supremacy within 12 months. Still, just a week after Oulton Park, at Snetterton, Jack was merely 1½ seconds off the pace and he finished third in the first heat behind Hill and Clark, although he retired from the second heat with a broken throttle linkage. Being a long-stroke engine, the Honda unit had more vibration than was usual and the throttle linkage would be a recurring problem. What nobody realized until late in the season was the engine was setting up a resonance which affected the fuel pump and prevented it from feeding the right amount of fuel to the engine. Once that problem was discovered it was easily solved by mounting the pump on a different bracket.

It took time to discover things like that, but there were other things to learn on the way. Tadashi Kume recalls: 'At one of the races the clutch broke and Jack-san was shocked and amazed to see that the clutch plates were made of synthetic plastic resins, like we used on motorcycles. Jack-san introduced me to Ferodo and they felt sorry for me and agreed to help. We removed our resin facings and took the clutch plates and drawings to Ferodo and we solved the problem. Jack-san got the worst of the deal for the 1965 season and I was really grateful to him for putting up with us during the worst time. He had enough patience not to get mad or say: "You people go home".'

Mr Kume paints a gentle picture, but back in Japan Nobuhiko Kawamoto was the recipient of his frustration. 'Mr Kume would phone me up, day and night, cross with me. But I was only a new employee who had been working with the engine group for only a year, so I didn't know what to do. There were only three engineers on the project and Mr Kume had to be chief engineer, chief mechanic and manager all at the same time and he had only two mechanics in England.'

The Brabham-Honda raced only once more, at Pau, before being taken back to Japan. The engine was too peaky to do well on a tight street circuit like Pau and once more Jack had throttle linkage problems.

By that time, there had been other developments. Ron recalls: 'Honda had fitted its own fuel injection system and the engine was peaky, with poor torque. We put it on a dyno and tested it against a Cosworth SCA, so we did our homework. Jack and I figured that we needed the Lucas system.'

Tadashi Kume remembers the test: 'We found that the power at the rear wheels was less than the Cosworth. Ron-san was not pleased. We drove back in silence, the Honda people in a Mini, Jack and Ron following us in another car. Then a Jaguar suddenly appeared, hit us broadside-on and drove off. Jack got us out of the Mini, then he got in and set off after the Jaguar.

'We were standing in the middle of the countryside, in the middle of nowhere, I can remember the birds were singing and we were dejected, and Ron-san suddenly started to talk about how we should redesign the engine. Even in those circumstances he did not stop. He gave us so much advice. For example, he once told me: "Your engine is too tall and top-heavy, which makes the car swing too much when cornering. Maybe you don't understand how race cars behave." Things like that taught me that horsepower is not everything.'

The Honda engineers went home in mid-summer – Mr Kawamoto says they returned with a broken heart and a broken engine – and managed to make some improvements to the unit. For the time being, Jack reverted to a Cosworth engine until late in the season.

Meanwhile, in Melbourne Repco was having a few dramas of its own. The first engine, a 2½-litre Tasman unit, was ready on March 21, 1965, but in initial testing it produced only 220bhp, which was less than a good Coventry Climax FPF. Frank Hallam put it down to Phil Irving's deviation from the initial design, especially the shape of the combustion chambers. The Tasman version never worked as well as the Formula One engine, although things did improve a lot when Lucas agreed to supply its fuel injection system.

As though that was not enough, Hallam was beginning to become agitated at Irving's interpretation of office hours, though it has to be said that the latter was employed as a freelance consultant; he was never officially appointed head of the project.

Then again, some parts ordered from England seemed to take forever to arrive. Among the items sent over was a Cosworth SCA camshaft. Time was running on and the realistic deadline for delivery of the first Formula One engine was advancing. It had to be shipped to England, installed and tested, and then the car had to be sent to South Africa for its first race on New Year's Day, 1966. Meanwhile, the initial budget of around £10,000 had more than quadrupled and more money had to be committed to the third stage of the exercise before a Brabham-Repco had even turned a wheel. In September 1965 it was decided to send a Tasman unit to Europe so that it could be run in a car. It came over as the hand luggage of the son of one of the Repco managers.

That same month Jack ran at Oulton Park with a revised version of the Honda unit, which was now producing 130bhp. He qualified 6.2 seconds quicker than he had in early April, and most unusually, the times were directly comparable because pole position time was identical on both occasions. Although Brabham was soon out of the race with clutch trouble, at least progress had been made.

Jack followed that at Albi with pole position, the fastest lap and second in the race to Clark – by six-tenths of a second after nearly two hours. That really did indicate that Honda could be a threat. Jack's fastest lap was 1.5 seconds quicker than his pole position time, which indicated how furious the pace had been.

In fact, even then the engine had not been right because it was running too lean and by the end the pistons were thoroughly roasted. Still, it was a promising note on which to end the season, allied to the fact that Honda had also won that very last race run to the 1½-litre Formula One.

Ron continues: 'We sent Honda a report and they asked us to fly to Japan. I agreed provided I could have a week in Australia – I hadn't been home for five years. Honda entertained us exceptionally well, listened to what we had to say, and agreed with our proposals. It is very simple doing business with Honda, provided you are straightforward yourself.

'The Japanese don't like to haggle, and in private they'll admit that's because they're no good at bartering, it's not part of their culture. They like things to be clear-cut and straight. I know people who now live in grand houses, paid for from the invoices they submitted to Tokyo. The invoices were settled, but those people no longer do business with Honda.

'Honda also placed an order for eight cars for their racing school. These were basically Formula Three chassis fitted with tuned Ford engines – they were Formula Ford cars before Formula Ford was invented.'

Jack says: 'Apart from anything else, the original Formula Two engine was the wrong shape, it didn't fit in the car properly and it was impossible to make the back end stiff enough. We were also getting too much vibration. We told them that we needed a brand new engine and we'd need it by the beginning of March if we were to do the job properly. They said "OK" and we went away, not for one moment thinking they could design and build a completely new engine in under five months But on March 1, 1966 we had one in our workshop with roller bearings, torsion-bar valve springing and 150bhp.'

It was a remarkable feat, and not easily achieved. Nobuhiko Kawamoto recalls: 'Mr Kume and I went to a hotel in a seaside resort, determined not to leave until we had sketched out a new design. We had no drawing board so we drew freehand using only rulers and compasses. Think of that, just Mr Kume and me in a hotel room with almost no word spoken and him constantly smoking.

'He was rather a difficult man to approach, so it was hard to become his friend even as a member of his group. He put a lot of pressure on me, it was always: "Haven't you finished this or that?" The sea I saw from the hotel window was blue, but it appeared grey to me. Nevertheless he was an outstanding engineer and to this day I have never encountered a better one.'

Tadashi Kume says: 'For the 1966 season we went through 180 degrees and in addition to a shorter stroke we had torsion-bar valve springing. The first engine was built during the New Year's holiday in 1966. Mr Honda was there as we checked the compression ratio of our engine. He was there when we found that it had a compression ratio of only 6:1. I went pale and felt faint. We had made this discovery in front of Mr Honda, but he did not say a word. Perhaps he was so shocked that he was completely lost for words.

"As we inspected the engine, we found that the valves were too big. We redesigned the cylinder head with smaller valves. We already had a deadline by which to develop the unit, but with the help of two engineers, Mr Shinmura and Mr Nakagawa, we finished two weeks' work in three or four days.

'While we were still working, people from the wood pattern shop came to ask for drawings. I told them that we had only drawn to the centreline and they said that was OK. They were professional craftsmen who could tell what sort of engine it was going to be just by looking at an incomplete drawing. They started making the patterns from unfinished drawings, then they came back as the drawings progressed. That's how everyone worked to complete the engine on time.'

While the Honda engineers were going through one sort of trauma, all was not well, either, in the MRD factory. Despite all outward appearances, with success at every level on the track and business booming, there was a growing discontent.

Ron says: 'At the end of 1965 I told Jack that I didn't want any more to do with Formula One. In fact I was pretty disgruntled all round. I was still on only £30 a week and although I owned 40 per cent of MRD, it wasn't paying me any money. Jack's accountants handled MRD's accounts and they advised him not to take money out of the company, and if he didn't take money from MRD, then I couldn't.

'Jack listened and agreed that I had a point. The upshot was that the company was restructured so I was an equal partner and my basic wage went up. The Formula One team became a 50/50 operation between MRD and BRO and that led, of course, to my active involvement in Formula One.'

It was not quite straightforward because Jack did not give in to Ron's demands without first looking at other alternatives. He approached every other racing car manufacturer – the Brabham Racing Organisation was, after all, a private team which could buy its cars from anyone.

In the event, Jack could not find a better deal, or at least one he could balance with his trade contracts, so he reassessed his relationship with Ron. He was like a husband whose eye strays over the field and then decides that perhaps the missus in the kitchen doesn't rustle up such a bad plate after all.

10

The golden year

To say that 1966 was a good year for MRD is a gross understatement for no other manufacturer of single-seater racing cars has ever won as many international races and championships at so many levels in the course of one season.

Jack won the Drivers' World Championship and Brabham-Repco won the Constructors' Cup. The first IndyCar race of the year was won by Jim McElreath's two-year-old BT12, and Mario Andretti took his second USAC title with a development of his Brabham-copy. Brabhams dominated Formula Three, as usual, and Harry Stiller gave the marque its first British Championship, while in Formula Two, Brabhams won every race. To be pedantic, a Brabham did not win the Formula Two class which was run concurrently with the German Grand Prix, all the leading Brabham drivers being involved that day in the main Formula One section of the race. But a Brabham won every race run exclusively for Formula Two cars.

Of course, the works Brabhams did have the advantage of Honda engines, but even if you eliminate Jack and Denny from the equation, and make the bold assumption that neither would have won had they been using Cosworth engines, the final score would still have been Brabham 9, Rest of the World 6.

'Rest of the World' included such players as Cooper, Lola, Lotus, McLaren and Matra. But Jack and Ron had worked for their advantage, and the reason why their cars did so well in 1966 is that they had given up a year of competitiveness in order to tutor Honda in the art of winning.

Meanwhile, Jack had cracked the problem of engine supply in Formula One, although the Repco engines were slow in arriving and Denny Hulme had to start the season with a 2.7-litre Coventry Climax FPF engine in the back of a modified BT11, and Bob Anderson did the same. Jack began the year with a Repco engine in the BT19, a one-off originally designed to take the 1½-litre flat-16 engine which Coventry Climax had built but not released.

Being a car originally designed for a 1½-litre engine, and now equipped with the most compact new engine in Formula One, the BT19 was noticeably smaller than its 3-litre rivals. Ron says: 'At first the engine produced about 290-300bhp, but that rose to about 310bhp.' It was not terrific, even by the standards of the day, but the engine was reliable and it meant that MRD had a full 3-litre engine which was reasonably light and compact. The reliability was remarkable since the engines were rebuilt in the workshop without having the benefit of a dynamometer to check the build quality and set the ignition and fuel injection timing. The normal procedure for each race meeting was to use the first part of practice to run the engines in before working them in anger to set a time.

In the early races, Jack tended to make fairly leisurely starts because the Hewland HD gearbox he was using had been built for 2-litre engines and was marginal with a 3-litre engine, but later he took delivery of Hewland's heavy-duty transmission, the DG300. Mike Hewland recalls: 'Although it was a heavier-duty gearbox, we had already used the designation HD for heavy duty, and then someone suggested that this was a different gearbox, so DG it became.'

The South African Grand Prix, which was run on New Year's Day, was dropped from the World Championship calendar because most teams were not yet ready to go racing, but Jack indicated how the season might develop by setting pole (with Denny third-fastest), and he led most of the way until the injector drive belt on his engine failed.

The fact that the Repco engine had come close to winning on its debut – and the component which failed was not a Repco part – caused delight in Melbourne. It has to be said, however, that the opposition in South Africa was relatively weak and the engine had not been over-stretched prior to it coming to a stop.

Both Brabhams were entered for the Syracuse Grand Prix in May, but they missed official practice, so Jack and Denny started from the back of the grid. As it turned out, they need not have bothered, because Jack retired after one lap with a problem in his fuel metering unit and Denny went out six laps later with an oil leak. Suddenly, things were not looking that bright.

But the cars' next outing was more promising and in the International Trophy at Silverstone, in mid-May, Jack put the BT19 on pole ahead of John Surtees in a works Ferrari. Surtees had been favourite to win the race, but Jack led every lap, posted fastest lap along the way, and took the flag just over 7 seconds ahead. By this time he had also won all four Formula Two races in which the works Brabham-Hondas had started.

Nobody could escape the fact that the Brabham-Hondas were in a class of their own in Formula Two. Ron says: 'Our Honda engines were so superior that we tried not to win by too great a margin, otherwise it would have destroyed the Championship. Since Jack and Denny were not to go flat-out there had to be team orders and Denny had the job of following Jack. I don't think he liked that too much. He'd follow Jack, then hang back and make a spurt so he'd get fastest lap, because in the French races you got prize money for that.

'If Denny thought about it, he was coming second in Formula Two, and he wouldn't have come higher than third with any other team because we had first and second sewn up. In Formula One, where there were no team orders, Jack proved that he was faster than Denny.'

Tadashi Kume brought over five engineers from Honda and David Mills recalls their arrival: 'It was long before there was any regular communication between the West and Japan and most of these guys had not a word of English. I simply got them to the hotel, got the keys to their rooms and left them there. There was nothing else I could do, but I do believe that they soon learned how to order whisky.

'What was amazing was to see the utterly methodical way in which they worked. One guy would come forward and do up a bolt, then he'd step aside and somebody else would step forward and do his bit. It was unlike anything I'd seen in motor racing, in fact it reminded me of the sort of system we had in the RAF for checking an aircraft's systems after work had been done on it.'

The first Formula Two race of the year had been scheduled for Oulton Park, but it was cancelled due to snow. At the Easter Monday meeting at Goodwood, however, Jack and Denny stroked home to an easy 1-2. Mr Kume says: 'When we won our first race at Goodwood, Jack poured champagne into the trophy and told me to drink it. It was sweet and wonderful and was the most memorable moment of the whole project so far as I was concerned.

'After two more races, both of which we won, I was sufficiently confident to return to Japan and have Mr Kawamoto take over. I am sure that he had a much easier time dealing with such difficult men as Ron-san and Jack-san than I did.'

Both Honda men tell of being at the sharp end of Ron's tongue at different times. Of course, that was part of the exercise. Nobuhiko Kawamoto recalls: 'It was a different world and I made mistakes. There was one big one which I've never told anyone about before. One of the MRD mechanics told me to fill the water tank. The nozzles for the fuel and water tanks were close together and I poured water in the fuel tank. The mechanics did not leave the works until nine at night, and it was only then that I was able to set about disassembling the filters and draining the tanks. I was not just an amateur, I was a stupid amateur. It was two in the morning by the time I finished. That was my fault but, in general, I had more jobs than I could cope with and I was usually pretty tired.'

There were also the ear-bashings from Jerry, the workshop foreman, when the young Kawamoto misused tools. In fact, one of Ron's catch phrases was 'Turn the nut, not the bolt'. Ron called Kawamoto 'Hong Kong Mechanic', and would observe that, had the War continued, as an RAAF pilot he might have been dropping bombs on Tokyo, which was interesting bearing in mind that Ron was trained on fighters! It's a wonder they have remained friends, but they have, and Mr Kawamoto said in 1997: 'Ron-san is one of the true engineers.' At the time, Mr Kawamoto was President of Honda and Ron was one of his trusted advisers and consultants.

The World Championship finally got under way at Monaco in late May. Only 16 cars were entered, since many were still not ready for the new formula. But after the promise of the International Trophy, Monte Carlo was a disappointment; Jack could qualify only 11th, while Denny was sixth, and they both retired before one-fifth distance.

Since Monaco was unusually late, it meant that there was no clash with Indianapolis so there could be a strong European presence at the 'Brickyard'. Stewart appeared to have the race in the bag until his Lola retired late on. Finally Hill took it in a Lola, from Clark's Lotus, and the race has since been presented as a British benefit. What people forget, however, is that 'over-the-hill' Jim McElreath in his old Brabham BT12 might have won had he not stalled in the pit lane and lost more than a minute. As it was, he came third, just 50 seconds down on Hill, 9 seconds behind Clark, and catching both men hand over fist.

Back in Europe, Jack qualified fourth and finished fourth in the Belgian Grand Prix, then won the French Grand Prix, with Denny, running with a Repco engine for the first time, in third place. The headline news was that it was the first time that a driver had won a World Championship race in a car which bore his name. Most popular newspapers gave the impression that Jack had built the car with his own hands!

Denny had a new car, a BT20, which was a tidied-up BT19 with a longer wheelbase, a stiffer frame and bigger brakes. It was the lightest 3-litre car in the field, but even so it was above the minimum weight limit.

Lorenzo Bandini's Ferrari had led the French Grand Prix for most of the way until his throttle cable broke and many people at the time suggested that Jack's was a fluke win. For all that it was a popular one. What the sceptics failed to notice, however, was that Jack never ran lower than second, and the race was held on the ultra-fast Reims circuit, so the Repco engine was clearly more powerful than many had assumed. The French Grand Prix, in fact, was the fastest World Championship race ever held to that date.

Ron says: 'The organizers at Reims used to give away vast amounts of champagne, 100 bottles for pole, another 100 for the winner. We not only won the Grand Prix, Jack won the Formula Two race as well. It came in very handy later at my daughter's 21st birthday.'

John Judd recalls a stroke that Jack used to pull during practice at Reims: 'At the hairpin before the start/finish straight he'd pretend to leave his braking late and would shoot up the escape road. Then he'd turn round and shoot out going a good 30-40mph quicker than he would have done had he had to take the hairpin. 'Gosh,' we suggested, 'Jack must have liked his bubbly.' 'He never touched it,' said John, 'he just liked winning it.' That sums up the racing driver's mentality.

Naturally, given the nature of motor racing, Colin Chapman was soon making overtures to Repco to sell him an engine, but the company was stretched to supply and maintain the engines that Brabham used. There were contractual reasons to refuse Chapman's overture, but there was also a feeling that Chapman wanted the engine less to put in the back of a Lotus than to pass it over to Cosworth Engineering to strip down and examine while Keith Duckworth was finalizing the design of his own V8 Formula One engine. Also, while Chapman was trying to winkle a Formula One engine out of Repco, Jackie Stewart was trying to winkle a Formula Two engine out of Honda. He wasn't successful, either.

Works Brabhams not only won the French Grand Prix, they also finished 1-2 in the accompanying Formula Two race. Afterwards there was a prizegiving dinner and Ron and Jack discovered that their Honda mechanics were not invited. They dug their heels in. Ron recalls: 'The organizers eventually relented and put our mechanics in an adjoining room. They went so far as to put a bottle of Scotch on their table. I don't think any of them can remember the evening.'

The following week there was a race at Rouen which resulted in an uncharacteristic failure of one of the Honda engines. Nobuhiko Kawamoto explains: 'Before the race I received a call from Mr Honda, who was concerned that the engines were lasting so long that we were not learning anything. He wanted us to run an engine until it broke, so I built one with used crankshaft and bearings.

'Jack-san did not finish the race because the engine seized four or five laps from the end and he spun. He walked back to the pits and we were apprehensive, thinking that he would be angry. Jack-san, however, smiled and pulled the gear lever out of his pocket so everyone, especially the journalists, thought that he had retired because of the gear lever. He did it, of course, to protect me and Honda. He was a demanding man, a hard man to work for, but he had a great heart.

'That night, as the rest of the team went off to the victory party, Mr Furusawa and I borrowed a key to the transporter and removed the sump from Jack's engine. Sure enough, we got covered in oil, but we were able to locate the seized bearing.

Then I had to find a telephone to call Honda in Japan to tell them. I got to bed at two or three in the morning. The following day a champagne company had everyone to dinner, but I was so exhausted that one glass of champagne sent me to sleep.'

Jack's revival continued at Brands Hatch, where he set pole for the British Grand Prix, led every lap and set fastest lap as well. Denny was second-fastest in practice, but he struggled in the wet conditions at the start, then as the track dried he moved up to second, crossing the line just 10 seconds behind his team-leader.

The team was on a roll, and Jack and Denny headed the grid for the Dutch Grand Prix, which Jack then duly won, but not until he had first performed a spot of theatre on the starting grid. Jack was now past his 40th birthday, and people in the media were suggesting that it was time he gave up, that Formula One was a young man's sport. So what does Jack do? He dresses up in a long black beard, grabs a jack handle to use as a walking stick, waits for everyone else to be in place on the grid, then emerges from his pit and hobbles slowly down the track towards his waiting car. The photographers had a field day! His victory, of course, was the icing on the cake, for it proved that he was far from over the hill. Next he headed for the Nürburgring, where he led every lap of the German Grand Prix – four wins in succession was a remarkable feat. Meanwhile, he'd now won six Formula Two races, with Denny picking up a seventh win for the works Brabham-Hondas.

Understandably, Honda was very pleased with its involvement, and in July, Yoshio Nakamura, Honda's competition manager, wrote to Jack offering to supply V12 3-litre Formula One engines to Brabham in 1967. This would have been in addition to the 'Honda-Honda' effort, although it was also suggested that BRO might run Honda chassis as well. In that case, Honda was prepared to talk about financial backing over and above the supply of engines.

Neither Jack nor Ron can recall the letter, but the tie-in with Repco is the most likely explanation for turning down an offer that most outfits dream of. There were also widespread rumours that Denny would leave Brabham to join Honda, but he stayed on at MRD for another year and took the World Championship in 1967.

John Surtees recalls being approached by Mr Nakamura at Monza, which led to him joining Honda the following year. John says: 'Things were getting very political back in Japan. Mr Honda had got set ideas, particularly about things like air-cooled engines, and he wanted to take the racing division down that route. Mr Nakamura thought that if he could make an alliance with Jack or myself, the competition department could continue to do things as they wanted to do them. Jack and I were both World Champions, we were both engineers and we had our own workshops. We both had the right combination of prestige and practicality, and I accepted the offer.'

Denny finished third in the Italian Grand Prix, only 6 seconds behind Lodovico Scarfiotti's winning Ferrari, although Jack was an early retirement with an oil leak after leading the race. When both Stewart and Surtees had also retired before half-distance, Jack became World Champion for the third time. Ron says: 'I had not realized that the title was that close to being settled, and when he retired we flew home. When we landed at Fairoaks airfield there were all these journalists waiting for the new World Champion.'

One of Ron's close friends, Greg 'Peewee' Siddle, says: 'The fact that Brabham won the title in a Brabham gave journalists a story. He was the first driver to win in a car of his own make, and some gave the impression he had designed the car. I think that, over the years, that has got to Ron.'

The new World Champion led home Denny Hulme at the International Gold Cup at Oulton Park, with just a tenth of a second separating them. By then they were so confident that they let the BRMs lead, knowing that they would retire, just so they could give the crowd a show. True to form, the BRMs duly retired and Jack and Denny came home first and second.

Jack then set pole for the United States Grand Prix and was leading the race when he retired with engine trouble, and the team ended the Formula One season with Jack finishing 8 seconds behind John Surtees' winning Cooper-Maserati in the Mexican Grand Prix, with Denny a lap behind in third place.

Jack's third World Championship, at 40 years of age, was a magnificent achievement from a man who had been considering retirement just a year before. It was also a great achievement by Repco, who had made a bargain-basement engine which had beaten Ferrari. The Italian company had been making Formula One engines for nearly 20 years, whereas Repco's business was making spare parts for road cars. It is so easy to get blasé and trot out the usual line *Brabham had a light, reliable, engine which was down on power but which did the job, etc, etc.*

That much is true, but Formula One has never been easy, and the fact remains that Repco, which in the way these things are measured has always been a small company, would win back-to-back World Championships despite the fact that it had little previous involvement in motor racing. Ask Porsche how difficult is Formula One. Ask Peugeot. Ask Yamaha. Ask Lamborghini. Then recall that Repco spent just three years in Formula One, yet won two World Championships.

Ron says: 'What you must also remember is that the engines were not dyno-tested after rebuild. They were just rebuilt by ordinary mechanics, not even specialist engine-builders. Our Honda engines were rebuilt in our workshop in the same way. It's a wonder we finished any races, let alone won them.'

Had there been a Formula Two Championship, Jack would have won that as well since he took 10 wins. In fact the French organized their races into a Championship, and Jack won that from Denny and Alan Rees in a Winkelmann Brabham. In fourth place, however, was Jean-Pierre Beltoise in a French Matra, both driver and constructor giving notice of their intentions.

The only time that the works Brabham-Hondas were beaten was in the very last race of the year, at Brands Hatch. Jochen Rindt won the first heat from Jack – Cosworth had done a lot of development on the SCA engine and Ron reckons it was very close to the Honda unit by the end of the season. 'Our engines came over from Japan and were simply worked on in our factory, so they never saw a dyno, but I reckon by the end of the year they'd lost a bit of their edge.'

In the final, Rindt and Brabham went at it hammer-and-tongs, and Brabham led as they came to lap a backmarker. This poor chap had his mirrors full of superstar drivers when his gear lever come off in his hand and he drifted over to Jack's line. That let Jochen through and he just held on, with the rubber on his tyres almost gone, to lead Jack across the line by a fifth of a second.

Formula Two was to be upgraded to 1.6 litres in 1967, and as Honda had no 1,600cc engine to use as a basis for a racing unit – the new F2 engines had to be based on a production block – they pulled out at the end of the year.

Ron and Jack prepared one of the works Brabham-Hondas and sent it to Japan as a gift. It was a gesture which was greatly appreciated and Mr Honda wrote to Jack: 'I was so thrilled to hear that you and Mr Tauranac are offering me the actual Formula Two Brabham-Honda raced by yourself this year as a memento of this very successful year, and it is my most pleasure to accept your offer which I believe will be a most honorable and memorable gift to all of us.'

Honda now leaves the Tauranac story until 1979, when Nobuhiko Kawamoto will re-enter it. To summarize the feelings of Messrs Kume and Kawamoto at the end of 1966: they achieved their objectives, but it had not been easy. They were handicapped by their limited command of English and they found Ron something of a conundrum. They had a mixture of fear and affection for him. They admired his personal integrity, that of his designs and the way he ran his factory, but they'd each received ear-bashings on occasion. He was a hard taskmaster, but he was also a profoundly influential teacher.

Ron is complex and sometimes contradictory. Take the following stories: Among the people working at MRD in 1966 was Bert Ray, who since 1971 has made the Ray Formula Ford cars as well as being part of the network of subcontractors which sustain the British motor racing industry. Bert recalls: 'I joined Brabham in 1964 as a fabricator and welder, and I used to work alongside Denny Hulme. I got £17 10s a week, Denny got £18 a week, plus he got to drive the cars.

'Ron had a phrase, "Naaa, that's no good". Over the years I've often done my Ron impersonation, but when I arrived at the 1996 Brabham Reunion Dinner, I found that everyone was doing it.

'At the time Ron didn't do any drawing, he'd tell you what he wanted and leave you to make it up. Then we'd get *"Naaaa, that's no good"*, and you'd be told to do it again. I think he'd got an idea in the back of his mind and needed to see something in metal which he could examine and work from. In a subtle way he wound you up to do better; he was never complimentary, but he made you want to please him.'

Ron is adamant that this happened only with prototypes, and then only with the installation. He points out that every bought-in item, which included the frame, had to be drawn in detail. There is also a legend that Cooper did everything on the hoof, which does not quite explain why the Cooper designer/draughtsman, Owen Maddock, still possesses the original blueprints.

Preston Anderson, who joined MRD in 1969, says although it was not easy working for Ron, he was genuinely concerned about his workforce. 'The only time in my working life that I have ever received a bonus was under Ron. It was £20 at Christmas and that was a week's wages.'

Michael Hillman says: 'After I'd been working for some time at MRD, I happened to tell Ron that I was getting married and he said: "You'll need more money in that case," and that was it. I got a raise. Ron has a very broad streak of kindness in him, even if he does his best to conceal it.'

In September 1966 the Argentine national motor club bought five Brabham BT16s for their local drivers so that they would have competitive cars to compete with the European drivers for the Temporada series of F3 races. 'Juan-Manuel Fangio came to Silverstone to look at the cars and to do a gentle drive around the track. He was in street clothes and wearing a cloth cap, but after a little while he got the bit between his teeth and was going at a fair speed. In fact he was within a second of the lap record when the officials black-flagged him.' This link with the Argentine national motor club probably led to their sponsoring Carlos Reutemann for Formula One in 1972.

In 1966, on top of all the successes in the more senior formulae, it was a rare Formula Three grid on which Brabhams did not out-number every other make combined. But this year the opposition fought back. Lotus made a determined bid to regain its market with the Lotus 41, which took its share of wins, while in France Matra also made an excellent car, and unlike most French outfits, the company was wise enough to use Ford engines.

Matra took nine important wins, including the prestigious race at Monaco, but it made very few cars and it concentrated on French races. Matra was in Formula Three as part of a learning process in order to take it to Formula One. Unlike every other company, it was not in Fornula Three to sell cars. In fact, the cars were built without regard to cost or customer requirements.

So Matra was a side-issue so far as the customer market was concerned, but a response was needed to the threat from Lotus. At the traditional Boxing Day Brands Hatch meeting, Derek Bell appeared at the wheel of a new Brabham Formula Three car, the BT21. It had a new chassis-frame, revised suspension and a new body, which was at least as slippery as the very slim Lotus 41.

Derek says: 'I'd started racing in a Lotus Seven and, when I was ready to move up to Formula Three, Lotus invited me to Goodwood with loads of other drivers – all the young hotshoes – for a test drive. I was green, I didn't have good advice and I was sucked in by the glamour of Lotus. It was the charisma of Colin Chapman. It was Jimmy Clark winning the World Championship. It was pretty heady stuff.

'So I bought a Lotus, and after I'd been upside-down a few times, I began to see the error of my ways. I knew that I had to have a Brabham. With the Lotus you could win on some circuits and be hopeless on others, but if you wanted a top-three finish in every race, a Brabham was the only car. It was reliable and it worked everywhere. I reckon that buying the Lotus put my career back a full season. We made the decision to switch to Brabham very early, so we had a car ready for the Boxing Day meeting.'

Derek's Brabham was a private entry at Brands Hatch, but Team Lotus entered Jackie Oliver in its 1967 car because the most important race of the season for a manufacturer to win is the last one, even if ostensibly it happens to be a relatively minor club meeting.

Derek Bell started from pole position, but the outside line was slippery, which is always a problem at Brands Hatch, so he was slow off the line and sat in second place for 12 of the 15 laps. Then he made his move and came through to beat a strong field, lapping everyone up to and including fifth place.

Orders rolled in, and eventually 110 of the BT21 series would be built, making it MRD's most popular model. Derek himself would race Brabhams not only in Formula Three but, later, in Formula Two and would become perhaps the company's most successful private entrant.

Derek, who was to have a fruitful relationship with MRD, recalls: 'They were good people to deal with, very straightforward and very organized. Ron wasn't the sort of person you'd stop and pass the time of day with, you felt that he was on another planet, but if you asked him a question about setting up the car, you got a good straight answer and you knew that everyone was being treated equally.

'In fact, if anything they were too fair. In 1970, for example, I was doing well in European Formula Two and I could have won the Championship. The problem was the new Tecno from Italy. Early in the season I phoned Ron and said that we needed something extra. He said: "How did you get on?" I told him I'd won. "It doesn't get better than that," he said.

'He was right in one sense, but he flatly refused to give me anything that his other customers didn't have. I think that was short-sighted because I could have won the Championship. As it was I was runner-up to Clay Regazzoni's Tecno. That's how they operated, straight down the line. If the worse came to the worse, then Jack would drive your car and sort it out for you. He did that for me once.'

Ted Croucher, the chief marshal at Goodwood, says: 'We had a guy here one day and he'd just bought a Formula Three Brabham. He was hopeless and his car was not much better. Jack was here and his leg was in plaster, so that'd make it 1969. Come the break for lunch and Jack went to the guy's mechanic and asked to borrow his tools. He then made adjustments to the chap's car, right there, doing all the work himself, and said: "That should fix it."

'He then went up to the bloke and said: "Follow me around for a couple of laps, and I'll show you the line." Jack was then not just a Formula One driver, he was three times a World Champion, and not only did he set up the guy's car for him, he gave him individual tuition. You couldn't buy that.'

That incredibly successful 1966 season was all the more remarkable in that all the design work was being done by Ron with the assistance of Michael Hillman. Not everything that Ron touched turned to gold, however. That was the year of the BT17, the last sports car Ron would design. 'Big banger' Group 7 sports car racing had taken off and was proving very popular with drivers, promoters and spectators, as well as being very profitable for manufacturers. McLaren, Lola and Lotus all made cars for it, and Jack and Ron also decided to have a go.

The BT17 was basically a beefier BT8A, with the body opened out to accommodate the new breed of wide tyres. It ran only twice, first with a 4.3-litre Repco engine, which proved so unreliable that it failed to make the start of the race. The main problems centred on the cast-in cylinder liners. Then a 3-litre Repco engine was fitted, and was run just once. Jack drove it in the 1966 Tourist Trophy, where it suffered oil feed problems. The works had too much on at the time to develop it, so it was put aside and later sold to a privateer.

Ron laid out drafts for a CanAm car several times, and had even got round to building a quarter-scale wind-tunnel model, but as he says: 'I don't really like the complication of building cars with sports car bodywork, and we were running a tight little factory building what cars we'd got time to build. I only had so much time to give to anything and that was a limitation on what we were able to do.' Jack says: 'I was keen to do CanAm, but the problem was that there was only one Ron. What we needed was an identical twin brother.'

For MRD, the failure of the BT17 was merely a blip, but for Repco it was a major setback since the sports car engine (like the Tasman engine) was supposed to be a commercial operation. The Formula One project was really only tagged on to the main business. That fact helps to explain some of the tetchiness which developed between Repco and Brabham.

At the end of 1966 Ron did something he had done only once before in his life. He took a holiday, but being Ron, it had to be a holiday with a point, a holiday with some action. He chose skiing, and ever since he has spent the fortnight over Christmas on the slopes.

11

The Repco connection – 2

In the autumn of 1966, the Honda engineers returned to Japan, happy with their excursion into Europe. Among the things they took with them was the memory of how Jack had saved face for them at Rouen when he had intimated that his gear lever had come off.

BRO had pleased one engine supplier, but in October Jack received a letter from Frank Hallam at Repco which positively spat blood. An article on Brabham-Repco, with a rare interview with Ron, had appeared in *Motoring News*, and Mr Hallam began his letter: 'I was absolutely furious to read the stinking write-up . . . from material which was obviously supplied by Ron Tauranac. I can only hope that it does not fall into the hands of any Repco Directors.'

After that breezy opening, Hallam got down to cases. The article had suggested that the Oldsmobile block cost £11, that the Repco RB620 engine had been developed in England, that it was an Oldsmobile engine converted to sohc, that modifications in England had raised the output from 290 to 310bhp. It was all true, but Mr Hallam took exception and declared that 'our engine is not a converted Oldsmobile but it incorporates an Oldsmobile block which has been converted to suit our purposes.' Later he would say that it would have been easier in the long run to have designed a new block.

The subtext of the letter was that Repco was not wholly convinced it was getting value for money. It had invested $A150,000 in capital expenditure and a further $A254,698 on the engines (that was around £200,000 at the time) and wanted to see at least that much returned in positive publicity.

Ford paid Cosworth £100,000 to produce the prototypes of two four-valve engines, the FVA and DFV, and when the DFV was made available to customers in 1968 the price was £7,500. Since the initial budget for the Repco family of racing engines was only £10,000 (including Phil Irving's salary) it would seem that the project was doing what so many motor racing projects do, it was bleeding cash.

Frank Hallam's position was delicate. He had seen his engine win a World Championship, and that had made Repco a household word and done wonders for the reputation of Australia. On the other hand, you cannot quantify things like that and the engine had been first proposed as a commercially viable replacement for the Coventry Climax FPF. It was supposed to generate profit, but in its 2½-litre form, it had been a flop. In the 1966/7 Tasman series Jack and Denny ran 2½-litre Brabham-Repcos and won only one race – they were soundly beaten by three-year-old BRMs and Lotuses with 2-litre engines.

Frank did not know that would happen when he wrote his letter, but he did know that even those local drivers who were able to pay $A7,500 for a Repco engine were having to wait for them because so much of the company's limited resources was being poured into Formula One.

After the Tasman series, enthusiasm for the engine took a sharp dive and Repco-Brabham was unable to rectify the position. So much effort was going into the Formula One project that, even though the workforce was putting in a huge amount of unpaid overtime, there were not enough resources left over.

Then again, the final design of the Tasman engine had been set as soon as Repco had placed an order for crankshafts with Laystall in England. Those, therefore, were the crankshafts which had to be used. While a change in the bore/stroke ratio would have been desirable, as everyone soon discovered, it was impossible.

There was the irony that, in 1966, BRO was dealing with two engine suppliers on the other side of the world and, despite all the problems with a different language, different culture, supposedly different level of engineering competence, and all the rest, it was Honda which caused the fewer problems.

The 4.3-litre sports car engine had proved a disaster on its one outing and it needed a comprehensive revision. This it received, and the capacity was increased to 4.4 litres, but only one had been sold by the end of 1966.

Frank Hallam felt that Jack had not done enough to promote the sports car engine. Ron says: 'Jack wasn't interested in selling them. He could have done had he wanted. There wasn't that much pressure during, and between, race meetings, but he basically didn't want anyone else to get their hands on them.'

It appears that there were also members of the Repco Board who were taking a personal interest in Jack, and who were his patrons. It would seem that he was given the odd nod and wink that Frank Hallam was not privy to.

Repco-Brabham was providing the Formula One engines at no charge to BRO – the money was being lost in the books – but by the end of 1966 customer sales were just under A$70,000 against a prediction of twice that. Formula One absorbed 75 per cent of Repco-Brabham's effort, yet produced not one cent of profit and most of the company's income was still coming from reproduction Coventry Climax parts. It is small wonder that Hallam felt sensitive, especially since most of Repco's Board did not understand motor racing.

Part of the trouble was that relationships such as Brabham had with Repco and Honda (and Lotus was forging with Ford) were relatively new in motor racing, and the parties concerned were having to create new rules of engagement. Commercial sponsorship did not arrive until January 1, 1968, so the relationship between a car constructor and an engine manufacturer was different to what it is now.

Then again, Ron had hardly ever been interviewed by journalists, and the piece in *Motoring News* was the first major profile of him to appear since he'd arrived in England. He'd been asked straight questions and had given straight answers. He had not put a PR spin on his conversation.

There remained acute problems of communication between Australia and the UK – this was the time when you used to book a phone call in advance and you were lucky if an airmail letter took less than a week. Air cargo was in its infancy, so most things went by sea and that took at least six weeks.

Frank Hallam would visit Britain in the summer of 1967, by which time the second-series engine, the RB740, had won races. Repco numbering was arrived at because machining on the prototype engine was given the job number 615. After that, the first digit referred to the block-crankcase unit and the second two digits indicated the type of cylinder head.

Design of the new engine had been going on almost as soon as the RB620 was up and running. There was, however, some change to the personnel. John Judd had joined BRO from Coventry Climax in 1965 and Jack proposed lending him to Repco-Brabham Engines in Melbourne. John was to stay there from March 1966 until late in 1967. He would not, however, have much experience of working with Phil Irving.

There had been a clash of personalities between Hallam and Irving early in 1966, and either Hallam dismissed his designer (his version) or Irving resigned (his account). It was a bit like an unsuited married couple going through a divorce, it doesn't matter who was in the right, the relationship was obviously wrong and Irving had stopped working for Repco before Jack had won the 1966 French Grand Prix.

John Judd says: 'I did not get on with Phil. In fact I was probably the catalyst which caused his departure since he stormed out every weekend. We parted on bad terms, but I have to say that he has never been given the full credit for what he did.

'It was Phil who worked away in an attic in Shepherd's Bush. There was poor communication between England and Australia and Phil had to sort out the problems which arrived with the engines. I don't think his contribution has been recognized.'

Norman Wilson replaced Irving as the project chief, and for 1967 there was a completely new crankcase and a revised cylinder head. The most visual difference was that on the second (RB740) series, the exhaust pipes were within the 'V' of the cylinder banks whereas they had been been on the outside of the block on the RB620. This had caused installation problems. Further, the new engine shed about 24lb in weight and power increased to 330bhp. It was a major revision.

Frank Hallam visited the MRD works just after the 1967 British Grand Prix; at this point Denny led the Drivers' World Championship from Jack and Brabham-Repco headed the Constructors' Cup. The threat from the Cosworth DFV, however, had come at exactly the right time if Ron and Jack were to get Repco to raise the level of its game. In fact, Norman Wilson had already spent several months working on a new four-valve cylinder head.

Following Hallam's visit, Ron set down the main points in a succinct three-page report. Frank was concerned about the Cosworth DFV, but Jack and Ron pointed out that the Lotus 49 had a problem putting all the power down on the road. Unlimited horsepower was not the solution that Repco thought it was.

Frank was also worried that the motoring press was not presenting Repco in its full glory. It was agreed that there should be a press handout and fortnightly bulletins on the progress of the Repco engine. One can imagine Ron's eyes glazing over at this point, but Frank being excited by the concept. It never happened, of course.

Jack suggested that substantial sponsorship could be obtained if Repco agreed to badge the engine in conjunction with a major manufacturer. Ford had its name on the DFV's cam-covers, and motoring journals were already referring to the Lotus-Ford.

It would be unfair to suggest that Frank Hallam went to the meeting only with bleats about the exposure Repco was getting. Among other things, he had ideas for cooling the gearbox oil and proposed a short-block engine and a relocation of the injector nozzles to help reduce drag.

Indianapolis and USAC racing was also on the agenda – a turbocharged 2.8-litre Repco engine was suggested for Indianapolis and it was thought that 550-600bhp could be obtained, while a sohc 4.2-litre normally aspirated unit was proposed for USAC road races.

Another item on the agenda was a four-cam Tasman engine to be run in a limited number of events. The idea was to use the Tasman Championship as a low-key evaluation exercise for a new Formula One engine. It was a sound idea in principle, but it was also far too ambitious given the timescale and available resources.

Frank Hallam's ideas were all sound, and when he returned to Australia he was able to report that MRD and Repco had a new understanding. But unfortunately, Repco did not understand motor racing. If Repco was to be in the business of selling customer engines – and as Cosworth was about to demonstrate, there was a good business in that area – then it had to gear up properly. It was no good taking the attitude that we have to make uncompetitive engines because we have ordered the crankshafts.

In mid-1967 Repco had more or less committed itself to a new Tasman engine which would lead to a new Formula One unit; two Indy engines, one of which would be turbocharged; plus various developments of the sports car engine, including a 5-litre version. In the meantime, Repco-Brabham would look around for subcontract work with major motor manufacturers.

That massive commitment was made without there being any clear idea about the financial structuring or standing of Repco-Brabham and with a significant faction on the parent Board being opposed to the whole idea. Worse, even those Board members who were in favour of the project did not really know enough about motor racing to know why they were in favour. If your allies do not know why they are supporting you, you are in trouble.

12

Double World Champions

On January 2, 1967 the Formula One season began with Jack and Denny occupying the front row of the grid in South Africa. In the race, Jack lost four laps in the pits with a dead engine and Denny lost two for a variety of other reasons, but it was altogether a bizarre race, which Pedro Rodriguez finally won in a Cooper-Maserati – it was to be Cooper's last Formula One victory.

Still, despite having lost so much time, Denny finished fourth and Jack sixth, so both came away with points to begin their World Championship campaign. They then headed to their homelands to take part in the Tasman series for the next couple of months, but there they found that their 2½-litre Repco engines were not as good as the 2-litre BRM and Climax V8s and, worse, they were not as reliable. Considering that Jack was returning home as World Champion, it was all a little disappointing. True, he won the final race in the series, but that would be the only Tasman race ever to be won by a Repco engine.

The Australian Gold Star, the premier home-series award, was won in 1967 for the second year running by Spencer Martin in a Brabham. The trouble was that the Brabham was fitted with a Coventry Climax FPF engine, which in turn was serviced with parts made by Repco. As Repco alone was keeping the venerable Climax engine going – as well as making some small improvements to it, as a result of which the old FPF 'four' continued to beat the Repco V8 – the whole motor racing side of Repco had all the ingredients of a nightmare.

Back in Europe at Brands Hatch, for the Race of Champions, Dan Gurney's Eagles had the new Weslake V12 engine installed and Dan duly won. But it was to prove a false dawn. As the season got under way it would have been a brave man who predicted that Brabham-Repco would take the title again. At the International Trophy, at Silverstone, Mike Parkes won for Ferrari with Jack second; it appeared that Ferrari, Eagle and Honda all had the measure of Brabham, and everyone knew that Lotus had a new car in the wings.

Jack set pole at Monaco from Lorenzo Bandini's Ferrari, but his engine gave up on the first lap while Bandini and Stewart began to take turns in the lead. Surtees was also well-placed in the early stages, but Denny was driving magnificently, and he hit the front on lap 15 and stayed there to the end, lapping the entire field. But his first Grand Prix victory was tarnished with sadness, for Bandini, tiring in his efforts to match Hulme's pace, crashed at the chicane and was fatally burned. Young, quick and glamorous, his loss to Ferrari was incalculable.

Denny was a laid-back guy, but on his day he could be mighty. Ted Croucher, the chief marshal at Goodwood, recalls Denny testing a CanAm McLaren there: 'All the quick guys were here – Surtees, Stewart, everyone. Denny was asleep on the pit counter, but when his car was ready he woke up, got in, demolished the lap record, got out and went back to sleep on the counter. He lapped in 61 seconds and that is still the unofficial record.' Ron says: 'Denny's idea of setting up a car was to kick the tyres and say, "She'll be right".'

Lotus arrived at the Dutch Grand Prix with their DFV-powered car and Graham Hill put his on pole. The future had arrived, and only Gurney's Eagle looked capable of offering it a challenge. Jimmy Clark, currently a tax exile living in Paris, had not previously driven the Lotus 49, so understandably he was relatively subdued in qualifying, but from the start of the race he was on the pace.

Ron recalls: 'Our engine discharged a lot of oil and the thing was that we'd collect it in a waste tank and every six laps I'd hang out a sign to Jack to remind him to switch on the Bendix pump, which would recirculate it. Jimmy was right on Jack's tail, so I didn't hang out the sign. For some reason Jimmy was suddenly keeping well back; I think he was expecting Jack's engine to go at any time.'

Hill led the early stages, but then retired, and Clark came through to win from Jack and Denny. The headlines were all about the sensational debut of a new car and engine; they tended not to notice that Denny was leading the World Championship – or that Jack had a new engine in his car, the RB740.

So far as the Brabham team was concerned, the Belgian Grand Prix was an unmitigated disaster due to oil surge in the sump. Neither driver could get within 7 seconds of Clark in qualifying – Denny was 12 seconds adrift – and both were out by half-distance with engine failure. Ron says: 'It was late in the day when we realized what the problem was. The nature of the track, with its long downhill sections, was causing a valve to stick open. The night before the race, Jack modified his car and I worked on Denny's, but we didn't get it right.' The next day Gurney scored a memorable victory with his Eagle-Weslake – it was to be the marque's only World Championship win.

It was at the Belgian Grand Prix that Jack's car appeared with small wings – trim tabs, Ron called them – on either side of the nose. Ron says: 'It was something I'd been thinking about, but it was not an original idea. I think you'll find that one or two people had been trying them in IndyCar racing. Jack did a few laps and said: "The tabs work OK, but it's at the back that we need them".'

In fact, the Formula Two Brabham which John Coombs entered for Graham Hill in 1965 sometimes ran with trim tabs similar to the ones Jack used at Spa, and Frank Gardner had run tabs on his Brabham Formula Junior car way back in 1962. The wonder is that they were never taken up by others.

After the Dutch and Belgian races, nobody gave Brabham much of a chance, but then Jack and Denny romped home first and second in France, a lap clear of the field. They had been on the pace throughout the meeting – Jack was second on the grid, only a tenth of a second behind Hill's Lotus – and they were in first and second places by half-distance. On the medium-pace Circuit Bugatti at Le Mans the car's sweet handling came into its own. It was giving away perhaps 75bhp to the Lotus-Cosworth – 325 compared with 400bhp – but everything stayed together while everyone else self-destructed.

At Silverstone, though, power made the difference, but even so Denny came home a strong second to Clark, with Jack fourth. It was after that race that Frank Hallam visited the works and went away with an extensive shopping list.

Neither Brabham driver had ever gone particularly well at the Nürburgring, but Hulme was second to Clark in qualifying and never ran lower than second in the race. First Clark led, then Gurney, and when they both retired, Denny was there to win, with Jack in second place.

By then Guy Ligier had switched from a Cooper-Maserati to a Brabham-Repco. Ligier, a former Rugby Union international for France, was never an ace, but the move was one more nail in Cooper's coffin. Then tragically, shortly after the German Grand Prix, Bob Anderson, one of the last of the old-style privateers, was killed while testing his car at Silverstone.

In early August, Repco sent over a number of bolt-on engine kits, which gave an extra 20bhp. The guys in Melbourne were really working hard.

The next race, the Canadian Grand Prix, was run in very wet conditions and Jack led Denny home for a Brabham 1-2, but he'd had his share of luck. Denny had had to pit twice with steamed-up goggles and Clark's engine had died when he was in the lead. Against all the odds, therefore, Brabham-Repco was coasting towards its second Constructors' Cup and Denny was in the lead of the Drivers' World Championship by a comfortable margin.

In the remaining three races, Jack took two second places and a sixth, but although Denny came away with only two third places, this was enough to secure him the title. One of Jack's second places was behind Surtees' Honda at Monza – by a car's length. Had he won this race instead of Surtees, his gross total would have been equal to Denny's, but he would then have had to drop 3 points since not every result was allowed to count.

You would have thought that after securing a second consecutive Drivers' World Championship and a second Constructors' Cup the Repco Board would have been overjoyed. In fact, some of them demanded to know why Denny (a Kiwi) had won and not Jack.

A friend of his recalls that Denny thought he was not supposed to win the title. 'Denny said that he'd be in the workshop and would notice that if there was a new bit it would always be on Jack's car. He'd be told: "We're just trying it out, you'll get it if it works." Denny was convinced that he was not getting equal treatment, and that thought prompted his move to McLaren the following year.' At the time Jack said: 'Kiwi driver in a Kiwi team . . . makes sense to me.'

Ron says: 'Denny was a Kiwi and a close friend not only of Bruce McLaren, but also of Phil Kerr (Bruce's co-director). A move to McLaren was a good arrangement for him. On the other matter, Jack did usually have the new parts first, because he wanted them, and Denny was content to let him try them. The result was that Denny's car was the more reliable.' Frank Hallam is on record as agreeing with that. Denny took the view, 'If it's not broken, don't fix it,' while Jack was always looking for new angles and advantages.

At this time Frank Hallam was facing mounting pressure from the Repco Board, some of whom felt that having scored consecutive World Championships it was a good time to retire. They were aware that part of the company's success was due to the fact that it had been ready when the opposition hadn't, and that to remain competitive was going to take increasing amounts of money. By November 1967, Repco-Brabham Engines had managed to sell just three units for the Tasman Championship and two for sports cars.

Denny had now decamped to join a team which would have Cosworth engines and a chassis drawn by Robin Herd, who was then regarded as the new superstar designer, and who will cross this story several times. On top of the prospects for the McLaren Formula One effort, there was the promise of the lucrative CanAm series, which the team would come to dominate so decisively that it became known as the 'Bruce and Denny Show', and which did their bank balances no harm at all.

On the other hand, Repco was sitting on a CanAm engine and had nowhere to place it. Apart from the purely physical limits to what Ron could achieve himself, the relationship was becoming unstitched. Hallam had managed to get as much done as he had because he was a man in the Tauranac mould, but there is rarely room for two personalities like that in one relationship. Before long there would be strife.

That autumn, another Australian entered the story, Ralph Bellamy, who had been walkabout, making the mandatory trip to Britain and Europe that so many young Aussies made. He would gain a reputation as a very reliable designer and he credits Ron with teaching him the fundamentals of racing car design.

Ralph says: 'If you are looking for saints, you'll find motor sport very barren ground, but Ron has characteristics which have allowed him to be successful and to survive in an extremely harsh environment which, as a matter of record, has taken its toll both mentally and physically of many of his contemporaries over the years.

'Ron is honest to his own standards, responsible and hard-working, but he is also ruthlessly competitive, egocentric and not particularly interested in other people's points of view. You work *for* him, not *with* him; he only needs you to help him do what he wants done. This is probably true of many high achievers and it brings me to the 'Thick line, thin line' story.

'When I went to work for MRD, I had been working as an engineering draughtsman for about 12 years and had always taken pride in my penmanship and the quality of my drawings. On this particular occasion I was drawing a wheel, and on the drawing we had a local convention of showing the cast surfaces in thin lines and the machined surfaces in thick lines, instead of normal surface finish symbols. I had almost finished the drawing, but I had chosen to draw the machined surfaces in ink instead of pencil so that when my original was run through the dyeline print machine to produce the working drawings the black ink lines would print much thicker and darker than the pencil lines and so achieve the desired effect.

'At that point Ron came into the Portakabin drawing office and had a look over my shoulder to see what I had done. "Naaaa, that's no good, look." He picked up one of my pencils and scrubbed it back and forth four or five times across the drawing saying: *"That's* a thick line," and then about an inch lower he took the pencil once across the drawing saying, *"That's* a thin line".

'He then put the pencil down and walked out. As you can imagine, Mike Hillman and Ted Marley were deeply impressed and gathered round to view and comment on this piece of wisdom which had been handed down to us so graciously.

'The point is, of course, that I had not done it wrong, I just had not done it *his* way, and with Ron there is only one way – *his* way.'

But if Ron wasn't easy to work for, at least he was successful, and Brabham continued to dominate the Formula Three market. Lotus had mounted a strong campaign in 1966, but Derek Bell's comments, recorded earlier, speak for many drivers of the time. Lotus was fast losing credibility as a maker of production racing cars.

As the season wore on, many Formula Three drivers looked enviously at the Matra MS5, but that was a factory effort plus favoured private teams, it was not a customer car. At the end of the season, the score in terms of international wins was Matra 23, Brabham 26. But the bare scoreline does not give the flavour of the match. If Matras had been as plentiful as Brabhams, nobody else would have got a look-in.

There was one unusual team in Formula Three that year. DAF wanted to promote its Variomatic transmission, an early form of CVT using rubber belts, expanding pulleys and no differential. TV commercials showed a driver with a simple gearstick: *Forward to go forward. Back to go back.* In fact, theoretically you could go as fast in reverse as forwards in a DAF.

DAF commissioned the Chequered Flag garage, which had made the Gemini Formula Junior cars, to run a team using the Variomatic transmission. The Dutch company had first conducted experiments on an Alexis Formula Three car, and then MRD was commissioned to build cars to take the unusual transmission.

Ron recalls: 'Jack did some development driving for them and he found that on certain corners, like St Mary's at Goodwood, he was losing 300rpm because there was not enough variance of ratio between the rear wheels, and the effect was like having a locked differential. So they put in a differential, which cured that problem, but there were others.

'From rest, the car had phenomenal acceleration – nothing could live with it – but it was tricky to handle because of all the extra weight at the back. Then again, the driver could not feather the throttle in corners because as soon as he did so, the transmission varied the gearing, so you didn't have control through your right foot.

'People have looked at CVT transmission for Formula One. Williams has experimented for years with it and I have told Patrick Head he'd always have that fundamental problem to overcome. I don't know if he paid any attention.'

In Mike Beckwith and Gijs van Lennep, Chequered Flag had two good drivers and, in wet conditions, the cars went well because they did not suffer from wheelspin. Late in the year, van Lennep won a race in Sweden, and Beckwith won the E R Hall Trophy at Brands Hatch, which was one of the biggest Formula Three races of the year – 19 of the drivers present that day later raced in Formula One, most of them with top teams. Beckwith was helped in that it rained in the final.

No fewer than 44 Brabhams, most of them BT21s, had been entered for the E R Hall Trophy against a total of 29 cars from Lotus, Matra, Merlyn, DAF, Tecno, de Sanctis, Pygmée, Titan, Cooper, Chevron, Alpine and Shannon. That one statistic tells its own story.

Delve a little deeper and we find that Lotus, which had dominated British racing in the late 1950s and early 1960s, had only nine cars on the grid; it was being edged out of production racing cars. John Miles brought his Lotus 41 home second in his heat (behind Piers Courage's Brabham) and third in the final behind Beckwith's 'Brabham-DAF' and Clay Regazzoni's Tecno, so the Lotus was not a disaster, it was just not a good customer car. Cooper built only two Formula Three cars in 1967, and they were the last customer single-seaters that the company would make.

Tecno was then just a blip on the horizon, but it would very soon become a serious competitor, though like most outfits which challenged Ron's cars, although it found an initial advantage, it couldn't sustain its development. The same went for Titan, a car which bore some resemblance to a Brabham – Roy Pike won the second heat at Brands Hatch in his. Roy would be a front-runner and race-winner in 1968, but by then Titan had stopped making cars.

In fact we need to consult reference books to pin down what happened to the others, with the possible exception of Chevron. Peter Gethin, who raced a wide variety of cars, says: 'You always knew you could win with a Lotus provided it stayed in one piece – which frequently it did not. With Brabhams and Chevrons you never had any doubt about that.'

Chevron enters the story as a rival maker. The cars were built in Bolton by Derek Bennett and a talented team which included Paul Owens and Paul Brown, who went on to become senior men at Reynard. Like Ralt, Chevron did not go in for a high press profile, but simply got on with the manufacture of racing cars of impeccable integrity.

In some ways Bennett was like Tauranac. They had both started in grass roots racing (Bennett with midget speedway cars), both were self-taught, both shunned the limelight, and both built fine cars. Bennett's best designs were 2-litre sports-racing and GT machines, which were superb, although his single-seaters were less consistent. There would be seasons, however, when they would challenge Ron's designs.

When the 1,600cc Formula Two arrived in 1967 virtually everybody ran the new Cosworth FVA engine. Jochen Rindt won the lion's share of Championship and non-Championship races in his Roy Winkelmann Brabham, but it was Jacky Ickx, in a Matra run by Ken Tyrrell, who took the title from Frank Gardner's Brabham. There were 10 races counting towards the European Championship and the result, in terms of outright victories, was Brabham 6, Matra 3 and Lotus 1. Seven of those races attracted graded drivers, and each of these was won by one of them: Rindt (Brabham) 5, Stewart (Matra) 1 and Clark (Lotus) 1.

As already mentioned, the batch of Brabham school cars which had been built for Honda over the winter of 1965/6 were, in effect, Formula Ford cars before the category had been thought of, but in the middle of 1967 the initial rules for the new formula were revealed, one of which was an upper price limit of £1,000.

That left very little margin for profit, so some people sold complete Formula Ford cars, and then the customer found that he had a bog-standard engine and a VW gearbox and needed to spend £200 on having his engine blueprinted and a further £200 to buy a Hewland gearbox. Ron called it 'Formula Fiddle' and declared at the time: 'I have always treated my customers honourably. I can't build a car for that price, I might consider doing one for £1,750, but I'm not going to resort to tricks.'

Even when the (optimistic) price regulation was eased and finally dropped, MRD declined to make Formula Ford cars. As Ron says today: 'I've always been more attracted to international categories. It's the old story, there's only so many hours in the day.'

There was no need for MRD to go trawling in unknown waters when production and sale of other cars remained strong, which was no wonder when you consider that Brabhams had won a record total of 10 championships for single-seater cars that year. In 1967 MRD made nine distinct models, which may also be a record (or on the other hand it may simply have been excessive). It is true that they shared many components, but as Michael Hillman has said, they were different cars.

While some of the 'International' cars were built for the Tasman series, with Repco engines, the most successful one in the series was the BT23D, which had an Alfa Romeo Tipo 33 engine and was built for Kevin Bartlett, who won the 1968 Australian Gold Star Championship.

Back at Repco-Brabham, the attempt to make a 2.8-litre turbocharged Indy engine using a Garrett-AiReseach turbocharger came to nothing. The men at Repco dubbed it 'Puff the Tragic Wagon'. The turbocharger was abandoned, yet it was the way to the future in Indy, but Repco was right to jump ship because it simply did not have the resources to pursue the option. Cosworth, which was a huge operation compared to Repco, waited another eight years before it attempted to move into the Indy market.

The little team in Melbourne was also hard at work on a new engine with four-valve heads. This new unit, the RB860, has been represented as being merely an Oldsmobile with new cylinder heads, but it was rather more than that – there was a new crankcase and sump for a start. But while that was taking shape the Repco Board was in turmoil, seemingly not knowing how to exploit the company's second World Championship, but instead demanding to know why it was not selling more engines. The fact was that the resources of Repco-Brabham were so stretched that the company could either go racing, or it could build engines for sale, but it couldn't do both.

Mario Andretti's 1965 IndyCar Championship-winning car was a copy of the BT12 produced by Clint Brawner and called a Hawk, but it was entered as the Dean Van Lines Special.

It can't get better than this! Brabham-Repco team-mates Jack Brabham and Denny Hulme lead Jim Clark early in the 1966 Dutch Grand Prix, which Jack went on to win. This was the year of his third World Championship.

The Brabham-Repcos were not the most powerful F1 cars in 1966 and 1967, but they were certainly the most effective and took Brabham and Hulme to their respective World Championships.

Ron's open-air wind-tunnel! His partner blasts down a runway with the F1 car bedecked with wool tufts to help identify the passage of the airflow.

Ron's only large-engined sports car, the 1966 BT17, was at first powered by a 4.3-litre Repco V8 engine, later by a 3-litre version, but was only raced by Jack once before being sold to a private entrant. Thereafter Ron concentrated on single-seaters, which he much preferred.

The master tries a Brabham for size. Juan-Manuel Fangio ordered a bunch of these chassis for the Argentine Temporada F3 series and subsequently signed this photograph for Ron's administration manager Alain Fenn.

A double-winged Brabham-Ford BT26 was amongst the line-up of F1 cars on the occasion of a royal visit to Goodyear's headquarters in Wolverhampton. Denny Hulme is just visible behind Bruce McLaren and alongside Goodyear's Leo Mehl as Princess Margaret approaches the Brabham.

An untypically quiet scene with a group of F2 and F3 cars left temporarily unattended in Ron's assembly shop at New Haw, Surrey.

Jack Brabham getting down to it with his BT24 in 1967, his Brabham-Repco carrying the number 1 reserved for the current World Champion.

When DAF decided to investigate Formula 3 in 1967 they asked Ron to adapt a chassis to take their infinitely variable transmission system. Jack tested the car, but he didn't like the lack of throttle control the system gave him.

Ron had developed his duck tail for this IndyCar a year before a similar solution was adopted in Formula One following the banning of the flimsy tall wings in 1969.

A smooth and quick driver in a smooth and quick car. Jackie Stewart at Thruxton at the wheel of John Coombs' F2 Brabham BT30 in 1970.

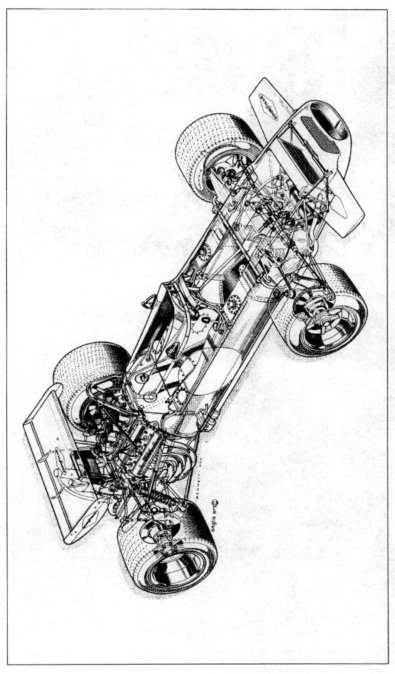

Ron's first Formula One monocoque was the Brabham BT33 with which Jack Brabham concluded his professional driving career in 1970. Bill Bennett's cutaway drawing, which appeared in *Autosport* early that year, highlights the neat packaging of components – a Tauranac trademark – the inboard and vertical front suspension units and the huge tyres which were fitted to 13-inch wheels that season.

There was no mistaking Ron's Brabham BT34 with its 'lobster claw' radiator intakes

Ever-practical, Ron found a simple solution when a photographer wanted to 'shoot' the BT34 in the workshop from above!

13

To finish first . . .

The 1968 motor racing season was dominated by tragedy, the death in early April of Jim Clark being followed by the loss in successive months of Mike Spence, Lodovico Scarfiotti and Jo Schlesser. Meanwhile, Formula One was becoming more competitive as the Cosworth DFV engine had been made available to other teams, the option being taken up by McLaren and by Ken Tyrrell, who was using Matra chassis and for whom Jackie Stewart was now driving, having left BRM. Every race but one would fall to a DFV-engined car, the exception being the French GP, which was taken by Jacky Ickx's Ferrari.

With Denny Hulme having left Brabham to join McLaren, a seat was available for Jochen Rindt, who had spent the previous two seasons struggling with a Cooper-Maserati in Formula One, while winning races in Formula Two with a Brabham. With Jochen came his mechanic, Ron Dennis, although he would then become Jack's mechanic instead.

Dennis says: 'There was a complete change of philosophy. Cooper was committed to monocoques whereas Brabham was making spaceframes. In terms of culture, I thought I was going backwards. Jack Brabham didn't just run a tight ship, I thought it was tight without reason. Only later did I discover how short money was, but even so everything was done to a budget, so we all had to travel to Grands Prix in a truck.

'Every morning we used to dread the sight of Ron's ghastly maroon Renault lurching into the factory. The Golden Rule was that you avoided him until he had his coffee break at ten. Until then he was unbearable, and if you said anything to him, he would take the opposite view. It was dreadful, but at the end of the day you have to say that he got more things right than he got wrong.'

Jochen Rindt made a big impact at MRD. Some thought that he was imperious, and Michael Hillman thought him utterly exotic. 'Jochen made a point of portraying the glamour of being a racing driver,' Michael says, 'it was part of his promoting himself – sharp clothes, beautiful wife. Jochen was a culture shock to us after Jack and Denny.'

Ron found a different man. 'He was totally natural, with a great sense of humour. We got on wonderfully and he was also Jack's favourite driver. We tried to save money where we could, and Jochen and I used to share a hotel room at the races. That was the sort of guy Jochen was, he was prepared to muck in with the team. When Jacky Ickx joined us and found that he was expected to share a room with me, he turned on his heel and booked his own room.

'Some teams had their pit popsies and lap scorers, but we tended to be an all-male outfit. It was only later, when Graham Hill drove for us, that Norma would come to the races because Graham would offer her a lift in his plane.

'Jochen definitely liked girls – he was a racing driver – but at race meetings he concentrated on the job in hand.'

Jochen was no stranger to the Brabham factory, of course, since he'd been driving Brabhams in Formula Two for four years – and had won 13 races in them. The combination of Jack's experience and ability to develop a car, combined with Jochen's blinding speed, looked formidable on paper, and another positive factor was that Jochen admired Jack above all others in motor racing. Also, Repco had a new 'quad-cam' engine on the stocks.

There was another movement in 1968 which in the long term would have an effect on the MRD part of the Tauranac story. On January 1, 1968 the FIA allowed sponsors' names to be carried on cars. The governing body recognized that costs were escalating and that something had to be done. They didn't want to go down the American route (with such as the John Zink Track Burner Special) and they stipulated that a sponsor's logo could be no more than a foot square. Within days of the rule coming into force, a Lotus raced in the Tasman series entered as a Gold Leaf Team Lotus and painted in red, white and gold, with John Player's logo occupying the mandatory one square foot.

Colin Chapman had read the rulebook, found his loophole and had driven a coach and horses through it. For better or worse, the motorized advertising hoarding had arrived, and it would be that which, more than anything else, ultimately caused Ron to sell Brabham.

Ron says: 'Jack was able to put together deals within the trade, but neither of us could handle the idea of putting on a suit and tie and going to some meeting in the Grosvenor House Hotel.' For the time being most of the Brabham budget was picked up by Goodyear, Esso and, of course, by Repco through the free supply of engines.

In 1968 the Cosworth DFV engine was no longer exclusive to Lotus and, with hindsight, Brabham should have used Cosworths until the new RB860 engine was ready to race. The political situation within Repco-Brabham, however, made this option impossible.

Ideas for the new engine had been floating around for over a year. The Apfelbeck head design, as used by BMW, was explored – but even BMW soon dropped it. Exploring that route, however, drained resources. Then subcontractors supplied substandard cylinder heads, and rectifying that delayed production of the new Formula One engine by about four months.

Nerves were getting frayed and Frank Hallam and Ron exchanged angry letters. Ron had stipulated a particular sump design for the Indy engine and he thought there was agreement on this point. But Hallam raged that a batch of sumps had cost a total of A$10,000 and perhaps Ron would like to trade in one of his cars on them.

Yet so far as the Brabham team was concerned, the start to the season was promising. Jochen and Jack occupied the second row of the grid in South Africa and Jochen finished a strong third behind the Lotuses of Clark and Hill and two laps ahead of Amon's Ferrari in fourth place. That was most encouraging, especially considering that Jochen was in the 1967 car. But by the time the works Brabhams next appeared, Jim Clark was dead, having been killed in a Formula Two race at Hockenheim, and fate was moving Jochen towards Lotus.

The new RB860 engine first ran in the Spanish Grand Prix in May. It had arrived so late that the team had to charter a plane to fly the car to Madrid. Since there was spare space on the flight, some of the MRD workers got a free weekend in Spain. One of them recalls vividly how impressed he was to see Jack at the end of practice without a bead of sweat on him, while Jochen was showing signs of extreme physical exertion, with bulging eyes, and red face veins out on his neck.

That eyewitness account from a reliable source could be taken as clear evidence of Jack's supreme ability to relax. But unfortunately on this occasion the reason why Jack was so unstressed was that a valve seat on the new engine had given up after just a couple of laps of practice, whereas Jochen, who still had the sohc RB740 unit, had been driving balls-out just to be ninth quickest of the 13 starters.

It was typical of Rindt's relaxed approach, however, that he was having a cup of tea in the transporter with his mechanics when they heard a noise. The field was off on the warm-up lap. Jochen had to sprint to his car and chase them. He started at the back and was the first to retire.

Meanwhile, Brabham unveiled the BT25 for Indianapolis, which was the first monocoque car MRD had built. Even then the construction was chosen mainly because USAC rules demanded bag-type fuel tanks. The Brabham was fitted with a 4.2-litre RB760 engine, but the most interesting part of the car was its body shape, with the rear deck sweeping upwards into an integrated spoiler. It was something which Colin Chapman would copy the following year during a period when suspension-mounted wings were banned following some serious breakages.

Jochen's schedule meant he could spend only one day qualifying at Indianapolis and, as luck would have it, it was on a damp track. But driving with the tail hanging out, in a way rarely seen at the 'Brickyard', he somehow managed to qualify – it shouldn't have happened, but it did. Ron called it sensational, and the organizers breathed a sigh of relief.

The regular drivers stayed off the track – you don't drive on a damp oval. But the fact that Jochen had driven and qualified meant that the organizers did not have to refund the spectators' entrance money. Come the race, however, and he was out after five laps with, of all things, a burned-out piston.

That same car was raced in 1969 by Peter Revson, who finished fifth in the Indianapolis 500 and also won a 150-mile USAC race at Indianapolis Raceway Park with it. It lays to rest the myth that the Repco 'quad cam' was a total failure because that win was the first in USAC by a non-American engine since before the Second World War.

Back in Europe, Jack alone had an RB860 engine for the Monaco Grand Prix, but after qualifying only 12th he crashed out of the race. Jochen managed to qualify fifth in the previous year's car, which was a good effort, but in the race a radius arm detached itself – it was most unusual for a Brabham to suffer a structural failure.

Meanwhile, the guys at Repco-Brabham were suffering from being 12,000 miles from the motor racing industry. On top of the serious problem with the cylinder heads they were having difficulties with quality control. To take one small example – gudgeon pins. You would not have thought gudgeon pins would be a problem, but they were, and eventually the difficulty was solved by using the gudgeon pins from a Petter diesel engine.

In Spain, Jack had a valve seat fall out because the wrong material had been used and the seats were shrinking. Ron takes up the story: 'It was at the Belgian Grand Prix at Spa-Francorchamps that the reason became clear. After practice on the day before the race, we stripped down an engine and discovered the problem.

'Jack contacted John Judd at BRO with a request to make new valve seats. He then flew back to England with two cylinder heads and collected the seats. In order to fit them he heated the heads in the kitchen cooker so that the seats could be shrunk into place. At three in the morning the smell of baking metal woke Betty Brabham, who was convinced that the house was on fire. It's just as well she went downstairs to investigate, or the fire brigade would have been around.'

Then Jack flew back to Belgium, snatched some sleep while the heads were fitted, and then raced on the most awesome circuit in the world. After all that, Jochen retired with a dropped valve seat and Jack retired with sticking throttle slides. Jack, a triple World Champion, had been baking engine parts in his kitchen at three in the morning of a Grand Prix taking place in a different country. No wonder Jochen worshipped him. Although many a driver in Rindt's position would have thrown the odd wobbly, he accepted it because he knew that everyone was working at full stretch.

In Melbourne the workforce of Repco-Brabham had risen from 19 employees in June 1966 to 59 in May 1968, and by then Repco's investment in Brabham had risen to A$553,000. The fact that the RB860 engine was delivered very late was due at least in part to the cylinder head design change from Apfelbeck to a conventional four-valve head. It had had a minimum of dyno-testing at Repco and there had been no time for car testing, so the difficulties that arose with the engine's accessories and their drives were to be expected. The Formula One engine revved to 9,000rpm, whereas the 4.2-litre version as used at Indy ran to only 7,500, so it lasted longer. But the ultimate problem, diagnosed with the benefit of hindsight, was its destruction of the Alfa Romeo cam followers due to torsional vibration of the camshaft.

A lot of bad press has hung around the RB860 engine, and it did have some fundamental flaws, in particular its very bad vibration and consequent frequent breakages of those cam followers, and because of the lack of adequate dyno-testing or track-testing, chassis and engine never became a harmonious unit.

Meanwhile, after Belgium, the team's headlines were earned not because Jack had flown home and back overnight, but because the Brabhams had sprouted a high-mounted wing at the rear, which worked in conjunction with front trim tabs. Ron says: 'We ran with them first, then Ferrari ran with them, and since theirs was adjusted hydraulically from the cockpit, they didn't just work them up overnight. We were obviously working on parallel lines, and just because we went out on the track first with a wing, it doesn't mean that I want to claim credit for this.'

Before long wings were sprouting on every car, often on tall pylons attached to the suspension. They became taller and bigger by the race, and it is fair to say that not everyone understood what they were doing. Ron conducted airflow tests with tufts of wool attached to the car in an effort to learn more about what was happening to the airflow.

Before the Dutch Grand Prix, Repco had supplied some replacement pistons and these had been fitted to the engines prior to the cars being dispatched by transporter to Holland. Ron takes up the story: 'After their departure we were informed by Repco that the pistons were too tall and would hit the cylinder head at high revs. So Jack purchased a couple of wood chisels, made a template to fit to the cylinder block and flew to Zandvoort. On arrival the cylinder heads were removed and, using the template to control the amount of metal removed, he proceeded to scrape .02in from the top land of each piston, whereupon the engines were reassembled and they performed well in qualifying.'

Despite all the hard work, there was a spot of light relief at Zandvoort when Jochen took Jack, Ron and John Judd to the local funfair and booked them all half an hour on the dodgems, where they let off steam!

The potential of the Rindt/Brabham/Repco combination was becoming obvious as Jochen was second-fastest in practice for the Dutch Grand Prix, then he would put his car on pole for the French Grand Prix at Rouen. But the races were both a disappointment. In Holland Jochen retired with excessive engine vibration, while Jack's auxiliary fuel pump flattened his battery so, when he spun, he could not restart, while in France Jack's fuel pump failed and Jochen's fuel tank split.

But these were trifling problems compared with those surrounding Honda, for whom John Surtees had been striving to do his best since the previous year, but was still being thwarted. 'The first car had been overweight, so we adapted a Lola IndyCar chassis, and Tadashi Kume was working on a new lightweight V12 engine. But back at the factory, Mr Honda insisted on having his own way, so we only received new cylinder heads, and the rest of the hoped for lightweight components never arrived. Instead, all their energy was diverted into building a car with an air-cooled V8 engine. I flatly refused to drive it.' So this car was entered instead for Jo Schlesser at Rouen. On the third lap the engine suddenly cut, Schlesser ran wide and hit a bank, the car flipped and caught fire. Poor Schlesser was killed and Honda withdrew at the end of the year.

It was not until the German Grand Prix in August that either Jack or Jochen was classified as a finisher, and even that was largely because the race was held in a downpour, so the engines were understressed. According to the history books, quite a number of failures were on the peripherals, like throttle slides and ignition. Ron says: 'When we could, we used to shoulder some of the blame to protect our suppliers. Jack was particularly conscious of this, but I wasn't as acutely aware of the importance of doing that until I gave that interview at the end of 1966 which had so incensed Frank Hallam.'

Regardless of the real reasons for retirements, the upshot was that Jochen, now considered to be the quickest driver in the world, finished the season with just two third places, while three-times World Champion Jack Brabham tied for last place in the table with 2 points. Having won the Constructor's Cup two years on the trot, in 1968 Brabham finished behind even Cooper, and Cooper was about to collapse.

In Melbourne, Frank Hallam felt he was being compromized politically within Repco-Brabham and he resigned. Repco-Brabham Engines had not been a commercial success, even though its involvement in Formula One had brought it into line for a number of lucrative contracts with road car manufacturers. But even then it failed to exploit its contacts as well as it might have done.

In the meantime, Jochen was being wooed by Colin Chapman, and Chapman came a-courting with more than chocolates and flowers. He came with large pay cheques, larger than anyone else could offer; Chapman had sponsorship well developed. Jochen had two realistic options, Brabham and Lotus. He wanted to stay with Jack and Ron (and Leo Mehl of Goodyear), but Lotus made him an offer which he had to take seriously, and long before the end of the season it seemed likely that Jochen would soon be heading for the exit. He was not keen to do so, and in this he was being influenced by his close friend Jackie Stewart, who had refused to drive Lotuses because he considered them to be unsafe.

Ron recalls: 'At the last race, in Mexico, Jochen told us what he had been offered by Chapman. I forget what it was, but he offered to drive for us for half of that. But we could not even meet that. Jack was prepared to give up driving and to run the team solely for Jochen – just as he'd been ready to do if Dan Gurney had stayed on. It was not something he was prepared to do for anyone.'

Brabham had had a rotten season in Formula One and things were not a great deal better elsewhere. Although Jochen had taken several wins in Formula Two, the Matra MS7 was clearly the car to have, and in Formula Three, the Italian Tecno, made by a kart manufacturer, was sweeping the board except in the parochial British series.

The Tecno incorporated a lot of thinking which originated with their karts. In particular, it had a short wheelbase, a wide track and it made very efficient use of space. As their performance on high-speed circuits showed, Tecnos were very efficient aerodynamically, but their real secret was in the way they exploited the latest wide, slick tyres. Of the 65 international Formula Three races run in 1968, Tecno won 32.

Although Repco had harboured ambitions to become a mainstream engine supplier, Jack and Ron had now made the decision to switch to Cosworth for 1969, so that brought the Repco line to an end. The company had been in Formula One for only three years, but had won two Drivers' World Championships and two Constructors' Cups, the best strike-rate ever. Also, things were not quite over for the engineers back in Melbourne because they would be at Indianapolis in 1969, but the adventure in Formula One ended in 1968.

John Judd, however, continued to work for the Brabham Racing Organisation and he designed special cylinder heads for Vauxhall and a Ford Indy engine which never raced. But 1968 had been a dreadful year for MRD. Sales, like wins, were down and it was beginning to look as though MRD was being left behind and that Ron was running out of both energy and ideas.

14

Towards the evening

When Jochen Rindt left Brabham to join Lotus, he changed the balance of power, not so much in Formula One – because this was destined to be another disappointing season for him at the top level – but in Formula Two. Since Jochen was now a Lotus driver, Roy Winkelmann Racing also switched to Lotuses and ran Rindt and Hill in what was virtually the Lotus works team. Jackie Stewart was still in a Tyrrell-run Matra (a manufacturer which had support from the French government) and Ferrari and BMW snapped up the best of the rising talent. There were some heavy-hitters in Formula Two, and BMW, entering single-seater racing for the first time in the company's history, ran not only chassis designed by Len Terry and built by Dornier, but also Lolas.

For the first time since Formula Two was revived in 1964, Brabham was not the dominant make, neither did it have a top team running its cars. Frank Williams Racing would enter up to four cars for any one race, but that was a case of Frank looking after cars for clients, it was not quite the same as the Winkelmann and Tyrrell operations.

Jack had edged away from the category at the end of 1967 while his new partner in the Brabham Formula One team, Jacky Ickx, had commitments in sports car racing which largely kept him away from Formula Two. To compound matters, there were serious production problems with both the BT30 Formula Two car and the BT28 for Formula Three.

Only four Formula Two races fell to Brabham in 1969 and only one of those was a round of the European Championship. The old BT23C was no longer competitive, other than in freak conditions, such as could happen with a slipstreaming battle, and while the BT30 was on the pace, there were few of them around.

Much the same went for the BT28. For the first time in years, the previous year's Brabham was off the pace and this year's car was slow in arriving. It was not until late June that as many as six BT28s were entered in any one race, which was a very low number for any Brabham model. A couple of years earlier it was nothing for Brabhams to outnumber every other make on the entry list, but in 1969 there were many races when there were more Tecnos present than Brabhams.

It is ironical that while MRD's production cars had, by the company's

103

standards, a pretty miserable year, in Formula One, Brabham bounced right back as a leading contender. Jacky Ickx was runner-up to Jackie Stewart in the Drivers' World Championship and Brabham was runner-up to Matra in the Constructors' Cup, all this being achieved with an 'old-fashioned' car with a spaceframe chassis and outboard suspension, which everyone knew to be years out of date.

Mike Bowron, subsequently with Penske, joined Brabham in 1969 and stayed until the end came for the production racing cars. He says: 'You were always put to work on fairly basic jobs at first, until you had proved that your work could be trusted. Then I graduated to helping build the Formula One cars and I'd do things like the uprights, drive-shafts and steering boxes.

'Most of the new workers were a bit afraid of Ron. His catchphrase "No, no, no, no," was a bit intimidating at first, until you realized that that was how he spoke to everyone. In fact you soon got to respect the guy, his commitment was total – he was a workaholic – and he would turn his hand to anything. He was also that rare thing, a totally honest man.

'People today wouldn't believe how many cars we built. In 1969 we built cars for Formula One, Formula Two, Formula Three, plus special cars for hillclimbs, and they were made to an incredible level of quality. People don't realize how few production racing cars are built to a very high standard, but Brabhams were. I never heard of anything breaking on a Brabham.

'People would race Brabhams for two or three seasons, not like today where they have to spend thousands on a new car each year. Over the winter they might bring them back to the factory to have work done, like having their wishbones reset, then they'd go out for another year's racing. I'm still in motor racing, so I know how it's changed, but I think that everyone who was at Brabham can look back and congratulate themselves on a wonderful job.'

When the 1969 Formula One season began, Honda was no longer part of the scene, and nor was Cooper. It had lost its production car business, and the Formula One team had become a makeweight. A car for the new Formula 5000 was displayed at the 1969 Racing Car Show, but it had no takers. So the first company to make production single-seaters in significant quantities had died after a 21-year history.

You could say that the rot had set in when Jack left the team, but that would be an over-simplification because it does not take account of the reasons why Jack, having won successive World Championships with Cooper, took the risk of setting up on his own. Had Cooper been going forward, perhaps Jack would not have felt the need to move, and Ron might have ended his working life as a factory manager in Australia.

When Jack was joined in his Formula One team for 1969 by Jacky Ickx, the Belgian had already won a Grand Prix for Ferrari – it was the very wet race at Rouen in 1968, and it had been Ickx rather than Ferrari who had been the victor that day. In fact, Ickx had been lying a strong second in the 1968 World Championship when, during practice for the Canadian Grand Prix, his throttle stuck open, causing him to crash and break a leg. Since that had been his first season in Formula One, Jacky was widely viewed as a future World Champion.

Ron says: 'I never got to know Jacky well. He didn't call in at the factory. What little testing we did was done by Jack, and at races Jacky would arrive at the very last minute. He wasn't one to socialize.' Ron is being diplomatic here, for others who were in the team at the time reach for terms like 'spoiled brat' and 'prima donna', but nobody denies the man's talent.

Ron says: 'Jacky came to us from Ferrari because Ford wanted him in their sports cars and they were picking up the tab. Part of the deal was that we got two free Cosworth DFVs.'

The BT26 was carried over from the previous year and fitted with the Cosworth engine, and since Jack put his on pole in South Africa it appeared to bode well for the season. It also made people wonder how the 1968 season might have panned out had Brabham not stuck doggedly to the Repco engine.

Ron relates: 'Jack found room for improvement in the Lucas fuel injection of the DFV. He has a feel for engine response and is able to translate this into the mixture control. Having found the throttle position which produced a flat spot he would hold a steady throttle, switch off the engine and coast back to the pit, where the mechanics would mark the position on the fuel cam and remove it so that the required amount could be stoned off. The procedure involved a bit of trial and error, but it always improved the theoretical cam shape. Imagine my feelings when Cosworth, having copied our cam from an engine sent back for rebuild, replaced those in our subsequent rebuilds and charged a fortune for them in addition to supplying the improvement to all other DFV users, thus negating our advantage.'

Neither car finished at Kyalami, nor in the Race of Champions, but Jack won the International Trophy (just ahead of Jochen Rindt) with Jacky fourth. In fifth place was Piers Courage, driving a BT26 for Frank Williams. Although Ickx was the young charger and Brabham was reckoned to be close to the end of his career, Jack was usually quicker than Jacky in qualifying. The first time Ickx was quicker than his boss was at Monaco, but even then it was only by a tenth of a second.

So far as the cars were concerned, it was the year when wings dominated Formula One. Rindt and Hill both came close to losing their lives when the rear wings on their Lotuses collapsed at the same spot during the Spanish Grand Prix. Ickx ran as high as second in this race, but he lost time in the pits having a new rear wing fitted after his broke up, and eventually his rear suspension began to fail, probably as a result of the downforce from the rear wings.

From his hospital bed, Jochen Rindt sent an open letter to journalists and a private, very angry, letter to Colin Chapman pointing out that in his entire previous career he'd had one breakage on his car, but he'd had three since joining Lotus. Chapman went ballistic.

The field arrived at Monaco and were promptly told that all wings which were not part of the bodywork were banned. They were promptly removed before the race and Graham Hill won in a Lotus 49 fitted with bodywork which was used only in that race and incorporated a ducktail rear deck. This has been touted as further proof of Chapman's perspicacity, but the idea had originated on the 1968 Brabham BT25 Indianapolis car. Behind Graham's Lotus at Monaco came Piers Courage in Frank Williams' BT26; 1969 would prove to be Frank's most successful year in Formula One until 1978.

The rules on wings had not been clarified by the time of the Dutch Grand Prix, where the Brabhams turned up with aerofoils sticking out of the engine cover. Since they were part of the bodywork they were deemed legal. Colin Chapman took one look at them, gathered up the appropriate staff, flew them back to Hethel and returned next day with similar bodywork. The Brabhams were not quite on the pace at Zandvoort, but Ickx was fifth and Brabham was sixth in the Grand Prix.

Soon afterwards Jack was at Silverstone testing some new tyres for Goodyear. He recalls: I was approaching Copse Corner when the nearside front tyre deflated and came off the rim. I was doing exactly 115mph, the car hit the bank and my left foot went through the undertray and was trapped. It was like an eel-trap where you can get in but can't get out.

'The engine was revving madly because the throttle was jammed open, but I managed to twist myself round and turn off the ignition. Then fuel started to pour out, but since I'd helped to put the car together, I knew that the fire extinguisher nozzles were directed at the exhaust pipes, so I fired the extinguisher.

'I was still in the middle of a pool of fuel, which spread out 30 feet all around me. When the crew arrived, Ron Dennis had them cover the exhaust pipes with foam and then they cut me out. It was the only time that we had a team car written off.'

Ron Dennis says: 'Jack was in pain, a lot of pain. He was half-in, half-out of the car with his foot trapped. The Silverstone crew wanted to use power tools to cut him out, but he was in the middle of an ever-widening lake of petrol and a spark could have sent us all up in flames. I was able to make a hole in the bodywork and stuck in a tyre lever. You find strength at times like that and I was able to apply enough pressure to release Jack's foot.'

Jack sustained a broken foot and missed the next few races. In his absence two things happened, one of which was that Matra, McLaren and Lotus all tried their four-wheel-drive cars and discovered what Ron had suspected all along, that to make a car heavier and bulkier while draining power though increased friction was no way to advance. There were other factors at play as well, one being that there were then no differentials up to the task – which Cosworth had discovered when testing its own 4WD car. Basically it didn't like turning corners, which is a handicap on a racing car.

There was also the advent of wings, plus the improvements in tyre technology had solved the problems teams had been experiencing in putting around 400bhp down on the road. Four-wheel drive became a footnote in Formula One history, but not before it had drained three of Brabham's rivals of human and monetary resources.

Perhaps it was because Brabham's rivals had been distracted, or maybe it was the fact that the Brabham team had only one car to service, but suddenly Ickx hit his stride. Third place in France was followed by second at Silverstone, then pole position, fastest lap and victory at the Nürburgring, where he beat Stewart by nearly a minute and sliced nearly 20 seconds from the lap record. It was a superb drive.

Jacky followed that with a win in the Oulton Park Gold Cup, against admittedly fairly thin opposition. In fact, the race was notable chiefly because Jochen brought his Lotus 63 home in second place, which remains the second best result by a 4WD car in a Formula One race after Moss' win at Oulton Park in the Ferguson P99 in 1961. The difference is that Rindt was driving with so much of the power split biased to the rear that he might as well have been driving a conventional car. It was typical of Chapman to continue to chase the theoretical advantage of all-wheel drive against all the pragmatic evidence.

Jack was back in the cockpit for the Italian Grand Prix, but neither he nor Ickx showed well in practice or in the race. Stewart clinched the World

Championship with a win at Monza, his sixth of the season, but in Canada Ickx led Jack for a Brabham 1-2 and, again, Ickx set pole and fastest lap. At Watkins Glen Piers Courage, in the Frank Williams BT26, held second place for most of the way ahead of Ickx and Brabham, but then Ickx's engine gave up and Jack had to call at the pits for more fuel, which enabled Courage to score his second runner-up spot of the season. Taking the chequered flag, though, for the first time in his Formula One career, was Jochen Rindt, but late in the race his teammate Graham Hill suffered a huge accident, which seriously damaged his legs and effectively ended his career as a front-line driver.

Despite breaking his duck with Lotus, Jochen again talked to Jack about driving for Brabham. His relationship with Chapman was uneasy, and he was deeply disturbed by the number of failures his cars had sustained. Jochen had exploited his fame and was running very successful racing car shows, but he still wanted to win the World Championship. Naturally, he also wanted a decent pay day, even though he would have taken a big cut in order to drive again for Brabham.

Jochen had a manager in Bernie Ecclestone, and they had been trying to put together a package which would have involved Robin Herd designing a car funded by outside sponsors. Eventually that fell through and Robin went off with a group of friends to form March Engineering. March actually offered Rindt a drive, which he refused, and instead in the end he signed up once more for Lotus.

The main reason for him doing so was the revolutionary Lotus 72, which Chapman (and Maurice Phillippe) had on the drawing board. Jochen was convinced that it could give him the Championship and, after that, he could retire and spend the rest of his life exploiting his title. It was typical of Rindt's self-belief that he could make such a decision even before he had won his first Grand Prix, let alone the title. In the end, after the flaws which beset the Lotus 72 had been sorted out, it would indeed give Jochen his title – in 1970 – but not before a breakage on the one he was driving at Monza had also cost him his life.

The formation of March Engineering was announced before the end of 1969. It was the first time that a group of highly-accomplished individuals had come together to form a company to build production racing cars. You had Max Mosley (later to become President of the FIA) wooing the punters, you had Robin Herd (later the Chairman of Oxford United Football Club) designing the cars, you had the late Graham Coaker building them and Alan Rees (later to be one of the founders of Arrows) managing the racing side of the company. When Alan Rees joined March he was followed by other ex-Winkelmann personnel, and that effectively ended the history of a private team which had won nearly 30 Formula Two races. There are still people in motor racing who speak of the Winkelmann team with awe.

March's Formula One effort was possible because of sponsorship, and the availability of the Cosworth DFV engine and Hewland gearboxes. Its production car business was possible because there was a motor racing industry which had been built up during the 1960s and to which Ron Tauranac had made a substantial contribution.

There are people who will tell you that Ron was a crusty old devil who demanded everything on the dot, to time, to price, to everything, but he was also that guy who paid in advance when a subcontractor he valued was having cashflow difficulties. Ron kept companies in business because he sent out cheques on the 22nd of each month without fail. He nurtured companies. He could, and at times did, give them grief, but they knew where they stood, so when he demanded that they raise their game, they raised their game.

By 1969 it had become possible for an outfit to get under way with not much more than a designer and a line of credit. In its first full year, March would build 50 cars. None was outstanding, but nevertheless March took sales from MRD.

In October 1969, John Wyer, who was then directing the JW-Gulf team, wrote to Ron to thank him for his help in developing the Mirage M3 sports-racer. This was basically the other side of the deal with Jacky Ickx – it was Ford and Gulf calling in a favour.

Wyer wrote: 'This was of the greatest possible value and the performance of the car was completely transformed. You may have noticed that in the Austrian 1000Km race at Zeltweg we made fastest lap time and led for more than half the distance, and later in the season were able to win the race at Imola. We were right on top of the opposition and I do not think that there is any doubt that the Mirage is, at the present time, the fastest 3-litre sports prototype in the world.'

Wyer was not free with praise, and most engineers would have framed the letter and hung it on the wall. Ron says: 'I know that I must have done something, because I've seen the letter, but I can't remember what it was.' Len Terry, who designed the Mirage, says: 'My guess is that Ron altered the suspension geometry. At the time tyres were constantly growing and companies were experimenting with compounds and construction. You had to dial them in.'

In his autobiography, Wyer called the Mirage 'the worst (car) with which I have ever been associated', yet Ron made it into 'the fastest 3-litre prototype in the world.' As he said, he must have done something. For Ron Tauranac it had been just another day at the track. There was a car which was basically honest, but things were not going right. They probably bundled down to Goodwood and Ron watched, listened and absorbed. Then he changed a few things. It's easy when you know how.

Of his approach to race engineering, Ron says: 'You will find some people get results by going through lists, step by step, and they eventually work it out that way. You could say that my approach is almost feminine. I tend to listen to everything that's said and then go by intuition. I'll take several steps at once.' As for the Mirage, it was pensioned off after its one victory. For 1970, JW-Gulf ran Porsche 917s for the Porsche factory.

15

The last days

The 1970 season was blighted by fatal accidents. Piers Courage died at the wheel of Frank Williams' De Tomaso in the Dutch Grand Prix, Bruce McLaren died during a test session at Goodwood in June, and Denny Hulme, still recovering from burns he received at Indianapolis, had to shoulder the burden of keeping the McLaren team together.

John Miles joined Jochen Rindt at Team Lotus – and his Formula One career would collapse in the wake of Jochen's death at Monza in the September. Graham Hill, too badly injured in an accident at Watkins Glen to still command a top works drive, was run by Rob Walker, to whom Chapman would sell a Lotus 72 as soon as its teething problems were overcome.

John Surtees, despairing of ever finding a team to give him the right working environment, decided to form his own, while BRM began to enjoy an upturn of fortune, thanks to a new chassis by Tony Southgate.

For the first time in a decade the Tasman series did not attract its usual crop of Formula One stars. There were two reasons, one being a change of formula to embrace the 5-litre stock-block Formula 5000 (which soon took over totally) and the other that Formula One drivers were increasingly being called upon to test in the winter months as the general pitch of competition increased.

Wider commitments also made it less likely for Formula One stars to be seen in Formula Two races, although it occasionally happened and Jack Brabham had three outings in a car entered by John Coombs.

From the perspective of this story, it is hard to say which had the bigger impact, the fact that at the end of 1969 Jack sold his share in MRD to Ron – so effectively becoming Ron's employee in 1970 – or that March Engineering had been formed. March was set up to build everything from Formula One cars down to Formula Ford and was the first such outfit since Jack and Ron had founded MRD. It was becoming much more difficult, however, to sustain success in both Formula One and in the manufacture of production racing cars and, within three years or so, March would be the only firm still trying to do so – Brabham, McLaren, Lotus and Surtees would all be Formula One teams pure and simple.

March started off by sending a Brabham customer into MRD's stores to buy a pair of rear uprights, supposedly for a friend who was building a special.

Special indeed, the prototype March 693 just happened to have Brabham uprights.

Since Matra was resolved to build only Formula One cars which used their V12 engine, and Jackie Stewart was convinced that he needed a Cosworth to be competitive, Team Tyrrell bought Marches for Stewart and Cévert. They would have been better off buying Brabhams, but Ken approached Jack, and Jack had said 'No', without reference to Ron.

What Ken did not know was that Jack had sold his stake in the company and that Ron was now the owner. There's nothing like keeping the opposition away from a good car. In addition to the Tyrrell cars, Mario Andretti appeared occasionally in a private March, as did Ronnie Peterson, while works cars were driven by Jo Siffert and Chris Amon.

March seemed to be unbeatable when Jackie Stewart claimed pole in South Africa, with Chris Amon alongside him with an identical qualifying time. Stewart already knew, however, that there was no development potential in the car, which is why work had already begun on the first Tyrrell.

Despite the fact that Jochen nearly caused a multiple shunt at the first corner – among other things, he ran over Jack's front wheel – it was John Arthur Brabham who came through to win at the end – and he set equal fastest lap on the way. For all the hype surrounding March, the Old Firm could still show everyone how things should be done.

Partnering Jack in the Formula One team was young Rolf Stommelen, whose passage had been eased by Ford of Germany. Stommelen was not an ace, but Ron and Jack had to bow to the changing conditions of Formula One.

If Bernie Ecclestone had been successful in putting together a package which would have taken Jochen back to Brabham, the BT33 might well have given Rindt the World Championship. Jack was ready to retire in order just to run Jochen, and Goodyear was willing to increase its contribution, but Chapman was desperate to retain Rindt and he had both tobacco sponsorship and a profitable road car company through which extra cash could be channelled.

Chapman trumped the deal between Brabham and Goodyear, not only with more money, but also with an offer of setting up Jochen in his own Formula Two team. Not only would he have the latest Lotus 69, but he would be able to use the magic words 'Team Lotus', something which guaranteed premium starting money.

Jochen Rindt Team Lotus, which was run by Bernie Ecclestone, would put either Graham Hill or John Miles, Jochen's number two in the Formula One team, in the second car. For a driver with one eye on retirement and the other on essaying his reputation into a future career, it was an irresistible offer, and the Lotus 69 gave Jochen several wins.

However, the Brabham BT30 was more strongly represented than any other type on the Formula Two grids, at many races accounting for half the field, which would typically include cars from Lotus, Tecno, Crosslé, Pygmée, BMW, Lola, Chevron and March. Formula Two had become a very competitive arena.

Much the same pattern was evident in Formula Three. Brabhams were numerically the most numerous cars on the grid, but while they won a lot of races, they did not dominate. In Britain, most of the important races fell to Lotus 59s, but there was a Lotus works team, while the privateers included drivers of the calibre of James Hunt and Carlos Pace. Lotus had established a division to build customer cars and the guys running it took a few leaves from

Brabham's book. They were strong and easy to work on, and they became a feasible alternative to Brabham.

Tecno still held a large part of the market and Chevron had made inroads, as did Martini from France and McNamara, which was an American outfit based in Germany. The Martini MW4 was a development of a car which was, well, inspired by Brabham, while the McNamara was not only built on Brabham lines, it incorporated some Brabham parts, and in Italy both Birel and de Sanctis were also of the 'Tribe of Ron'.

When the European Formula One season got under way, Jackie Oliver's BRM led the first few laps of the Race of Champions – the first time a BRM had been on the pace for some years – but Jack soon went by. He was stroking away from Stewart, Rindt and Hulme when, with a couple of laps to go, his coil expired, whereupon his misfortune gave March its first win.

In what was to be his last driving year, Jack with his BT33 was clearly a serious contender for the World Championship. Just as Ron had made a monocoque IndyCar to accommodate bag tanks, so, when the same rule arrived in Formula One, he was forced to build a monocoque Formula One car.

Dave Luff, later to become a freelance race engineer, worked for Brabham from 1964 until 1971. He says: 'Ron was the most difficult man on earth to work with, but everything I know about motor racing I learned from him. In 1970 I was put on the building of the Formula One cars, and I was working on the first one with Ron Dennis.

'You have to remember that Ron (T) never drew anything, but would tell us what he wanted, and in this case he wanted brackets for oil coolers on each side of the gearbox. He had to see the part in three dimensions, to see how it fitted with everything else.

'Ron (D) and I listened to what he said and made a pair of brackets. "No, no, no, no, no." We made another set. "No, no, no, no, no." I think we made nine sets of brackets and then he was satisfied with something we showed him. The set he was happy with was the very first one we'd made. He was not easy!'

Ron (T) says: 'I think what Dave means is that we didn't draw some of the things that we made in the factory. Chassis-frames, wishbones and things like that, which were subcontracted out, were all drawn. When we came to assemble the cars, however, we had to see where things would fit.

'I suspect that was true of everyone making cars with tubular chassis. I can't see any other way of doing it with what we had then. Nowadays you have computer-generated graphics, which allow you to see everything in three dimensions. Back then you only saw the picture when you had the finished car.'

At Jarama, for the Spanish Grand Prix, Jack set pole, but spent most of the race running second behind Stewart's March. At two-thirds distance Jack was preparing to take the lead when the crankshaft broke. It was a new engine, which had been fitted to ensure reliability, but Cosworth had a batch of faulty crankshafts. With a little more luck Jack should have had three wins under his belt, two of them counting for the Championship.

Dave Luff remembers: 'We flew back from Jarama in Jack's plane. It was chronically overloaded and I was sitting on the loo seat, which was probably the safest place to be. Jack was at the controls and Ron was in the co-pilot's seat. We set off around midnight, and throughout the whole flight they bickered about the car's fuel system. Jack reckoned Ron could never design a good fuel system and he liked to do that himself.

'While they argued, everyone else tried to snatch some sleep. About six in the morning, as the sun was coming up and the white breakers of the Solent were underneath us, one of the engines started to misfire, then coughed and was silent. Then the other did the same. We were dropping like a stone and all you could hear was the whoosh of the air outside and these two at the front arguing about what was to be done. The thing was that they'd been so engrossed in their own private drama that they'd forgotten to switch over fuel tanks.'

Jack retired from the International Trophy with engine trouble, but it was bad judgment, not bad luck, which cost him the next race, the Monaco Grand Prix. He had taken the lead on lap 28 out of 80 and had a reasonably comfortable cushion with a few laps to go when he was unintentionally baulked by Jo Siffert's March. Jo was swinging his car from side to side to pick up fuel, but it cost Jack 12 seconds and Jochen was on a late charge. With two laps to go Rindt had closed to within 5 seconds of Brabham, but even then overtaking was not easy. However, going into the very last corner, Jack went off line to lap Piers Courage, and as a result he braked on the 'marbles', slid into the barrier and Jochen nipped by to take the flag.

While Jack cursed himself after the race, the champagne corks were popping in the Lotus camp. But Jochen, knowing what his friend and rival was going through, had champagne sent over to the Brabham pit.

Alain Fenn, who was commercial manager at MRD, says: 'Jack blamed himself for making a mistake and Ron maintained that there was a problem with the brakes. This seemed to us to be an admirable difference of opinion because both men were taking the blame on themselves, whereas every other driver and team manager would be blaming each other.'

Although one of the reasons for Jochen staying with Lotus had been the Lotus 72, there were endless problems and breakages and it was John Miles, who was as good an engineer as he was a driver, who was usually assigned the 72 to race.

Jack and Jochen both retired from the Belgian Grand Prix, so Jack still led the World Championship, but Jochen took over the lead in the series after the Dutch Grand Prix, which was the first race to fall to the Lotus 72, which by then had coil-spring instead of torsion-bar suspension. Chapman had been forced to discard a lot of theoretical thinking, as a result of which the 72 had become a fairly practical car. Jack had problems in the Dutch Grand Prix and finished four laps down.

Jochen won again in France, where Jack finished third and was therefore still in the hunt. Then, in the British Grand Prix at Brands Hatch, Jochen set pole, but Jack was alongside him with an equal qualifying time – a fact to be savoured.

Rindt led for much of the race, with Brabham shadowing him, and then Jochen missed a gear change and Jack was by. But going into Clearways, the very last corner of the last lap, Jack's engine coughed and he coasted over the line out of fuel; Rindt had been close enough to pounce and so take the win.

The fact that nobody else could take advantage of Jack's misfortune, as he trickled over the line, shows just how clear of the field he had been. In fact, he still finished more than 20 seconds ahead of Denny Hulme in third place. There had been a cock-up over the number of churns of fuel which had been used in

The last days

his car. The fact remains that, at the mid-point of the season, Jack could have been the winner of four Grands Prix plus the Race of Champions.

After the British Grand Prix Jack did not score another World Championship point, yet even in his very last race, the Mexican Grand Prix, he qualified fourth and was running strongly in third place when his engine gave up. So ended a great career.

Before long MRD would be in decline. It had been a double-act with Jack contributing not just his peerless ability to develop a car, but also a great deal in the background. It was Jack who had the connections to use the facilities at MIRA, it was Jack who had made the initial contacts with Repco and Honda, and it was Jack who picked up the last batch of Coventry Climax FPF engines around which the BT8A sports-racer (and also many hillclimb and Tasman Brabhams) were built.

When HRG quietly wound down in 1965, Jack bought many of the machine tools and recruited a chap called Ron Cousins as workshop manager. John Judd was on the staff, and the workshop basically looked after the engines of his own racing cars.

Before he left for Australia, he converted this into Engine Developments Ltd, with John Judd as its principal. Judd and Engine Developments will re-enter the Tauranac story in the early 1980s.

At MRD, Jack did most of the fixing and negotiating, leaving Ron to run the factory. Ron says: 'After Jack went back to Australia things were not the same. I had the responsibility for the factory and for the Formula One team and that meant raising sponsorship, and I wasn't really much good at that. It wasn't much money by today's standards, about £100,000, most of which was met by Goodyear and Esso.' The Goodyear deal brought free tyres and £33,336 a year with a £1,000 bonus for a win, £500 for second and £250 for third. Esso paid £20,000 a year.

Ron says: 'Formula One eventually became a gamble that I could not afford to take, especially since, at the time, I was paying off Jack for his shares in the business. My motivation was anyway not to make money, it was to win races.'

Brabham production cars did their fair share of winning in 1970. In Formula Two the wins were shared between Brabham, Lotus, BMW and Tecno, but Brabhams took most of the points finishes. Brabham would win more races in the five years of the 1,600cc Formula Two than any other marque, just as it had done in the 1-litre Formula Two.

John Watson remembers working at the factory with his mechanic to get his BT30 finished on time for the first race at Thruxton. At least he got his finished – quite a number of drivers missed that race because their BT30s were not ready. Ron says: 'The reason was always that people had not put down their deposits in time or had not paid. I didn't start building until I had the money.' It was simple business ethics.

John was a novice in Formula Two and his car did not turn a wheel until he arrived at Thruxton to practice for the meeting. He was third on the grid in his heat behind Rindt and Ickx and that is about as good as you can expect to get. There has never been another maker of production racing cars who has turned out machines to such consistency that a novice driver could do that in a car which had not even been shaken down, let alone undergone serious testing. Wattie was well over a second faster than Chris Amon in a works March. For all the hype surrounding its launch, March did not shine in the lower formulae in

1970. It had tried to do too much too quickly, but it would recover.

In his last three Formula Two races Jack showed he had lost none of his speed and was still capable of qualifying on the front row and finishing on the podium. Among the other drivers who raced Brabhams in Formula Two were Derek Bell – who was runner-up to Clay Regazzoni (Tecno) in the European Championship – and Jackie Stewart.

MRD's last IndyCar, the BT32, had a turbocharged Offenhauser engine and was bought by A C Agajanian, the legendary IndyCar owner, who renamed it the Sugaripe Prune Special – there's nothing like a snappy name. Although it was a 1970 car, engine problems kept it from contention until the following year. Bill Vukovich Jr took third place in the 1971 USAC Championship, albeit without winning a race, and he finished fifth in the Indianapolis 500.

At the end of 1970, when it was clear that Jack Brabham was retiring, Ron Dennis and fellow mechanic Neil Trundle left MRD to start their own racing team, Rondel. It was virtually the Brabham Formula Two works team since it ran Graham Hill and Tim Schenken, MRD's Formula One pairing, and Rondel also ran a car for Bob Wollek.

Ron Dennis recalls: 'Between the United States Grand Prix and Mexico, the mechanics went on ahead and most of us took a short flight to Acapulco while we waited for the cars to arrive. Jack had entrusted me with cashing his cheque from the US Grand Prix and I had his money in a suitcase. I saw how much it was and I realized that I was in the wrong game. I passed over the simple fact that we had no capital, but that is where Ron Tauranac helped out.'

Rondel Racing had the aim of running a Formula Two team to the standards of Formula One. Despite all Ron Tauranac's protestations to the contrary, Rondel was loaned cars on the basis that they'd be paid for at the end of the season, and Ron (T) was also easy when it came to spares, providing them to Rondel on a sale-or-return basis.

Ron Dennis says: 'If it had not been for Ron's generosity, it is highly likely that I would not now be head of McLaren. I would have taken a different direction in my career. To a certain extent it was a two-way street because Rondel Racing delivered the goods, and that helped MRD. The thing about Ron is that he can be cantankerous, but he's completely honest. In fact, he would have been more successful commercially had he been less honest because he has a level of naivety. He never asked anyone to do anything that he was not willing to do himself. I still stick to that. And he taught me to.'

'Turn the nut, not the bolt,' was a phrase that everyone who worked with Ron can remember. Ron himself explains: 'By turning the nut you get a better feel for the tightening torque; if you turn the bolt the friction of the bolt shank gives an incorrect torque reading.'

For 1971 Ron ran Graham Hill and Tim Schenken in the Formula One team. He says: 'We reckoned we were going to need sponsorship and we did a deal with Graham. We paid him a retainer of £5,000, plus his share of the prize money, and he was going to try to raise sponsorship both for the team and in order to pay him a bigger salary.

'Racing drivers have a reputation for being tight-fisted, but not Graham. He'd fly the team, journalists, Norma and me to the races and he liked to take the team out for dinner before the race. He was very good like that. Nick Goozée remembers: 'If the mechanics were working late at the factory, and Graham was in the vicinity, like he and Bette had been to some function, he'd make a point of popping in to say a few words and crack a few jokes.'

Graham was still a big star, but he was no longer a top driver. The injuries to his legs had been substantial, but he was still capable of springing the odd surprise.

One was victory in the International Trophy in the BT34, nicknamed the 'lobster claw'. It was a hugely popular win, especially as most teams except for Ferrari were present.

Ron recalls one incident from the year: 'Graham always wanted to set up the car just as he liked it. He'd have a mechanic go to the four corners with a gauge to check the camber. We were pushed for time when we were preparing the car for the Dutch Grand Prix at Zandvoort, so I told the crew not to bother about checking the corners. "Graham will do that for us," I said. Sure enough, Graham went through his usual routine and was most upset when he discovered that all the settings were out. I told him, in a very pleasant way, that perhaps it was enough to have one team on the job.'

Following his win in the International Trophy, Graham scored an astonishing win for Rondel at Thruxton in a race named after Jochen Rindt. Graham had shown that he still had greatness in him by winning his heat and coming second overall on aggregate in a race at Hockenheim the week before.

At Thruxton he started from pole in his heat and won it. Then in the final he led until his exhaust pipe began to work loose, causing a loss of power. That enabled Ronnie Peterson in a works March to haul him in and overtake as they entered the last lap. A backmarker got in the way round the back of the circuit and Graham pounced to win a brilliant victory. Hats were thrown into the air (really) and there was not a dry eye in the house.

Overall, however, the season belonged to Ronnie Peterson and March. Still, with seven Formula Two wins in 1971, and Carlos Reutemann second in the European Championship, it was not exactly a disastrous year for Brabham.

New regulations were scheduled for Formula Two in 1972, but during the five years of the 1,600cc Formula Two, Brabham won 32 races to the 18 wins of both Lotus and Matra. The fourth most successful marque, surprisingly, was the newcomer, March, with 11 wins, all of them gained in 1971. Tecno took 10, Ferrari five, BMW four and Lola two, with cars they had sold to the BMW works. No other manufacturer – and the list included names like Cooper and McLaren – scored a win. Between 1964, when Formula Two was revived, and 1971, Brabham took 61 Formula Two victories, and no other constructor came close.

Brabham also held up well in Formula Three but, again, it was not dominant in 1971. Many French drivers had turned to the Martini MW7 or the Alpine A360, both of which were good cars and there some highly professional teams running them. Tecno was on the wane, partly because it was preparing for its disastrous entry to Formula One and partly because it had been an outfit with only one idea.

Other outfits were springing up, probably because March had reminded many people that there was a market to be tapped. In Britain there were cars from Ensign and Palliser – both of which were serious about series production – while March recovered from a poor initial season and offered both spaceframe and monocoque designs. The latter worked very well and March took its share of wins. Times, however, were changing. For a start, Ron was employing assistant designers. Michael Hillman describes himself as Ron's pencil; he doesn't claim to have been a designer.

During 1971 Ron began to edge towards the idea of off-loading some of the responsibility of running both a factory and a Formula One team. He says: 'Bernie Ecclestone had started to talk to me, and his first approach came at the Monaco Grand Prix. Of course, I knew Bernie because he'd been Jochen Rindt's manager and had also had an involvement with Graham Hill. The deal was that he'd buy me out for the value of the assets of the company, which we agreed at £130,500. Further, I would stay on on much the same basis as before, designing the cars and running the works. The deal included the BT34, two BT33s, six Cosworth DFV engines and three Hewland gearboxes. Then just before we were ready to do the deal, Bernie phoned and offered me £100,000 instead. I was caught off guard and accepted.

'A number of things happened soon after he took over. For a start, I was not impressed to find that a new van I'd ordered for MRD was on the forecourt of one of Bernie's garages with a 'For Sale' sticker in the windscreen, and I was surprised when someone arrived at the works with a load of breeze-blocks and instructions to extend the spares department.

'I think that, as Managing Director, I might have been told. Then I went off for my annual skiing holiday and when I returned I found that someone else, Colin Seeley, was basically doing my job. There was no point in me going into the factory so I started to work from home.

'Over the years Jack had often talked about CanAm, so I worked on a design for that, along with 2-litre and 3-litre sports cars. In the meantime, Ralph Bellamy, Gordon Murray and Geoff Ferris were designing the single-seaters.'

Colin Seeley had made motorcycles with some success and Bernie also had an agreement to buy out his company, Colin Seeley Developments, of Belvedere, Kent. At the time there were plans for an Ecclestone-backed motorcycle Grand Prix team. Part of Bernie's business background was in motorcycles, and he'd built up a major motorcycle business, Compton and Ecclestone.

Bernie has always insisted on fastidious standards and, unlike the usual run of motorcycle shops, which were dingy, oily and decidedly downmarket, the premises of Compton and Ecclestone were light, bright and clean.

Mike Bowron recalls: 'Colin Seeley had built motorcycles, but I don't think that he understood the problem of building cars. It's a very difficult business, building quality production racing cars. In the old days, just before the first meeting of the season, the road outside would be one long row of trucks and transporters. Inside, drivers and their mechanics would be finishing off the cars. There were drivers who became very big names, like John Watson, getting stuck in during the build season.

'Ron and Jack kept open house. You go to a modern racing car factory and you don't get two feet without a swipe card. At MRD there was a storeman called Stan, who kept the spares sheets, and people would go up to him and say "such-and-such a team, two uprights please," and they'd be handed over and ticked off on the sheet.

'Ron and Jack ran the company like it was one extended family. You bought a Brabham and you bought part of them. I don't think that Bernie could operate like that. He's a very strong, decisive man, and Ron would sometimes hum and haw, and think things over and perhaps dig his heels in. The relationship was not going to work.

'On the other hand, Gordon Murray was there and he was young, and was probably easier for Bernie to give direction to. Gordon is a very nice guy, and he showed he could do the business. Eventually he not only became chief designer, he finished up running Brabham because Bernie was so involved with FOCA.

'I also think that Bernie was irritated because restrictions on the lease meant that he could not have the factory as he wanted it. As soon as the lease was up he moved to Chessington and to his idea of what a modern factory should be. That's how it seemed from the shop floor, but I could be wrong. I think we were more concerned about the future of the company rather than who was running it.'

In fact, Gordon Murray was not promoted immediately as Ralph Bellamy would first be chief designer. It is true that Colin Seeley had no experience of building production racing cars, but he did have production experience. His motorcycle business employed 30 people (MRD then employed 58) and had a comprehensive engineering shop. Seeley took over the production of a number of components and standardized others.

Ron says: 'I think that Bernie thought that he could solve some of our delivery problems. His attitude was that if you get the parts made, you get the cars made. That's all very well provided you know beforehand that the car will work.'

Bernie Ecclestone says: 'I wanted to go into Formula One and I bought Brabham rather than set up my own team from scratch because everything was in place. I kept the name because you can't improve on it. It was always officially Motor Racing Developments, but you don't play around with a name like Brabham any more than, if you bought Marks & Spencer or Halfords, you would mess around with them.

'In retrospect, the relationship was never going to work. Ron is not the sort of guy who can cooperate with some other guy who is also making decisions. He and I are two of a kind, we both take the view: "Please be reasonable, do it my way."

'I have to admit that I wasn't really interested in production racing cars, I didn't want to be in that market in order to make the Formula One team commercially viable. With production racing cars you put your fate in the lap of the gods and that's not something I like. You build a car and then some young hotshoe buys someone else's car and then you get worried. You begin to beg people to buy your car. It was inevitable that we would split, but I had the utmost respect for Ron then, as a man and as a friend, and I have the utmost respect for him now.'

Geoff Ferris designed the BT38, which was the main customer car and the first customer car to have a monocoque. It was never a great success and Ron says: 'For a start he put too many curves into the tub; it was going to be too expensive to make. Then I could see that it was not going to work because the aerodynamics were wrong. It had a chisel nose, which was generating far too much downforce; you couldn't dial out the oversteer when running a low-downforce set-up.

'I was still determined to make the relationship work, so I went testing at Goodwood with the car, even after I had officially parted company with MRD. I made some suggestions, but they didn't really want to know.'

At the opening round of the 1972 World Championship, in Argentina, Carlos

Reutemann, in his debut Grand Prix, put the BT34 on pole. The BT34 has never been regarded as a particularly wonderful car, but what percentage of car types (let alone individual cars) ever sit on pole? It cannot be high.

In Argentina there was a new designer (Ralph Bellamy), new team manager (Keith Greene, promoted from racing manager and answerable to Ron) and a new chief mechanic (Bob Dance) as well as Ecclestone himself.

Reutemann's pole position was to be the highspot of the season apart from his win in the non-Championship Brazilian Grand Prix, with team-mate Wilson Fittipaldi third in a BT33. However, there were only 12 starters that day.

Brabham scored only 7 points in the season and failed to take a single championship in the lower formulae. The customer cars were late, largely because there was uncertainty about wheel sizes until very late the previous year. Worse, for customers, there was not the traditional help from the factory, so they had to iron out the bugs themselves.

The Formula Two cars fared better than the Formula Threes largely because the teams that ran them tended to be more professional and therefore less reliant on factory back-up. Jean-Pierre Jaussaud (BT38) was runner-up to Mike Hailwood's Surtees in the European Formula Two Championship, although he was a long way behind. Many drivers who began the season with Brabham Formula Three cars subsequently switched to other makes, in particular newcomers Ensign and GRD, both of which flourished for a short while..

As the season panned out, Ron was not part of the Brabham set-up. He says: 'Frank Williams asked if I'd go to South Africa with him in early March to engineer for him. He was running a March for Henri Pescarolo, so I spoke to Bernie and sought leave to go.' Ron went and did not return to MRD. While he was in South Africa Bernie released him from his contract. It came as a surprise to nobody, for the rumours had been flying all winter.

Ron returned home to find that his wages had been stopped, that he had to hand back his company car and the standing order to pay an allowance each month to his mother had been cancelled. That still rankles.

After the split, Bernie was reported as saying: 'I think he missed Jack and, although he initially seemed happy to work with Colin, Gordon Murray and Ralph Bellamy, it didn't take long for the situation to come to a head. It was a peculiar situation for, on the one hand, I think he honestly wanted us to make a go of it all on our own and be successful ... but somehow he also tended to resent anyone making a success of the name Brabham without his being involved.'

With hindsight, it is hard to see how it could have worked. Ron says: 'I've had dealings with Bernie since, like buying equipment from him, and there's been no problem whatsoever. He's been very straightforward to deal with.'

About a month later, graffiti appeared in the works toilet: 'Come back Ron – all is forgiven'. Before long Brabham had stopped making production racing cars and so had Lotus, Surtees and McLaren. Building production cars and running a Formula One team had been proved to be incompatible activities and although March continued to attempt it, it was hardly a shining example. Other outfits sprang up to service the production car market, but most thrived for just a short time and then folded. Very few firms have been able to sustain success in the production racing car market, and most of those that have have done so by concentrating on particular niches.

No company has made as many models which have won races as Brabham did when Ron was in charge. For 10 years MRD was the standard-setter, the only failure being the one-off BT17 sports-racer, mainly because of the inadequacies of the Repco engine combined with Ron's indifference to the genre. No other company in motor racing comes close to a record like that.

16

Interlude

For the first time in his life Ron was at a loose end, and inactivity is his idea of Hell. He did, however, work on a number of projects. Some are fairly well-known, but others may come as a surprise.

He did some consultancy work for Guy Ligier, who was then making a sports-racer. 'It came about at the suggestion of Jabby Crombac. Ligier arranged my trip over and I made a few suggestions which they took on board. We hadn't discussed a fee, and I was just glad of the break, but as I left, they pressed a great wodge of money in my hand. That was nice.' Typical Ron, he wanted to work more than he wanted to be paid.

He also went out to Italy to give Tecno a few pointers on its Formula One project. 'I think Chris Amon got me in on that one. They asked how much I wanted, so I thought of something outrageous and they agreed. I looked at everything: suspension geometry, roll centres, everything. They really did need help because almost nothing had been done well. They asked why I was charging them so much, and I pointed out how much money I'd saved them by telling them that their oil tank was all wrong and they'd blow their engines. It was all academic because I never did get paid.'

Then there was work for Frank Williams. 'The original FX3, Frank's first car, was designed by Len Bailey, who left the project when it was 80 per cent complete. I finished it off. The same was true of the second Williams. It was designed by John Clark, and this was also about 80 per cent complete when Frank and John fell out and I was brought in to complete it.'

The Williams/Tauranac relationship fluttered here and there in the period 1969-74. Frank himself had driven a BT18 erratically in 1966. 'It was me who was erratic,' he says, 'not the car. That was wonderful. I called in Ron because he was so practical and straightforward. In fact he is the most honest, straightforward and blunt individual I've met, with the possible exception of Patrick Head.

'He was a most remarkable one-man show. He had the highest standards and I held him in the highest regard. He was definitely part of my educational process and that is not just bullshit for a book. He is a remarkable individual.

'Even he can be wrong, though. I remember we were outside the gents in the paddock at Monza in 1973 when my two cars had just qualified 20th and 23rd

Interlude

and he told me: "Face it, Frank, you're never going to win a race".'

Ron was at Monza to engineer Frank's cars, and one of the drivers, Howden Ganley, says: 'Ron brought a sense of sanity to the team. He was exactly what Frank needed, and what Frank later found in Patrick Head.'

Ron's most promising offer came from Colin Chapman. Ron says: 'People tell me that Chapman and I could never have worked together, but I think we could have done.' Chapman made his bid as soon as Ron was a free agent and he pursued his man throughout the year. Ron and Norma seriously considered returning to Australia and they went there for an extended stay. Chapman sent telegrams. On offer was the post of Technical Manager for Team Lotus, initially for one year. Pay was to be 10 per cent of the profits of Team Lotus, with a guaranteed minimum of £4,000 per annum – Chapman assured Ron that a realistic target was £7-8,000 pa. There would be a further £4,000 for other work within Group Lotus, although this work was going to be nominal.

Basically, Chapman did not want to upset other employees – including Peter Warr, who was doing the footwork – so was using the full range of his group of companies to bump Ron's salary up. There was also to be a Ford Cortina as a company car and an annual travel grant of £1,000 to enable Ron to keep abreast with the latest developments worldwide. Ron's salary would therefore be around £10,000 plus a Cortina and a travel allowance. It was an excellent package for the time.

Ron recalls: 'Colin laid out the red carpet, he flew us up to Hethel, we looked at houses and schools, and we agreed on a deal. I think that it was the following morning when he phoned and said he wanted to discuss the matter with someone. I don't know who for sure, but I snapped down the phone, "If you can rethink, maybe I can, too." I don't know why I said it, I think it was a case of being annoyed and speaking before I'd thought the matter through – which I sometimes do. Anyway, that was that, and we proceeded no further.

'Some time later I bumped into Colin, who said: "It's a shame we never got together, I'm still interested . . ." But by that time both my daughters were settled in their schools and I didn't pursue it.'

Had Ron gone to Lotus, and had the relationship worked, motor racing history would have been completely different. Perhaps Lotus would have maintained a presence in the customer car market for longer. What is certain is that some of Chapman's ideas in Formula One would have been moderated.

Lotus pursued a number of ideas which were not bad, but too often they were before their time. The technology did not exist to make them into viable realities. Chapman sometimes needed someone who could tell him 'No'.

Brabham production remained reasonably healthy through 1973, but no more customer cars were built after then. Ecclestone then concentrated on Formula One, like most of the others were doing. From early in the 1970s, Formula One teams had become more focused, and even Ferrari gave up sports car racing, the type of racing which had made its reputation.

For several years McLaren had farmed out production of its customer cars to Trojan, a company which had once made its own cars and vans and had since diversified into a number of fields, including karts, scooters, bubblecars and the Elva Courier sports car. When McLaren decided to concentrate on Formula One, it left Trojan with spare capacity and a gap in the market, so at the end of 1972, with the Lotus offer clearly not going to materialize, Ron accepted a commission from Peter Agg, who owned Trojan, to rework a McLaren Formula

Two design for Formula 5000.

A memo from Peter Agg dated April 30, 1973 emphasized that Trojan wanted Ron 'body and soul'. Agg said that he did not want to expand his staff too much, or to aim for high production figures, but he wanted to expand Trojan's range to include an IndyCar and either a 2-litre sports car or a Formula Three or Atlantic car. Even at that point Agg was talking about Formula One and asked Ron if he could outline a Formula One budget.

Agg clearly had big plans for Trojan, and he went so far as to ask if Ron could find and appoint a production manager. Ron says: 'Peter Agg felt that he had to do the right thing by his workforce, so he was looking for ways to employ them. What he didn't know was that most of them were hoping to be laid off so they would pick up redundancy pay. I thought it was my duty to tell him this and so he dropped his plans.'

Ron did a thorough revision of the McLaren, and the result was offered as the Trojan T101. In fact there were few takers, partly because F5000 had begun its decline, but it was a car capable of winning races. Jody Scheckter won the 1973 Formula A series in America using a Trojan, while Keith Holland was a strong third in the European F5000 Championship.

While running MRD, Ron could have built a Formula 5000 car had he wanted, but he had not wanted. He says: 'I thought it was a 'bitza' formula and it never appealed to me. Then you had the complications of tuning the engine and so on. It was different at Trojan because they were set up to do it. They'd been making CanAm cars, which were not that different.'

For 1973 Ron Tauranac designed the T102, which bore some similarity to his Brabham BT34 'lobster claw', but the planned season for Keith Holland fell through when he and Agg fell out. Brian McGuire later drove one for a few races before switching to a Lola.

This was not a good year to be in the production racing car market since, in the wake of the OPEC oil crisis, there was economic instability on an unprecedented scale in 1973. Ron suggested to Peter Agg that instead of being involved in Formula 5000, he might as well be in Formula One – the budget was much the same and he at least stood a chance of some starting money.

Ron adapted the Trojan T102, with assistance from a youngster called Patrick Head, and the whole thing was done on a total budget (including all wages and two DFV engines) of £50,000. 'We had almost no testing,' he says, 'and just two mechanics. We were always behind. Then Tim Schenken, our driver, got married and I think that modified his view of the risk business.

'I made mistakes on the car as well. I specified a Hewland DG gearbox instead of an FG because I thought it might cut down the chance of breakages. What happened was that the extra mass of the gears cut down acceleration – and we had a pinion bearing fail at Monza, which happened to be a carryover from the FG.

'The rear suspension geometry was not ideal, either – but that was something I did not discover until I'd carried over the same mistake to the Theodore and the Ralt RT1. Think of the forces generated under acceleration and braking as North/South, and those under cornering as East/West: part of the job of the suspension is to absorb those loads. The way I had it was that the loads were trying to rotate the chassis.'

The T103 was a thoroughly conventional 'British Formula One Kit Car' – aluminium monocoque, Cosworth engine (rebuilt by John Judd at Engine

Developments) and a Hewland gearbox – which raced a few times in 1974 entirely without distinction.

Patrick Head recalls: 'I think that there wasn't much wrong with it, but the front end which Ron carried over from the BT34 'lobster claw' was not that clever. Our main problem, though, was lack of money. Towards the end of the season we were at Goodwood and Ronnie Peterson was there with the Lotus 72. We persuaded Ronnie to have a go in the Trojan and, within three laps, he was quicker in it than he had been in the Lotus. I don't think there was a lot wrong with the car.

'I had first met Ron at Silverstone, where I was looking after Richard Scott's Formula Two car which I had designed. Ron liked the look of the car and he had heard a few positive things about me. I had intended to go into engine tuning when Ron offered me a job at Trojan, helping him on the Formula 5000 car and designing a CanAm car. The CanAm car never happened, which was just as well for me because I wasn't ready for it.

'When I had been at Lola it was frowned upon if anyone from the drawing office ventured into the factory, which was the reverse of how Ron operated. Ron used to do the basic layout and the details tended to be done on the job. When I went to work for him I was something of a purist, but from Ron I learned that you always have a certain amount of time in which to reach a practical solution and you have to work within those parameters. He taught me how to be practical.'

More than a quarter of a century on, Peter Agg also retains vivid memories of working with Ron. 'He could be a miserable so-and-so, yet I always felt that deep down beneath that hard and uncompromising exterior there was a genuinely warm person trying to get out. Technically and practically he was brilliant, except that he insisted on keeping everything in his head – it used to infuriate me that he would never commit anything to paper. I always found him to be scrupulously honest, but our relationship wasn't helped by the fact that he seemed to have no sense of humour whatsoever. To be honest, it wasn't a particularly good time to be in the racing car production business, what with the changes in regulations, the decline of sports cars and various developments on the political scene, so I thought that if I was to continue pouring money into a lost cause it might help if occasionally we could at least have a laugh about it. But that was not Ron's style.'

In truth, the relationship between Ron and Trojan was never easy – Ron operates best as an outside consultant or as the boss, and at Trojan he was neither one nor the other. He also had other offers, one of which came from the American outfit Vel's Parnelli. This had been set up by Velco Miletich and a former USAC star, Rufus Parnelli Jones, with the idea they could clean up in both USAC and Formula One. Since they had Mario Andretti in the cockpit and Maurice Phillipe at the drawing board, it was not a far-fetched notion, but for various reasons the reality did not match the concept.

Maurice Philippe became the scapegoat – he was actually a designer for whom Ron had the highest regard – and overtures were made to Ron to name his price and join the team. But if Ron was not going to move to Norfolk, he certainly was not going to cross the Atlantic.

Meanwhile, Norma was having to put up with him being under her feet most of the day with not enough to do and it was straining her patience. Even Ron admits that. Then Larry Perkins, an Australian who had come to Europe to race in Formula Three and was spending most of 1974 as Chris Amon's mechanic, approached Ron for some advice. Ron recalls: 'Larry had bought a GRD and thought it needed improving. He brought it to the house, I took a good look at it and said: "There's nothing to be done with this, it would be easier to start from scratch."'

Ron cannot remember precisely what he objected to, but in general terms he says of looking at another man's design: 'You notice mechanical things, small details, which are not efficiently done. You can't necessarily assess a spaceframe, but you can see where tubes are missing, because all spaceframes are based on tetrahedrons. You get a general sense of geometry, although geometry has become less important since about 1982, when downforce made suspension so much stiffer, so there was less pitch movement of the car. The importance of geometry increases with the amount of suspension movement. Before we were getting significant under-car downforce, good geometry was essential because we were relying on mechanical grip.

'As for aerodynamics, you just get a feel for it except when people come up with new concepts. I try to imagine the vehicle breaking through the air and I try to guess how much air it displaces. These days you can have access to very sophisticated programs in the field of Computational Fluid Dynamics, which can save a lot of time in the wind-tunnel, although they do not yet replace it.

'Larry Perkins' GRD got me going, and I started to draw a car at home. Word got out what I was doing and Ulf Svensson, who had been the Brabham agent in Sweden, heard about it and said that he wanted to buy a couple of cars. Then Chuck McCarty, who had handled Brabham in Italy, wanted a couple as well.

I checked with Bernie Ecclestone to make sure that there was no conflict of interest, and that was fine. Norma located a 2,000 square foot workshop in Woking through a small ad in the local paper. We stayed there until 1978, when Bernie moved Brabham to a new factory in Chessington and I could buy the old MRD works at New Haw from Jack.

Alain Fenn, who had been with me at Brabham, heard what was going on. He phoned from America and announced that he was coming back to work for me. I told him that he had no job, but that didn't deter him. He came back and moved in to answer the phone and to order parts.'

Alain recalls how he first became involved with Ron when, in late summer 1965, he applied for a job at MRD: 'Invited by telephone to attend an interview on a Saturday morning, I turned up at the offices at New Haw and found them open but empty. I moved down to the workshop, where the large sliding door was also open. I entered and approached the cleaner, who I could see was sweeping the floor below a part-built Formula Three chassis on stands, and asked where I might find Ron Tauranac. "That's me", he replied, "you must be Alain Fenn..."

'The first half of the interview continued there and then without interruption of the floor sweeping. Then once he had finished we moved to his office, where he sat down and pronounced: "I'm useless at interviews. People either give me loads of bullshit that I swallow, so I give the job to someone who can't do it, or else they say too little so don't get the job when they should. So really, we're wasting our time. Do you want the job?" I took it.

'I left Brabham in 1972 after Bernie took over and, about that time, I visited Ron. On his desk stood a Porsche air-cooled cylinder casting, with integral (aluminium) liner.' Ron explained: 'I was at Hockenheim – there was an

Interseries race on, so I walked down the pits to have a look at the cars. Whilst looking at the works Porsche, one of their engineers recognized me and came and asked if I liked their car. I said it was typical Porsche – badly designed in the first place then developed over a long period till it worked very well. A few weeks later he sent me the cylinder. Proves my point – they can't even spell!' The liner was indeed engraved: 'To Tarnac, to make him like Porsche.'

'One of Ron's catch-phrases was "Don't push me, I'm not ready yet. If you have to have an answer today, it has to be No." This philosophy applied extensively to Ron's dealing with correspondence – most letters hung around so long the answers were no longer expected.

'When it came to building the cars, other guys who'd been with me at Brabham turned up and we were on our way. There are plenty of stories of how difficult he was to work with, but it's amazing how many people stayed the full distance. And came back.'

Ron recalls: 'I wanted a simple car, with as little overhang as possible, and which, aerodynamically, was built to the law of areas. The one monocoque served for Formula Two, Formula Three and Atlantic, and the only difference between them was the specification of the brakes and the number and size of the fuel tanks. Originally I wanted to do the cockpit area as it eventually finished up, with high rounded sides, but in order to get things under way I went for a style which I thought customers would accept. When Ian Flux first tested this cockpit he reported back saying that although he got the same revs it made the car oversteer and this he didn't like. Alain Fenn suggested that he could adjust the rear wing to regain the balance if he hadn't already tried this. He hadn't, the new cockpit was cleaning up the airflow to the rear wing, so knocking off rear wing gave more revs on the straight, with consequent lap time improvement. Once you start winning races, you can take chances.

'At first we called the company Ron Tauranac Racing, and that was good while we were dealing with people in the sport. It helped to get us launched. Then we changed it to Ralt Cars; it was easier when writing cheques, and the last thing you want in your name is the word 'Racing'. You'll find, for example, that the insurance premiums for your road cars will go up.'

Then the motor racing press began to run stories with headlines like 'Tauranac to Build People's Racing Car' – how very 1970s. It was a good time to move into Formula Three because the category was reinventing itself. In 1974 it had been in the doldrums, partly as a result of the aftermath of that OPEC oil crisis. Even rounds of the British series sometimes had a grid in single figures, and many of the more ambitious young drivers had opted for Formula Atlantic.

Then the Formula One Constructors' Association made it clear they thought Formula Three was the main learning category, and there were a number of moves to give that thought substance. FOCA arranged for a Formula Three race to support the British Grand Prix, for example, and encouraged the organizers of other Grands Prix to do the same. BP was persuaded to sponsor the British Championship, and with the name of a great company behind it the series acquired status. Things began to move forward, and Ralt moved with them.

17

Ralt revived

Designing the Ralt RT1 meant that Ron started with a clean sheet of paper for the first time since 1960. Every previous Formula Three car he had drawn had been a development of a line which had begun with MRD-1. It was also Ron's first production monocoque, although he had modified the tub of Geoff Ferris' BT38 to make it more practical to manufacture. Although Ron had been far from inactive after he left Brabham, none of his work had been in production racing cars, and there had been considerable changes in them during this period.

He says: 'Before starting a new design, you first have to study the rule book and find where you can get your best advantage. It's like a driver setting up a car to get the best lap. Certain things are set for you. You know what engine you're going to use and what gearbox – and their shape and weight. You know that you have to go for a 40/60 front/rear weight distribution because that is what the tyres are designed for. You must operate within 1 per cent of the 40/60 balance.

'The driver, fuel cell, engine and gearbox will settle your wheelbase, while the track is settled either by the regulations or by aerodynamics. If it is a car for a formula with no aerodynamic aids you go for a wide track for optimum roadholding. When you have aerodynamic aids you can usually obtain more downforce than you need, so when you're designing primarily for speed, you go for a narrow track. It comes down to your judgment as to how narrow you make it.

'Brakes virtually settle themselves. Before we had significant downforce you might consider inboard brakes in order to reduce unsprung weight, but once we had wings that became less important. You therefore choose brakes that will fit inside the wheels and you choose ventilated or non-ventilated depending on what use they are going to have.'

Ron makes it sound easy. In principle no other designer would disagree, which begs the question: 'If the parameters are as tight as all that, why is it that some designers get most of their designs right, but most designers get few of them right?' Tauranac, despite having designed more racing cars than anyone else, has hardly a blip on his CV.

Much of his secret is contained in that word 'harmony'. It's like when an orchestra plays a certain piece of music – different conductors will produce different performances, and one, by common consent, will be the best.

A run of 10 Ralts would be made in 1975, and the new marque's debut came at Thruxton on March 31. Larry Perkins, driving for Team Cowangie, put his Ralt in second place on the grid with a time equal to that of Alex Ribeiro's works March and quicker than Gunnar Nilsson's sister car. Larry finished fifth, but a front-row position was enough to get Ralt noticed.

At that time Formula Three was dominated by March, but there were also cars from GRD, Modus, Royale, Ray, Lola, Ehrlich, Palliser, Hawke, Alexis and Safir, and that was just in Britain. On the Continent there were outfits like Martini, not to mention the people still running Brabham BT35s.

Larry Perkins, who was soon joined in Team Cowangie by his brother Terry, made people sit up when he set fastest lap in practice for the Monaco Grand Prix support race. He then won his heat and was lying second in the final on the road, but as the leader had a penalty for a jumped start Larry had the race in the bag. But he made a mistake and crashed.

Ron recalls: 'There was a guy helping him (part sponsor David MacKay) and when the leader got his penalty he was all for signalling him with the news. I told him not to because I know drivers, and I figured that Larry would lose concentration. David ignored my advice, hung out the pit board and, sure enough, Larry crashed.'

Larry's first major win was the Gran Premio Della Lotteria at Monza. This was one of the premier Formula Three races of the year because the prize fund was so good. It was a sweepstake – punters could buy tickets and, if they were lucky, they drew a car. Who knows what some Italian punter thought when he drew Larry Perkins in a car nobody had ever heard of! No doubt, though, Larry became a hero to someone that day.

Then he won a race in France and Terry Perkins won in Denmark. Next, a couple of rounds of the British Championship fell to Larry, along with some podium positions. The European Formula Three Championship was not a high-profile series, but nevertheless Larry Perkins won it.

In other races on the Continent, Bertram Schäfer was doing much the same as Perkins, putting together wins and high finishing positions. Just as in the early days of Brabham, a good story was spreading about the cars; they were simple and safe and they responded to the driver.

Formula Three was not yet the highly professional category that it became a few years later. One reason was that the idea of sponsorship was still permeating down through motor racing and through business. British drivers (and businesses) were slow to capitalize on sponsorship and consequently British representation was relatively thin.

There was also the fact that in some other countries the tax laws made sponsorship more attractive. If you could offset a budget against tax, it obviously helped. If you were in a country with a weak currency and, perhaps, restrictions on monetary movement, but you could get your sponsorship budget to a hard-currency country like the United Kingdom, that was an incentive as well.

Because Formula Three was still in a state of flux, you didn't necessarily need a new car to win, as Rupert Keegan proved when he won the first three British Formula Three races of 1976 in a two-year-old March. Mike Keegan, Rupert's father, had bought the racing car maker Hawke, and commissioned a

Formula One design from a young Adrian Reynard. Adrian was well under way with the car when Mike Keegan decided that he first wanted a Formula Three car. So the Hawke Formula One car was put on the back burner, and today Adrian admits that it is probably as well that it was not made, although the Formula Three car was.

One of the mechanics at Hawke recalls: 'We told Adrian that if he wanted to know about Formula Three, he'd better go and look at a Ralt. So he went to the factory and came back with eight Ralt uprights, which Ron had sold him. We began to wonder how good our car would be if the designer was buying essential parts from the maker he was supposed to beat!

'In fact, the front end of the car wouldn't speak to the back end because the tub was flexing in between. Adrian had made a reasonable copy of an RT1 – and the Hawke and Ralt tubs were both made by Mo Gomm – but Adrian had skimped on the rear bulkhead on the Hawke.'

A little more than 10 years later, the success of Reynard's cars would contribute to the financial crisis which would cause Ron to sell Ralt to March Group plc. A year further on and Adrian would come within 24 hours of buying March and, therefore, Ralt.

At the time, March had the Formula Three market sewn up. They had an established network of agents and they ran works cars. Lola was also in Formula Three and so was Chevron with a particularly good car, the B34. There were times when only one or two Ralts were in a race, or even none at all. It was an uphill struggle in Britain, but even so production trebled in 1976.

The fact that Larry Perkins won the 1975 European Championship was probably the reason why sales were strong in Europe, but that also meant that many of the sales went to the backwaters of Formula Three: Scandinavia and Germany.

Cars were built for Formula Two as well, but in 1976 Renault supplied a small number of French drivers with a superb V6 engine and only the works March-BMWs could live with them. Freddy Kottulinski gave Ralt its first Formula Two win at the Nürburgring in his BMW-powered RT1, but neither the Renault nor the March team was present. Even so, the field consisted of the cream of privateers, so it was a case of Kottulinski winning against his own type. Typically, he would be halfway up the grid when the serious boys were present, which still made a positive statement about the RT1.

Ray Mallock raced his Atlantic-engined car in Formula Two on occasion. At mid-season Eddie Cheever was in an RT1-Hart run by Ron Dennis, and by the end of the year was qualifying it in the top six. That was a good effort in the circumstances. In fact, Cheever even finished third at Pergusa ahead of Jean-Pierre Jabouille, who won the Formula Two title.

So Ralt was doing OK and a good story was spreading. Further, Ron was making good money and he re-invested in machine tools so he could make a more consistent product. This would be crucial to the success of Ralt, because nobody else seemed to be doing it. The bottom line was that a spare from Ralt fitted the car, you didn't have to take a file to it.

Ron also knew what his cars cost to make and he kept his margins tight. Nobody at March had the faintest idea what their cars actually cost them to make; the list price was taken out of the ether and was a vague notion of what the sales manager thought the market could stand. And that information comes from a former March sales manager!

Dan Gurney rounds the Rouen hairpin during his winning drive in the 1964 Brabham-Climax BT7. It was the first victory in a World Championship race for the Brabham marque.

Denny Hulme had scored his first GP success at Monaco three months earlier, and here he is heading for another victory at the Nurburgring, where he and Jack made it a Brabham-Repco 1-2 with their BT24s in the 1967 German Grand Prix.

Jack leads team-mate Jacky Ickx in their 'bi-plane' Ford-powered BT26s round the Barcelona street circuit during practice for the 1969 Spanish Grand Prix. This was the last race for the tall wings, which were banned after both Lotus cars crashed heavily when they failed. Ickx's rear wing also buckled, robbing him of second place.

Ickx scored two wins during his 1969 season as a Brabham driver, although he had to settle for third place in the French GP here at Clermont-Ferrand with his BT26.

Ron back in the cockpit again, but only for the photographer at the press preview of the new Ralt RT1 Formula Three car at the New Haw factory.

The new Ralt, like its Brabham predecessors, was 'user-friendly' in every sense, quickly became the most popular customer F3 car and took drivers to a host of race victories.

The Ralt RT2 Formula Two car was built exclusively for the Toleman team, for whom Brian Henton, seen here during a test session, scored wins at Mugello and Misano with the Hart-powered car during the 1979 season.

Celebrating another successful Tauranac-Honda partnership. As in the Brabham days, Honda power helped Ron's cars dominate Formula Two and in 1982 Ralt's first F2 Championship was won by Geoff Lees, seen here next to Mike Thackwell, still on crutches after a serious accident on the Thruxton circuit.

The cars Tauranac designed for Honda's racing school were assembled at the Japanese company's own UK facility in Langley, where Ron was also provided with office facilities.

School time at Suzuka. The fleet of Ron's single-seaters lined up at the circuit and ready for another day's driving tuition.

Throughout Ron's career as a designer and manufacturer of racing cars he has tended to operate out of modest premises, but there were few if any compromises with the quality of the machinery installed in them. This was the main machine shop in the Ralt days, where much of the equipment was computer-controlled.

In 1996 Formula Renault gave Ron the inspiration for this neat spaceframe car running on slick tyres. Originally called the Ronta FR1, it was intended to be run by a company which would also acquire the design rights, but when the deal fell through Ron took the car back and later passed it on to the owner of the Hawke name, who so renamed it.

Ron Tauranac the family man. Ron, Norma and their younger daughter Julie joined Jann on the day of her graduation from University, and below, more celebrations as Julie takes charge of the bottle and Jann, Ron and Norma smile into the camera.

The early days of Ralt did not quite mirror the early days of Brabham because every level of motor racing had become more serious. You would not get the equivalent of John Watson and his mechanic turning up to build their Formula Two car, but it still happened with the Formula Three cars. Increasingly, however, it would not be a driver and mechanic, but mechanics employed by a team that was running the driver.

Today, team owners say things like: 'Not everything that Ron did was perfect and we used to make our own modifications.' The complaints diminished year by year, however, as the re-investment in machine tools caused the Ralt product to become ever more reliable and consistent. It also has to be said that, in some cases, teams made more of their 'secret' contribution to the car than was strictly merited, and who can blame them? Every team was hoping to attract the best driver and package.

There was a small incident that deserves recording – and to understand its significance, it should be remembered that Ralt Cars had been established for little over a year when it occurred. Lotus had been in the doldrums in Formula One, and its new car for 1976, the 77, appeared to be an unmitigated disaster when it first came out. Nobody was used to seeing Lotus cars in the last two places on the grid, especially when the drivers were Mario Andretti and Ronnie Peterson. Things were so bad that, after the first race, Ronnie defected to March.

Much of the problem came down to flexing of the front suspension, because the suspension had been designed to be fully adjustable. Further, the car's front brakes were mounted inboard, where they provided no heat input to the front tyres.

Len Terry, Colin Chapman's first-ever design assistant, takes up the story: 'I felt sorry for Chapman and I phoned him with a suggestion. I thought he needed a more conventional set-up, with the brakes in the wheels, where their heat would warm the tyres. I went to Ron Tauranac, obtained some Ralt uprights, and we designed the suspension round those. Gunnar Nilsson qualified it fourth at the British Grand Prix and a Lotus 77 won the last race of the year.'

Ralt was still on an upward curve in 1977. One of the designers that year was Ian Bailey, who had first worked with Ron for a spell in 1965, and again from 1968 until 1977 and would stay with Ralt until 1990. He worked with Ron in the drawing office longer than any other person on the design staff, although workshop foreman Roy Billington remained with him through most of the MRD and Ralt years and at Trojan on top.

Ian Bailey says: 'The big difference between Ralt and MRD was the absence of Jack Brabham. Jack had a lot to say about things like engines, brakes and clutches, but Ralt was run in Ron's own idiosyncratic style. I think he took the view that almost anyone could be turned into a worker at Ralt provided they were prepared to knuckle down and do things his way. He called the training process intensive care – you survived it or you didn't.' (If you did, it set you up for a job anywhere in motor racing: Formula One teams were known to advise young applicants to spend a year or so at Ralt.)

'What was a shock to many people was his forthrightness. Australians did not have the same hang-ups that we Brits had. They got right to the point, and it was a shock to the system. It was not unusual for people to leave after a week or a month; I think the record was one and a half days. More than once I got up and left the works, telling Ron that I would not stay and be spoken to in that way.' But Ian still worked for Ron longer than he worked for any other company, and his employers have included Jaguar and Lotus.

During 1977, in only its third year of existence, Ralt made 51 customer cars while March made 57. Even that does not tell the true story because March was well established in the USA, so a large number of cars were made for Formula B, which had yet to discover Ralt. In Formula Three, Ralt made 30 cars to March's 18. That was the real underlying story.

Ralt was taking March's market hand over fist, but again, most cars went abroad. Still, they were starting to get into the hands of good drivers. Nelson Piquet, for one, began the European Championship with a March, but switched to a Ralt. In Britain, Derek Warwick began with a Chevron, but ended the season with an RT1, and although he won no races, he took several second places. Jack Brabham's eldest son, Geoff, made a name for himself in a private Ralt run from the factory by fellow Australian Greg 'Peewee' Siddle. Geoff won several races in 1977 and went on to a successful career in IndyCar racing.

March not only had Ralt to contend with because the Chevron B38, though made in smaller numbers, was also an excellent car. During that year, Chevron, March and Ralt shared the honours. It was becoming noticeable, however, that whereas Chevron and Ralt made cars to a consistent standard, only March cars run by professional teams scored wins.

As the 1977 season went on, Ralts became more numerous and, in Italy, Elio de Angelis switched from a Chevron to an RT1 and went on to take the Italian Championship. By mid-season Ralt was frequently the most highly represented marque on a Formula Three grid in Europe – in only its third year of production. At the Österreichring in August, for example, there were 20 RT1s against eight Chevrons, seven cars from March and three from Argo. Ron was proving that the consistent success of Brabham in Formula Three had been no fluke.

In Formula Two, however, the Ralt representation was light, but an RT1-BMW run by Ron Dennis for Eddie Cheever came close to taking the European title. Cheever was just 19 years old and was considered to be a prodigy. He did, however, make mistakes. Eddie should have won at Enna and Misano, but in the former he crashed while leading late in the race, and in the latter he lost the lead through a lapse of concentration. That kissed goodbye to 13 points and Eddie was runner-up, just 12 points behind René Arnoux, so he could have taken the title.

For the most part, Formula Three was, as it had always been, one driver and one mechanic, but in 1978 Derek Warwick decided to put his operation on a more professional footing. The headline was that he no longer drove the truck to meetings.

While Ron Dennis' Project Four and Dave Price's David Price Racing, the two best-funded and glitziest teams in British Formula Three, ran Marches, most owner/drivers lined up behind Ralt. March would make only 11 cars for Formula Three and SuperVee in 1978 while Ralt would make 36, further evidence that.Ralt was rapidly eroding the position of the most successful production racing car company of the 1970s.

Warwick won the first two Formula Three races of the year, finishing both of them ahead of Chico Serra in a Ron Dennis-run March. Nigel Mansell had a works March for the International Trophy meeting, and he set pole and led the race until he spun. He finished second to Piquet and spent the next two decades telling anyone who'd listen that the March was rubbish and he'd been ripped off.

The British Formula Three races really came down to Warwick, Piquet and Serra, and there was a long period when Serra led both British series. In fact, Chico might have won both had he not been sidelined for several weeks following a crash in testing which was none of his making. Many regard him as the great Brazilian talent that slipped through the net.

After strong showings early in the season, Warwick began to take second place to Piquet. While Derek spent his days welding trailers in the family business, Nelson had nothing to occupy himself except his racing, and in Peewee Siddle he had a good tutor. They found fractions of time in areas such as fitting lighter universal joints to the drive-shafts.

Ron says: 'That was something that I did for them, and the car went quicker. They swapped engines and the car was still quicker. That taught me a valuable lesson about inertia, and it set me looking at other areas of the car. It influenced my thinking on all my later cars. We were all on a learning curve.'

There was very little to choose between Piquet and Warwick and they each won a championship in Britain, with the other the runner-up. After his early dominance, however, Derek panicked when Nelson began to cut into his lead. Les Thacker, BP's competition manager, arranged for him to try a March. Derek tested it, elected to race it, and it broke the rhythm of his season. At the time he first drove the March, Derek and his RT1 had won more Formula Three races in Britain than any other driver. After a few races, Derek was back in his Ralt, but the excursion had spoiled his season.

Nelson did actually have a job apart from racing, which was sweeping the Ralt factory floor at the end of the day. Nelson says: 'Me being the cleaner did not prevent Ron from taking me seriously, and between sweeps he'd listen to my ideas.

Ron taught me something very important, he taught me how to handle success. He was already twice a World Champion constructor, yet he treated me as if I was the World Champion.' Who knows how much psychological edge that gave Nelson? Derek did not have someone like Ron in his corner – and a boxer's second does more than wipe the fighter's face with a wet sponge.

When Bob Sparshott bought a McLaren M23 to enter in Grands Prix he looked around for a likely driver, and as Nelson was then doing most of the winning in Formula Three he got the chance. At the beginning of the following year, Nelson was a works Brabham driver while Derek was at the start of a nightmare season in Formula Two.

While Piquet and Warwick slugged it out in Britain, Ralts dominated Formula Three in Europe as well. Jan Lammers won the European Championship from Anders Olofsson in a tight finish (they were equal on points with four wins apiece and Lammers won on second places). In fact, Ralts won every Formula Three Championship apart from the Italian series, which went to Siegfried Stohr's Chevron.

Almost unnoticed was an American, Bobby Rahal, who raced a Wolf WD1 with reasonable success. The 'W' in the car's designation was for Walter Wolf, and the 'D' stood for Gianpaolo Dallara, a name which will appear again later in the story. Rahal went on to become a triple CART IndyCar Champion.

The big news of 1978, however, was the Lotus 79, with its sliding skirts and ground effect. Everyone wanted ground effect, but hardly anyone knew what it meant. Not even Lotus, the team which had discovered the 'something for nothing' system, really understood it, as the Lotus 80 (the car which, Colin Chapman said, was going to make the Lotus 79 'look like a double-decker bus') soon proved.

Ron was also in Formula One that year, albeit at arm's length. He had designed a conventional Formula One car for Teddy Yip, an entrepreneur who owned a huge casino in Macau. Teddy liked his motor racing and he sponsored a number of cars and drivers, without really finding the resources, or the focus, to do the thing properly. He just liked being there, at the show.

The Theodore TR1 was recognizably the bigger brother of the Ralt RT1. Two cars were made, but Ron had little to do with them after their creation. He says: 'The team manager, Sid Taylor, arrived with a rear wing off a Wolf and told me that was what I was to use. I couldn't cope with people providing help like that.' Ron put them in touch with Len Bailey, who finished off the project.

Most of the time the TR1 failed to even pre-qualify, let alone qualify for races. Eddie Cheever drove it a couple of times, then gave up on it. Then Keke Rosberg managed to put it on the grid – just – for the South African Grand Prix, but he retired in the race. In his autobiography, Keke wrote: 'The car was really not that bad. I kept up with the pace and was only a second behind Lauda in testing. Otherwise, the team was a disaster: everyone was busy fighting everyone else. There was no team spirit of any sort.'

The next race for the Theodore was the International Trophy. It was one of the last of the non-Championship Formula One races, and while it was short on numbers, it was high on quality: Lauda, Hunt, Andretti, Fittipaldi and Peterson headed the cast. Keke, in only his second Formula One race, qualified 11th (from 17 entries – only Wolf and Ferrari did not send at least one car). That suggests that the TR1 did have some potential when it was dialled into a circuit.

On race day the skies opened. Two drivers refused to start and most of the others were soon throwing their cars at the scenery, but Keke kept the TR1 on the road, resisted constant pressure from Emerson Fittipaldi, and won by just over a second. Most of the credit went to Rosberg, and rightly so because it was an astonishing performance, but Keke could not have won if his car had been flawed.

It was at the International Trophy that the Lotus 79, the first car to be designed around sliding skirts, made its debut. Mario Andretti put it on pole position, but it was part of the scenery by the third lap. But as soon as the Lotus 79 had proved its worth everyone set about designing ground-effect cars.

But something else happened in 1978 which would affect the production racing car industry. In March, Derek Bennett, the founder of Chevron, died following a hang gliding accident. The team that Bennett had assembled, which was led by Paul Owens and Paul Brown, who were soon designing and building Maurer Formula Two cars and later became senior members of the Reynard organization, could have continued the Chevron line. But unfortunately, because so little was known about the company, it was commonly believed that Chevron was a one-man band, and so when Bennett died, customers lost confidence.

Because Derek had owned most of the shares, which passed to his sisters, who did not understand the business, the company did not have the financial resources to engineer a new car. Instead they brought in Tony Southgate to design a ground-effect package around the existing tub – they thought that they had to put a name behind the car – but the existing tub was too wide to utilize ground effect, and after the first few races of 1979, during which the Chevrons struggled, it was as good as over. It was another example of how precarious the motor racing business can be. Neither was Ralt immune to the fickleness of the business, and in 1979 its production would drop from 55 cars to 25, (how many conventional manufacturing companies – washing machine makers, say – could survive a drop like that in 12 months?) Also, for the first time in his career, Ron built a new Formula Three car which did not win a single race during the year.

18

Treading water

During 1978, Ron was approached by Toleman to design a car for Formula Two. Ted Toleman had made his fortune by transporting new cars from the factories to the showrooms. For a time, he had raced cars himself, but then his brother died in a racing accident, so Ted hung up his helmet and went powerboat racing instead while sponsoring a modest team in Formula Ford 2000.

Toleman had run works-assisted Royales and Ted had persuaded the cars' designer, Rory Byrne, to work for him. The move from Formula Ford 2000 to Formula Two, with cars specially commissioned from Ralt, was the first step towards Ted building his own Formula One team and Rory emerging as one of motor racing's top designers.

Since ground effect had arrived, Ron laid down a new generation of Ralts. For 1979 there would be the RT2 (Formula Two), RT3 (Formula Three) and RT4 (Formula Atlantic), but all were to the same basic concept involving a sheet aluminium monocoque, inboard rocker-arm suspension and ground-effect aerodynamics. Rory Byrne was loaned from Toleman for three months and Toleman's mechanics were also loaned to do the car assembly. 'We got on quite well,' Ron recalls, 'there were no problems at all with Rory.'

But practically everyone was at sea in the new ground-effect area. Spring rates had suddenly quadrupled and monocoques, which had been perfectly adequate before, began to crack and break under the increased stresses they now had to endure. Designers also struggled to find a balance between downforce and straight-line speed, and there was the problem of the sliding skirts. When a car was going at speed and the skirts were in contact with the road, the low-pressure area created under the car caused the skirts to be sucked inwards, deforming them. It was a steep learning curve for everyone.

March, the most experienced and successful team in the 2-litre Formula Two, ran a four-car team and would start every test and practice session with each car on different settings, then they would adopt those of the car which seemed the most promising.

The RT2 was late, the first one arriving only just in time for the first race of the season. So Toleman ran the Ralt-Hart for Brian Henton – 'Super-Hen' to his many British fans – while the team's second driver, the quiet South African Rad

Dougall, was given a March 782.

After the first three rounds, Rad Dougall and the proven and uncomplicated pre-ground-effect March 782 led the Championship, Rad having finished second at Hockenheim and first at Thruxton. But after four races, Brian was second to Rad in the series, although he chose to race the team's well-sorted March 782 at the Nürburgring, where he finished second behind Marc Surer's March 792. But most revealingly, third place in that race went to Manfred Winkelhock, who was driving his 'obsolete' RT1, with which he also set the fastest lap; his car didn't have ground effect, which was causing everyone else a lot of grief. Although one would have thought that the 1979 Formula Two cars with their ground-effect aerodynamics would have been quicker than their predecessors, in fact only two lap records (out of 12) were broken during 1979.

Rad Dougall didn't get his Ralt RT2 until June, by which time Henton had pushed him down into second place in the series. Brian was on a roll by this time and had won two races in his Ralt, at Mugello and Misano. He had also crossed the line first at Enna, only to be disqualified under contentious circumstances. He had taken to an escape road to avoid an accident, but had not actually stopped before rejoining the race.

At the time of the final round at Donington, Henton's home circuit, an appeal was still outstanding over the Enna disqualification, but regardless of the outcome of that, Henton still led the series by a single point. Observers wrote that the Ralt had become the car to beat and wondered how the season would have panned out had Ron been able to deliver the cars earlier.

Henton led the Donington race, but on the last lap his car ran out of brakes and he spun down to fourth. By finishing second, Marc Surer took the Championship for March, at least provisionally. The title was not confirmed until two months later when Henton's appeal against disqualification at Enna was finally rejected.

At Donington Brian had made no excuses, and in the pits immediately afterwards he blamed the loss of the title on the fact that his helmet was painted green; he changed the colour to blue and won the title the following year! Some time after he had retired from the sport Brian said: 'On the way to the meeting Toleman's chief mechanic was killed in a road crash. Apart from the team's emotional response to the tragedy, it set us back a day and as a consequence we didn't do our normal brake wear tests, so we had to go by guesswork, and we guessed wrongly.

'As the race progressed my front pads wore away until we had no pads at the front and no fluid in the front brake cylinder, only air. I braked heavily in the closing stages, but there was nothing left at the front, the rear wheels locked and I spun.' That cost Brian – and Ralt – the Championship.

Although Henton would return the following year and win the title for Toleman, it would be in a Toleman T280, which was actually a Ralt RT2 built with aircraft-grade materials that Ron felt to be unnecessary. Having scored a 1-2 in the Formula Two Championship, Toleman then moved up to Formula One in 1981, but granted a licence to Lola to build replicas of the Formula Two car.

Quite how Toleman felt it possible to grant Lola a licence to make a Ralt remains a mystery, but they were good enough to win the odd race. Of course, there were denials that the car was a Ralt, but all the spare monocoques which Lolas made finished up with SPA Fabrications, suppliers to Ralt, who say that rivet for rivet they were identical. Some of these Ralt-Toleman-Lola tubs then became the basis of the successful Rowan hillclimb cars.

Work on the Ralt RT2 for Toleman delayed progress on the RT3 Formula Three car and only one RT3 appeared in the British series. With Ralt hobbled and Chevron out of the picture, March bounced back with a ground-effect car which, truth be told, was little more than a body kit with sliding skirts on an existing chassis. It was not serious technology, it was a marketing exercise – and it worked.

If ground effect had been all it had been cracked up to be, one would have expected wholesale demolition of Formula Three lap records. In fact, just four new records were set in Britain, all in the second part of the season, whereas during the previous year, without ground effect, six circuit records had been broken.

Formula Three cars had not taken a quantum leap, but everyone 'knew' that you had to have a ground-effect car. In Britain, every Formula Three race bar one fell to March – and the exception went to Chevron. At most circuits drivers could not beat records established by RT1s, but nobody thought that you could win in an RT1.

There was an added complication: the authorities decided that sliding skirts would be permitted in Formula Three, but only for one year. So far as Ron was concerned, this meant a redesign, so he advised potential customers to go elsewhere.

Eventually Eliseo Salazar appeared in an RT3, but it was not without problems. The sliding skirts were made of plastic sheeting, and as referred to earlier, they were being deformed through being sucked into the low-pressure area that they were helping to create under the car; when they became stuck they would cause variable downforce and a change to the centre of pressure.

Dave Price, who was running Brett Riley and Nigel Mansell in Marches fitted with down-on-power Triumph Dolomite engines, says: 'I told my drivers to get behind Salazar. That Ralt was so big that it cleared the air and towed them along.'

Rob Wilson, who did much of the testing on the car, says: 'When I first drove it, it was the worst racing car I'd ever driven. After six months it was the best.' The RT3 highlights the Tauranac philosophy. March did wonders with a piece of clever marketing, while Ron worked away at a proper ground-effect machine. March reaped short-term benefit – it made 25 Formula Three cars to the six of Ralt – but the RT3 would eventually wipe March out of the Formula Three market altogether and, soon after, from the Atlantic/Formula B market as well.

19

The Honda connection – 2

After an absence of 10 years from motor racing, Honda began to reconsider its position and decided to return to Formula One, but only after first becoming involved once again in Formula Two. Honda sought the advice of Jabby Crombac about this, and he recommended Ralt. Because of their past connection, John Surtees had also been considered, but he had decided to wind up his team at the end of 1978.

At first, though, there had been an approach to March, because Ralt was virtually unknown in Japan whereas March had been the regular winner of the Japanese National Formula Two Championship since 1973. So Honda entered preliminary negotiations with March Engineering, who found their offer tempting, except that it would have had to be an exclusive deal, which meant that March would no longer be able to claim that 'Our cars are the same as the customer cars.' Also, March went back a long way with BMW; Robin Herd being a very close friend of Paul Rosche, BMW's chief engine man, the company had kept faith with BMW on a previous occasion when it had been offered Renault engines in Formula Two.

Conventional thinking has it that Ralt eventually landed the Honda deal because when the Japanese company had been in Formula Two previously it was in partnership with Brabham. Ron certainly believes this to be the case, and since he wasn't building production Formula Two cars, he could run a works team exclusively for Honda and not be competing against his customers. He says: 'We had been building and selling cars, it's as simple as that. We had not been running a team, but when the chance came along we took it, as we did with Toleman, and we used Formula Two as a development exercise.'

In the meantime, Nobuhiko Kawamoto, 'Hong Kong mechanic', had risen within the corporation. So had Tadashi Kume, who had taken over from Mr Honda as President of the company. Nobuhiko Kawamoto remembers: 'In 1979 I had a strong urge to return to racing, so I made some drawings at home in secret. Then I asked Mr Kume if it was OK to develop the project, and he replied that he would turn a blind eye to what I was doing.

'I went to a hotel with Mr Ichida as my assistant, just as I had accompanied Mr Kume to a hotel room in 1965. I told Ichida that he could sleep, eat and drink at any time, but we would not be going back to the factory until we had finished the design.' The result was a 2-litre V6 engine for Formula Two.

If it seems odd that both the 1966 and the 1980 Formula Two engines were designed in hotel rooms rather than in a drawing office, it is because of certain restrictive practices agreed with the trade unions in Japan. By going to a hotel in a seaside resort Messrs Kawamoto and Ichida could claim they were not working, but were simply on holiday.

'After we had finished the engine we had to decide which chassis to put it in and the first person I thought of was Ron-San. He was doing a fantastic job on chassis design with his Ralts and he was also the only person I knew well. We consulted other people for their advice, then in 1979 we went to England to see Ron-san.

'It was Ron-san and Jack-san who taught us various criteria relating to things like reliability, power characteristics, maintenance, weight distribution etc, when we did not know much about automobiles. We had thought that to make an automobile engine all we had to do was to put two motorcycle engines together.

'After we suspended the Formula Two project at the end of 1966, the Formula One project went on with a 3-litre engine. Again, I don't think we knew what we had to do to win Formula One races. We thought that all we had to do was triple the size of the 1-litre Formula Two engine. That concept did not work and eventually we withdrew from Formula One as well. In contrast to the Brabham, which combined a simple V8 engine with a light chassis, our Formula One car was a monster. Ron-san taught me how to win motor races.'

When the Honda V6 engine was delivered, Ron could see a problem which had not occurred to Honda. The exhaust pipes were on the outside of each block and, being a V6, they pointed downwards. Unfortunately, ground effect had arrived and this meant that the exhaust pipes intruded into the ground-effect tunnels. So Ron suggested new cylinder heads, with the exhaust ports raised, and Honda accomplished this in an astonishingly short time. They completed the casting for a single cylinder in three weeks and sent it to Ron for approval. It was a repeat of 1965/6, when Honda had designed an engine in isolation without giving sufficient thought to its installation.

But that was not the only trouble with the engine. There was a problem with the oil scavenge system. Ron says: 'We sorted that out. The thing about Honda is that they understood cylinder heads, but they didn't understand oil flow in a racing engine and things like how to scavenge a dry-sump engine properly. In fact, that was something I don't think anyone understood until Keith Duckworth came along and showed us how to do it.'

Oil scavenge and engine installation are important themes in Ron's work. In the early summer of 1997 he spent a few days advising the TWR Arrows team on engine installation and suddenly the Yamaha engine became both more reliable and more powerful. At the end of the season, team boss Tom Walkinshaw admitted that they had been losing 50bhp through a combination of poor engine installation and deficient inlet ports.

Mr Kawamoto continues: 'Ron-San still had a sharp tongue, but during one of my visits to England he invited me to his house for dinner. I thought that women were bosses in their homes in Western countries, but in his case Ron-san's only interest was racing. I thought that his wife was a remarkable woman to allow him to do whatever he wanted to.

'He also had two beautiful daughters. One time one of them brought a car to Ralt to be fixed. His face lit up with a smile and he was a gentle and caring father. In my mind he had changed from being a hard-headed and sharp-tongued man to being gentle and broad-minded, yet he remained very straightforward and honest.'

Roberto Moreno recalls that since Mr Kawamoto knew that he could always find Ron at the works, which was only a short drive away from the Honda facility at Langley, he would often call in if he wanted advice or to discuss a problem.

When Honda returned to four-wheeled racing, sponsorship costs were escalating, partly because some people had become greedy. There has been more than one occasion when a major manufacturer with a long relationship with a racing company has split for unspecified reasons, but it has come down to the fact that they have been presented with outrageous invoices, which they've settled, and then gone elsewhere.

Among Ron's papers are some estimates for running a Formula Two team. They are undated, but they appear to relate to 1983/4. A one-car team would cost £249,503.50. We're less than £500 from a quarter of a million, so most people, putting in a bit for expenses, would look at that and call it £275,000, but Ron's estimates come down to the penny. His estimate for a two-car team was £406,370.41. The odd pennies came from an actuarial calculation of depreciation on capital assets. If something which costs £1,000 is written off over three years, then you get £333.33 each year, plus a penny somewhere. Ron explains: 'You add it all up and if it comes out to odd pennies, then it comes out to odd pennies.'

His figures break down into fine detail. The drivers were paid £15,000 each. Each car cost £30,000. There would be two cars and 10 support personnel for a one-driver team and three cars and 15 support personnel for a two-driver team.

A one-day test at Silverstone with one car would involve four people, and their food and the fuel for one truck and a Ford Granada would come to £60. The fuel for the race car was worked out at 100 laps at 6mpg. The circuit hire (it was not an exclusive booking) came to £50. The total day, including wear and tear on chassis and gearbox, two dog rings per car and brake pads, came to £433.

An exclusive one-day test with two cars at Brands Hatch (on the Club circuit) was £2,328.50, which included expenses for three marshals and the attendance of an ambulance and a breakdown truck. All were carefully itemized: the payment to the marshals was £12.50 each, exclusive circuit hire was £954 and the breakdown truck and ambulance cost £75 apiece.

The golden rule in motor racing seems to be that expenditure rises to meet the amount of the available sponsorship money, no matter how much that is. Nobody in the sport apart from Ron has acquired a reputation for being parsimonious with sponsor's money while still turning an honest profit. That may explain why Honda has dealt with Ron-san for more than 30 years.

20

Formula Ralt

The race is won by someone in a Ralt. Someone else, driving another Ralt, comes second. A third person, in yet another Ralt, finishes third, followed by three more, all of them driving Ralts, who cross the line fourth, fifth and sixth.

Formula Three would become like that over the next few years – it would come to be known as Formula Ralt, although this had seemed extremely unlikely during the early weeks of the 1980 season. If you had been asked to nominate the outstanding Formula Three car after the first few races, you would have been hard pushed to decide between the March 803 and the Argo JM6 – there were more Marches on the grid, but the Argo won proportionally more points in both Britain and on the Continent. Kenny Acheson, who was being run by Murray Taylor, actually used a 1979 March for some circuits and a 1980 March for others, and he was in contention for the title until the very last race.

In the European Championship, the Martini Mk 31 did most of the winning, but the tyre rules in Europe were different – the Brits ran crossply control tyres with a hard compound – so it is not possible to make a direct comparison. In fact, Michele Alboreto won the series in a March, largely because the top Martini runners took points off each other.

People began to write off Ralt. Few drivers were running an RT3 and, in Britain, it was not until the eighth round of the series that one scored a points finish. This happened at Silverstone, where Rob Wilson, who had taken pole, finished third. Rob was unable to translate that into a string of successes, but four rounds later he was on pole again, and this time he finished second. Rob didn't have the advantage of a professional team behind him, and he had a living to earn as well – playing the guitar in London nightclubs.

When Rob took his second place, Roberto Guerrero (Argo) and Kenny Acheson (March 793/803) were tied at the top of the table on 67 points and Stefan Johansson (March 803) was in third place with 45 points. The main flaws in the March were concerned with the aerodynamics and poor traction and it was not until mid-season that these were addressed. March brought out an update kit, with rocker-arm rear suspension and a new body with a narrower nose and revised sidepods, but update kits in mid-season are never popular and are no way to spread goodwill.

Johansson was being sponsored by Marlboro and run by Ron Dennis, who at the time was in negotiation with Marlboro about taking a stake in McLaren. It was therefore desirable for Ron Dennis' long-term ambitions that Johansson should win the Championship, and soon he was trying different engines.

Then Rob Wilson began to put together a string of strong finishes, including a win in a heat of a race at Silverstone, and by this time other drivers had also made a switch to the RT3, notably Eddie Jordan, who says: 'One difference between a March and a Ralt was that a March spare – a wishbone, say – always looked good even if, perhaps, it didn't fit properly. March was, well, artistic and Ralt was practical.

'Marches were nicely made and they looked the business. A Ralt was nothing but brackets on brackets on brackets, but they were effective. And they were easier to work on. March spares were more expensive, and there was always more fuss dealing with them. If you went to Ralt the storeman would say: "That's it, mate. She'll be all right."

'Then there was testing. Robin Herd at March had a very quick stopwatch for testing. These days you have computers and telemetry, but back then you had watches and everyone was quick when Robin was timing them. The best car was the RT1, which I raced a few times in Atlantic. It had so much bodywork to put sponsors' stickers on. That full-width nose was sheer bloody magic!'

The number of brackets was a common criticism of Ralts, but Ron says: 'My cars were notable for their simplicity and their ease of maintenance. They were easy to understand and to set up. This was achieved by long hours of work and the critical appraisal of the developing project. That often meant changing the position of ancillary components so that the connections between them took the best route.

'This was the time before the advent of CAD in racing car design. CAD allows you to prepare a layout, see it in three dimensions and change it if necessary. Many complicated cars were designed during the Ralt era by some quite clever designers, who set their designs on the drawing board. Quite often they built themselves into a corner and had to take a complicated way.'

Dick Bennetts, who had been assisting Ron Dennis' Formula One project (which would become the McLaren MP4), took note of the performance of the various Ralts and suggested to Project Four that they try one. Dick says: 'It took us a month or so to understand the car and make it work, but when we did understand it, we dumped the March.

'One of the first things we did was to dump the fuel system. It was heavy and hideously complicated. Rob Wilson was having fuel pick-up problems and so was having to run with extra fuel. We substituted a simple system we took from a March.'

Murray Taylor recalls: 'At Silverstone Ron Dennis said to me: "Do you enjoy winning? Make the most of what you've won because I'm about to turn up the screw." What he meant was that he was about to buy a Ralt.

'Kenny's sponsor offered to do the same for us, but we were in charge of the Championship and leading by miles. We saw our main threat as Roberto Guerrero, not Stefan, and it didn't make sense for us to swap cars at that stage of the season.'

Kenny Acheson remembers other factors, like the promise of the Formula Two drive he would have if he stayed loyal to March. 'The trouble is,' he says, 'there was nothing in writing.' Kenny never did get a Formula Two drive with March, but he got one with Ralt.

Stefan Johansson arrived at Mallory Park on September 28 with his RT3. At the start of the race, Acheson was on 84 points, Guerrero on 79 and Johansson was down on 58, and there were just four rounds to go. It seemed an impossible task. But Johansson won at Mallory Park, then won, and won, and won – and he took the Championship by 2 points. He was helped by the fact that Kenny Acheson had red mist before his eyes at the last round – he had only to finish fifth to take the title, but he tangled with Rob Wilson at the chicane on the first lap and broke his nosecone.

The headline was that Stefan came from a long way behind to take the series and he had switched from a March to a Ralt to do so. Then a couple of weeks later Rob Wilson rounded off the season by winning the televised non-Championship race at Thruxton.

Naturally the RT3 became the object of many a driver's desire, and something else changed in Formula Three. Even in the late 1970s you would find drivers running their cars with a single mechanic.

Glenn Waters, who set up his Intersport Formula Three team at the beginning of 1981, says: 'Ron was largely responsible for the sudden emergence of professionally-run Formula Three teams. There had been one or two teams around, but Ron took the view that the cars were getting too complicated for a driver with a single mechanic to work on, at least if they were to be competitive. Ron actively encouraged the change by helping people like myself to set up in business.

'I stuck with Ralt in Formula Three because Ron was totally straight. He helped me to grow my business, he gave me excellent professional advice, and I finished up buying 23 cars from him. I stopped only when he was no longer Ralt's Formula Three designer.

'I had spent eight years working with Lotus – I was Mario Andretti's chief mechanic when he won the World Championship – but the RT3 was the first racing car I worked on which was properly engineered. Everything was done correctly and everything fitted. The only other car I've worked on that you can say that about is the Dallara Formula Three cars we run today.'

While Stefan Johansson came out of nowhere to take the Formula Three title for Ralt, the first Ralt-Honda Formula Two car had been completed and raced. Although given the designation RH6, it was essentially an update of the RT2. The main difference was that, whereas on the RT2 the four-cylinder Hart engine was mounted on an A-frame, the Honda engine was a stressed unit.

It was the year during which the Toleman-Harts of Brian Henton and Derek Warwick finished 1-2 in the Championship. It was a case of a works team with an exclusive deal with Pirelli. It also helped Toleman that its first car was actually a refurbished and developed Ralt RT2.

The driver of the first Ralt-Honda was Nigel Mansell. It was a big break for him, although it does not rate a mention in his autobiography save to boast that the Honda Formula One engine was based on the Formula Two engine which he had helped to develop.

The selection of Mansell raised many an eyebrow because, while he had his adherents, others thought that he was a waste of space. Ron explains his decision: 'I was approached by David Phipps, who was close to Chapman. Lotus had signed Mansell as a test driver and Phipps told me that they thought he was the coming man. It was mid-season and most of the likely drivers were signed-up, so I took Nigel as a favour to Lotus.

'We've already mentioned the problem with the exhaust pipes and the engine oil scavenge system, but when the engine was first delivered it was peaky and the fuel injection wasn't good enough. They'd fitted a Lucas unit which they'd taken from a Triumph saloon. It worked fine in a Triumph, but it was not much use over 6,000rpm and the Honda unit revved to 11,000rpm. To make it work we had to increase the fuel pressure from 110 to 160psi. The problem was solved, however, after we consulted Lucas, who suggested that we replaced it with a unit they made for a Ferrari V12. We had a V6 so we ran it at half engine speed.'

Another problem was that the (mechanical) fuel injection system was designed for a 90-degree engine and Honda's was a 76-degree unit. The injection system was always problematical, and electronic systems were still some way off. Yet another area of potential problems was the integrity of the exhaust system. To ensure that every pipe was exactly the same length, Ron used to fill them with ping-pong balls. You dropped the balls down the pipe and if one pipe held, say, 14 balls and another would take only 13, something was amiss. It was rough and ready, but it worked.

Mansell did not exactly set the world back on its heels. In four races he was 11th, retired (an accident), fifth, then was second at Hockenheim. By that time Geoff Lees had joined the team and it even seemed for a time that the two Ralt-Hondas would finish 1-2 at Hockenheim, but then Geoff suffered a puncture and Nigel had a mechanical problem late in the race.

By the end of the season Mansell had earned a seat with Lotus in Formula One, while Lees kept his place with Ralt. Ron says: 'Alan Howell, who managed our team, suggested Geoff to me, and by the time he drove for us he was already a mature driver.' Howell, who had managed drivers and teams in F1, F2 and F3, says: 'I was really brought in to be a race engineer, but nothing was that simple at Ralt. I was race engineer, chief mechanic, team manager, everything. But that merely reflected what Ron was. He was everywhere.

'I was with him for 11 years and I don't think we ever discussed anything in his office, it was always in the yard between his office and the race shop. Wages, work conditions, everything was thrashed out in the yard. The only way you could guarantee to meet Ron was on a Thursday. You poured a cup of coffee, opened your copy of *Autosport*, and within 10 seconds he was by your side.'

Many people thought that Honda would steamroller the opposition. The logic was sound: a V6 engine developed by a major company should be unstoppable, just like the Renault V6 had been in the mid-1970s, added to which there was Ron's track record, and the fact that in 30-year-old Geoff Lees and 19-year-old Mike Thackwell he had two superb drivers for 1981.

But there were problems with the engine, as John Judd explains: 'At the end of the season Ron was pretty frustrated with the Honda engine and he persuaded them to bring one up to us and run it on the dyno. We were able to make an immediate improvement, up to 20bhp in some parts of the power curve, simply by advancing the ignition. It was a fluke. It so happened that the airflow in our test rig was the same as in a car, whereas the air in Honda's dyno was less agitated. Consequently, they had set up the engine in one environment and transferred it to another, and the airflow, when running in a car, was upsetting the mixture in the trumpets.

'Anyway, we achieved an immediate improvement. Mr Kawamoto was impressed and asked if we had any more ideas. We took an engine apart and saw that their inlet ports were completely different to what had become the norm since the introduction of the Cosworth DFV engine. Inlet ports had become smaller.

'What we did then was to weld sleeves into the inlet ports and that found an extra 15bhp at the top end, with an extra 35bhp in mid-range. Geoff Lees won at Spa in 1981 with the cylinder heads we'd bodged together and Honda then produced a proper casting. Within four or five weeks they had productionized our modification.'

At the end of the 1980 season Toleman moved up to Formula One (and later metamorphosed into Benetton) so the sharp end of Formula Two would be works teams from March, who had that special relationship with BMW, and the two Ralt-Hondas.

Meanwhile, Johansson's late charge in Formula Three meant that everyone wanted a Ralt. Stefan's car was sold to a new team, West Surrey Racing, which was built around Johansson's former race engineer, Dick Bennetts. The driver was Dr Jonathan Palmer, who went on to win the British Formula Three Championship.

Dick, who became a guru in Formula Three and won more championships than any other team manager, says: At the end of 1980 I could have gone to McLaren with Ron Dennis to run the Formula One test team, but I didn't want to be one person among 200, so I went on my own.

'When we started to run Ralts we made a lot of new stuff for our cars. It then occurred to me that I could make suggestions to Ron, he could make the parts, and we could test them. That would save us money and we would get the good bits first, although the reality is that you can test 10 items and only two may make an improvement.' Ron was receptive to the idea, so Dick established a special relationship with Ralt, although Dick's was by no means the only team which tested new parts.

During 1981, Ralt made 76 cars for the junior formulae and March made 26. March had been the chief beneficiary of the withdrawal of Brabham and Lotus from the production racing car market in the 1970s, but now Ralt was about to knock it out of the Formula Three market.

Alan Howell says: 'One of the problems at Ralt was that Ron would never accept that any team car was ever finished. He always wanted to fiddle, so you might have three cars on stands with no corners on. In fact they had previously had their corners on and had been set up properly. At one o'clock Ron would drive home for his lunch and there would be frenzied activity. The idea was to get the three cars completed and into the transporter before he returned at two.' But Ron says: 'Alan always liked to cut corners, and often the cars would be loaded unfinished, to be completed at the circuit.'

March did well in the European Formula Three Championship, but as already mentioned the tyre regulations were different there. Whereas in Britain the crossply control tyre was mandatory, there was a free choice in European Formula Three and most drivers used radials. Robin Herd, by then the head of March, says: 'We had so little money that we had to make a straight choice between building a car for Europe, or building one for British Formula Three. We chose the former and created a car with low drag since we reasoned – correctly – that the softer European tyres would compensate for the lack of downforce. Had we gone for downforce we would have overloaded the tyres and the car wouldn't have worked in Europe, just as it didn't perform well on the hard Goodyear control tyres used in Britain.'

The results back Robin's statement. March did very well in Europe, but Ron says: 'I didn't make different cars, I just altered the amount of negative camber and fitted stiffer rollbars to the cars bound for Europe. It was noticeable, however, that the Italians preferred more rear braking, which is a legacy from karting, although ultimately it's not the quickest way to go. Dallara's fitting of equal-sized Brembo brakes all round gave them a head start in the Italian market. In the UK we ran a smaller caliper at the rear.

'Brakes are one reason why Anson never quite made the grade in Formula Three. They used double calipers at the front, which was not necessary for Formula Three. All they did was to add unsprung weight and cost.' Ansons were designed by Gary Anderson, who later became Jordan Grand Prix's chief designer, and was then already a man with a background of Formula One at Brabham and McLaren. The Anson came quite close to being competitive and one of them took the German Formula Three Championship, while it was well-received in North American SuperVee, where Ed Pimm won several races with one.

Ron says: 'Anson also used aluminium honeycomb for the monocoque with a carbon composite integral top. The engine block had the gearbox mounting ears cut off to allow wider aero tunnels and special gearbox side plates were cast to provide the mountings. Add to this the (balanced braking) front brake calipers and you have a very costly and time-consuming car to make.'

On the back of their first successful season in 1982, when two cars were sold, Anson received 22 orders for 1983, but they struggled to produce them. Also, the cars didn't make money and Gary himself says that the 1983 car wasn't much good. However, he thinks the 1984 car was a good one and when an offer was received for the company it was accepted, largely because Gary was tired of combining engineering and running a business. Great plans were announced, but the buyer had insufficient funds to carry them through and Anson soon went into liquidation.

Ron continues: 'When people come into Formula Three from Formula One they tend to look at lift/drag, a ratio between downforce and drag. A Formula One car has plenty of power so you can pile on a lot of downforce at many circuits. The drag becomes almost incidental. But with the power that Formula Three cars have, drag becomes critical and there are many circuits where you want to shed all the downforce. What becomes more important is pitch sensitivity.

'To put this as simply as possible, if you have a 40/60 weight distribution, you need the same ratio of downforce and to maintain a constant centre of pressure. If the centre of pressure moves back and forward under acceleration and braking, then you get a change in handling. If the centre of pressure moves to the front, the back becomes loose and you get oversteer, but if it moves to the rear you get understeer.'

By the end of 1981, British Formula Three had again virtually become Formula Ralt, but in 1980 the start of the year had been somewhat different. The 1980 season had ended with a three-way battle between March, Ralt and Argo. When Argo announced a new ground-effect car, the JM8, some drivers pinned their faith in it, but they soon wished that they hadn't. When *Autocar* published a photograph of it someone screwed up the caption, but the result was one of the most telling misprints ever. The picture of the JM8 was captioned: *The New Allegro*.

Another design which appeared in 1981 was the Tiga 381, which was run by Team Tiga along with two Ralts. The principals of the outfit were former Formula One drivers Howden Ganley and Tim Schenken. The car was not fully developed, but it did win championship points on one occasion.

Howden says: 'The car was a bit of a problem, but I'll never forget the sight of Ron trying to help Tim to sort it out. Can you imagine anyone else doing that for a rival?' It must have helped that Tim is an Aussie and Howden is a Kiwi.

Howden continues: 'In the late 1960s, I was working as a mechanic at McLaren and I wanted to buy a Brabham BT21. Like everyone, I had heard that Ron was absolutely strict about money. I told him that I wanted to buy a car, but I wouldn't have the money until late in the year because I would be in North America with the CanAm team. When I got back I went to the factory and said: "I suppose I've lost my place in the queue." Ron said: "No, there it is. You said you wanted one and I've made you one".'

While there were more Ralt RT3s than any other new car in 1981, some drivers stuck to proven chassis, such as the Argo JM6 and the older Marches, until the position became clearer. After all, Stefan Johansson had benefited by a big budget and by being run by an ultra-professional team, which put a skew in anyone's calculations. One driver who took the conservative route was Dave Scott, who bought the ex-Roberto Guerrero Argo on the grounds that it was a known quantity and a developed car. By mid-season he had swapped to a Ralt and had won his first Formula Three race. That raised a few eyebrows since previously he had won just one minor Formula Ford race.

By the end of the season, Dave had been invited to test for Lotus and he turned the chance into a test contract. Although he failed to convert that into a place in the race team, part of the reason was internal politics in the wake of the death of Colin Chapman.

Roberto Moreno also had a test contract with Lotus, partly as the result of winning a race at Silverstone mid-season. He says: 'I had come to Britain to do Formula Ford in 1979, and at the suggestion of Nelson Piquet I was looked after by 'Peewee' Siddle. I was always short of cash and the team I had hoped to go with demanded too much money.

'Peewee had a few words with Ron, who said that if we cleared out an old shed next to the factory, put in some lights and put something on the floor, we could use that. He charged us nothing, although I was supposed to sweep the factory after work and at weekends. I did it only once, but Ron never raised the matter.

'I started 1981 with no money, as usual, and no prospect of a drive. Then one of the drivers in a Dutch team contesting the British Formula Three series was injured in a road accident and I got half a season in the car. My third race was one of those where the British drivers on control tyres ran concurrently with European drivers on free rubber. I was entered in the British section when suddenly Ron appeared and said: "I've got a set of Bridgestones. D'you want them?" "Why?" I said. "So you can run in the international section."

'We fitted them and I set pole and won the race. Since I beat the top guys in Europe as well as the British runners, it helped me no end. Ron has always been there for me.'

Mike White, a South African, had landed the works March drive and he opened the season with a strong second to Jonathan Palmer's RT3. Palmer won the first three rounds, but White ran well and the Ralt-versus-March debate was by no means settled.

The fourth Formula Three race in Britain was the Donington Park round of the European Championship, so tyres were 'free', and there, running on Bridgestones, White ran away and hid from the opposition, and the top Ralt finisher was down in eighth place. But that was due in part to most of the British Championship regulars staying away because they couldn't get hold of the right tyres.

March, meanwhile, had discovered how much money was to be made in IndyCar racing, so gave up on Formula Three. The works effort was handed over to David Price Racing, but the factory had nothing to do with it. So, although Mike White finished a close second (by a few feet) to Palmer at Mallory Park and took a win at Thruxton in early May, the car made no progress and White's career slid down the tubes.

Jonathan Palmer won the British Championship from Thierry Tassin (who had started the season with an Argo) and Raul Boesel – all in Ralts. Mike White, who had held second in the series after the early races, was fourth with 38 points – but that was 41 points adrift of Boesel. Virtually every other points finish was taken by a Ralt driver.

At the end of the year March announced that it was no longer to make cars for Formula Three, Formula SuperVee or Formula Atlantic. So Ralt had seen off March in the junior formulae, but there was still the matter of Formula Two and March assembled a particularly strong three-car team in Corrado Fabi, Thierry Boutsen and Christian Danner.

Robin Herd was prominent within the March Formula Two team, but he no longer had an active rôle in design. Ron, meanwhile, had appointed Alan Howell as his Formula Two team manager, but he was still looking over everyone's shoulder. He was designing cars for Formula Two, Three, Atlantic and SuperVee, and on top of that portfolio he was running a factory and was very actively involved in the Formula Two team.

Ian Phillips, who covered Formula Two for *Autosport* at the time, recalls: 'Ron was everywhere and the only time I can recall him missing a race was one year at Vallelunga, when he caught an early plane home on the Sunday. Apparently a contractor was going to lay a new factory floor on the Monday and he had to be there to supervise it. It made you wonder why there was nobody at the factory he could trust to do a simple thing like that.'

Several people tell a story on the following lines: It was around 1988 and a 'pikey' arrived at Ralt and offered to lay tarmac in and around the factory. The car park was breaking up and there needed to be slopes to some of the factory doors and so on. Everyone except Ron knows that pikeys are not quite professional craftsmen, but there is Ron checking the work with a camber gauge and arguing over the depth of the tarmac. The pikey, a huge Mick, was heard to say: 'If that booger comes out again, I'll lump him one.'

Alan Howell says: 'It would be in the Formula 3000 days, and we were at Enna. The race had been delayed after two false starts. Our drivers were out on the track, we were booked on a plane, so with about 18 laps to go the entire team apart from two truckies left the circuit and drove to the airport.

'Before we left for the airport we did a deal with a Lola team – if one of our boys came into the pits in need of tyres, they'd change the wheels.' The reaction of the drivers, who finished a race only to find that their team had gone home, is not recorded.

In Formula Two the Honda engine had about 10 per cent more power than the BMW and Hart units, the best of which gave about 315bhp. But against that the RH6 was overweight by about 100lb and the Honda had a peaky power curve, so the equation was slightly more complex than the raw power figures suggest.

The Honda engine began the season with a power curve which was an improvement over 1980 due to John Judd's accidental discovery, but it was not until near the end of the season that it received new cylinder heads developed by Engine Developments.

Ralt seemed to be in a different class in the opening round of the Formula Two Championship as Thackwell and Lees dominated the International Trophy at Silverstone. Mike led until he had to slow when he started to run out of fuel. Then Geoff, who was running on marginal tyres in damp conditions, spun his lead away with less than two laps to go. Young Mike then cruised to an easy win – it was the day before his 20th birthday.

A Ralt 1-2 appeared certain a week later at Hockenheim, but Thackwell again began to run out of fuel, Lees spun, and victory went to Johansson's Toleman-Hart, which was effectively a Ralt RT2 anyway. Then Roberto Guerrero's Maurer-BMW won the third round at Thruxton, but as far as Ralt was concerned, the major event was a terrible accident to Thackwell during unofficial practice.

Ron says: 'We sent Mike out with the car set low to get a base line to set it up. We told him to take it easy, but being young and keen he got stuck in. The car bottomed at Church Corner, which is high-speed, and when it bottomed Mike lost grip and spun off the track.

'He was trapped in the car by his left foot, which was wedged between the clutch and brake pedals. His ankle was very badly sprained – not broken, as some reports had it – but that was not the main problem.

'Somebody calculated that he had survived an impact of 26g, so the whole of his insides, including his brain, had been given a severe shaking. Apart from a sprained ankle, Mike appeared fine on the outside, but he was damaged internally. I don't think that doctors understood as much about such injuries in those days as they do now. Mike was never the same man again.'

One way and another things were not going well at Ralt in Formula Two; it was not gelling as a team. Part of the reason was that it was a new outfit and Ron had not run a team for 10 years. Before the beginning of 1981 Ron's team had run in only four races, and three of those had been with just one car. They had started the season with Pirelli tyres, since Goodyear had withdrawn from Formula Two, and the Ralt wasn't working well on them.

Geoff Lees had his confidence undermined by a combination of poor handling and the slow pick-up and peaky rev-band of the Honda engine, and the fact that his team-mate had been badly injured did not help matters. Ron switched to Bridgestone tyres at Thruxton and that helped Lees because at least the car was now predictable, but Geoff could finish no higher than fifth at the Nürburgring, which was the last circuit on earth on which to have to cope with the characteristics of the Honda engine.

But try telling that to Honda; March-Hondas were doing well in Japan, yet

Ralt was not delivering the goods in Europe. So a March-Honda was parked in Honda's unit at Langley, just as a hint, but ready to be used if Ralt did not buck up. But this was Ralt's first full season of Formula Two, and with all the dramas associated with a debut season, it was only after Vallelunga that the team had the luxury of a day's testing. From then on the picture changed, for not only did the car go better, but Geoff Lees regained his confidence and he finished second in the next round at Mugello. Mike Thackwell made his comeback at Mugello, but it was too soon after his accident – as he will admit today – and it would be the best part of two years before he regained his old form.

Part of the reason for the performance improvement was the fact that Bridgestone had raised its game. Mr Hiroshi Yasukawa, motor sport head of Bridgestone, says: 'Our lack of experience of European tracks at this level was keeping us off the pace and it would not be unfair to say that a certain amount of tension and frustration was building up within the team.

'Our Tokyo Head Office Technical Centre, responsible for the development of the race tyres, had tried several options, but were struggling to make any significant improvements. Ron Tauranac decided it was time for drastic action. He offered us a piece of advice which has proved invaluable ever since. He said: "If in doubt, don't mess about with finicky changes, try something radical, something off-the-wall. You have to make a big step to find the way you should go."

'We had always been rather conservative in our approach and it was quite difficult to persuade our engineers to take a leap in the dark. However, thanks to Ron's dogged persistence and encouragement, leap they did. Fortunately, the changes we adopted proved to be in the right direction and we soon had the cars on the front of the grid – first winning races, and then winning the Championship.

'In subsequent years, breaking into other major categories, including Formula One, we have had several occasions on which to ponder and employ Ron's original advice. Without doubt, Bridgestone owes its current success in world motor sport at least in part to Ron Tauranac's encouragement and determination.' So said Mr Yasukawa shortly after Bridgestone had won its first Formula One race, the 1998 Australian Grand Prix.

Geoff Lees won the Formula Two race at Pau from Thierry Boutsen (March), then at Enna Boutsen took his second win of the year while both Ralts retired. It was Lees from Boutsen at Spa – with the bodged cylinder heads – and Lees from Fabi (March) at Donington. With two second places in the final two rounds Geoff secured the title from Thierry Boutsen.

According to Alan Howell, the team paid a visit to Japan and Geoff Lees declared that he wanted to live there. The following year he cut off all his roots in Britain and did just that. 'He's a god in Japan,' says Alan.

Although Honda had won the Championship in its first full season, it was not entirely happy. After all, it had provided Ralt with the most powerful engine in the field, but had won only four races to BMW's six and Hart's two.

John Wickham, who was Boutsen's race engineer in 1981, had excellent contacts in Japan, where he spent part of his time representing March, and a March-Honda had dominated the Japanese National Championship. Wickham was soon talking earnestly to both Honda and Bridgestone about an alternative to Ralt.

The upshot of Wickham's overtures was Team Spirit, which would build and run two Formula Two cars, powered by Honda with Bridgestone tyres and with sponsorship from Marlboro. The designer would be Gordon Coppuck, who had been responsible for most McLarens in the 1970s but who was then at March. Gordon was unhappy because March was not using him as a pure designer, but rather as a troubleshooter.

Part of Team Spirit's attraction to Honda was that it would be dedicated to winning the Formula Two Championship, with no distractions such as building customer cars, and there would be no compromises in the construction of the cars. The drivers would be Thierry Boutsen and Stefan Johansson.

Robin Herd says: 'Halfway through the 1981 season Honda offered March an enormous amount of money to use their engine the following year. Had I been sensible and ruthless I'd have accepted. As it was, John Wickham saw the ball bounce, grabbed it, and scored a touchdown.'

It was a blow to Ralt because it was a public vote of no confidence, but against that, the customers were flocking to buy cars for Formula Three, Atlantic and SuperVee. That was just as well because 1982 would be the worst year Ron would ever experience while running a team, even though his cars would win 10 championships.

21

Champions!

At the beginning of 1982 Ralt had the British Formula Three market well under control. The British and the European Championships continued to be divided by tyres, Avon crossply control tyres in Britain, a free choice in Europe. Thus it was that while a March 813 was regarded as hopeless in Britain, a March 813 given a little development and renamed a Euroracing 101 dominated the European series. Oscar Larrauri took the title easily from his team-mate Emanuele Pirro, who in turn was clear of the third man.

There were few Ralts in the European series, although when James Weaver entered the odd race in his Eddie Jordan Ralt RT3, running on Yokohama tyres, he was on the pace. In four outings, James took three wins and a second and finished in fourth place overall in the series.

The British Champion was Tommy Byrne, driving for Murray Taylor, and second was Enrique Mansilla, who was run by Dick Bennetts. Mansilla was an Argentine driver and 1982 was the year of the Falklands War. That undoubtedly affected his confidence and led to financial problems with his Argentine sponsors. In third place was Dave Scott, who was run by Glenn Waters' Intersport team. All were in Ralts.

Byrne was the only one of the trio to make the start of a Grand Prix. He was entered by Theodore in five races, qualified for two of them, but spun off in both. In contrast, for most of the late 1980s and throughout the 1990s a majority of the drivers on a Formula One grid would have driven a Ralt at some time in their career, yet Ron knew very few of them intimately.

For example, he has no special memories of Ayrton Senna, Jacques Villeneuve, David Coulthard, Gerhard Berger or Damon Hill, or any of the dozens of others, yet in 1997, half the drivers engaged in the F1 World Championship had driven a Ralt at a crucial stage in their careers. The same went for drivers in CART Champ Car racing, starting with Michael Andretti and Al Unser Jnr.

Part of the reason was that, during most of the 1980s, Ron was looking after his Formula Two/Formula 3000 team. Another was his natural reticence. Some heads of companies have made it a policy to go to junior formulae races in order to nurture relationships. For instance, Adrian Reynard used to do so on the grounds that the guy who is racing a Reynard Formula Ford car today may be a customer for a Formula 3000 car the day after tomorrow. It worked for Adrian, but then he is an outgoing bloke, he ran his factory on completely different lines to Ron, and in Rick Gorne he had a very active partner.

Another reason why Ron did not form relationships with drivers was the sheer number of his customers. In 1982, Ralts won a total of six Formula Three series, three Atlantic Championships plus North American SuperVee. The latter was second only to IndyCar in North American single-seater racing and the top 12 drivers in the series drove Ralt RT5s.

The only time in history that a manufacturer had previously won 10 championships in a single season had been MRD in 1967, although on that occasion the championships included the Formula One titles for both drivers and constructors.

The figure of 10 championships in a year would be beaten by Reynard, but it would be bolstered by the Ford formulae and one-make categories. The only constructors to have won 10 international class championships in one year are still Brabham and Ralt.

With 82 cars made in 1982 business was booming for Ralt, but not everything was wonderful because in Formula Two Ron suffered the worst season of his career. Although the cars for the junior formulae received only minor revisions, mainly to enable them to be manufactured more accurately, the RH6/82 Formula Two car was extensively revised and ran on Bridgestone tyres.

The works drivers were Jonathan Palmer and Kenny Acheson and it was not a united team. Kenny was not Ron's choice, but had come at the recommendation of Alf Briggs, a former motorcycle racer, whose contacts with Honda ran long and deep. After all, Kenny had won three Formula Ford titles in one year (1978) and been one of the strongest runners in Formula Three. Kenny says: '1982 was the worst season of my career. It was nobody's fault, we just didn't gel.' And that's it.

Jonathan Palmer says: 'Every driver has to assert his authority over his team-mate, even if they remain friends away from the track, and I certainly tried to get the upper hand. Anyway, Ralt was not a place for a sensitive driver, and Kenny was perhaps too sensitive. You couldn't wish to meet a nicer guy, but Ralt was not the right environment for him.

'You had to stand your ground; Ralt wasn't a team for shrinking violets. If Ron thought you were talking crap, he'd tell you so. You had to be prepared to argue your corner, and when the inevitable dispute occurred you had to be confident in your opinion or else you'd crumble. If you went through a logical process, you would be respected. There is no doubt that working with Ron toughened a driver.'

There was also the fact that Kenny had had only one race since the previous May when he crashed and broke his leg in the Formula Two race at Pau. Ron says: 'We saw Kenny at the last race of 1981 and he convinced us that he had recovered, but I don't think that he had.'

Kenny was not particularly adept at feedback, while Jonathan was the other way, he was very precise. That precision appealed to Dick Bennetts, who jokes against himself that he has a reputation for very small adjustments whereas Ron has tended to go for the big jump. Of course, the difference is that Dick was teasing advantages from a customer car whereas Ron was in charge of design.

As well as March-BMW, which had a new car designed by Ralph Bellamy,

Ralt faced opposition in Formula Two from Spirit-Honda, Maurer-BMW and BMW-powered cars from Minardi and AGS, and there were also Ralts, Tolemans and Lolas in the field.

Everyone expected a Honda walkover, so much so that BMW almost withdrew. The decisive element in BMW staying in the game was again that close friendship between Robin Herd and Paul Rosche.

In fact, the Honda engine had been flattered by the 1981 Ralt package because while it was powerful, it was powerful over too narrow a rev-range. There was also a tyre war going on. Michelin supplied favoured BMW teams, Bridgestones were used by Ralt and Spirit, while others used M & H, Pirelli and Dunlop. Jonathan Palmer is convinced that one of the deciding factors of the season was the choice of tyres. He says: 'I drove the RH6 in testing at Silverstone before the season and I thought it was fantastic – and don't forget I was the Williams test driver at the time.

'Bridgestone was part of the Anglo-Japanese package, as it was with Spirit. Whereas Spirit used the Bridgestone crossplies, Ralt was working with Bridgestone and we were using the radials, which had a very short life. Well before the end of the year I was urging Ron that we had to change to Michelin.'

Stefan Bellof won the first two rounds of the Championship for Maurer, and that rocked everyone because nobody then knew what a superb talent Stefan was. Unfortunately, however, there have been many accusations that Maurer was cheating. One senior man at March was of the opinion that Maurer was running with oversized engines and he claimed that the numbers on the engine blocks proved it.

Ron knows, however, that Maurer had a system for holding the suspension below the legal level. He says: 'It was a form of locking pin. At speed, ground effect caused the car to go down on its springs and this device locked it in that position, giving it a lower ride height than was legal. That meant it benefited from ground effect, even in the slower corners.

'To return the car to a legal ride height, because it might be examined at the end of a race, the driver operated a Bowden cable. That released the locking pins and the car rose on its springs. It came to light when one of the Maurers stopped on the Mugello circuit and one of the engineers sprinted to it. With no downforce being generated, the locking pin was wedged in place and the car had an illegal ride height. The man from Maurer had to bounce up and down on the chassis so that he could release the locking pins.' After a couple of wins, Willi Maurer believed that he'd cracked Formula Two. But he interfered with the team, which was based at the old Chevron works in Bolton, and everything fell apart.

Meanwhile Ralt struggled. Ron says: 'I was using aluminium honeycomb for the first time and I had taken on John Baldwin to design the Formula Two car. Honeycomb was something we both had to learn about, and we'd been able to visit the Fittipaldi team and learn from Dr Harvey Postlethwaite.

'John was on three months' trial either way, and just before the three months were up he announced that he'd accepted a job with Spirit. That put us back because I was busy working on the customer cars, running the factory and so on.

'John had enjoyed the run of our factory, had access to all our drawing office information and had spent three months researching and laying out our Formula Two car. That knowledge could have done Spirit no harm at all, while his leaving Ralt set us back.'

The Ralt RH6 was finished in a rush, it needed testing – which it didn't get – and the fact that both drivers crashed heavily in the first race did not help matters because the races came thick and fast. Also, there is no doubt that Michelin was making the better tyre. Both Ralt-Honda and Spirit-Honda had the mortification of seeing Satoru Nakajima in a March-Honda finish second to Stefan Bellof's Maurer in the first race at Silverstone. The only works Ralt or Spirit to be classified as a finisher was Jonathan Palmer, down in 15th place – and he was a non-runner at the end. Ron says: 'Nakajima used his knowledge of Bridgestone tyres. They made their 'wets' with different depths of tread and Nakajima had a great deal of experience of wet-weather racing in Japan.'

Thierry Boutsen (Spirit) finished second to Bellof (Maurer) in the second round at Hockenheim and Kenny Acheson was second at Thruxton, but that was to be one of only two podium finishes achieved by the Ralt team that year. The same number of podium finishes were earned by Mike Thackwell, who drove a private March in just half a dozen races.

By the end of the year, however, Ralt had caught up. The team had managed to get in some testing and, in particular, had refined its spring rates. Both Acheson and Palmer were top-six qualifiers for the last race. There was nothing to choose between them in performance, but it was a long way from the Honda steamroller which had nearly caused BMW to give up.

March, meanwhile, operated as a team and got the package right, and Corrado Fabi finally won the Formula Two title – March's fifth – by a single point. Fabi's team-mate, Johnny Cecotto, won as many points, but he had to discard one of them.

At the last race, which took place at Misano, Thierry Boutsen, who had won three of the earlier rounds, could still have taken the title for Spirit, but the decision of the organizers to delay the start laid the foundation for an Italian to win both the race and the title.

Bridgestone made a durable crossply slick as well as radial slicks and 'wet' tyres, but the radial slick had a short life. Therefore, if a race started in wet conditions and the track subsequently dried, the Bridgestone users would then be committed to their short-lived slick radials because the radials and crossplies had different diameters, so there was no way that a car could be switched from one size to another in under 10 minutes.

It was raining at Misano when the race was due to start and, with the benefit of local knowledge, the organizers decided to delay the start. Boutsen went into the lead on his radial Bridgestone wets, but then the rain stopped, the track dried and he had to change to the radial slicks, which were useless after 20 laps. So Corrado Fabi and March won the race – and the title – after a little help from the Misano organizers.

Things did not seem to bode well for Ralt as far as Honda was concerned, especially when it became clear that Honda would be sticking with Spirit for a toe-in-the-water exploratory foray into Formula One. In fact, Mr Kawamoto had suggested a Formula One project to Ron, who had responded in characteristic fashion by considering the problem and expressing doubt about his ability to do it alongside his production car responsibilities. Most times when a company president holds a Formula One deal in his hand, his arm is ripped off at the socket, but Ron was his usual self and began by considering the objections, and Mr Kawamoto had assumed that he was not interested.

Actually, Ron was interested in Formula One, but he did not want to say 'Yes' first and then consider the problems. So the contract to take Honda into Formula One went instead to Spirit. It was a low-key data acquisition project, which did not last long. Williams subsequently got the proper deal, and the rest is history.

In fact, when Mr Kawamoto had asked Ron which of the current Formula One teams Honda should go with, he had had no hesitation. 'Williams,' he said. Also, when Mr Kawamoto realized that he had not assessed the earlier situation correctly, it was to Ron that he turned to design a Honda IndyCar, which was drawn but not built. Oddly, this phantom car would play a big part in the long-term future of the Honda-Tauranac relationship.

Ralt was to win nine championships in 1983, but two of them stood out. One was the British Formula Three series, the other was the European Formula Two Championship. The early rounds of the British Formula Three series were dominated by Ayrton Senna (Ralt RT3), run by Dick Bennetts, with Martin Brundle in an Eddie Jordan Ralt, who finished second to Senna in eight of the first nine rounds. It seemed as though Martin would be the eternal bridesmaid, but then, at Silverstone in June, there was a joint European/British Championship race. Senna and Brundle both opted to run in the European section and Brundle won it. In fact he not only won the race, but he rattled Senna into making an error which caused him to crash. From that point on, Brundle grew in confidence and seemed to be the driver with the tougher mental attitude.

Martin won three of their next four encounters, all in the British series, and in a late-season charge he narrowed the gap on Senna, a gap which had once stood at 22 points. As the two men went into the last round at Thruxton, Martin was one point ahead in the series, but if he finished in the points he would have to drop his lowest points finish, which would be a third place. Senna did not have to shed any points because he had finished races less often than Martin, largely because he crashed more often. This is something which is usually overlooked by the keepers of the Senna legend.

Nobody who followed the season closely could quite believe the news that spread along the grapevine prior to the final race at Thruxton. Ron Tauranac had been playing around with some new tweaks and had given the 1984 aerodynamic package to Dick Bennetts for Senna to use and the 1984 suspension revisions to Eddie Jordan for Brundle. Reports from test sessions suggested that Ron had virtually given the title to Ayrton.

Ron says: 'I just didn't think of it that way. I had this arrangement with Dick so he got the development parts. It never occurred to me to think in terms of the Championship.' Dick Bennetts says: 'What people did not realize is that although Jordan and we were both running Novamotor Toyota engines, Jordan's were rebuilt in Italy whereas ours were rebuilt in Britain. Further, Jordan had done a deal whereby he had new engine tweaks ahead of us.

'Before the last race, Ayrton took his engine to Italy and he stayed there while it was rebuilt. We went testing at Snetterton and Brundle was there at the same time. We ran both with and without the new sidepods and Ayrton was quicker than Martin whatever bodywork we were running. The crucial difference at the last round was the engine. At last we had an engine which was very nearly as good as the one Brundle had.'

Eddie Jordan says: 'That's a wonderful story, I hope you don't believe it! As soon as we heard that Dickie was going to receive the prototype '84 floorpan and underbody we knew we were sunk. Ron always tried to play things fair and we got things to try as well. But Dickie spent a lot of time at the factory and, if he got special favours, that was part of his dividend.'

Ralts won every single round of the British series and all but one of the European Championship – the prestigious Monaco race fell to Michel Ferté's Martini. In all of the other junior categories, the position was much the same, although the North American SuperVee Champion, Ed Pimm, also used an Anson SA4 in his campaign, and won two races with it.

Ron was making good money. The 83 cars he built in 1983 turned a handsome profit (and every racing car needs a lot of spares). His personal needs have always been modest, and remember that his daughter, Julie, had once assumed that her father was poor because he drove such cheap cars.

Ron is not naive in financial matters, but he's not flash. He preferred to reinvest much of his profit in machine tools. That ensured that he stayed ahead of rivals by improving production standards rather than by attempting to make quantum leaps in design.

In 1983, Steve Hollman, later to become one of the principals of Bowman Race Cars, joined Ralt. Steve recalls: 'My official title was Office Manager, which is typical Tauranac understatement. Every customer dealt with me and I acted as Ron's PA as well. There had been a time when teams came to the factory to build their cars, but that had stopped before I arrived. We did take on mechanics from the teams over the build season, but they were working for us, not for their teams. Ron always maintained that the last people who should build racing cars are racing mechanics because they are too pernickety and take too long.

'You would see the team owners at the factory around Christmas, but you never saw any drivers except for the Ralt Formula Two team. I joined Ralt the year Senna won the Formula Three Championship, but we never saw him. We were a production company which happened to make racing cars. Ron would go away with the Formula Two team, but to find out what had gone on I had to wait until *Autosport* came out on the Thursday.

'From early January until early April life was hectic. We built at least a car a day and then there was a hiatus and we'd paint fresh lines on the car park. Then we'd be making spares, we made an awful lot of spares, and later in the year we'd make Formula Atlantic cars for racing Down Under.'

Ron says: 'It was about that time that I employed a factory manager who did me a lot of harm, though I didn't find out about it until much later. He antagonized some of our best people so they left. We did a lot of painting during the summer because this guy insisted on maintaining everyone on 10 hours overtime each week whether we needed the work or not. He even turned away John Thompson, who then went away and established his own company.'

John Thompson is a legend in the motor racing industry – he is the fabricator's fabricator. John is the man who built a McLaren from four paint marks on the factory floor where Bruce McLaren reckoned the wheels should go. John is the man who created a monocoque for Ferrari and drove to Italy with it on his roof rack. He used the trip as an excuse to give his wife and kids a continental holiday. If John Thompson asked you for a job, you didn't ask for references.

Steve Hollman recalls: 'We used to call the place the Rat Factory since you had a building here and a building there, like a maze for laboratory rats. Ron would run between them – he never walked if he could run and he was everywhere.

'Ron could be infuriating. One day I needed to speak to him on something I thought was important and it took me all morning to get his attention. Eventually I managed to pin him down, but as I was talking his gaze was going over my shoulder and concentrating on a crack in a window pane.

'Then he went outside and examined the window, which was metal-framed. He came back in and said: "There's a design fault in that window." He then listened to what I had to say, but it was typical of him that he could pursue the main thread of the plot while not missing any detail.

'One day he went in the loo and saw a guy washing his hands. He said: "No, no, no, that's not the way to wash your hands. This is the way you wash your hands." And he showed the guy how to do it. The infuriating thing is that he was probably right.

'We used to hang our oil tanks on the outside of the engine/transmission and then, I think it was in 1985, we were looking at having an integrated oil tank, just like Lola and Reynard had. Ron phoned Mike Blanchet at Lola and Mike sent him down one of their units – can you imagine them doing it for anyone else?

'Ron said: "How much will it cost to make?" I said that it would be around £700, but other people were selling it at around £3,000. He said: "Sell it at £700, don't put on a margin." Ron wanted it in the cars for the sake of the customer and for the sake of having the best cars in the field, and that meant more to him than making a quick profit.'

Ron admires the way how, in the 1990s, Dallara has re-invested in plant and machinery in order to make a consistent product. It makes it so much harder for anyone except for an eccentric millionaire with a craving to win Formula Three races to get a look in.

Ron's standards were different to other people's. Ralph Bellamy says: 'It is my opinion – and I have told him so – that Ron is the only constructor to have genuinely brought industrial production engineering techniques to the manufacture of racing cars. In the late 1980s I had a small involvement with a Ralt Formula Three car and I asked Ron where the centreline of the chassis was. He said: "That rivet in the front bulkhead is on the centreline." I said: "I don't doubt that it's close, but I need to be exact." He replied that it was exactly the centreline. Then he explained how the chassis was made by accurately punching all the rivet holes in the flat sheet before it was folded. I was absolutely amazed, I could hardly believe that it could be done, but Ron had figured out how to do it, and all Ralt cars were made that way.'

Ralt had the production car market tied up, but it had unsettled his business in Formula Two. Thackwell's performances in a private March convinced Ron that he was fit enough to return to Ralt alongside Jonathan Palmer. Not only had Kenny Acheson not enjoyed his season with Ralt, but he wanted to move up to Formula One. In 1983, Kenny would struggle to qualify in a RAM-DFV for seven Grands Prix, and make the grid only once.

Team Spirit moved into Formula One on a low-key basis and its 1981 Formula Two cars were sold to privateers who fitted BMW engines. The two main teams in a formula in which people were rapidly losing interest were still

March and Ralt. Costs were rising and it was increasingly difficult to attract sponsors to a category which received little media coverage. Meanwhile, Formula One had become an established fixture on television and was attracting most of the available money.

In Formula Two, Ralt switched to Michelin tyres for 1983, but due to communication problems did not get the best from them until mid-season. Ron says: 'March had been with Michelin for some time and they were working with engineers from France. We had someone from the British end, a nice bloke but not an engineer. We simply didn't have the technical input.'

That would change mid-season when there were rumours about a switch to Bridgestone, partly as a result of Honda breathing down Ralt's neck. That caused Michelin to raise its game – Michelin makes its money by selling tyres to motor manufacturers, not by supplying teams like Ralt, and Honda is a major motor manufacturer.

Thackwell was second to Beppe Gabbiani's March in the first two races and Palmer won the third, and in mid-season Mike Thackwell also won a race. Jonathan Palmer says: 'I think that Ron had a soft spot for Mike; Mike respected both Ron and Alan Howell, and although he and I got along well, I didn't always understand him.

'Most of the time we were a good team, but I do remember the time when Mike and I were travelling with Ron in a hired Fiat in Italy. Ron was in a bad mood and was driving in his normal aggressive style. Neither Mike nor I dared tell him that the car had a fifth gear so we had two hours of valve bounce down an autostrada.'

Alan Howell recalls the time, it would have been at Enna in 1981, when the Ralt team had hired three vehicles, two little Fiat 127s and a minibus. Alan says: 'Ron had the key to the minibus so the entire team packed into the two Fiats; you wouldn't have believed so many people could have got into so small a space. One guy was late off the mark and he was Ron's passenger.'

After seven rounds from 12, Gabbiani led the Championship with 36 points to Palmer's 30, but he scored only another 3 points in the remaining five rounds. Mike Earle, who was running the works March team – and Gabbiani – under the Onyx banner, says: 'About mid-season the car started to go backwards because of chassis flexing. We sent our cars back to the factory and they added carbonfibre cockpit surrounds. That cost us a bomb, but our drivers could feel no difference and since no more ideas were coming out of the factory we faded away.'

What was needed was not a patch job with carbonfibre, but for the cars to receive new monocoques. They had conventional sheet aluminium tubs, but their longevity was compromised by shaping the tub to fit the aerodynamic package.

In common with AGS and Maurer, Ralt was using dual springing. The rules said that cars had to have 4cm of ground clearance – Formula Two still allowed ground-effect tunnels and the ride height rule was to lessen their effectiveness. The dual-spring system had a very soft spring on top of a stiff spring. In the paddock it allowed a car to pass the ground clearance test, but on the circuit, downforce compressed the soft top spring so it was virtually solid. This brought the ground clearance down to about 1.5cm and the lower, stiffer, springs then operated as normal. The Ralt's soft springs were enclosed in adjustable sliding canisters to control the length at which they became solid.

After the race at Jarama, March slapped in a protest against Ralt's lowering device, which they did not understand. The protest was upheld as Ron didn't wish to explain the system to the stewards in front of the March rep, but Ralt's subsequent appeal was also upheld. It was merely coincidence that March was seriously off the pace for the first time in 1983.

Jonathan Palmer recalls: 'On the day before practice at Donington I learned that we could not run our dual springs because of the Jarama decision. The news came at noon and it was devastating because I had come to understand our system and was able to exploit it. By midnight, though, I had worked out an alternative strategy, and luckily for me Ron was always open to radical changes.

'Ron and I had developed a very good working relationship and he trusted me on things like settings. Quite often I would fax him what settings I thought we should start practice with and he would go along with that.

'What we did was to build up the bump stops and run with relatively soft springs. We set it up in the garage and reached the settings by first Ron deciding what ground clearance we should have. Then we duplicated the downforce we expected to generate at 130mph by having members of the team stand on the car. It was literally a case of two blokes on the front and three on the back. It was rough and ready, but it worked, and I set pole by the biggest margin in my career – 1.4 seconds over Mike Thackwell.'

It was the first time in the season that Ralt had taken the top two places on the grid. Then Ron overheard them discussing how they would race each other to the flag if, with 20 laps left, they had disposed of the opposition. At that point Ron laid down the law and he insisted that Jonathan should be helped to take the title since it was his second year and that was the custom. Mike could win it next year. Mike agreed.

Jonathan says: 'The fact is that I was quicker and there was no need for team orders. I was so much quicker at Donington in any case and that was a most satisfying win. In fact that season with Ralt was the most rewarding of my career.'

Jonathan's win at Donington moved him ahead in the series, and then he won the final four races. It was the first time in the history of Formula Two that a driver had won five races in succession; not even Jack Brabham had managed that in his triumphal 1966 season with the Brabham-Honda.

He had worked hard for his advantage and had honed his car to perfection. Ron suggested that he should stay on for a third year, but Jonathan was set on a drive in Formula One. Mike Thackwell was runner-up in the Championship and he did stay on for 1984; he was designated Champion-elect and he duly secured the title with assistance from his team-mate, Roberto Moreno.

More than 15 years on, and long after he had retired from motor racing, it was clear that Mike Thackwell retained strong memories of his time with Ron and he was generous with his recollections. 'Ron was a tenacious problem-solver, innovative and always critically invective. He was genuinely inquisitive, and he would work with meticulous expediency until the one-minute board to instigate success.'

Thackwell also recalls Ron's surprising tolerance. 'What Championship-leading boss would let his top driver risk his neck racing off-road motorbikes every other weekend? What team chief would allow his mechanic (Ian Dyer, my mechanic in 1984) to mark each victory by sticking to the car's bodywork aeroplane silhouettes cut from Fablon? What team boss would deliberately prevent his drivers from using qualifying tyres to avoid them lapping too fast and then during the race ask them not to win by too much for fear of dominating the racing? That was Tauranac.

'I had the good fortune to drive to victory many of his cars. Three seasons from 1983 to 1985 yielded over 20 F2/F3000 victories, bringing the team first and second places in the Championship in both '83 and '84, and second and fourth in '85. Our partnership with Tauranac was not as public as the one Ron had with Sir Jack Brabham in Formula One, but it can be shown race-for-race to have been extremely successful.

'Despite the superlatives or criticisms about Tauranac's work, I prefer to recount what's always been of more value to me. If a measure of a true friend is one who never keeps reminding you of what they've done for you; if another measure is that they never hold grudges or make one feel obliged; if it is someone who asks few favours but will give freely of their time when asked ... in my own personal experience, this was Ron Tauranac, and the foundation of his success.'

Ralt had won six successive races in Formula Two in 1983, which nobody had done since Brabham in 1966, and was destined to dominate again in 1984. Many people assumed that Ralt's superiority was due entirely to horsepower, but Ron had stumbled upon a happy accident in the wind-tunnel. He says: 'You have to be an expert aerodynamicist to use small-scale wind-tunnel models. In most cases wind-tunnel work is best used as just a guide. Sometimes, however, you can stumble on things by accident, as Lotus did when they first discovered ground effect, and as we did when we were preparing our 1983 cars.

'We ran our models with the venturi tunnel in each sidepod adjustable for height and there was a misunderstanding between the model maker and me. I thought we'd started testing with the tunnels at the lowest setting, but we were actually at the middle setting. I then took the tunnels up to what I thought was the middle setting, but which was actually a setting which I would not otherwise have tried.

'We got a big gain from that, which was entirely unexpected because the conventional thinking was to run everything close to the ground. It didn't work in Formula Atlantic, however. Most Atlantic drivers are amateurs, who generally prefer to run on softer springs, and their cars already run higher as a result of that.

'In Formula Two our chief advantage over March was not the engine, it was the aerodynamic package. You'd see the effect on high-speed corners, like Stowe at Silverstone. Our drivers might take a corner flat, but you'd see March drivers change down.'

Joining Mike Thackwell in the Formula Two team for 1984 was Roberto Moreno, who recalls: 'I had decided that if I was going to save my career I had to do a full season of Formula Three and do it properly. I arranged to borrow money from two friends and I was due to be run by Dick Bennetts. We went to a test session at Thruxton and Ron came over and gave me a hard time. It went like this:

'Ron: "Why are you doing Formula Three when you should be doing Formula Two with me?"

'Me: "Why didn't you ask me?"

Tim Schenken setting off for another test lap in the F1 Trojan. Ron is alongside Champion's John Glover, with Trojan boss Peter Agg partly hidden behind him.

The Theodore TR1, another of Ron's F1 commissions during his early 'Ralt' years. Two cars were built, and Keke Rosberg took the second of them to victory in the International Trophy race at Silverstone in 1978.

Many a top driver has competed in cars designed by Ron Tauranac. Here is Nelson Piquet in a Toyota-powered Ralt RT1 during a BP Formula Three Championship race in 1978.

Geoff Lees was the first driver to win the Formula Two European Championship for Ron in 1981. Here his Ralt-Honda is heading for victory at Donington.

A successful team. From the left behind Mike Thackwell's Ralt-Honda are Thackwell, Yoshio Nakamura, Geoff Lees, Ron, Nobuhiko Kawamoto, Katsumi Ichida and Bruce Carey.

Jonathan Palmer's Ralt-Honda RH6 laid bare during a break in early-season testing.

Mike Thackwell out in front on a wet Pau circuit in 1983 with the Ralt-Honda, with Beppe Gabbiani leading the pursuit in his March-BMW.

Another successful partnership. Ron with his F2 drivers Roberto Moreno and Mike Thackwell during the 1984 season, which once again the team dominated.

Ralts holding the first four places at Macau in 1985, with Mauricio Gugelmin in the lead in his VW-powered RT30, followed by Emanuele Pirro, Jan Lammers and Mike Thackwell in the third of the Marlboro team cars.

Another Ralt driver on his way up. This is Ayrton Senna in his Toyota-powered RT3 in 1987.

A Brabham in a Ralt, but this time it is Gary, the second of Jack's three sons, who raced an RT32 into second place behind Damon Hill's similar car in the Grand Prix-supporting F3 race at Silverstone in 1988.

The evidence. Christian Fittipaldi went testing at Oulton Park in 1990 with his Ralt's rear wing end plates and flap coated with oil so as to check the airflow, which was found to be spot-on.

Rubens Barrichello won the 1991 British Formula Three Championship with this Ralt-Honda RT35. A little over a year later he would be in Formula One.

The two ends of the Ralt production range in 1991. On the left the RT23 F3000 car and on the right the RT35 F3 model.

A decade of difference. In the foreground, Ayrton Senna's Ralt from 1983, and behind it the 1993 Dallara from the company which in recent years has maintained the high standards of racing car design and production established so long ago by Ron Tauranac.

Ron comparing notes with Hiroshi Yasukawa, 'Mr Bridgestone', with whom he has enjoyed a long and fruitful relationship.

Italians are not the only people who speak with their hands! Ron in animated conversation with Jonathan Palmer while Mr Yasukawa listens in.

Time to celebrate. Ron with Honda's Yoshio Nakamura and Nobuhiko Kawamoto raise their glasses, while Mike Thackwell hangs on to the silverware.

'Ron: "Didn't I?"
'Me: "No."
'Ron: "Anyway, why don't you come and do Formula Two?"
'Ron squared it with Dick Bennetts and, instead of having to borrow money, I got paid for the drive. There were team orders, but I never accepted them – I'm in racing to win. They were forced on me in the background.
'Take the first race at Silverstone. Mike Thackwell set pole and I put on a set of new tyres simply to scrub them in for the race. I was supposed to do one flying lap, but I did two and took pole from Mike. When I arrived at the pits, the doors were shut and I was given the biggest bollocking of my life. The fact that I had done two laps rather than one was more important to Ron than the fact that I had set pole.' Ron comments: 'Mike also had his laps restricted, and he could have gone faster. We only wanted pole, we didn't want to destroy the formula.'

The 1984 season would mark the end of an era for Ralt. It would be the last year when it did not face a strong competitor in Formula Three and it would be the last year of Formula Two, which was dying on its feet.

Palmer's five-in-a-row (and Ralt's six-in-a-row) did not help Formula Two. When Bruno Giacomelli won eight races in a works March-BMW in 1978, it did not damage Formula Two, it caused people to queue up to buy Marches. Unfortunately, you could not buy a Ralt-Honda, and for 1984 BMW withdrew factory support from the category. But that still does not quite explain the margin of Ralt's superiority in 1984. There was also an aerodynamic advantage and a story did the rounds at the time suggesting that, since Honda had cemented its connection with Williams, Ralt was able to use the Williams windtunnel.

Ron says: 'Patrick Head had worked for me, and I had worked for Frank, so we knew each other. We had a commercial arrangement, however, and I would use their tunnel when there was a change of regulations, such as when we went from ground-effect tunnels to flat bottoms. I had one-day sessions on three occasions, which were paid for at the going commercial rate.' Ron had also learned a lot about building a honeycomb monocoque during the previous season, and the chassis of the RF6/84 was considerably stiffer and more refined than the 1983 car.

That last year of Formula Two had shades of 1966, when the Brabham-Hondas had dominated the category. There had to be team orders or it would have wrecked the Championship. Mike Thackwell was duly designated to win the series and Roberto Moreno would get the star treatment in 1985, if he stayed with the team.

Although Roberto received that tongue-lashing at Silverstone after he had stayed out for an extra lap in practice, he was still designated to win the race. Unfortunately, though, he got carried away when, in the closing laps, Mike tried to make it look like a real race to the finish. Roberto spun on the last bend of the International Trophy and so Mike won.

At the second race Roberto received his win (Mike was right on his tail) and then Mike stamped his authority on the series. From 11 races he scored seven wins, six poles and nine fastest laps. Roberto won twice for Ralt while the other two races were taken by March and AGS.

Roberto recalls: 'Mike was usually quicker than me in the early part of the season. Then, at Misano, three races from the end, I was quicker than Mike. Ron took me aside and said that Mike had to win so that he would clinch the Championship, and once we had done that, Ralt could switch from Michelin to Bridgestone in preparation for Formula 3000. I have never been so hurt in my life. I stood there and cried like a baby.'

On past form, Roberto would have stayed on for a second year, but he says: 'In Formula 3000 Ralt would not enjoy the same level of superiority. I tested for Toleman in Formula One, landed a drive, and then Toleman lost their tyre contract. It looked like Toleman was out of racing, so I accepted a drive in America.'

As usual, Ralts dominated the junior categories in 1984. Johnny Dumfries led yet another Ralt Formula Three steamroller in Britain, trailed by the quiet Canadian, Allen Berg, who like Johnny enjoyed a brief Formula One career. Dumfries should also have won the European series, which was finally awarded to Ivan Capelli, who drove a Martini-Alfa Romeo. Capelli's team had been caught red-handed with an ingenious way of admitting more air to the engine than the rules permitted. Everyone expected that the authorities would penalize the Italian's team, but they didn't. Why not was to remain a mystery because it had seemed to be an open-and-shut case for disqualification.

Johnny was run by David Price Racing, and Dave says: 'We were the last team to switch to Ralt because March had made us such a good offer to run their works car in 1981. I ran Martin Brundle in a Ralt in 1982, and Calvin Fish in '83, but I never got close to Ron. I think it was because he always gets on best with people like Dick Bennetts and Glenn Waters, who are from the engineering side of motor racing, whereas I am one of the entrepreneurs. And he likes winners.

'Ron changed his attitude to me a little in 1984. I had a fabrication business and I made my own version of Ralt monocoques incorporating changes and using different materials. Ron never complained about that, but some makers would have. The 1984 RT3 had pushrod front suspension, which was tricky to set up, but it also had a new aerodynamic package. After back-to-back tests we decided to go with our version of the '83 chassis with its simple rocker-arm suspension in conjunction with the '84 aerodynamics. Johnny flew right from the start of the season and Ron began to warm to us. We were doing things he approved of. We were applying a bit of engineering to the problem but, above all, we were winning.'

When Formula Two ended at the end of 1984 – except in Japan, where the category was retained for another year – Formula 3000 became its logical successor for 1985. Apart from providing a sensible stepping-stone towards Formula One, Formula 3000 was a neat way of making use of the many Cosworth DFV engines which had been made redundant in Formula One by the move to turbocharging. The engines were to be restricted to 9,000rpm to keep down costs, and the new formula presented a fascinating problem to designers and to customers.

Going from 2 to 3 litres posed such questions as whether you uprated a Formula Two machine or used a Formula One car. That was a technical problem, but Ron also faced a commercial threat, which was the appearance in Formula Three of Reynard Racing Cars. This was a serious matter because the Tauranac and Reynard attitudes to the business of selling production racing cars was entirely different.

In some respects, Adrian Reynard was like Ron in that he had built his first racing car so he could go racing, and from being a special builder he had turned into a constructor. That was the traditional route – Cooper, Lotus and Lola had all started that way – but Adrian may very well be the last mainstream constructor to emerge from that tradition. You need more than ingenuity and a set of welding equipment to set up a business today, but Reynard had little more than that when he started a company called Sabre Automotive with Bill Stone in 1973.

Subsequently, Adrian had his ups and downs, but his fortunes turned when he was able to persuade his friend and former racer (and customer) Rick Gorne to join him in business. Rick could sell you your own left leg. Further, when Reynard attempted to move up from the Ford formulae to Formula Three, Rick had a unique selling point with which to impress the punters – it was a carbonfibre monocoque, which was a first in Formula Three.

22

Changing times

Reynard sold 24 Formula Three cars in 1985, which was remarkable for a debut car. In Britain, however, all the established teams stayed with Ron. They knew where they were with him. Reynard only sold cars to teams from the Ford formulae which were making the transition to Formula Three.

New regulations called for flat bottoms and Ron took the opportunity to build an entirely new car, the RT30. The rear springs were mounted on top of the gearbox, pushrod front suspension replaced the earlier rocker-arm system, and there was some use of aluminium honeycomb in the monocoque. The most surprising thing, however, was the asymmetrical body with just one radiator, mounted in a sidepod, on the left-hand side. On the right side was simply a platform with the mandatory side protection panel.

Glenn Waters, head of Intersport, got together with the other team managers and they offered a conversion, which Intersport made, to update Ralt RT3s to satisfy the new rules. Without such a kit, the teams' existing cars could not easily find buyers. In all, 48 update kits were sold, some going as far as Japan, but in Britain these were mainly sold to drivers in Class B, for cars a year old.

For 1985 Reynard had Russell Spence in a car run by PMC Motorsport, while Andy Wallace and Tim Davies were paired in cars run by Swallow Racing. Madgwick Motorsport secured a works engine deal from Saab for its pair of Reynards, but that was a disaster, mainly because the engine had been developed in isolation rather than with the car under racing conditions.

In effect, the Reynard threat came down to just three cars, but even so Reynard won the first six rounds, with the scoreline Spence 4, Wallace 2. In third place, however, was Mauricio Gugelmin in a Ralt RT30 run by Dick Bennetts.

Dick says: 'Over the years I've had my run-ins with Ron and the RT30 was one of them. Mauricio was a very good test driver, and he was complaining that he wasn't able to feel what the front end of the car was doing.

'We tried softer springs, but the front end wouldn't go down at speed, so we were losing downforce. After the second race at Silverstone the car was parked on rough tarmac and I took Ron over to see it. I bounced on the front and said: "The front end won't bottom." Ron said: "That's because it's parked on a rough surface." I couldn't believe what I was hearing. I was speechless and had to walk away.

'We knew that there was a problem with the front suspension geometry so we drove straight back to our workshop and spent hours fiddling with the front rocker spring ratios. What was happening was that the angle between the rocker and the pushrod was causing the suspension to stiffen and lock.

'Next day we managed to buy a set of unmachined rockers, machined them ourselves, fitted stiffer springs and took the car to Mallory Park. There was an immediate improvement. Then I phoned Ron and said: "I know that you have a problem with the front suspension because we've just fixed it." We wanted to keep the secret up our sleeves for a few races, but Ron was galvanized. It was not long before he found why the mistake had been made at the factory; it was a mistake between the drawing and the metal. It was a rare moment to hear Ron admit to having made a mistake.'

From then on Gugelmin moved up the Championship. He had a narrow lead from round 14 (of 18) and went into the final race with 5 points in hand over Andy Wallace. Mauricio didn't put a foot wrong, however, and won the race – and the title – with Andy runner-up in both.

David Price Racing had begun the year with 1984 cars fitted with the flat-bottom update kit. Dave says: 'After the first few races, when our drivers weren't winning, they said that they had to have Reynards. After Ralt it was a culture shock. You spent all your time keeping it together. It was a nightmare. I'd run Marches, and March, like Reynard, was based in Bicester. I began to think that there was a Bicester School of Racing Car Construction.' Andy Miller, who ran the French side of David Price Racing, called it the Reynard Diet. 'Run a Reynard and you spend so much time working on the car that you never have time to eat.'

The Championship went to Gugelmin, not only because Dick Bennetts sorted out and improved his Ralt, but because Reynard scored an own goal. After winning six races in a row, Adrian Reynard decided that he had cracked Formula Three, so he and Rick Gorne, and their partners, took off to the Greek islands for three weeks.

Since Adrian and Rick had been high-profile in the Formula Three paddocks in the early races, their sudden absence was the more noticeable – nobody was surprised if Ron was not present. Their absence had an effect and today Adrian regrets in particular that he was not on hand to be in Russell Spence's corner. After those first six straight wins, only one further British Formula Three race would fall to Reynard in 1985.

But there were factors other than the Reynard holiday. One was that Swallow Racing had been set up to run Tim Davies, with Andy Wallace as an addition. Andy, however, proved to be the quicker, so the team formed around him and Tim tried too hard to compensate. Frequently he and Wallace seemed intent on driving each other off the road and Davies was dropped by mid-season.

Russell Spence's position was slightly different. He was supremely confident in the first races of the season, but then his team, PMC Motorsport, entered Formula 3000 with an ex-works Williams FW8C for Lamberto Leoni. Spence was no longer the centre of the team's attention, and that affected him.

While the Formula Three branch of PMC had the potential to win the Championship, there were big problems with the Formula 3000 branch. The trouble was that, as everyone else who tried a former Formula One car discovered, the larger fuel cell did not make for optimum weight distribution when running with smaller wings and tyres. Lola encountered precisely the same problem when it entered Formula 3000 with a car based on its IndyCar tub.

March and Ralt, however, both built Formula 3000 cars which were developments of their 1984 Formula Two machines. The Cosworth DFV engines, which everyone used, when equipped with a rev-limiter to restrict them to 9,000rpm gave about 125bhp more than a typical 1984 Formula Two car, but they were considerably more reliable than a BMW or Hart engine and were much cheaper to run as a consequence. As in Formula Three, a flat bottom was mandatory.

Bridgestone sponsored the Ralts, so in recognition of that, the new car was called the RB20. March made customer cars, whereas Ralt ran just a works team, Mike Thackwell being paired this time with the Dane, John Nielsen.

There was a bit of a spat before the season started when Bridgestone announced that it would supply exclusively to Ralt, and the tyres would be radials. Since the only other supplier was Avon, with its crossplies, this was deemed to be unfair, so there was a rule change which stated than any tyre maker had to be prepared to supply up to 30 per cent of the field. In the end Bridgestone and Avon shared the honours, and of the 12 drivers who led races, six were on Avons and six on Bridgestones.

Mike Thackwell was unlucky not to win his second title. He won the first race, was second to Emanuele Pirro's March in the second, and was in command of the third round until the rev-limiter caused his engine to misfire, which allowed team-mate John Nielsen to win. That was bad luck for Mike because the rev-limiter was a mandatory fitting to supposedly level the playing field. That failure probably cost Mike the series and, perhaps, the chance of a regular Formula One drive.

At the final round, Christian Danner (March), Pirro and Thackwell all had a chance of the title, but Pirro and Thackwell took each other off at the first corner and that let Danner through to win both the race and the title. Thackwell was second, Pirro third and Nielsen fourth.

The two Ralts won four of the 11 races (plus a non-Championship event in Curacao) and every other event was taken by a March, but March had made 16 cars. Looked at objectively, therefore, honours had finished up fairly evenly, especially since everyone had used the same engine and there had been no apparent advantage in the choice of tyre.

For the following year Ralt would make a total of eight RT20 Formula 3000 cars (four for the works and four for sale). The Bridgestone connection in the numbering was dropped because, in order to keep costs down in Formula 3000, a control tyre was specified and the contract went to Avon.

The works Ralt team of Nielsen and Satoru Nakajima, however, did have different engines to the rest of the field because the Honda name appeared on the cam covers. At this time Honda was making large inroads in the United States with its road cars and thought that it would like to try IndyCar racing. Mr Kawamoto still felt badly that he had misunderstood Ron's reaction to his suggestion about going into Formula One, and so he asked him to design an IndyCar for Honda.

This brought in John Judd and Engine Developments, who had made dramatic improvements to the previously peaky power curve of the Honda V6

Formula Two engine, and whose relationship with Honda had begun way back in 1966. So Engine Developments designed a 90-degree V8 engine, which was largely the work of the Chief Engineer, Neil Walker, who had once been with BRM. The first engines were made in Rugby, with Honda technical input aided by the frequent use of the fax machine.

John Judd says: 'We had done quite a lot of the rebuild work on the Honda engines for both Ralt and Spirit, and our suggestions had probably saved Honda a year or two's development time on the engine. We hadn't asked them for much money, so giving us the engine to design was our reward. We supplied some engines to Honda at an early stage of development and they were worked on in Japan.'

Ron did the general layout of the chassis design, which was then handed over to Tony Southgate – at that time operating as a freelance – to finish. Ron says: 'We had more or less finished the design when Kawamoto came to see me, obviously embarrassed. When a Formula One Williams-Honda won in Dallas in 1984 and in Detroit in 1985, it gave the Honda dealers in the States a pitch to sell cars on. They didn't want this spoiled by Honda appearing in IndyCar racing and possibly failing. I told Kawamoto: "No problem. Pay us for the work we've done and we'll forget it." Kawamoto was astonished that we took that attitude, and to show his appreciation he gave us some assistance.'

Over at Engine Developments, John Judd asked Mr Kawamoto whether they could carry on with their IndyCar engine, and EDL was told that they could keep everything they'd done. In fact, Honda knew that it would need a Formula 3000 engine for 1986 (the Japanese changed from Formula Two to Formula 3000 a year after Europe) and duly placed an initial order for 12 units.

Just as the Cosworth DFV was reduced in size and modified to become the DFX, a turbocharged Indy engine, so the Judd AV 2.65-litre Indy engine (which was badged 'Brabham-Honda') was modified to become a normally aspirated 3-litre engine, the Judd BV, but badged 'Honda'.

Honda helped with sponsorship, and Satoru Nakajima joined the team. Nakajima was a huge star in Japan, having been the national (Formula Two) Champion four times by the start of 1986. He would add a fifth title that year, also scoring a hat-trick, as he commuted between Europe and home.

Although Nakajima's Formula One career was ultimately a disappointment, he was blindingly quick in Japan, as visiting Europeans could testify. As a member of the Ralt-Honda Formula 3000 team, however, he could do no better than a fourth place and two fifths.

The RT20 had a new monocoque and revised front suspension, and as it was under the weight limit it was ballasted. While the works team had the Honda unit, the four customer cars used the Cosworth DFV. The works cars won a race when Mike Thackwell deputized for Nakajima, and so finished higher in the Championship than either of the regular drivers. Privateers Pierluigi Martini and Luis Perez Sala, in Cosworth-powered cars, each won two races. The private Ralts came on song in the latter part of the season when Avon introduced a harder compound, and the season ended with March and Ralt each taking five wins and Lola the one remaining race with a new car designed by Ralph Bellamy.

On the surface, it would appear that the Judd/Honda engine was not as good as a Cosworth, but as John Judd says: 'When you go through a season of 12 races and in only three of them do both cars complete the second lap, it really does limit one's chances of success. When Mike Thackwell substituted for Nakajima at Pau and won, it showed what a really good, motivated driver could do.

'I want to stress, though, that in my view there was no real difference between any of the engines in Formula 3000; the regulations were framed according to the laws of physics and there's no way round that. People's perception of engine power, on the other hand, is a different matter.

'You get these trends in racing and we benefited when everyone in Formula Three decided they had to have one of our VW engines. We won every British Formula Three race in 1984, '85 and '86. What happens is that a particular engine becomes part of the package which is sold to the sponsor, so success becomes self-generating.

'Even when we were winning everything in Formula Three, I maintained that if we took an old Toyota chain-driven unit and did a proper job on it, we could put it into a winning car and it would still win. In 1976/7 a good Toyota produced 158bhp, but our VW engine rarely saw more than 162bhp. After 10 years we managed to build an engine which produced 4bhp more than the Toyota, but if you listen to the claims which are made every year, when people introduce new cylinder heads or ignition systems, and add them all up, we should have had about 190bhp.' Since only eight Ralt RT20s were made compared with the 20 cars from March, and they split the wins exactly, with Lola virtually nowhere, it suggests that the Ralt was the better car.

Meanwhile, March had started its period of decline. During 1986 it became the first racing car manufacturer to be launched as a public company. For a time it meant that it was awash with cash, and outside managers were brought in to run the company as a sensible business. The trouble is that making production racing cars is not a sensible business. The product is assessed after every race. You don't ditch your cooker just because a sponge doesn't rise or the beef is overdone, but if a racing car does the equivalent it is likely to be dumped. No other product has to be the best, week by week, in order to sell. March would buckle under the constraints of trying to become a sensible business, although before long it would own Ralt.

Judd engines won every Formula Three race in Britain in 1986, but the series was taken by Andy Wallace in a Reynard run by Madgwick Motorsport. Wallace won by 38 points, which gives the impression that he dominated the season, but he only took the lead in the series past the halfway mark, and it was the Brazilian, Maurizio Sandro Sala, who won three of the first four races.

The series was a classic example of the importance of driver psychology. The balance of the season changed even before it began. Dick Bennetts was due to run the promising young Canadian, Bertrand Fabi, in an RT31, but Fabi was killed while testing at Goodwood before the start of the season and West Surrey Engineering withdrew from the series, which was a major blow to Ralt.

The Ralt in which Maurizio Sandro Sala won three of the first four rounds was being run by Eddie Jordan and there was controversy over the fuel some of the other teams were using. Loose wording in the rulebook had caused some teams to increase the octane rating of their 4-star fuel. Others lodged protests, stuck to pump fuel, and sat back confident that penalties would be imposed on the transgressors, which included Wallace. Jordan and Sala held out for longer than most, but no penalties were imposed. This rankled with Sala, who believed that he was being unfairly treated and that others were cheating, and

Changing times

it rubbed the edge off his performance. It probably cost him the Championship.
The ironical thing is that the advantage that some people had through their fuel was probably less than that which Sala enjoyed, naturally, over the rest of the field. Sala was considerably smaller and lighter than any other driver, and weight translates into notional horsepower. So while Sala out-psyched himself, Andy drove with supreme confidence and, in the latter half of the season, he dominated the series. Eventually he was so confident that he would tell his team on which lap of practice he intended to set pole. Some members of the Madgwick team had begun the season convinced that their star would be Perry McCarthy, but Perry, with similar equipment, took only one podium position. The final score of wins was Reynard 8, Ralt 10. Wallace, however, went on to win the prestigious international events at Macau and Fuji.

Ralt made 49 Formula Three cars to Reynard's 20 in 1986. They each won two Formula Three Championships, but ever growing in strength was the Italian firm Dallara, which had gained new confidence since the introduction of the new rules in 1985.

For several years past, Ralt had split the lion's share of the European Formula Three market with the French outfit Martini. It had been roughly 60/40 in favour of Ralt, but in 1986, Martini, which took its ninth French Championship in 10 years, seemed to be running out of ideas. Although in 1987 Martini introduced an all-new car with a carbonfibre monocoque, and Jean Alesi began his successful campaign in the French Championship in one, he would soon dump it in favour of a Dallara.

The racing car market was in a rare state of flux. In 1986, when March Engineering, buoyed by the profits from its IndyCar successes, was launched as a public company, the launch price of its shares gave it a value of more than £14 million. The game plan was for the company to move out of the risky, seasonal production racing car business and into high-value relationships with major manufacturers. March already had joint projects with Nissan and BMW and would soon form alliances with Alfa Romeo and Porsche. It had its eye on specialist consultancy and design work while using Formula One as its flagship.

In the early 1970s every Formula One team except March had dropped its production racing car side (whereas March carried on to the end of 1977 but dropped its Formula One side), but now March was apparently showing the way forward to other racing car makers. Consultancy was the buzzword in motor racing in the 1980s – everyone desired it, and talked about it, but not much consultancy actually took place.

Meanwhile, despite Andy Wallace's fine performances in Formula Three in 1986, Reynards continued to be relatively thin on the ground in Britain in 1987, even though 58 Formula Three cars had been made compared with the 43 Ralts. The Reynards were being sold abroad, while most of the leading British teams preferred to stay with Ron.

One who didn't was Eddie Jordan Racing, which put together a package consisting of Johnny Herbert, a Reynard chassis and a VW engine tuned by the German firm Speiss. Eddie says: 'I got tired of standing behind Dave Price in the queue at Judd's and I looked around for an alternative. The difference between me and teams like Dickie Bennetts' is that we looked for the drivers that we wanted and we made it happen for them. We put together the entire package – the car, the engine, the sponsors, everything.' Apart from his racing team, Eddie Jordan runs a management company and handles the careers of a number of drivers, many of whom drove for him at a crucial stage of their careers.

Herbert won four of the first five rounds and by June he had a lead of 21 points. Then the Ralt brigade, which included Martin Donnelly, Gary Brabham and Damon Hill, caught up, but they tended to share the wins amongst themselves, which made Johnny's life a little easier.

Reynard won nine races to the eight of Ralt in Britain, while Ralt won three to Reynard's two in the revived EFDA European series, although the series as a whole went to Dave Coyne's Reynard. Reynard won the European Formula Three Cup at Silverstone, but Ralt took the important Monaco and Macau races.

Oddly enough, it was only the second occasion that a Tauranac car had won in Monaco, the other being the Brabham BT28 driven by Tony Trimmer in 1970. In 1987 the winner was Didier Artzet, who led home Jean Alesi and Johnny Herbert. Artzet's only other major accomplishment was a third place in Formula 3000 in 1990.

Ralt and Reynard had their horns locked, and while Ralt continued to retain the cream of the British Formula Three teams, Reynard was making progress in other markets, as was Dallara. Ralt still had healthy markets in Formula Atlantic and SuperVee, however, and it was a good spread of products because most of the parts on an RT4 and RT5 could be made during the English summer, when things were traditionally slack for a racing car manufacturer.

However, trouble was looming on the horizon. Formula SuperVee was in decline, and while Atlantic continued to be relatively healthy in North America and the Antipodes, the American company Swift now had its eye on those markets. Swift had gone through the Ford formulae with great success, indeed its Ford cars were paid the compliment of being copied by Reynard in 1985, and for a time there was a UK branch of Swift.

Formula Atlantic was a natural progression for Swift, but Atlantic has its own culture. People tend to hang on to their cars and develop them. Take the Ralt RT4: around 40 cars were sold in both 1981 and 1982, then sales ticked along at around a dozen a year, plus spares. Ralt could handle a sales graph like that because it was in other categories and, being based in England, had a huge subcontractor industry within easy reach.

In Formula 3000, there was a new Ralt for 1987, the RT21. Not only was the monocoque stiffened by a greater use of aluminium honeycomb, but there was also some carbonfibre. Ron says: 'Everyone had decided they had to have carbonfibre tubs without realizing that some carbonfibre construction was a long way short of Formula One standards. I have seen a car break up just because it bottomed, and everyone said: "Wow, look at the strength of carbonfibre, the driver's unhurt", but it should never have broken in the first place.'

The final victory score at the end of the season was March 5, Ralt 4, Lola 2, with Stefano Modena in a March taking the title. Modena was guided by Mike Earle, who suspected that the chassis of the all-new March was flexing and had adjusted the suspension settings accordingly.

Roberto Moreno rejoined the Ralt team for 1986. He says: 'I had made myself financially stable in America, and flew over to take part in the Birmingham Superprix Formula 3000 race for Bromley Motorsport. Ron came up and said:

"What are you doing here?" I told him, and he said: "Why don't you come and drive for me next year?" Within two minutes of meeting him we'd shaken hands on the deal and I had a drive for 1987. That was Ron all over, we never had a contract, merely a handshake.'

Roberto was paired with Mauricio Gugelmin, also from Brazil, and Ron says that they're the two best test drivers he has ever worked with. Between them they set six pole positions and Roberto might have been Champion except for a run of mechanical failures. Roberto says: 'Four times I was leading when my car failed within a few laps of the end. And there was no pattern to the failures.'

He led at Enna on the last lap. He came through the last corner with a dead engine, apparently running out of fuel within sight of the finishing line. After all the other bad luck, Ron could not believe it. Roberto continues: 'When I could see the second-placed man in my mirrors, I put the car into second gear and roared across the line. I'd done it to wind Ron up. He was furious!'

At least Roberto and Mauricio each ended the season with their reputations intact and with a win apiece, Gugelmin at Silverstone, Moreno at Enna. Luis Perez Sala took two wins with a Lola-Cosworth and was runner-up to Modena's March in the Championship, but with Moreno and Gugelmin third and fourth, it was quite a strong year for Ralt, especially considering how thinly represented it had been on the grid compared with March and Lola.

There was nothing to suggest that Ron could not keep fighting his corner as he had done for 25 years, first with MRD and then, after a break, with Ralt, but he was about to be caught in a pincer movement.

23

Decline and fall

It was in 1988 that Ron lost control of Ralt. In a nutshell, his two works Formula 3000 drivers, Russell Spence and Eric Bernard, left the team, taking their sponsorship (£400,000) with them. The irony is that observers at the time declared the Ralt RT22 to be the best engineered car in the field, although it had problems. Simultaneously, sales of the junior formulae cars fell from typically 60 to 70 a year to just 42. That's the story in brief, but like most things in motor racing, the real picture was somewhat different.

SuperVee production was down to a mere three cars in 1988 because the category was in decline in North America and there were enough RT5s knocking around to keep everyone happy. The American company Swift had tried to take on Ralt in SuperVee and had failed, although it had done remarkably well in the Ford formulae in which Ralt had not been involved. An RT5 had won 10 of the 11 SCCA SuperVee Championships from 1980 to 1990, during which time there had been no fewer than 43 other manufacturers in the category. So 44 manufacturers had given SuperVee their best shot, and they included heavy-hitters like Lola and March as well as barely remembered names from Europe and America, but Ron had beaten them all. In many cases he (or Ralt) had wiped them out altogether.

In North American Formula Atlantic Swift delivered a good car and stole a lead on the RT4, which had won every Championship since 1981. Swift got the upper edge for a while, but no outfit has controlled Atlantic like Ralt. Ron has already said that one of the ingredients of success for the maker of a production racing car is that you have to guess the strength of the opposition, then do just enough to stay ahead. The arrival of Swift in Formula Atlantic was a rare instance of Ron not getting it quite right.

North American Atlantic had once allowed any make of engine, but the organizers had done a deal to turn it into a one-engine category and the engine was to be Toyota. To assist the transition from one set of rules to another, Toyota-engined cars were given a weight advantage.

There was nothing wrong with that, it was a typically pragmatic American solution, but the height of the Toyota engine did not suit the RT4 as it stood. Ron says that he could not get his hands on a Toyota engine, or even drawings of it, in order to mate the unit to the chassis and that finally he decided that the market was not big enough to justify too much effort, so he let it go.

Meanwhile, Reynard had made inroads into Ron's Formula Three market overseas, although his traditional British customers remained loyal. Rick Gorne at Reynard sometimes let cars go for nothing because he knew he could turn a profit by supplying spares. From the moment Rick joined Reynard, at the end of 1982, his business plan had incorporated the fact that, on average, a racing car has an accident once every eight or nine starts.

As well as Reynard, with its aggressive marketing, Dallara had also made inroads into Ralt's Formula Three market in Italy and in some other European countries. Ron says that he made a mistake on the RT32 and the magnesium rear uprights were flexing, but despite that several drivers in Britain switched from Reynard to Ralt during the season. Ron says: 'The problem with the rear uprights was not so bad in Britain, where we were running Avon crossplies, which flexed, but it was an acute problem in Europe, where people ran on Michelin radials.'

Steve Hollman recalls an earlier occasion when Ron came bouncing into the factory saying: 'It worked. It worked. The car's undriveable!' Steve says that Ron had suspected that the rear uprights on a car were flexing, so he had made an upright with extra bracing so that it was ultra-stiff, and he had run the car with a standard upright on one rear corner and the stiffened upright on the other. The car was undriveable because the rear uprights were out of harmony, which proved to Ron that the standard upright was flexing.

The brilliant Finn, JJ Lehto, won the British Formula Three Championship for Reynard, but the next five places were filled by Ralt drivers of the standard of Gary Brabham, Damon Hill, Martin Donnelly and Eddie Irvine – who tended to take points from each other. In fact, in Britain, Reynard and Ralt ended the season on nine wins apiece.

It was the erosion of the overseas markets which had made Ralt vulnerable. Swift used its success in North American Formula Atlantic to attack the New Zealand Atlantic series and, since Ron's eye was off the ball, it made progress. That affected Ralt considerably because the cars which it had been building each year for New Zealand, though relatively few in number, had helped to spread the racing car build season. They had been made during the English summer, when otherwise the guys at Ralt would have been twiddling their thumbs or making spares.

The problems which surrounded the RT22 Formula 3000 car were a little more complicated, not least because in 1988 the conditions under which Ron was making it were different from before. Now there were paid-for works drives and not much in the way of customer representation. Ron explains: 'This was the first time that I had run drivers who were paying for the ride and they were very demanding. Instead of doing what I call workshop testing, going over things in detail, they insisted that they call the tune.'

Some people, complaining of a handling problem, tried to point a finger at the car's carbonfibre tub, but in fact there was nothing wrong with the tub at all. Ron explains: 'The problem arose because I had decided to locate the rear suspension links 3 inches forward of the tyre contact patch, so that adjustments could be made without altering the corner weights. I had done a good job on the geometry, but unfortunately the magnesium rear uprights were flexing, just as they had been on the RT32 Formula Three car, and of course the problem was magnified because of the greater loads generated on the Formula 3000 car.

'There was also another little problem. I was employing a designer, David North, who had Formula One experience and later went on from me to McLaren. Normally I used needle roller bearings in the front suspension rockers, but David produced a miniaturized version, a Formula One arrangement, using Glacier DU plain bearings. There seemed nothing wrong with that, but at the first race Andy Miller, who was running Gary Evans in a Ralt, called me over and demonstrated that if you depressed the front suspension suddenly, by bouncing down hard on the tub, the front suspension could seize.

'That was easy to fix, but fixing the rear suspension was a more long-winded affair, but even so, Russell Spence was heading for fourth place in the opening round of the Formula 3000 Championship until his engine's ring gear detached itself from the flywheel, and Eric Bernard finally finished sixth. We thought that we could develop the car, but Russell left after two races and used a Reynard for the rest of the season. I think part of the trouble was that I got on the wrong side of his manager.

'There had been a major change to the engine for this season, the sump having been reduced in depth by 20mm, which allowed the installation to be lowered a similar amount. This, of course, changed the engine's oil scavenge system, which became suspect as we had lost 200 revs over the previous year, but as it was a completely new car it was difficult to pin down the cause.'

Spence was not the only driver to switch to Reynard. The 88D won on its debut and kept on winning. March, which had won the first three European Formula 3000 Championships, was still using a development of its 1984 Formula Two car, while the 1988 Lola was nothing special and, of course, Ralt had its own problems. Reynard began the season by building seven cars, but 15 more would be ordered during the year.

The Champion in 1988 was Roberto Moreno in a Bromley Motorsport Reynard, having scored an unprecedented hat-trick on his way to the title. Roberto says: 'The difference between the 1988 Reynard and the 1987 Ralt was that the Reynard was an 'aero' car, with virtually no suspension, while the Ralt had fantastic suspension and no aerodynamics.

'I think that when Ron didn't do the wind-tunnel testing he began to lose his grip. I think that basically he did not have the patience to spend day after day in a wind-tunnel, logging data.' Ron explains: 'By then we had free use of a wind-tunnel, but we didn't have the back-up facilities. To use a wind-tunnel properly we needed to have modelmakers within the team and the budget didn't run to that. Roberto is right, to a degree, I didn't have the patience to spend day after day logging data, but the sticking point is that we didn't have the back-up.'

Mike Thackwell came out of retirement to guest for the works team at Pau and finished seventh – Eric Bernard was fourth – and then Mike turned his back on motor racing. It was almost the act of a mystic. At the beginning of 1998 Mike was teaching children with physical difficulties.

The crunch for Ralt came in the fifth round, at Monza, where both the works Ralt drivers, Eric Bernard and Marco Greco, failed to qualify. It was the first time in the history of Ralt (or Brabham for that matter) when a works car had failed to qualify, let alone two works cars. Ron was quoted at the time as saying: 'The whole thing this year has escalated beyond belief. The Reynard is very quick, there's no doubt, and I imagine that the amount of effort being put in by March, Lola and ourselves is probably up five times. Formula 3000 has always been very competitive, but the drivers are improving and the teams are getting more professional all the time. It is a different ball game to last year, being up at the front.'

Eric Bernard switched teams after Monza. 'He had a French sponsor with whom I got on quite well,' Ron recalls, 'so when he phoned up and asked if he could defer one of the payments I said "OK", so Eric got some free races and I never did get paid.

'By then there were rumours that Ralt could be up for sale and I was approached by Eddie Jordan, who said that he was interested. I suspect that Eddie had been the one to put the rumours about in the first place so he could open up the conversation. We had the assets of the company valued, agreed a price and Eddie's lawyer paid me a deposit of £5,000 while Eddie went out to find the finance. Eddie thought that he had got together a consortium of investors, but they were slow in stumping up the money.'

Meanwhile, March was in deep trouble. When it had been launched as a public company in 1986 it seemed at first to be headed for success. In order to run it like a modern business, some of which were plain daft, like an idea to try to market the March name as a glamour product. It was thought that there could be products like March aftershave, although outside motor racing everyone thought that March was a month, and not a particularly nice one at that.

Then there was the idea of a March supercar, which reached quite an advanced stage, but nobody had any idea what engine to use. Further, there was nobody on the workforce who had even designed a door with wind-up windows and regular locks.

Jabby Crombac recalls the time when Guy Ligier asked him to approach Ron to design a roadgoing coupé. 'Ron said: "I have never designed anything that needed doors like that".' That was also the reaction of Lamborghini when March spent tens of thousands of pounds on a proposal to design the successor to the Lamborghini Countach.

The March wind-tunnel, which had been touted as the most advanced in the world, was a disaster. The insulation material used for it was 16,000 times more effective than was needed. As a result the tunnel became a pressure cooker which produced useless information. The irony is that the superb 1988 March Formula One car was developed in the wind-tunnel at Southampton University because it was cheaper to hire. Meanwhile, Lotus ceased to be a top team because it hired the March tunnel, which sent it in the wrong direction.

Then there was March Composites, which was another opportunity to lose money. It dropped half a million pounds on the mid-engined Panther Solo GT car of which just a dozen were made before Panther pulled the plug. In early 1989 the new management team was even talking about approaching Bentley to develop carbonfibre bodies.

Then March's 1988 Formula 3000 car had been a problem, particularly in Japan, where Leyton House, March's Formula One sponsor, was forced to drop the cars after one race and switch to Lola. March had sold 37 Formula 3000 cars in 1987, but only 22 in 1988. After March had won the first three European Formula 3000 Championships, it won just a single race in 1988, and that was a fluke.

Before the end of the year its Formula 3000 project had been sold to Leyton House, whose boss, Akira Akagi, had meanwhile become a major shareholder in March Group plc. As such he had a seat on the Board, although in practice he sent a deputy.

March had done remarkably well in IndyCar racing, but had lost the thread of the plot. Lola was making great strides in the IndyCar market largely because March had been taken away from the racers. Customers in America were delivered sub-standard parts. There were even instances of bodywork being sold with 'rejected' painted on the inside. March's new management team, brought in from outside the motor racing industry, did not understand the demands of motor racing.

Robin Herd, as President of March Group plc, had negotiated exclusive works IndyCar deals with Porsche and Alfa Romeo and was looking for an exit from the production racing car market. James Gresham, March's sales manager, said at the time: 'I don't know why we are in the production car market because we're not very good at making production cars.'

If March was to stay in the production car market it needed Ralt, if only to reaffirm its core values. Ralt had been knocked down largely by circumstances beyond its control. Ron had been making a good profit each year, but had invested much of that in machine tools for his factory. If March was to sustain two IndyCar programmes for Porsche and Alfa Romeo it needed two separate facilities. Buying Ralt would solve that problem and, further, Ralt was a possible profit centre.

By then, John Cowen had been appointed Chairman of March Group plc. He was a City businessman who had been brought in to rationalize the company and there had been blood-letting. One day his secretary phoned Ron and asked if John could have an appointment.

'I wanted to know why, and she wouldn't tell me. I'm like that, I didn't want to waste time. Eventually we got together and we more or less got the deal done in one meeting. We agreed that March would buy Ralt for the asset value – we didn't include anything abstract like goodwill. March would rent the factory for 20 years and could exercise an option to buy it within three years.

'Having done all the homework for the sale to Eddie Jordan, I had all the facts and figures at my finger tips. John was most impressed. Being Chairman of a public company, he had to go back to his Board and he had his own assessors check the value of the assets. He said later that he was amazed how straight down the line my statements had been. In fact, the only area of disagreement was over the value of our transporter, but the guy who assessed that did not realize that racing teams do relatively low mileages and it costs a lot to kit them out inside.

'We – that's Norma and me, the two equal shareholders – sold the company for £1.25 million. We agreed that the value of the factory was £1 million and rent was to be paid on that basis, at roughly 10 per cent of the value. There was some haggling; John wanted the first three months rent-free and offered me a salary of £80,000 per annum as a consultant, which would be taxed by PAYE. But I wanted a long-term arrangement and I didn't want it spoiled by unrealistic figures. I reckoned that £60,000 was my market value, which was agreed on in lieu of the three months rent holiday.

'Norma and I went up to London, signed the contracts and received the cheque, and when I got home I thought it would be polite to fax Honda to inform Kawamoto what we'd done. At nine the following morning I had a phone call from Tokyo telling me not to do anything. Half an hour later Mr Noguchi, later to become head of Honda's motorsport division, arrived from Langley. He wanted to know things like what our wage bill was, and how much sponsorship we had. Then he said: "We'll cover you so you can carry on." But it was too late. I'd done the deal, and besides, I'd had a gut-full of running the business.'

Ron was relieved of some responsibilities, which left him free to be creative and to direct the new company. He says: 'I had always rated Maurice Phillippe as a designer; he was a very good all-rounder. I suggested that March should try to get him, and he joined us from Tyrrell to work on the Alfa Romeo IndyCar project.'

Tragically, Maurice had not long been working at Weybridge when he committed suicide. Alan Howell, who had given him a lift to an airport in Italy, says that everything had seemed normal, but within hours Maurice was dead. But he did have a history of depression.

So John Baldwin joined March/Ralt to head the Alfa Romeo project, but Ron's feeling is that John's attention was not entirely focused and that he missed being in Formula One. Meanwhile, Ron concentrated on Formula Three with the RT33. Production of Ralts was down to 37 Formula Three cars in 1989, but the operation made a profit.

Reynard made almost twice as many Formula Three cars, but Ralts took the first three places in the British Championship and took the German series, which had become the second most important Formula Three Championship. Once again Ron had proven his mastery of production racing cars. But, ironically, at the end of the year Adrian Reynard came within 24 hours of buying March and, with it, Ralt.

As a director of March, Leyton House's Akira Akagi had access to all financial matters, and one of his assistants realized that March had a severe cashflow problem. He thought that by withholding sponsorship money that was due he could bring March to its knees and buy the entire company for peanuts. At the beginning of 1989 he nearly succeeded, and shares in March, which had once been at nearly twice the launch price, dropped to 50p, whereupon trading in them was suspended. Things were so bad at March that there were instances of employees paying for parts from their own pockets because suppliers had cut off credit.

Leyton House was due to take delivery of its new Leyton March Formula 3000 cars, ready for the first race in Japan in early May (the Japanese motor racing season runs about six weeks behind Europe's). John Cowen told Akagi that he was not going to get his cars and, moreover, the Japanese press would be informed that it was because he had failed to make his payments.

Cowen assessed, rightly, that the loss of face would be too much for Akagi to bear; a deal was quickly thrashed out, the sponsorship money came at once and Leyton House bought both the Formula One team and the wind-tunnel. As part of the deal, Leyton House bought the right to use the name 'March' in both Formula One and Formula 3000 for seven years. That is why March used the Ralt label for its subsequent Formula 3000 cars.

In May 1989, Robin Herd handed over the running of what remained of March, the racing car maker, to Dave Reeves. March then consisted of Ralt, two IndyCar projects, and the hope that it could generate other business. Meanwhile, the parent, March Group plc, would diversify into financial services.

Dave Reeves had been one of the first employees. He began as a fabricator, became production manager, and had hauled March from the coals more than once. In particular, he had done more than anyone else to make the first March IndyCars a success and that had led to March's period of prosperity.

But Dave was being handed a poisoned chalice. He was not the optimum choice to become Managing Director of March Engineering at that particular time. Robin Herd and his advisers had made many bad decisions and Dave was not equipped to pull all the broken pieces together. In fact, it is hard to imagine who could have done.

Dave found himself Managing Director of a company to which he had devoted nearly 20 years of his life. He was a shareholder – thanks to Robin, who had given to loyal employees £1.5 million of shares on the launch. Dave could feel that he had done well for himself, but he was lulled into a false sense of security.

March production was down to 22 cars in 1989 and 10 of those were for ARS, the one-make sub-IndyCar formula later known as Indy Lights. In other words, nearly half the production was for a contract, it was not for racing cars in a competitive market. Almost all the remaining 12 cars had been ordered pre-season and would soon be dumped.

Within a few months March Group plc was prepared to sell the entire motor racing operation. Adrian Reynard had been trying to break into IndyCar racing, but he needed a partner to share the risks. He had been talking about this to Carl Haas, who was the North American agent for Lola as well as for Reynard – Lola supplied the heavy metal and Reynard catered for the junior formulae.

Reynard negotiated to buy March (and Ralt) with the deal to be underwritten by Haas. At stake was entry into IndyCar racing for Reynard and the Porsche and Alfa Romeo IndyCar deals for Haas. Nobody had given any thought to what would happen to Ralt, which came as part of the deal. Adrian thought he might close it down, while Rick Gorne relished the idea of having the two rival marques each turning out its own cars at different ends of a building.

There is no problem between Adrian and Ron. They accept that they are different and there's nothing to be done about that. Indeed, subsequently, Adrian approached Ron with the idea that he might design a Reynard for the Toyota Atlantic series. 'Lola also approached me,' says Ron.

Ron and Adrian had been head-to-head in Formula Three since 1985, and now, in October 1989, Adrian had come within 24 hours of buying his rival. But his accountants discovered that all was not as it seemed. There were loans between different branches of March which had not been settled, and the deal was suddenly not as attractive as it had first appeared. And that kept March/Ralt independent, at least for the time being.

24

Mad March days

In 1990 Ralt once again dominated the British Formula Three Championship, with Mika Hakkinen taking the series from Mika Salo. Ralt won every single round, yet Reynard – whose cars were suffering from a flexing gearbox casing – took the French and German titles. Of course, when the German Champion is Michael Schumacher (Reynard) and the close runner-up is Otto Rensing (Ralt), you may wonder whether it was the singer or the song. Also, when Mika Hakkinen took his Ralt to one of the German races he beat Schumacher into second place.

For Ralt it should have been business as usual, but Ron's destiny was now tied to March – like a Siamese twin. The March side of the operation had all kinds of difficulties in IndyCar racing and most were not of its making. A late change in regulations meant that its Porsche car had to be modified in a desperate rush and so it finished up overweight. It did, however, win a race.

But the Alfa Romeo engine in the other March Indy project did not deliver the goods and all sorts of shenanigans resulted. IndyCar engines, leased from Ilmor, found their way to Alfa Romeo, where they were stripped down and inspected in complete disregard of the lessee's contract – writs flew around the world. In early 1992 Robin Herd said of the Alfa Romeo case: 'It's pathetic to say it, but March's biggest financial asset is its outstanding legal cases.'

Meanwhile, while everything was falling apart, Dave Reeves, as Managing Director of a publicly quoted company, revelled in his new status. The trouble was that he had taken on the trappings of a successful businessman without realizing that his business was not successful.

The Ralt factory was not glamorous, so plans were mooted to build a new facade, a reception area with potted plants and so on, to impress the important people who would be flying in to monitor progress on the March-Alfa Romeo IndyCar. Or perhaps not.

Then, instead of sprucing up the Ralt works, it was decided to move the entire March and Ralt operation to a new facility at Colnbrook, close to Heathrow airport. It was a factory unit which previously had been used by the Carl Haas Formula One team, variously known as Beatrice or FORCE.

This meant that March had factory units in Bicester, the empty Ralt factory in Weybridge on which it was committed to paying rent, and a sparkling new factory which was costing £350,000 per annum in rent. It was nonsensical, especially since March was even having difficulty in paying Ron the rent for the Ralt factory. 'Eventually they sub-let part of it,' says Ron, 'and pocketed the rent. I'd agreed they could sub-let, but as a means by which I could be paid. I had to insist that the rent for sub-letting came directly to me.

'In the meantime, I could not sell the factory and property values were in decline. Apart from the thousands of pounds March owed me on unpaid rent, I lost more than a quarter of a million pounds on the factory when I was eventually able to sell simply because I'd been held up and the market had declined.'

When March moved into the new factory it unveiled two cars. There was the RT35 Formula Three, which was one of the best cars that Ron ever designed, and the RT23 Formula 3000 car, which was to win one race and be downgraded from a second win for an alleged jumped start.

Jean-Marc Gounon was the driver of the RT23 on both occasions, and it must be no more than a coincidence that his one-minute 'jump start' penalty came at Enna and that his misfortune allowed an Italian to win. Video evidence shows that Gounon did not jump the start, but Enna is in Sicily . . .

In the first six races of the year Gounon took two poles, three fastest laps and twice took the flag first. Mike Earle, who ran him, said at the time: 'If anyone else came into Formula 3000 with a new car which won its second race everyone would say how good it was, but because it's a Ralt they're not impressed.'

Ron says: 'I was working on the RT35 Formula Three car, the Atlantic car, which became the RT40, as well as the RT23 Formula 3000 car. There's a limit to how much one person can do, so John Baldwin finished off drawing the Formula 3000 car. When I first went testing with it I discovered a big problem. The bottom of the carbonfibre monocoque had been made with a curve in it, so when you tried to fit the flat floor it distorted and as a result the car was very difficult to set up.

'I went back to the factory and said that the problem had to be rectified, but the production manager said that it was OK, and that it had been passed by John Baldwin, but I'm not sure that John knew this.

'Basically everyone was in a panic. To rectify the problem would have cost money and held up production, and they were desperate that neither should happen.

'John Baldwin, who is a very good race engineer, looked after Jean-Marc Gounon for 3001 International and I was race engineer for David Brabham, who was driving for Roni Motorsport. Even though we had the problem with the shape of the tub, results in pre-season testing were promising. We were using a John Nicholson-prepared Cosworth engine which March supplied. Come the actual racing and Roni Motorsport fitted a Cosworth tuned by Heini Mader, which should have been on the pace but was not.

'David Brabham struggled in Formula 3000, then he got an offer to drive for Tom Walkinshaw in the Jaguar team and he snapped it up. Later I asked Heini why his engine had not been very good. It turned out that Roni had not paid their bills and so they got a second-rate engine. Roni went broke before the end of the year and I don't think that March ever got paid for the car. In fact, I believe that quite a number of cars went through the door and no money, or very little money, came in.'

In Formula Three, Rubens Barrichello won the British title from David Coulthard, both in Ralts, with Gil de Ferran in third place in a Reynard. Ralt drivers took the first two places in the French series, the top three places in Germany, and in Italy Domenico Schiattarella was runner-up in his RT35, swamped by Dallaras, but only 4 points adrift.

The Ralt RT35 was a brilliant car, and not only on the track. It outsold the contemporary Reynard by nearly two to one and it also had a direct effect on Dallara. Alan Docking, who was running RT35s in British Formula Three, allowed Dallara to examine his cars. He had friends in the Dallara camp and he says: 'People in Italy couldn't understand why they couldn't sell cars in Britain. Part of the problem is that they made them for a different style of circuit. They don't have too many high-speed corners over there and, back in 1991, a Reynard or a Ralt would drill a Dallara in a corner like Copse.

'Dallara made point-and-squirt cars, the front end was soft, the back end was stiff. They looked at our Ralts and made changes, mainly in the spring rates, and they adopted the same wheel bearings that Ron used. They got their eye on the ball and away they went. But they still didn't sell any cars in Britain, so we told them to send one car over and we'd develop it on British tyres, with our engines and on our tracks, and that's what they did. We gave Dallara the advice they needed to break into the British market.'

The Ralt Formula 3000 project had potential, but was flawed because the tub was not made properly and nobody at March was prepared to invest on a sensible basis. By now March Group plc, the parent company, had diversified into financial services and among its purchases had been a private firm of stockbrokers. After a time it decided to sell the company and it agreed terms with a major bank. Within an hour of the contract being signed, there came a phone call from the bank – discrepancies had been found.

One of the senior executives had been creaming off money and had been doing so before March bought the firm. The time was ripe to sell off the racing car side of the group in order to generate cash. A new name enters the story: Andrew Fitton. He had once been an amateur rally driver and he had made his name, and his money, as a company doctor, turning ailing businesses around in return for a stake in them. He had built up an impressive reputation in the City and in 1990 *The Sunday Times* Business News had nominated him as one of 'Ten To Watch In The Nineties'.

Andrew says: 'In 1989 I was speaking in a seminar at the Institute of Directors, which John Cowen attended. I engineered the place next to him at lunch and he told me that March was going into financial services. My reaction was that he was mad to be thinking of that and that he should be building a group of engineering companies, using March as the flagship.

'Two years later March was in deep trouble, having lost millions buying into a company of stockbrokers, and I wrote John a note saying: "I don't want to say I told you so, but . . ." Next day I had a call asking me to see him and I agreed to go in as a consultant for a month. At the end of that time I wrote a fairly frank report, which did not go down well with Cowen and the board. The upshot was that we parted amicably and the existing management bought the company.'

With backing from the Japanese March agent, plus key members of the management team putting in their own money, and even putting their houses on the line, the company became March Cars Ltd. Ralt was now merely an asset to be disposed of, along with the machine tools.

The new company could not possibly work. For a start it had massive and unnecessary overheads. Ron says: 'Their accountant put together a business plan which said that in order to survive they had to build 15 to 20 Formula 3000 cars and 50 to 60 Formula Three cars. They were never going to do it, but because that was the target, they thought they were going to build that number of cars and so they bought in all the stuff to make them. There was a massive amount of spares on the shelves doing nothing except losing value.'

The new management team had lost the thread of the story and was acting as though they were employees of a successful plc, who needed only to put in an expenses sheet for the expenses to be paid. They had not taken on board the idea that the money first had to be earned. Salaries were top-whack, people were flown around the world, and work began on a customer sports-racing car.

There were two problems with this. One was that the design got no further than drawings and a model, and anyone would have their work cut out to try to sell a racing car on promises. The other problem was that sports car racing was going down the tubes. None was made.

On top of all its other blunders, the management team at March had become focused on the company's image and decided to project a statement about youth. Ron had just designed the RT35 Formula Three car, which had won 12 of the 16 rounds of the British Championship in 1991. To build on this, March decided to drop Ron from the Formula Three programme and bring in Andy Thorby. Thorby was a bright young designer whose TOM'S Formula Three car had won one of the four races in Britain in 1991 which had not gone to a Ralt.

Many British Formula Three teams had stayed with Ralt through thick and thin because they trusted Ron, and that loyalty was not necessarily transferable. The biggest problem that Reynard had faced in Britain when it entered Formula Three was any design with Ron's signature on it. There were times, as in 1985, when Reynard should have dominated in Britain, but none of the experienced teams would take the risk of defecting from Ron, so Reynard had to go with new outfits.

In Formula Atlantic the Ralt name still counted for something, but Ron had never been known as a personality in North America. Therefore the sensible thing would have been to have put Andy Thorby on the Atlantic project. However, not only was Andy set to work on the RT36, but one of the design parameters he was handed was to use a male mould for the carbonfibre tub. The reasoning behind this was that they could pop out a monocoque every day because it was easier to lay-up the material than when using a female mould.

McLaren used a male mould for its monocoques, but the difference was that the March mould was solid and the McLaren mould could be dismantled. Using a solid mould meant that in order to be able to remove the finished tub, the mould had to be tapered. In turn, that meant that the tub was too wide behind the driver's shoulders, so the aerodynamics were compromised. The quality of the finish was not very good either.

At this point Ralt began to lose some of its traditional customers. Ron did not endorse the RT36 and some team managers lost confidence in Ralt, yet the RT36 was still a pretty successful car. The problem was that it was not a good customer car. One team manager says: 'It was OK if you were running a Formula One-style operation, but you can't run a customer car if it takes half an hour to change the battery.

'You don't get many words out of Ron, but he does know how to engineer cars for customers. The Ralt RT36 should have been billed as "Ron Tauranac with Andy Thorby". Andy could have done the main work, with Ron just helping him out, showing him how to make a customer car that works within the limits of the testing available, the expertise of the teams running them and so on. Instead, we finished up with a reasonably good car, with no name to it and which was not a customer car.'

Dick Bennetts, who had had a connection with Ralt since 1980, defected to Reynard. He says: 'Rick Gorne had been pursuing me for years and we did a back-to-back test with the Reynard 923. The driver set absolutely identical times, but we went with Reynard because it was easier to drive and much easier to work on. The Ralt was a quick car, but not a good customer car.'

Glenn Waters, who also defected to Reynard after a long association with Ralt, says: 'I think that the management put Ron up to getting me to go to the factory to look at the car. He looked a bit uncomfortable and quietly said: "I don't think it's any good".'

The RT36 was not a failure in terms of results, but it was the car which was to send Ralt into a nosedive and it didn't deserve to do so. Even so, there was an element of luck involved. The first round of the British series was won by the young Dutchman Marcel Albers (Ralt), then Albers set the fastest lap in the second round, but sadly he crashed and was killed during the race.

Had Albers not died he would surely have won more races. The RT36 is perceived as a failure, but Phillipe Adams used one to finish runner-up to Gil de Ferran (Reynard) in the British Formula Three Championship. In Italy, the only race not won by a Dallara went to Giancarlo Fisichella, having a late-season outing in an RT36, while in the German series the final score was Ralt 14 – Reynard 12.

Another car made by Ralt that year was the Formula 3000 RT24, which was an update of the RT23 farmed out to Simtek, a new outfit being run by ex-March designer Nick Wirth. Only one RT24 ever appeared in a race.

Another car was prepared for a consortium in which Nelson Piquet figured. Ron says: 'It was going to be run for some rich kid from Monaco. Nelson suggested the Ralt because of his connection with me. He tested it and I think he was caught out by the tyres, which were much harder than those he was used to in Formula One, and he crashed.' The car had used a clever rollbar construction which saved top weight, but unfortunately went through the airbox, where it no doubt caused turbulence, restricting top-end performance. To change it meant new certification, which under the circumstances was not going to happen.

The car which made it into a race was driven by Giabattista Busi, the reigning Italian Formula Three Champion. In 1991 Busi led the Italian Formula Three Championship from the first round, and to give some idea of the quality of the field, fourth was Luca Badoer, the 1992 Formula 3000 Champion, and down in sixth place was Jacques Villeneuve.

Busi could be said to have been a promising talent, but in Formula 3000 he failed to score a single point, in fact he failed to finish a race. It is true that he had more than his fair share of accidents, but neither he nor his team could have been assisted by the fact that, a few days after the opening race of the season, March Cars announced that it was withdrawing from Formula 3000.

Meanwhile, Reynard made an effort to establish itself in the Formula

Atlantic market, where the main rival would prove to be Ralt, this time a Tauranac car. Reynard was still recovering from an adventure into Formula One which ate money, failed to produce a car, and brought the company to within a few days of bankruptcy.

Reynard had its eye on the IndyCar scene as a way of securing its recovery from the Formula One disaster, but to prepare the way Adrian had agreed a deal with Mike Earle, head of 3001 International. The idea was that 3001 would field a two-car team in Toyota Atlantic and Adrian himself would engineer the cars. Since Atlantic rounds frequently supported CART IndyCar events, it would give Adrian an opportunity to scan the scene and make himself known to IndyCar owners.

The new Reynard 92H Atlantic car easily won the first three races of the series, but what happened next was a perfect illustration of the fact that different countries have different motor racing cultures and that there is more to winning than having the quickest car and driver.

Martin Dixon, who ran the US operation, says: 'We underestimated the task of transporting an English team to the States. For a start, if you want something done in England there are dozens of people to choose from, all close to hand, whereas there isn't the same industry in the States.

'Then our engines proved fragile. The 1,600cc Toyota has been around a long time and has been stretched to its limit. It does not give local drivers much trouble, but it could not cope with the sheer aggression that European drivers have – it's a case of a different culture. Late in the season the new Ralt RT40 arrived. It was a very good car, their driver did a lot of testing and we were well beaten.'

Ron's Atlantic cars came late in the season in 1992, but they took the Championship every year from 1993 to 1997. March Cars Ltd had put their most experienced designer on the North Atlantic market and had won it back, but the North American Atlantic market is a small one, and as explained earlier, drivers tend not to buy a new car every year.

Andrew Fitton now re-enters the story. He says: 'I kept myself informed of March's situation and eventually received a call from one of the directors suggesting a meeting. He was surprised that I did not ask why he wanted to speak to me. "How many cars have you sold?" I asked. He told me. "You've lost £800,000," I said. He was flabbergasted and said I was spot-on. "I wasn't expecting the call for another two months," I said.

'Dave Reeves was against my being involved because he'd been told by somebody that I was an asset-stripper. He eventually asked me why I wanted March and I told him that I had made a mistake when I left motorsport in 1981 and had not really enjoyed a single day at work since then. When Dave heard that, he swung behind me.

'I enjoyed the cut-and-thrust of the City and the thrill of the chase, but something was missing. One of my companies makes air conditioning units and, believe me, when you've seen one air conditioning unit, you've seen them all.'

Andrew Fitton enlisted the aid of his old rally co-driver Steve Ward. Steve had sold carpets from the back of a van and had parlayed that into the Steve Ward chain of carpet warehouses. He had sold at the peak of the market and had gone off to California to live a life of leisure. But his old friend's suggestion that he might like to run March and Ralt appealed to the romantic in Steve and he returned to England.

Andrew Fitton made some sound decisions. For a start he moved the company to a smaller unit in Wokingham and saved more than a quarter of a million pounds in rent. Then he trimmed down the design staff. He inherited no fewer than three chief designers and whittled them down to one, Chris Radage, while keeping on Ron as a consultant.

Fitton set Radage on the design of a new Formula Three car for 1994. At the time he spoke about building cars for the spaceframe formulae, but never got around to it, even though he had the most accomplished designer of spaceframes in history as a consultant to his company. He spoke about entering IndyCar racing on the back of Ralt's success in Atlantic, and did not rule out Formula One.

Meanwhile, at the beginning of 1993 March caused Ralt to suffer its biggest humiliation ever. Despite the RT36 producing better results than is often perceived, teams in Britain which had been loyal to Ron deserted Ralt when it became merely the company for whom he was working. In Britain, only Edenbridge Racing ordered RT37s, everyone else going for Reynards apart from a new outfit which ordered a pair of Dallaras.

Ron was given the task of designing the RT37, which actually came down to putting together whatever components were in the March spares bin, which included the unloved monocoque which first appeared on the RT36. He says: 'Steve Ward insisted that I had to use the RT36 monocoque because they had eight in stock. I told Steve it was a loser, the composite work wasn't good enough on the leftovers and they weren't properly engineered.'

Ward insisted, but Ron was proven right. One might suggest that being an amateur rally co-driver and successful carpet salesman does not necessarily make one expert at making racing cars, even if one does have several months' experience of the business.

The RT37, predictably, was a disaster. Reynards filled the top six places in the first race of the 1993 British Formula Three Championship and then won the next four races. After the first race, however, Peter Briggs, the boss of Edenbridge Racing, decided to return his Ralts – they were so bad that he refused to pay for them – and to switch to Dallaras.

That was to damage Reynard as well because other teams looked at the Dallaras and switched chassis. Although Reynard won the first five races, it won no more. Dallara wiped both Ralt and Reynard out of the Formula Three market in a matter of weeks.

Dallara had been in Formula One and consequently had a very high level of machine tools. It also had its own wind-tunnel and so it brought a new dimension to the manufacture of production racing cars. Also, unlike some other outfits with Formula One experience, Dallara knew that Formula One thinking did not necessarily translate to the lower formulae.

Ron admires Dallara because, having gained the advantage, it ploughed back its profits into production systems, just as he did. By investing in machine tools to produce components more accurately, Dallara has not only drawn away from the opposition, it has made it less likely that anyone can catch up unless there is a fundamental change in the rules.

Alan Howell recalls the time when Ron Tauranac visited his workshop, took a critical eye to the 1997 Dallara and said: 'I now know why I don't make Formula Three cars.' Alan also remembers the time when Robin Herd looked over a Ralt RT3 and said, of Ron: 'I'll never make another Formula Three car while that man's alive.'

Ron says: 'Dallara has productionized many parts of the car, for instance the wishbone mounts are investment castings. If you look at a Dallara tub you'll see that there are recesses moulded into it so that the castings for the wishbone mountings fit in it precisely. In turn, that makes the tub very smooth on the outside. It's that sort of detail that is only economic to do in quantity, making it difficult for anyone to challenge Dallara.'

So by April 1993, March/Ralt had just the Formula Atlantic market and blueprints and trophies from the past. The blueprints were part of the business plan. Nearly 1,500 March racing cars had been made, and the growth of Historic racing meant there was a steady demand for replacement parts. Andrew did not want the headache of making odd parts, but decided instead to sell duplicate works blueprints so that owners could have spares made.

Other than that, and the small but steady market in Formula Atlantic, all March had was the hope that the Ralt 94C being designed by Chris Radage would relaunch them in Formula Three. Ron says: 'Chris had been a Formula Ford driver and he'd worked for me for a time. He did a good job, but he wanted to do an Open University degree, so he got a job with Brabham, where the working hours were a bit more stable than at Ralt. Chris is very thorough, but he had little race engineering experience. He had worked in Formula One, where the main aerodynamic parameter is lift over drag, but in Formula Three a car must be able to run with little downforce and must not be pitch-sensitive.

'It so happened that a student had borrowed our wind-tunnel model of the RT35 for a project for his degree. We had all his figures and it turned out that the Ralt 94C was 13 times more pitch-sensitive than the RT35.

'March invested £350,000 in the 94C, with the body buck done on CNC – it is very accurate and nicely made. When you make an investment like that, however, you have got to sell a lot of cars to recoup your money – 60 or 70 cars for year after year. The car wasn't that far away from being good, but they rushed it. I think they panicked. They spent a lot of time in a wind-tunnel and that costs £1,000 a day, just to hire the tunnel. On top of that you have the cost of the model and all the alternate parts and undertrays. I used to do one day in a tunnel and I expected what I learned then to last me three years.

'Fitton made a big point of talking efficiency, but there were more people in the office than in the workshop – and the office people included a full-time accountant. I'd run Ralt with just one girl, who looked after the books – and she worked just 22 hours a week.'

Initial testing showed that the Ralt 94C had problems, and it was impossible over bumps. To try to improve its fortunes, and to drum up business, March hired Jacques Villeneuve to run in the prestigious end-of-season races at Macau and Fuji. Jacques had driven a Ralt RT40 in Toyota Atlantic, but even he could do nothing with the new car.

A two-car works team was announced for 1994, but four races into the season it was obvious that there was nothing to be done. The team withdrew, leaving two very aggrieved drivers and some very aggrieved sponsors.

By that time Ron was out of the picture. He says: 'Andrew Fitton wanted to cut back, but although he wanted to keep me on, it would be on a half-time and half-pay basis. He did not realize that my contract said that I was on 12 months' notice. So we compromised. I said I would take six months off, but would be on the end of a phone line if they encountered problems.'

In the air was the sort of deal that could have helped to save March. It was to supply a number of special cars for the Honda racing school at Suzuka. Mr Kawamoto had approached Ron, who as soon as he was on unpaid leave of absence flew to Tokyo and clinched the deal.

Much of the subcontract work on the three prototype cars was put March's way, and more might have gone that way except the company was wound up. Andrew Fitton took the March name and the blueprints.

Steve Ward took the Ralt name, moved to modest premises near Oxford and continued to make and service Ralt RT40 and RT41 Formula Atlantic cars. The RT41 was a light revision of the RT40 with the cockpit closed in over the steering wheel to stiffen the monocoque.

At the beginning of 1997 Toyota Atlantic became a one-make series and the American company Swift was the chosen make. There was, however, a proviso that existing cars, or new cars made to an established design, were eligible to compete. Existing cars such as the Ralt RT41, however, were not allowed update kits – this was to allow a gentle transition.

A Ralt RT41 driven by Alex Barron still won the series, and some teams – experienced and successful teams at that – preferred to stick to Ralt for 1998, even though the car was supposed to be obsolete. In fact, the Swift had serious chassis and engine installation problems.

Meanwhile, as this is being written, March and Ralt both exist as brand names and either can be revived in the future . . .

25

Free agent

When Ron began work on the Honda school car, he brought in Dave Wynne, a young Australian designer who had been at Ralt. Dave had arrived in England on the usual young Australian's tour. He had first worked for Ron in 1988, but left after a fortnight. Ron says it was because Dave was schooled in the metric system whereas he used imperial measurements and Dave needed to learn to do the same. Dave says he left because he and Ron couldn't stand each other.

He says: 'I think Ron has mellowed a lot over the last three or four years, but when I went to work for him again at Ralt in 1990, the first 18 months were absolute hell. Today, you can see his mellowness in his driving. He used to be very aggressive, and some people were frightened to ride with him, but he's changed.'

John Judd says: 'I first met Ron in 1966 and thought that he was on a terribly short fuse. Yet everyone else tells me that he was already so much more mellow by 1966, and that I should have seen him in the early days of Brabham!'

Dave Wynne continues: 'He was very difficult to work with – I think sometimes he was difficult just for the sake of being difficult. I received a lot of criticism, but now I bless him for it. I had done a degree in mechanical engineering at the University of Melbourne and we spent just half a term on technical drawing. I had a lot to learn and Ron was very pernickety, but now I expect the same standards.

'Our relationship changed when we worked on the Atlantic car and he's since been marvellous to work with. If ever I have a problem I talk to him about it, he never fails to make a contribution, and his breadth and depth of knowledge is remarkable.'

The Honda school cars were built on Formula Three lines, but with a 1.6-litre engine. Ron says: 'March thought that they should have got the contract, but it wouldn't have worked. For a start, there is no way that the Japanese could have worked with Steve Ward.' Anyway, Mr Kawamoto was not approaching March, his approach was directly to Ron and it was couched as a formal invitation for Ron personally to submit a proposal and tender.

Ron was given his own office at Honda's discreet facility at Langley, where he had all the design facilities he could wish for – he has kept abreast of all the latest developments in computer design. He produced the design and subcontracted the components. There is a pleasant irony in that he was able to do this because over the years he had done more than any other individual first to create and subsequently to sustain the British motor racing industry.

After the three prototype cars were completed and tested, Honda asked him to make 12 production cars. Ron says: 'We were at the Suzuka circuit in Japan and Satoru Nakajima had tested the car and was very enthusiastic about it. To make a batch of cars involved an impossible schedule, however; it was then the beginning of August and they wanted them by December. They offered me a verbal order there and then because big companies take too long to do formal paperwork. Then they took me to the office so I could phone Dave Wynne.

'Dave was just about to go back to Australia, and I phoned in from the circuit to ask him to stay put. We needed to re-draw the car to imperial, not metric measurements. The reason for this is that we use aircraft bolts in the construction of cars and they are made in imperial measurements, mainly because of the American influence. We use aircraft bolts partly because of their quality and partly because of the way they are measured. They measure the shank, and the screw thread is just long enough for a washer and nut. Everyone in motor racing uses them. If you see Japanese metric tubing, you do not see 25mm tubing, you see 25.4mm – they have simply translated from imperial measurement.

'We subcontracted all the parts, and the assembly was mostly the work of one man, although sometimes Dick Bennetts would lend us one of his men when we needed a bit more help.' The cars Ron built received warm praise from Mr Kawamoto and at the end of 1996 Honda placed an order for a further four cars.

Meanwhile, another project caught Ron's eye. 'I went to the launch of Formula Renault at the Williams factory and thought that it looked reasonably sensible. Dave Wynne needed a job, and I like to be kept employed, so we made a car for Formula Renault.' The result was the Ronta FR1, a neat little spaceframe car with slick tyres, wings and, of course, a Renault engine.

Remember that back in 1961 Ron had been asked to conduct torsional stiffness tests on two spaceframe chassis and that the Lotus 18 chassis had recorded 1,400lb.ft per degree of deflection, whereas that of the Vanwall had been just 660lb.ft/degree. With the aid of the engine as a stressed member, the Ronta's spaceframe chassis recorded no less than 6,500lb.ft/degree deflection wheel to wheel, which according to Ron was roughly on a par with a monocoque chassis made from sheet aluminium.

He says: 'Someone was going to set up a company to run a team and buy the rights to the design. I am sure that he has his own version of events, just as I believe that he has had a chequered career in motor racing. He had a backer whose son was to drive the car. Various monies were not paid and I received the car back. It ended up with a chap called Barry Playle, who had once worked for Hawke and subsequently owned the Hawke name.' The Ronta became a Hawke.

In addition to the school cars and the Ronta, at the end of 1995 Ron became a consultant to Honda Japan, with a special responsibility for the Japanese Touring Car Championship. He made regular visits to Japan and, at his suggestion, Dave Wynne spent 1996 in Japan working on the car. Honda won the JTCC in both 1996 and 1997.

In the summer of 1996, Trevor Elliott, of Honda Motor Europe, was dissatisfied with the performance of the Honda Accords being run by MSD in the British Touring Car Championship, and he called on Ron for help. Ron says: 'I did some work on the car in May '96 and tested at Silverstone and Pembrey. I made some changes, which basically unlocked the door and made the car conducive to development. Once we'd done that it was possible for MSD and Mike Pilbeam, the designer, to take it forward.' A few weeks afterwards, Honda won its first-ever BTCC race.

At the end of 1996 the contract for the Honda BTCC car went to Prodrive and Ron had little to do with the project after that. His contract to advise on BTCC matters expired in May 1997, but in September that year Ron became an adviser to Mr Suzuki, who was in charge of Honda Motor Europe. His specific brief was to keep his eye upon Touring Cars in Britain and the rest of Europe. Also, from August 1997 Ron became a consultant to Honda Motorsport, the brief in this instance being to assess and offer advice on CART engine installation, which meant visits to both the United States and Japan. Ron says: 'I can't say too much about any of this work for Honda because of confidentiality clauses in my contracts.'

In the early part of the 1997 season, the two TWR Arrows Formula One cars suffered some appalling engine reliability problems. Further, when the cars were running they were relatively slow. Then suddenly, around mid-season, they started to hold together and they also moved up the grid. Indeed, Damon Hill came agonizingly close to winning the Hungarian Grand Prix, but then a hydraulic failure two laps from the end kept his car stuck in one gear and he was overtaken by Jacques Villeneuve and his Williams-Renault on the last lap.

The background is that John Barnard had been appointed to head the design team, and at about the same time Ron was also engaged as a consultant. He spent five or six days liaising with Barnard on engine installation while Barnard simultaneously tweaked the chassis.

TWR Arrows' Yamaha engines were actually about 95 per cent the work of Engine Developments. Ron says: 'Word got around that the engine was 100bhp under power, whereas in reality it was producing 720bhp, which was within 30bhp of the very best engines in 1997. Part of the reason why that story got around is because of incorrect calibration of the dynamometer at TWR, which was reading too low. Then the engine was losing power because the oil was being overheated by heat from the gearbox. It suited some people at TWR not to correct the public perception of the engine.'

During 1998 – Ron's 73rd year – he was still to be seen regularly at various British circuits, either for testing or for racing, and if you were really quick you might have spotted him rushing through the departure lounge at Heathrow airport on one of his trips to Japan or the United States on Honda or other related matters.

His schedule would probably tire most men half his age, but then, he is probably fitter than most men half his age. He has always been meticulous with his diet, and every day he is working at home he will pause for his midday swim.

Clearly, Ron Tauranac loves his work, which is why, as I indicated when writing my Introduction to this book, retirement is not an option.

Brabham . . . Ralt . . . Honda . . . this really is an ongoing story.

APPENDIX A

Ron Tauranac's design philosophy for production racing cars

Author's note:
Many of the people I talked to in the course of researching the Ron Tauranac Story have already been quoted in the main text of this book, and a number of them have expressed opinions regarding Ron's design philosophy as they have interpreted it.
    But what about Ron himself? How would he describe the fundamentals of the design philosophy he has applied to the manufacture of his customer racing cars? What set him off along a design path which has proved so effective for so long? How, having produced a new car, does he go about fine-tuning it at the race track to ensure that it can deliver its full potential? And what about some examples of his practical approach in the search for that optimum performance? These were just some of the questions I put to him, and this is what he had to say in response to them:

'I like to think that any success I have achieved in designing racing cars has come about through being able to apply the correct balance between theory and practicality. Theory is very important, of course, but it is the practical application of it which makes it work on the race track.
    My goal in designing a production racing car – as distinct from a works team car, where the requirements quite obviously are very different – has not been to make the fastest car possible, but one that is capable of winning more races than the opposition. It must also be easy to maintain and set up, economic to produce, and leave room for improvements to be made from year to year. So I try to make all the set-up adjustments obvious and not particularly sensitive, so that relatively inexperienced team members can get the best from their car.
    This means that as far as is possible the geometry adjustments should not interact one to the other. This is particularly important for the common pit-lane adjustments of wheel toe and camber, neither of which should affect each other or the corner weights. Suspension stiffness, with a lack of hysteresis and friction, is also important, and with this in mind I have always tended to use larger spherical bearings than most to obviate the development of play during the course of the season.
    To use a modern expression, I have always tried to make my cars driver-friendly, as well as mechanic-friendly – cars which handle predictably and respond clearly to set-up adjustments. A racing driver is unlikely to be successful unless he has complete confidence in his car, knowing not only that it is unlikely to let him down, but also that it has no hidden vices to land him in trouble. This means giving him a car that is strongly built and comfortable to drive, with easily adjustable chassis and suspension settings to enable handling characteristics to be tailored to his own and the circuit's requirements as rapidly as possible.

My own first experience of car handling came as a kid with a Billycart. It had two iron wheels and two that were rubber-tyred – all of them of the same diameter, fortunately. There was a steep hill nearby which led down to a crossroad, and I started to experiment with the wheels. I discovered that whichever end had the iron wheels fitted to it was the first to lead the spin, and in order to turn into the crossroad successfully I had to fit both iron wheels down one side. This was in 1939, and fortunately traffic was almost non-existent, or I might have learnt a rather different lesson!

It was many years later that I discovered that what was happening was called understeer and oversteer, or as the Americans prefer to describe it, push (at the front) or loose (at the rear), which seems to me much more expressive. I have tended to follow this experimental or practical approach throughout my life. Initially it was because the theory was not known to me, but even when it was I still found that from practical experimentation I could usually get the more definitive answers I was looking for.

Back in the early Sixties I can remember going to Brands Hatch with our then current F1 car and Jack driving it in order to quantify various design characteristics. To determine the amount of anti-dive that was needed, the mountings for the front wishbones were made to take spacing washers, which could be added or removed so as to vary the amount of wishbone inclination from the horizontal. I stood beside the track at the braking point and observed the amount of dive, which was then balanced against driver feel, and in the end we settled on 4 degrees inclination of the lower wishbone. To optimize scrub radius a range of packers allowed us to experiment with wheel offset, and to our surprise we found that the steering effort decreased as the scrub radius was increased to about 2in.

Our top front wishbones consisted of a transverse and a longitudinal member. I had estimated that the forward component of braking torque produced by the caliper at the top wishbone attachment to the upright was approximately equal to the retardation force from the tyre contact. To test this theory we removed the bolt attaching the longitudinal wishbone member to the frame, with the driver observing the movement of the top of the upright under braking. Fortunately, the assumption proved correct!

At Ralt, in the RT1 series started in 1974, the rear suspension comprised transverse links to the gearbox for the lateral loads and radius rods running forward to feed the longitudinal loads directly into the monocoque side skins. This worked well structurally and in effect provided upper and lower wishbones with their axes inclined to the centreline of the car. However, as the series developed it was thought that the arrangement could result in the acceleration and braking forces trying to rotate the chassis about its longitudinal centreline, so in a test car we provided additional mountings to allow for the radius arms to be moved inboard to provide a wishbone axis parallel to the car centreline. In testing it was found that the rear anti-roll bar could be reduced in stiffness by approximately 50% to give more consistent handling with better traction.

With the arrival of ground effect in 1980 a method of supporting the gearbox and rear suspension was required that didn't intrude on the space needed for the ground effect tunnels.To use the engine as the structural member would have meant making new sumps and cam covers with provision for attachment to the tub, but with the large number of engines involved this would have been both costly and time-consuming, so the sheet aluminium boxes attached to the sides of the basic tub of the RT2, 3, 4 and 5 series were developed by modelling in cardboard and applying the appropriate loads. This method allowed us to vizualize distortion and to test various cures, but of course today this work would be done using FEA (finite element analysis).

When starting a new design I first of all analyze the regs and try to focus on the most important performance area, then think ahead to where development might lead and allow room for this. A particular formula will almost always require an overall size envelope and determine such things as tyre size, maximum width, minimum weight, and so on. Working within these regulatory guidelines I then try to achieve some fundamental design parameters, but since there will normally be a conflict here, one has to be prepared to compromise, whilst still giving priority to the areas offering the maximum performance potential. There are a number of basic rules which I have applied to both design and development, for example:

WHEELBASE: Longer is better if you can achieve it within the weight limit. It helps to achieve a low polar moment of inertia (as much of the weight as possible concentrated towards the CofG) to give the driver more reaction time. There seems to be a popular conception that you need a short wheelbase for tight corners, but I have never found this to be the case, and whenever circumstances have dictated that I go longer, the result has always been an improvement.

My first memory of this was the BT12 IndyCar, which was based largely on its F1 counterpart except that the regulations specified a minimum wheelbase, which we subsequently carried over to our next F1 car and produced a gain from it. This experience has since been repeated many times, most of them initiated by having to fit longer engines.

TRACK: This, of course, influences both straight-line speed and cornering force. For a non-wing formula such as Formula Ford you should go for the maximum. However, where wings are permitted and contribute so much to adhesion, a narrow track will be beneficial for the lower-powered formulae unless the circuit has a preponderance of slow corners. In both cases I like to keep the line between the front and rear contact patch centres parallel to the car centreline when cornering with maximum g-force.

WEIGHT DISTRIBUTION: Rear-wheel-drive cars have traditionally had 60% of the weight on the rear as the tyres were developed around this distribution and a deviation of as little as 1% was enough to restrict performance. However, with the advent of an increasing number of regulations restricting overall tyre width, the front tyres have become wider in relation to the rears and therefore have needed to take a similarly increased percentage of the total weight. Current F1 and mid-engined GT cars, for example, carry about 58% at the rear. The governing factor is tyre operating temperatures, which should be the same at the front and the rear. It goes without saying that a car's CofG should be as low as possible, and to this end formula cars should be constructed as lightly as possible, consistent with safety and durability, so that any required ballast to bring them up to the minimum weight limit can be added at floor level.

ROLL CENTRE: I start with it on the chassis base and try to minimize its movement, particularly laterally, to keep its distance to the contact patch constant so as to give cornering stability on bumps when cornering at maximum g.

CENTRE OF PITCH: This is determined by the relative front-to-rear wheel frequencies. For rear-wheel drive I use a lower rear frequency such that the car pitches about a point approximately three times the wheelbase in front. The softer rear helps to put the power down.

ANTI-DIVE, ANTI-LIFT: The amount used depends on how much downforce can be obtained from under the car (ground effect) and how pitch-sensitive the car is. The more you use the less the mechanical grip, but the more consistent the ground effect, so it becomes a trade-off.

SPRING PRELOAD: At the front it is almost always an advantage to preload the springs to the point where the car has enough load to break through the preload on the slowest corner. The advantage is gained by increasing the front sprung weight by the addition of the unsprung inside wheel. The wheel runs out of droop travel as the car rolls due to the cornering force and lifts under acceleration, helping to reduce understeer. The exception is on a very bumpy track. At the rear it is almost always a disadvantage as during braking, with the weight transfer to the front, the suspension runs out of droop and tends to lift the rear wheels from the road surface. The potential advantage is in long fast corners, where roll attempts to lift the inner wheel, thereby reducing roll.

CORNER WEIGHT: A quick check on whether the adjustment is correct is for the driver to wind some additional bias onto the front and brake hard in a straight line, checking the smoke from the front tyres. If they smoke together then all is well, but if one lights up first then put some more weight into that wheel and repeat until they come in together.

TESTING: One needs to make a distinction between development testing and pre-race preparation, where the aim is imminent performance. A driver given a choice will go for a balanced car which gives confidence, so when time is short you should go for this. However, in development testing you are looking at various ways of improving maximum adhesion, and this can initially unbalance the car. If you make a change to the front of the car and you induce understeer, or reduce oversteer, then you have reduced grip, so you then go the other way. Similarly, a change to the rear needs to produce understeer in order to be an improvement. This method is particularly appropriate for setting dampers as the effects of specific changes are not widely understood.

It can also speed up the testing procedure as it is usually quicker to make an immediate change and run again before the tyres have lost temperature, then reverse the direction if it proves to be wrong, than to spend time pondering and then having to get the tyres up to temperature again – it is vital that they operate within their correct temperature range throughout testing. Cambers are adjusted according to the distribution across the tyre, but not so much attention is paid to the front-rear distribution, which can tell us a lot about the car balance. For example, if the front tyres are hotter, this generally indicates understeer, requiring either a larger distribution of downforce or less roll stiffness on the front. If the rear tyres are hotter it indicates oversteer, so the adjustments should be in the opposite direction.

When testing I usually select a couple of safe corners, a fast one for aerodynamic settings and a slow one for mechanical adjustments. By not pressing hard over the whole circuit the driver can focus more precisely on car response on each element of the chosen corners, such as turn-in, mid-corner

Appendix A

and power-on for the exit. With this approach the tyres also remain consistent for longer and the engineer can be more focused.

When making adjustments I tend not to go for the softly-softly approach, which I find takes too long. Instead, I prefer to go for the extreme change, and if it happens to be too far, this will immediately become apparent and give you a clue as to where the next change should be. This is why I always say that an essential requirement of development testing is a lack of ego!'

APPENDIX B

The first Ralts

Ralt Special
A mid-engined 500cc Formula Three car, built 1949/50; with double-wishbone front suspension; swing-axle rear with lower transverse leaf spring. Tauranac-modified Norton ES2 pushrod engine, eventually bored-out to 600cc. Originally fitted with motorcycle wire wheels, later with Tauranac-designed cast wheels. New low-pivot swing-axle rear suspension with low roll-centre and long swing-arm length from late 1951. This was possibly a world first as it predated the Mercedes-Benz W196 of 1954. Car was sold in 1955 and subsequently driven with considerable success by Merv Ward.

Ralt 1100
A cycle-winged sports car built 1949/50 and powered by four-cylinder side-valve Ford E93A engine lightly tuned by polishing ports and fitting stronger valve springs. Four-speed Standard 10 gearbox and Morris Eight brakes, wheels and back axle.
Ron Tauranac-designed square-tube chassis; front suspension by Armstrong shock absorbers, upper radius arms and lower transverse leaf spring; rear suspension by semi-elliptical springs. Aluminium-panelled body over steel tubular frame with sheet steel tail section. Weight approximately 500Kg, height 2ft 9in. Considered to be the outstanding Australian special of its day. Mainly built and used by Austin Tauranac, who fitted 10:1 compression ratio cylinder head and twin Amal carburettors for occasional competition outings. Car sold when Austin married in late 1950.

Mk III
Based on successful Formula Three Hooper Special, but developed, re-engined and given a body - it had none when bought. Originally had 19in wire front wheels (from prewar Morris Eight) and 16in rear wheels from Raleigh three-wheeler. Eventually received Tauranac cast alloy wheels. Used for 18 months by Austin Tauranac with great success.

Mk IV
Vincent-powered mid-engined single-seater begun early 1956 with spaceframe, double-wishbone front suspension, de Dion rear suspension with a transverse leaf, and glassfibre body. Used couple of times by Ron before accepting an offer and using money (about £700) to lay down series of five cars.

Mk V
Front-engined single-seater for Austin begun at same time as Mk IV. Featured

Appendix B

spaceframe and similar suspension to Mk IV and would probably have had Peugeot engine and gearbox, but sold, uncompleted, by Austin on his retirement from racing.

Lynx
In 1958/9 Ron Tauranac laid down batch of five cars for what was nominally 500cc Formula Three but as racing class was virtually dead first production Ralts were expected to be used for hillclimbs, *Formule Libre* races, handicaps, etc. Multi-tubular frame, front suspension by coil springs and double wishbones and rear suspension by a transverse leaf spring and lower wishbones. Rigidly mounted engine/gearbox contributed to chassis stiffness. On departing for England Ron sold the drawings, wheel patterns and completed parts to Lynx Engineering and design formed basis for Lynx Mk II Formula Junior car of 1962, although double-wishbone rear suspension replaced original leaf-spring arrangement. Later Lynx Mk III was essentially a new design.

APPENDIX C

The MRD/Brabhams

Production details have been extrapolated from records compiled at the works after Ron Tauranac left, with amendments based on additional information supplied by him.
Only combined production figures are available for the years 1969-70.

BT1 (Produced 1961 – 1 made.)
Formula Junior car, originally known as MRD but retrospectively renamed as first Brabham in BT series. Spaceframe car with aluminium body, Ford engine, modified VW gearbox, drum brakes inboard at rear. Front suspension by coil springs, lower wishbones, single upper arms and Y-shaped radius rods. Rear suspension by coil springs, broad-based upper wishbones, lower links and twin radius rods. Car bought and successfully raced by Gavin Youl, winning Australian National Formula Junior Championship in March 1962.

BT2 (Produced 1962 – 11 made.)
Development of BT1 Formula Junior car but with Hewland Mk 5 gearbox and glassfibre body by Specialised Mouldings. Girling disc brakes all round and rear brakes now mounted outboard for easier maintenance and to avoid possible problems with oil on discs.

BT3 (Produced 1962 – 1 made.)
Formula One car built along similar lines to BT2 but with Coventry Climax 1.5-litre V8 engine, 6-speed Colotti gearbox, later changed to 5-speed Hewland before car sold to Ian Raby. Rear suspension featured parallel transverse lower links. Initially ran with Lola rear wheels, later changed to Brabham wheels.

BT4 (Produced 1962 – 3 made.)
'International' car powered by Coventry Climax FPF engine, mainly used in Australasian Tasman series run to 2.5-litre Formula One rules until 1970. Different engine bay from BT3. Jack Brabham won 1963 Australian GP and Graham Hill 1964 Tasman race at Longford driving BT4-Climax.

BT5 (Produced 1963 – 2 made.)
Sports-racing car powered by 1.6-litre Lotus-Ford Twin Cam engine and sharing many components with BT6 Formula Junior car. One car sold to Ian Walker for Frank Gardner and Paul Hawkins to drive.

BT6 (Produced 1963 – 20 made.)
Further development of BT2 Formula Junior car, some examples adapted to

Formula Two and Formula Three specification in 1964. Italian firm De Sanctis built copies of BT6 in 1964.

BT7 (Produced 1963 – 2 made.)
Development of BT3 with longer wheelbase, Hewland gearbox, revised bodywork and rear suspension by upper wishbones and lower transverse links.

BT7A (Produced 1963 – 3 made.)
Similar to BT7 but fitted with 2.5-litre Coventry Climax FPF engine. Jack Brabham won 1964 Australian GP with a BT7A-Climax.

BT8 (None made.)
Car designed but not built in this form. Wheel and tyre sizes changed leading to redesign as BT8A.

BT8A (Produced 1964-6 – 12 made.)
Sports-racing car produced to use batch of 2.0, 2.5 and 2.7-litre Coventry Climax engines after prototype initially raced with 2-litre BRM V8 engine. Roger Nathan adapted his BT8A to take 3.5-litre Oldsmobile V8, but experiment was unsuccessful. Many components common with BT11 F1 car.

BT9 (Produced 1964 – 13 made.)
Further development of BT2 Formula Junior car with Jack Knight gearbox derived from Hillman Imp transmission. Silvio Moser used BT9 to win four international races.

BT10 (Produced 1964 – 17 made.)
Formula Two development of BT6 single-seater, usually with Cosworth SCA engine and Hewland gearbox. Steel sheeting welded to bottom chassis tubes for added stiffness and to achieve minimum weight requirements. Pendant pedals in place of floor-mounted pedals of FJ/F3 cars, a distinction which continued until 1968 and the BT23 series. BT10 won nine of 18 F2 races in 1964. Some cars raced in Italy powered by dohc engine based on Fiat block. French firm Alpine bought cars, kits and the right to manufacture BT10s.

BT11 (Produced 1964 – 5 made.)
A revision of the BT10 built around the smaller and wider 13in tyres introduced by Dunlop.

BT11A (Produced 1964 – 5 made.)
A version of the previous car usually fitted with a Coventry Climax FPF engine. Certain BT11A chassis components supplied to LDS specials manufacturer Doug Serrurier for use in South African Gold Star Championship races by Sam Tingle. The last of Serrurier's line of LDS models came in 1965-6 with two cars based on the Brabham BT16.

BT12 (Produced 1964 – 1 made.)
IndyCar commissioned by John Zink and entered as John Zink Track Burner Special with 4.2-litre Offenhauser engine and Hewland DG300 gearbox.

Retired at Indianapolis in 1964 but subsequently won four Championship races in hands of Jim McElreath (once with Ford V8 engine). Clint Brawner was permitted to copy BT12, his version being called a Hawk, though entered as the Dean Van Lines Special. Mario Andretti won the 1965 IndyCar Championship with this car which was then further developed and although still essentially a Brabham, was commonly referred to as the Brawner or the Brawner-Hawk.

BT13 (None made.)
Number not allocated – Ron was certainly not superstitious about 13 as this is the date of his birthday, so he thinks it was because Jack Brabham was against it.

BT14 (Produced 1965-6 – 10 made.)
Formule Libre single-seater used for this class of racing at club level as well as for hillclimbing. From the BT14 would emerge the design of a Formula A/Formula 5000 car in the late 1960s.

BT15 (Produced 1965-6 – 58 made.)
Formula Three car sharing the same chassis with the BT14 and BT16, but fitted with Girling brakes and Hewland Mk 6 gearbox. Nearly all cars fitted with Cosworth Ford MAE engine. Very successful car, winning 42 major races.

BT16 (Produced 1965 – 12 made.)
Formula Two car, mainly powered by Cosworth SCA engine although some cars used BRM units. Jack Brabham ran a BT16 with a Honda dohc engine in three late-season races in 1965 before using them for the works team in 1966.

BT16A (Produced 1965 – 21 made.)
A Formula Three car built largely to Formula Two chassis specification.

BT17 (Produced 1966 – 1 made.)
Prototype Group 7 sports-racing car, basically a stretched BT8A with wider wheels (front 13x8in, rear 13x10in), bigger brakes etc. Originally fitted with 4.3-litre Repco engine, then by 3-litre version. Car later sold to private owner.

BT18 (Produced 1966 – 6 made.)
Formula Two car with 2.5in longer engine bay for improved acceessibility and longer uprights to copy with greater stresses generated by ever-wider tyres. Customer cars powered by Cosworth SCA engine but works team ran dohc Honda engines and had rubber doughnuts attached to drive-shafts.

BT18A (Produced 1966 – 32 made.)
Formula Three version of the previous car.

BT18B (Produced 1966 – 8 made.)
Car built to special order for the Honda racing school with a tuned Ford Kent engine. Essentially a Formula Ford 1600 car produced some 18 months before this formula was officially launched.

BT19 (Produced 1966 – 1 made.)
One-off car originally designed for the stillborn Coventry Climax 1.5-litre flat-

16 engine in 1965, then converted to run with 3-litre Repco RB620 V8 engine and Hewland DG300 gearbox. Wheel sizes 15x8in front, 15x10in rear.

BT20 (Produced 1966 – 2 made.)
Improved BT19 with longer wheelbase and stiffer frame, but still with RB620 engine and DG300 gearbox.

BT21 (Produced 1966-8 – 50 made.)
Further Formula Three development of BT18 single-seater with Hewland H6 gearbox and virtually all cars fitted with Ford-based engines. Shallower spaceframe than previous cars and detail revisions to suspension, including wider track, and slimmer body. Arrived late in 1966 but destined to become most popular Brabham model.

BT21A (Produced 1967 – 10 made.)
Formule Libre car with Lotus-Ford Twin Cam engine.

BT21B (Produced 1967-8 – 31 made.)
Update of BT21 with 13x7in front and 13x9in rear wheels and Hewland FT200 gearbox. Birel built by Ernesto and Vittorio Brambilla was a BT21 copy.

BT21C (Produced 1967-8 – 18 made.)
Formule Libre version of previous car.

BT21X (Produced 1968 – 1 made.)
Works development Formula Three car with stiffer spaceframe based on BT23.

BT22 (Produced 1966 – 1 made.)
Formule Libre car with 2.5-litre Coventry Climax FPF engine, originally built for a Scottish customer but later sold to New Zealand driver Jim Palmer for Tasman series races. Car based on BT11A but with BT19 suspension geometry.

BT23 (Produced 1967 – 9 made.)
Formula Two car with spaceframe stiffened by stress-bearing panels and engine bay reinforced with additional small tubes. Fitted with Brabham-made uprights and stub-axles.

BT23A (Produced 1967 – 1 made.)
International version powered by 2.5-litre Repco engine and used by Jack Brabham for 1967 Tasman series, winner at Longford.

BT23B (Produced 1967 – 3 made.)
Hillclimb version of BT23 powered by Coventry Climax FPF engine.

BT23C (Produced 1967-8 – 13 made.)
Formula Two version powered by 1.6-litre Cosworth FVA engine driving through Hewland FT200 gearbox.

BT23D (Produced 1967 – 1 made.)
Tasman car powered by Alfa Romeo Tipo 33 engine built for Kevin Bartlett,

who won 1968 Australian Gold Star Championship with it.

BT23E (Produced 1967 – 1 made.)
Tasman car with Repco V8 engine.

BT23F (Produced 1968 – 1 made.)
Car built for SCCA Formula B (Atlantic) racing with Lotus-Ford Twin Cam engine and Hewland FT200 gearbox

BT23G (Produced 1968 – 2 made.)
Similar to BT23F but with Hewland Mk 5 gearbox.

BT24 (Produced 1967-8 – 3 made.)
Formula One car following design of BT23A Tasman chassis apart from wider engine bay. More powerful Repco V8 engine, designated 740 and producing 330bhp, driving through Hewland DG300 transmission. BT24 almost as compact as current F2 car.

BT25 (Produced 1968 – 2 made.)
Indianapolis car – first Brabham to feature tubular chassis reinforced with stressed aluminium panels to meet requirement of bag-type fuel tanks. Fitted with 4.2-litre Repco V8 engine and Hewland LG500 gearbox. Wheels 15x8.5in front, 15x9.5in rear.

BT26 (Produced 1968 – 3 made.)
Further development of BT24 Formula One car, longer and with wider track. Fitted with dohc four-valve Repco RB860 engine. Wheels 15x11in front, 15x14in rear.

BT27 (None made.)
Type number reserved for 4WD Formula One car which did not progress beyond design study.

BT28 (Produced 1969-70 – 42 made.)
Formula Three car based on BT21X with stiffer frame and new bodywork. Tyre widths increased to 9in front, 12in rear.

BT29 (Produced 1969-70 – 29 made.)
Formula B car, closer in specification to Formula Two than Formula Three. Tyre widths 10in front, 14in rear. One or two cars subsequently uprated to run in Formula Two.

BT30 (Produced 1969-70 – 26 made.)
Formula Two car with more complicated spaceframe than Formula Three sibling. Wings appeared in Formula Two in 1969. Bag tanks housed in distinctive bodyside bulges.

BT30X (Produced 1969 – 2 made.)
Hillclimb car developed from BT30 with 1.8-litre Cosworth FVA engine, stronger drive-shafts, smaller brakes and tiny fuel tank.

Appendix C

BT31 (Produced 1969 – 1 made.)
International car fitted with Coventry Climax 2-litre V8 engine and used in Tasman series.

BT32 (Produced 1970 – 1 made.)
Indianapolis car with turbocharged 2.6-litre Offenhauser engine, Weisman gearbox and 15x10in front and 15x14in rear wheels..

BT33 (Produced 1970 – 4 made.)
First monocoque Brabham Formula One car. Cosworth Ford DFV engine driving through Hewland DG300 gearbox. Wheels 13x11in front, 13x16in rear.

BT34 (Produced 1971 – 1 made.)
Formula One car nicknamed the 'lobster claw' because of its twin water radiator nacelles ahead of the front wheels, with adjustable aerofoil section linking them. Built for Graham Hill with slab-sided monocoque and outboard suspension and front brakes. Front track of 62in, 4in wider than BT33.

BT35A (Produced 1971 – 3 made.)
SCCA Formula Atlantic version of multi-formula car with inboard rear brakes, Ford 1600 Twin Cam engine and Hewland FT200 gearbox.

BT35B (Produced 1971 – 7 made.)
Formula B/Atlantic car with 13x10in front and 13x14in rear tyres, outboard rear brakes and Hewland FT200 gearbox.

BT35C (Produced 1971 – 27 made.)
Formula Three version with 13x9in front and 13x10in rear tyres and Hewland Mk 8 gearbox.

BT35X (Produced 1971 – 4 made.)
Hillclimb car with heavy-duty drive-shafts. Two cars fitted with 1.6-litre Cosworth Ford Twin Cam engine and one with 1.8-litre Cosworth FVC engine, all with Hewland FT200 gearbox and Formula Atlantic-size wheels. One car with 5-litre Repco V8 engine, Hewland DG300 gearbox and 16in wide rear wheels, used by Mike MacDowell to win RAC Hillclimb Championship.

BT36 (Produced 1971 – 9 made.)
Formula Two car similar to BT35B but with Cosworth FVA engine.

(Ron Tauranac left MRD at the beginning of 1972.)

BT36X (Produced 1972 – 1 made.)
Hillclimb car with 5-litre Repco V8 engine, Hewland DG300 gearbox and 16in wide rear wheels.

BT37 (Produced 1972 – 2 made.)
Revision of Ron Tauranac's BT33 by Ralph Bellamy with conventional front radiator and slightly narrower front and rear tracks.

BT38 (Produced 1972 – 16 made.)
Formula Two car, designed largely by Geoff Ferris but with suspension similar to BT36. First customer Brabham with monocoque chassis. Chisel nose, side radiators and tubular frame behind cockpit.

BT38B (Produced 1972 – 5 made.)
Formula B version of BT38.

BT38C (Produced 1972 – 14 made.)
Formula Three version of BT38.

BT39 (Produced 1972 – 1 made.)
Formula One car based on BT38 chassis but fitted with Weslake V12 engine and Hewland FG400 gearbox. Tested but not raced.

BT40 (Produced 1973 – 28 made.)
Formula Two (9 built) and Formula B (19 built) car.

BT41 (Produced 1973 – 21 made.)
Formula Three car.

BT43 (Produced 1973-4 – 1 made.)
Formula 5000 car.

Appendix C

BRABHAM by model	1961	1962	1963	1964	1965	1966	1967	1968	1969	1970	1971	1972	Total
BT1	1												1
BT2		11											11
BT3		1											1
BT4		3											3
BT5			2										2
BT6			20										20
BT7			2										2
BT7A			3										3
BT8A				9	2	1							12
BT9				13									13
BT10				17									17
BT11				5									5
BT11A				5									5
BT12				1									1
BT14					9	1							10
BT15					26	32							58
BT16					12								12
BT16A					21								21
BT17						1							1
BT18						6							6
BT18A						32							32
BT18B						8							8
BT19						1							1
BT20						2							2
BT21						4	45	1					50
BT21A							10						10
BT21B							4	27					31
BT21C							2	16					18
BT21X								1					1
BT22						1							1

BRABHAM by model	1961	1962	1963	1964	1965	1966	1967	1968	1969	1970	1971	1972	Total
BT23							9						9
BT23A							1						1
BT23B							3						3
BT23C							3	10					13
BT23D							1						1
BT23E							1						1
BT23F								1					1
BT23G								2					2
BT24							2	1					3
BT25								2					2
BT26								3					3
BT28									42*				42
BT29									29*				29
BT30									26*				26
BT30X									2				2
BT31									1				1
BT32										1			1
BT33										4			4
BT34											1		1
BT35A											3		3
BT35B											7		7
BT35C											27		27
BT35X											4		4
BT36											9		9
BT36X												1	1
BT37												2	2
BT38												16	16
BT38B												5	5
BT38C												14	14
BT39												1	1
TOTAL	1	15	27	50	70	89	81	64	100	5	51	39	592

Appendix C

BRABHAM by category	1961	1962	1963	1964	1965	1966	1967	1968	1969	1970	1971	1972	Total
FJ	1	11	20										32
F1		1	2			3	2	4		4	1	3	20
Internat'l		3	3	5			3		1				15
Sports			2	9	2	2							15
F3				13	47	68	49	29	42*		27	14	289
F2				22	12	6	12	10	26*		9	16	113
Indy					1			2		1			4
F Libre						9	2	12	16				39
School								8					8
F Atlantic								3	29*		10	5	47
Hillclimb								3		2	4	1	10
TOTAL	1	15	27	50	70	89	81	64	100	5	51	39	592

* Denotes combined production for 1969 and 1970. Individual year figures are unavailable but are believed to be approximately equal within the total production figure of 105 cars over the two years.

APPENDIX D

MRD/Brabham racing record, 1962-72

During 1962-5 the Brabham Racing Organisation was a customer of Motor Racing Developments. Contrary to popular belief, therefore, BRO was essentially a private team and not MRD's official works team.

Chassis numbers: The first car was numbered FJ/1. From 1962 until the end of 1966 chassis plates bore a type designation, a frame number and the year of manufacture. Thus F3-1-63 was the first Formula Junior car to be made that year. From the beginning of 1967 cars bore a BT number followed by the number of the chassis. Thus BT30-5 was the fifth BT30 to be made. In the interests of clarity and consistency, the latter system has been used throughout.

Race and championship results: All Formula One races which had an international entry in which a Brabham appeared are detailed. World Championship events are marked in bold. In the 1960s there was also a healthy series in Southern Africa which complied with Formula One rules.

One has to draw a line somewhere, and anyone requiring even more comprehensive entry lists and results than those which follow are recommended to consult the works published by the Formula One Register, without whose valued assistance there would have been some large gaps in what follows here. The address is: 4 Station Road, Esholt, Shipley, West Yorkshire BD17 7QR, England. Telephone: 01943-877388; Fax: 01943-877204.

We also acknowledge Peter Higham's *The Guinness Guide To International Motor Racing* (Guinness Publishing Ltd, 1995), which supplied some of the more obscure championship winners.

Occasional inconsistencies in recording the results of some intermediate championships arise through their fluctuating importance. For example, from the early 1970s the British Formula Three Championship has been regarded as the most important F3 race series whereas in the 1960s the most talented drivers tended to concentrate on a series of European races which, though they were not organized into a championship, were universally regarded as the most important. These included support races to Grands Prix. From 1970 onwards, the main criterion in selecting which championships to list has been the way in which the results reflect the changes within Formula Three.

1962

German Grand Prix, Nürburgring, 5.8.62

		Qual	race	
BT3	Brabham	24	rtd	throttle linkage

International Gold Cup, Oulton Park, 1.9.62

BT3	Brabham	5	3

United States Grand Prix, Watkins Glen, 7.10.62

BT3	Brabham	5	4

Mexican Grand Prix, Mexico City, 4.11.62

BT3	Brabham	7	2

Although the Mexican Grand Prix attracted some leading Formula One runners, it was the first time the event had been staged and therefore was a non-Championship trial run prior to being awarded full Championship status in 1963.

South African Grand Prix, East London, 29.12.62

BT3	Brabham	3	4

Drivers' World Championship:
 1 Graham Hill (BRM)   42 (+10)
 2 Jim Clark (Lotus)   30
 3 Bruce McLaren (Cooper)   27 (+5)
 4 John Surtees (Lola)   19
 5 Dan Gurney (Porsche)   15
 6 Phil Hill (Ferrari)   14
 9 Jack Brabham (Lotus & Brabham) 9

Figures in brackets indicate a driver's additional points score over the season which under the scoring rules had to be discounted.

Constructors' Cup:
 1 BRM   42 (+14)
 2 Lotus-Climax   36 (+2)
 3 Cooper-Climax   29 (+8)
 4 Lola-Climax   19 (+1)
 5 Porsche   18
 Ferrari   18
 7 Brabham-Climax   6

Australian Formula Junior Champion: Gavin Youl
French Formula Junior Champion: Jo Schlesser

1963

Dan Gurney joined Jack Brabham in the Brabham Racing Organisation team. David Prophet entered some races in a BT6 powered by a 1,500cc Ford engine tuned by Cosworth. This was by no means an uncommon route and several makes of chassis were run as 'Formula One' cars using what was basically a

Ford Cortina engine, among them being Jo Schlesser's BT2. These cars mainly appeared in non-Championship races, and while no match for factory entries, in the hands of good drivers they frequently saw off less competent privateers in superior equipment.

Races for the South African Gold Star Championship were nominally run to 'Formula One' (1½-litre) rules, but were restricted to four-cylinder engines. Listed in this Appendix are only those races which were run to the FIA Formula One, without restriction of the number of cylinders. In practice this meant races which saw European participation alongside cars built to the local formula. All of these races took place in South Africa, although other races in the Southern African series were staged in Rhodesia, now Zimbabwe, and Mozambique. The national series attracted some fine drivers and good locally-built cars.

		Pau Grand Prix, Pau, 15.4.63			
BT2-5	Schlesser	8	rtd	engine	

		Glover Trophy, Goodwood, 15.4.63			
BT3	Brabham	3	6		

		Imola Grand Prix, Imola, 21.4.63			
BT2-5	Schlesser	7	4		

		BARC 200, Aintree, 27.4.63			
BT3	Brabham	2	DNS	piston	

		International Trophy, Silverstone, 11.5.63			
BT3	Brabham	4	7		

		Monaco Grand Prix, Monte Carlo, 26.5.63			
BT7-1	Gurney	6	rtd	crownwheel and pinion	

Jack Brabham had engine problems in qualifying and was loaned a Lotus 25 by Team Lotus. He qualified, and finished, last.

		Belgian Grand Prix, Spa, 9.6.63			
BT3	Brabham	6	rtd	fuel injection pump	
BT7-1	Gurney	2	3		

		Dutch Grand Prix, Zandvoort, 23.6.63			
BT7-2	Brabham	4	rtd	accident	
BT7-1	Gurney	14	2		

		French Grand Prix, Reims, 30.6.63			
BT7-2	Brabham	5	4		
BT7-1	Gurney	3	5		

		British Grand Prix, Silverstone, 20.7.63			
BT7-2	Brabham	4	rtd	con-rod	
BT7-1	Gurney	2	rtd	con-rod	

Solitude Grand Prix, Solitude, 28.7.63
| BT3 | Brabham | 2 | 1 | |

German Grand Prix, Nürburgring, 4.8.63
| BT7-2 | Brabham | 8 | 7 | |
| BT7-1 | Gurney | 13 | rtd | gearbox |

Kannonloppet, Karlskoga, 11.8.63
| BT7-2 | Brabham | 1 | 3 | |

Mediterranean Grand Prix, Enna, 18.8.63
| BT2-5 | Schlesser | 13 | 11 | |

Austrian Grand Prix, Zeltweg, 1.9.63
| BT3 | Brabham | 2 | 1 | fastest lap |

Italian Grand Prix, Monza, 8.9.63
| BT3 | Brabham | 7 | 5 | |
| BT7-1 | Gurney | 5 | rtd | oil feed |

International Gold Cup, Oulton Park, 21.9.63
| BT7-2 | Brabham | 11 | 4 | |
| BT7-1 | Gurney | 16 | rtd | oil leak |

United States Grand Prix, Watkins Glen, 6.10.63
| BT7-2 | Brabham | 5 | 4 | |
| BT7-1 | Gurney | 6 | rtd | cracked chassis |

Mexican Grand Prix, Mexico City, 27.10.63
| BT7-2 | Brabham | 10 | 2 | |
| BT7-1 | Gurney | 4 | 6 | |

Rand Grand Prix, Kyalami, 14.12.63
| BT5-5 | Prophet | 12 | 5 | |

South African Grand Prix, 28.12.63
BT7-2	Brabham	2	rtd	accident
BT7-1	Gurney	3	2	
BT6-5	Prophet	14	rtd	oil leak

Drivers' World Championship:
- 1 Jim Clark (Lotus)   54 (+19)
- 2 Graham Hill (BRM)   29 (+5)
-    Richie Ginther (BRM)   29
- 4 John Surtees (Ferrari)   22
- 5 Dan Gurney (Brabham)   19
- 6 Bruce McLaren (Cooper)   17
- 7 Jack Brabham (Brabham)   14

Constructors' Cup:
1 Lotus-Climax   54 (+20)
2 BRM   36 (+9)
3 Brabham-Climax   29 (+2)
4 Ferrari   26
5 Cooper-Climax   25 (+1)
6 BRP-BRM   6

Australian Gold Star Champion: Bib Stillwell

1964
Formula One privateer Ian Raby bought BT3 and ran it with a customer BRM V8 engine and six-speed Colotti gearbox. Bob Anderson had BT11-5 with a V8 Coventry Climax engine and five-speed Hewland transmission. Rob Walker bought BT11-4 and BT11-6, used BRM engines and six-speed Colotti gearboxes, and entered cars for Jo Siffert, Jo Bonnier and, on occasion, Jochen Rindt and Hap Sharp. Walker later acquired BT7-2, which retained its Coventry Climax engine.

John Willment Automobiles entered BT10-4, a converted Formula Two car with a Cosworth-tuned Ford engine and Hewland gearbox, for Frank Gardner and, later, Paul Hawkins.

Formula Three replaced Formula Junior this year. The main difference was a reduction in engine size from 1,100cc to 1,000cc and tighter tuning restrictions.

Formula Two was revived for cars with engines of 1,000cc and no more than four cylinders. Overhead camshafts were permitted.

		Daily Mirror Trophy, Snetterton, 14.3.64			
BT7-1	Brabham	5		rtd	scavenge pump
BT3	Raby	11		rtd	accident

		News of the World Trophy, Goodwood, 30.3.64			
BT7-2	Brabham	1		rtd	broken wheel rim
BT3	Raby	12		rtd	ignition

		Syracuse Grand Prix, Siracusa, 13.4.64			
BT3	Raby	6	8		

		Aintree 200, Aintree, 18.4.64			
BT7-2	Brabham	2	1		
BT7-1	Gurney	20		rtd	transmission doughnut
BT3	Raby	21	15		

		International Trophy, Silverstone, 2.5.64			
BT7-2	Brabham	2	1		
BT7-1	Gurney	1		rtd	brakes binding
BT3	Raby	19		rtd	piston
BT11-5	Anderson	18		rtd	clutch

Appendix D

Monaco Grand Prix, Monte Carlo, 10.5.64

BT7-2	Brabham	2	rtd	fuel injection
BT7-1	Gurney	5	rtd	gearbox
BT11-5	Anderson 1	2	rtd	gearbox mounting

Dutch Grand Prix, Zandvoort, 24.5.64

BT7-2	Brabham	7	rtd	ignition drive
BT7-1	Gurney	1	rtd	steering wheel
BT11-5	Anderson	11	6	
BT11-6	Siffert	17	13	
BT11-4	Bonnier	12	9	

Belgian Grand Prix, Spa, 14.6.64

BT7-2	Brabham	3	3	
BT7-1	Gurney	1	6	not running at end
BT11-6	Siffert	13	rtd	piston
BT11-4	Bonnier	14	rtd	driver unwell

French Grand Prix, Rouen, 28.6.64

BT7-2	Brabham	5	3	
BT7-1	Gurney	2	1	
BT11-5	Anderson	15	12	
BT11-6	Siffert	17	rtd	clutch

British Grand Prix, Brands Hatch, 11.7.64

BT7-2	Brabham	4	4	
BT7-1	Gurney	3	13	
BT11-5	Anderson	7	7	
BT11-4	Bonnier	9	rtd	brake pipe
BT11-6	Siffert	16	11	
BT3	Raby	17	rtd	accident
BT10-4	Gardner	19	rtd	accident

Solitude Grand Prix, Solitude 19.7.64

BT7-2	Brabham	8	rtd	accident
BT11-5	Anderson	7	3	
BT11-6	Siffert	10	7	
BT11-4	Bonnier	13	5	

German Grand Prix, Nürburgring, 2.8.64

BT7-2	Brabham	7	12	not running at end
BT7-1	Gurney	3	10	
BT11-6	Siffert	10	4	
BT11-4	Bonnier	12	rtd	electrics
BT11-5	Anderson 1	3	rtd	suspension

Mediterranean Grand Prix, Enna, 16.8.64

BT11-6	Siffert	1	1	
BT10-4	Gardner	11	rtd	piston

Austrian Grand Prix, Zeltweg, 23.8.64

BT11-1	Brabham	6	9	
BT7-1	Gurney	4	rtd	front suspension
BT7-2	Bonnier	9	6	
BT11-5	Anderson	12	3	
BT11-4	Rindt	13	rtd	steering
BT11-6	Siffert	14	rtd	accident

Italian Grand Prix, Monza, 6.9.64

BT11-1	Brabham	11	14	not running at end
BT7-1	Gurney	2	10	
BT11-6	Siffert	6	7	
BT7-2	Bonnier	12	12	
BT11-5	Anderson	14	11	

United States Grand Prix, Watkins Glen, 4.10.64

BT11-1	Brabham	7	rtd	piston
BT7-1	Gurney	3	rtd	oil pressure
BT7-2	Bonnier	9	rtd	stub axle
BT11-6	Siffert	12	3	
BT11-4	Sharp	18		not classified

Mexican Grand Prix, Mexico City, 25.10.64

BT11-1	Brabham	7	rtd	ignition, when third
BT7-1	Gurney	2	1	
BT7-2	Bonnier	8	rtd	wishbone
BT11-6	Siffert	13	rtd	fuel pump
BT11-4	Sharp	19	13	

Rand Grand Prix, Kyalami, 12.12.64

BT11-4	Hill	23	1
BT10-4	Hawkins	3	2
BT11-5	Anderson	4	3

Drivers' World Championship:
1 John Surtees (Ferrari)   40
2 Graham Hill (BRM)   39 (+2)
3 Jim Clark (Lotus)   32
4 Lorenzo Bandini (Ferrari)   23
   Richie Ginther (BRM)   23
6 Dan Gurney (Brabham)   19
9 Jack Brabham (Brabham)   7
10 Jo Siffert (Brabham)   5
11 Bob Anderson (Brabham)   4
15 Jo Bonnier (Brabham)   2

Appendix D

Constructors' Cup:
  1 Ferrari   45 (+4)
  2 BRM   42 (+9)
  3 Lotus-Climax   37 (+3)
  4 Brabham-Climax   33
  5 Cooper-Climax   16
  6 Brabham-BRM   7

Brabham Formula Two victories:

Driver	Circuit
Jochen Rindt	Crystal Palace
Alan Rees	Reims
Denny Hulme	Clermont-Ferrand
Jack Brabham	Karlskoga
Denny Hulme	Zolder
Jack Brabham	Albi
Jack Brabham	Oulton Park
Jo Schlesser	Vallelunga
Jack Brabham	Montlhéry

There was no European Formula Two Championship in 1964, the closest thing being *Les Grands Prix de France*, a six-race series run at traditional non-Championship circuits like Albi and Pau. The series was won by Brabham from Hulme and Rees.

Argentine Temporada (F2) Champion: Silvio Moser

Brabham Tasman Cup victories:

Driver	Race
Denny Hulme	Levin
Jack Brabham	Australian Grand Prix
Jack Brabham	Warwick Park
Jack Brabham	Lakeside
Graham Hill	Longford

Australian Gold Star Champion: Bib Stillwell

1965

The Brabham Racing Organisation continued to use combinations of the three 1994 cars it had bought from MRD. The cars' drive train now included rubber doughnuts as well as universal joints – a first in Formula One. Rob Walker Racing entered BT7-2 for Jo Bonnier and BT11-6 for Jo Siffert. John Willment Automobiles bought BT11-4 from Rob Walker and continued to enter BT10-4. The cars which Rodney Bloor and John Cardwell raced occasionally in Formula One races were Ford-powered.

South African Grand Prix, East London, 1.1.65

BT11-1	Brabham	3	8	
BT11-2	Gurney	9	rtd	ignition
BT7-2	Bonnier	7	rtd	clutch
BT11-5	Anderson	12	16	
BT11-6	Siffert	14	7	
BT11-4	Gardner	15	12	
BT10-4	Hawkins	16	9	
BT10-10	Prophet	19	14	

Race of Champions, Brands Hatch, 13.3.65

BT11-1	Brabham	5	rtd	oil leak
BT11-2	Gurney	13	rtd	accident
BT7-2	Bonnier	4	3	
BT11-5	Anderson	8	rtd	throttle linkage
BT11-6	Siffert	12	6	
BT11-4	Gardner	14	4	
BT3	Raby	15	9	

Syracuse Grand Prix, Siracusa, 4.4.65

BT7-2	Bonnier	3	4	
BT11-6	Siffert	4	rtd	con-rod
BT11-5	Anderson	10	6	
BT3	Raby	11	8	

Sunday Mirror Trophy, Goodwood, 19.4.65

BT11-1	Brabham	5	3	
BT11-2	Gurney	7	9	
BT11-5	Anderson	4		disqualified, missed chicane
BT7-2	Bonnier	8	5	
BT11-6	Siffert	9	rtd	accident
BT14-6	Bloor	13	12	
BT14-8	Cardwell	14	11	

International Trophy, Silverstone, 15.5.65

BT11-1	Brabham	6	rtd	
BT11-2	Hulme	7	rtd	oil leak
BT7-2	Bonnier	8	5	
BT11-4	Gardner	10	rtd	clutch
BT11-5	Anderson	14	14	
BT3	Raby	18	12	

Monaco Grand Prix, Monte Carlo, 30.5.65

BT11-1	Brabham	2	rtd	con-rod
BT7-1	Hulme	8	8	
BT11-5	Anderson	9	9	
BT11-6	Siffert	10	6	
BT11-4	Gardner	11	rtd	engine mounting
BT7-2	Bonnier	13	7	

Belgian Grand Prix, Spa, 13.6.65

BT11-1	Brabham	10	4		
BT11-2	Gurney	5	10		
BT7-2	Bonnier	7	rtd	ignition	
BT11-6	Siffert	8	8		
BT11-4	Gardner	18	rtd	ignition	

French Grand Prix, Clermont-Ferrand, 27.6.65

BT11-2	Gurney	5	rtd	engine	
BT11-1	Hulme	6	4		
BT7-2	Bonnier	11	rtd	alternator drive	
BT11-6	Siffert	14	6		
BT11-5	Anderson	15	9		

British Grand Prix, Silverstone, 10.7.65

BT11-2	Gurney	7	6		
BT7-1	Hulme	9	rtd	alternator drive	
BT11-4	Gardner	12	8		
BT7-2	Bonnier	13	7		
BT11-5	Anderson	15	rtd	gearbox	
BT11-6	Siffert	16	9		
BT3	Raby	18	11		

Dutch Grand Prix, Zandvoort, 18.7.65

BT11-2	Gurney	5	3		
BT11-1	Hulme	7	5		
BT11-6	Siffert	10	13		
BT11-4	Gardner	11	11		
BT7-2	Bonnier	15	rtd	valve spring	
BT11-5	Anderson	16	rtd	head gasket	

German Grand Prix, Nürburgring, 1.8.65

BT11-1	Brabham	14	5		
BT11-2	Gurney	5	3		
BT7-1	Hulme	13	rtd	fuel leak	
BT7-2	Bonnier	9	7		
BT11-6	Siffert	11	rtd	engine	
BT11-4	Gardner	17	rtd	gearbox	

Mediterranean Grand Prix, Enna, 15.8.65

BT11-1	Brabham	8	6		
BT11-6	Siffert	3	1		
BT7-1	Hulme	5	4		
BT11-4	Gardner	6	3		
BT7-2	Bonnier	7	rtd	oil pressure	
BT16-1	Rees	10	rtd	piston	
BT16-2	Rindt	12	rtd	drive-shaft	

Italian Grand Prix, Monza, 12.9.65

BT7-1	Baghetti	19	rtd	con-rod
BT11-2	Gurney	9	3	
BT11-1	Hulme	12	rtd	front suspension
BT11-6	Siffert	10	rtd	gearbox
BT7-2	Bonnier	14	7	
BT11-4	Gardner	1	6rtd	engine

United States Grand Prix, Watkins Glen, 3.10.65

BT11-1	Brabham	7	3
BT11-2	Gurney	8	2
BT7-2	Bonnier	10	8
BT11-6	Siffert	11	11

Mexican Grand Prix, Mexico City, 24.10.65

BT11-1	Brabham	4	rtd	oil leak
BT11-2	Gurney	2	2	
BT11-6	Siffert	13	4	
BT7-2	Bonnier	14	rtd	front wishbone mounting

Rand Grand Prix, Kyalami, 4.12.65

BT11-2	Brabham	1	1	
BT11-6	Siffert	8	5	
BT11-5	Anderson	4	rtd	oil pressure
BT11A-5	de Klerk	3	2	

Race run to 3-litre formula; Brabham used car already sold to a customer, fitted with 2.7-litre Coventry Climax FPF engine. De Klerk's car was to International spec. Strictly speaking this was not a Formula One race because it occurred 27 days before the official start of the formula.

Drivers' World Championship:
    1 Jim Clark (Lotus)   54
    2 Graham Hill (BRM)   40 (+7)
    3 Jackie Stewart (BRM)   33 (+1)
    4 Dan Gurney (Brabham)   25
    5 John Surtees (Ferrari)   17
    6 Lorenzo Bandini (Ferrari)   13
    10 Jack Brabham (Brabham)   9
    11 Denny Hulme (Brabham)   5
       Jo Siffert (Brabham)   5

Constructors' Cup:
    1 Lotus-Climax   54 (+4)
    2 BRM   45 (+16)
    3 Brabham-Climax   27 (+4)
    4 Ferrari   26 (+1)
    5 Cooper-Climax   14
    6 Honda   11

Appendix D

Swedish Formula Three Champion: Picko Troberg
Australian Gold Star Champion: Bib Stillwell
New Zealand Gold Star Champion: Jim Palmer

Brabham Formula Two victories:
  Denny Hulme   Oulton Park
  Graham Hill   Snetterton
  Jochen Rindt   Reims
  Jack Brabham   Karlskoga
  Alan Rees   Pergusa
  Silvio Moser   Syracuse

Brabham Tasman Cup victories:

  Graham Hill   New Zealand Grand Prix
  Jack Brabham   Sandown Park

1966
This marked the start of the 3-litre Formula One and was the last year of the 1-litre Formula Two. The Southern African Championship was also run to a 3-litre Formula, and jumped the gun by holding its first race in late 1965. The Brabhams which were raced in it – Dave Charlton's BT11-2 and Piet de Klerk's BT11A-5 – were fitted with Coventry Climax FPF units. In December 1966 Luki Botha acquired de Klerk's car.
  Denny Hulme's BT11 was fitted with a Coventry Climax FPF engine, as was Bob Anderson's. Rob Walker's BT11-1 (run for Jo Siffert) received an FPF unit at the French Grand Prix. Chris Irwin was occasionally entered in BT11-1 after Hulme switched to BT20-2.

South African Grand Prix, East London, 1.1.66

BT19	Brabham	1	rtd	injector drive belt
BT11-1	Hulme	3	rtd	gearbox
BT11-5	Anderson	8		disqualified, outside assistance
BT11-2	Charlton	10	4	
BT11-6	Siffert	12	2	

Syracuse Grand Prix, Siracusa, 1.5.66

BT19	Brabham	10	rtd	fuel metering unit
BT11-1	Hulme	11	rtd	oil leak
BT11-6	Bonnier	4	5	
BT11-5	Anderson	DNQ		piston

International Trophy, Silverstone, 14.5.66

BT19	Brabham	1	1
BT11-1	Hulme	5	4
BT11-5	Anderson	8	7
BT11-4	Taylor, J	9	6

Monaco Grand Prix, Monte Carlo, 22.5.66

BT19	Brabham	11	rtd	gearbox
BT11-1	Hulme	6	rtd	drive-shaft coupling
BT11-5	Anderson	8	rtd	engine
BT11-6	Siffert	13	rtd	clutch

Belgian Grand Prix, Spa, 13.6.66

BT19	Brabham	4	4	
BT11-1	Hulme	12	rtd	crash

French Grand Prix, Reims, 3.7.66

BT19	Brabham	4	1	
BT20-2	Hulme	9	3	
BT11-1	Siffert	6	rtd	overheating
BT11-5	Anderson	13	7	
BT11-4	Taylor, J	15	6	

British Grand Prix, Brands Hatch, 16.7.66

BT19	Brabham	1	1	
BT20-2	Hulme	2	2	
BT11-1	Irwin	12	7	
BT11-5	Anderson	10	13	
BT11-1	Siffert	11	12	
BT6-2	Bonnier	15	rtd	clutch

Dutch Grand Prix, Zandvoort, 24.7.66

BT19	Brabham	1	1	
BT20-2	Hulme	2	rtd	ignition
BT11-5	Anderson	14	rtd	engine
BT11-4	Taylor, J	17	8	

German Grand Prix, Nürburgring, 7.8.66

BT19	Brabham	5	1	
BT20-2	Hulme	15	rtd	ignition
BT11-5	Anderson	14	rtd	engine
BT11-4	Taylor, J	24	rtd	fatal accident

Italian Grand Prix, Monza, 4.9.66

BT19	Brabham	6	rtd	fuel problem
BT20-2	Hulme	10	3	
BT11-5	Anderson	15	6	
BT11-6	Amon	DNQ		

International Gold Cup, Oulton Park, 17.9.66

BT19	Brabham	1	1	
BT20-2	Hulme	2	2	
BT11-5	Anderson	6	rtd	engine

Appendix D

		United States Grand Prix, Watkins Glen, 2.10.66			
BT20-1	Brabham	1		rtd	engine
BT20-2	Hulme	7		rtd	oil pressure

		Mexican Grand Prix, Mexico City, 29.10.66	
BT20-1	Brabham	4	2
BT20-2	Hulme	6	3

Drivers' World Championship:
1 Jack Brabham (Brabham)   42 (+3)
2 John Surtees (Ferrari and Cooper)   28
3 Jochen Rindt (Cooper)   22 (+2)
4 Denny Hulme (Brabham)   18
5 Graham Hill (BRM)   17
6 Jim Clark (Lotus)   16
17= Bob Anderson (Brabham)   1

Constructors' Cup:
1 Brabham-Repco   46 (+7)
2 Ferrari   31 (+1)
3 Cooper-Maserati   30 (+5)
4 BRM   22
5 Lotus-BRM   13
6 Lotus-Climax   8

Brabham Formula Two victories:

Driver	Circuit
Jack Brabham	Goodwood
Jack Brabham	Pau
Jochen Rindt	Nürburgring
Jack Brabham	Barcelona
Jack Brabham	Zolder
Jack Brabham	Crystal Palace
Jack Brabham	Reims
Denny Hulme	Rouen
Jack Brabham	Karlskoga
Jack Brabham	Kaimola
Jack Brabham	Montlhéry
Denny Hulme	Le Mans
Jack Brabham	Albi
Jochen Rindt	Brands Hatch

The only Formula Two race of the year not won by a Brabham was the Formula Two section of the German Grand Prix – when the principal Brabham drivers were involved in the Formula One section. As in 1965, there was no European F2 Championship, but the French races formed a series, with the results: 1 Brabham (36 points), 2 Hulme (28), 3 Rees (Brabham BT18-Cosworth – 14 points). Jack Brabham also won *The Autocar* British Formula Two Championship

British Formula Three Champion: Harry Stiller
Italian Formula Three Champion: Tino Brambilla
Argentine Temporada (F3) Champion: Charles Chrichton-Stuart
Australian Gold Star Champion: Spencer Martin

1967
New Formula Two which stipulated engines of no more than 1,600cc and a maximum of six cylinders. The engine had to be derived from a production unit of which at least 500 examples had been made. There was a minimum weight of 420kg.

From the British Grand Prix onwards Guy Ligier drove BT20-2. Bob Anderson was killed whilst testing his car on the Club circuit at Silverstone on August 16.

South African Grand Prix, Kyalami, 2.1.67

BT20-1	Brabham	1	6	
BT20-2	Hulme	2	4	
BT11-5	Anderson	10	5	
BT11-2	Charlton	8	7	not running at the finish
BT11-5	Botha	17	8	not running at the finish

Race of Champions, Brands Hatch, 12.3.67

BT20-1	Brabham	5	9	
BT20-2	Hulme	13	rtd	camshaft drive belt
BT11-5	Anderson	16	rtd	ignition

Spring Trophy, Oulton Park, 15.4.67

BT20-1	Brabham	4	1
BT20-2	Hulme	2	2
BT11-5	Anderson	7	7

International Trophy, Silverstone, 29.4.67

BT20-1	Brabham	6	2	
BT20-2	Hulme	4	rtd	oil leak
BT11-5	Anderson	7	8	

Monaco Grand Prix, Monte Carlo, 7.5.67

BT19	Brabham	1	rtd	engine
BT20-2	Hulme	4	1	
BT11-5	Anderson	DNQ		

Anderson's time was equal 12th fastest, but he was eliminated by the method of seeding employed by the organizers.

Dutch Grand Prix, Zandvoort, 4.6.67

BT19	Brabham	3	2
BT20-2	Hulme	7	3
BT11-5	Anderson	17	9

Belgian Grand Prix, Spa, 18.6.67

Chassis	Driver	Grid	Result	Cause
BT24-1	Brabham	7	rtd	engine
BT19	Hulme	14	rtd	engine
BT11-5	Anderson	17	8	

French Grand Prix, Le Mans, 1.7.67

Chassis	Driver	Grid	Result	Cause
BT24-1	Brabham	2	1	
BT24-2	Hulme	6	2	
BT11-5	Anderson	14	rtd	ignition

British Grand Prix, Silverstone, 15.7.67

Chassis	Driver	Grid	Result	Cause
BT24-1	Brabham	3	4	
BT24-2	Hulme	4	2	
BT20-2	Ligier	21	10	
BT11-5	Anderson	17	rtd	engine

German Grand Prix, Nürburgring, 6.8.67

Chassis	Driver	Grid	Result	Cause
BT24-1	Brabham	7	2	
BT24-2	Hulme	2	1	
BT20-2	Ligier	17	6	

Canadian Grand Prix, Mosport Park, 27.8.67

Chassis	Driver	Grid	Result	Cause
BT24-1	Brabham	7	1	
BT24-2	Hulme	3	2	

Italian Grand Prix, Monza, 10.9.67

Chassis	Driver	Grid	Result	Cause
BT24-1	Brabham	2	2	
BT24-2	Hulme	6	rtd	head gasket
BT20-2	Ligier	18	rtd	dropped valve

International Gold Cup, Oulton Park, 16.9.67

Chassis	Driver	Grid	Result	Cause
BT24-1	Brabham	1	1	
BT18	Gardner	4	rtd	ignition

United States Grand Prix, Watkins Glen, 1.10.67

Chassis	Driver	Grid	Result	Cause
BT24-1	Brabham	5	5	
BT24-2	Hulme	6	3	
BT20-2	Ligier	17	rtd	camshaft

Mexican Grand Prix, Mexico City, 22.10.67

Chassis	Driver	Grid	Result	Cause
BT24-1	Brabham	5	2	
BT24-2	Hulme	6	3	
BT20-2	Ligier	19	11	

Spanish Grand Prix, Jarama, 12.11.67

Chassis	Driver	Grid	Result	Cause
BT19	Brabham	7	3	
BT21-30	Lambert	14	12	
BT23-4	Rees	10	11	
BT21A-8	Lamplough	18	rtd	gearbox

Non-Championship race run in order to qualify for Championship status in 1968.

Drivers' World Championship:
1 Denny Hulme (Brabham)	51
2 Jack Brabham (Brabham)	46 (+2)
3 Jim Clark (Lotus)	41
4 Chris Amon (Ferrari)	20
John Surtees (Honda)	20
6 Graham Hill (Lotus)	15
Pedro Rodriguez (Cooper)	15
15= Bob Anderson (Brabham)	2
18= Guy Ligier (Brabham)	1

Constructors' Cup:
1 Brabham-Repco	63 (+4)
2 Lotus-Cosworth Ford	44
3 Cooper-Maserati	28
4 Ferrari	20
Honda	20
6 BRM	17

Brabham Formula Two victories:
Jochen Rindt	Snetterton*
Jochen Rindt	Silverstone*
Jochen Rindt	Pau
Jochen Rindt	Nürburgring*
Robin Widdows	Hockenheim*
Jochen Rindt	Reims
Jochen Rindt	Rouen
Frank Gardner	Hockenheim
Jochen Rindt	Tulln-Langenlebarn*
Jochen Rindt	Brands Hatch*
Jochen Rindt	Ahvenisto

* Denotes round of the European Championship

European Formula Two Championship:
1 Jacky Ickx	Matra MS7-FVA	41 (+4)
2 Frank Gardner	Brabham BT23-FVA	33
3 Jean-Pierre Beltoise	Matra MS7-FVA	27
4 Piers Courage	McLaren M4A-FVA	24
5 Alan Rees	Brabham BT23-FVA	23
6 Chris Irwin	Lola T100-FVA	15
Johnny Servoz-Gavin	Matra MS5-FVA	15

Graded drivers like Rindt and Stewart competed but were ineligible to score points.

Brabham Tasman Cup victories:
Jack Brabham	Longford

Appendix D

British Formula Two Champion: Jochen Rindt
French Formula Two Champion: Jochen Rindt
The Autocar Formula Two Champion: Alan Rees
British Formula Three Champion: Harry Stiller
Swedish Formula Three Champion: Reine Wisell
Australian Gold Star Champion: Spencer Martin
New Zealand Gold Star Champion: Roly Levis
South African Drivers' Champion: John Love

1968
Denny Hulme left BRO to join McLaren and was replaced in the works team by Jochen Rindt. The Swiss privateer Silvio Moser bought BT20-2.
  In Southern Africa, Scuderia Scribante ran BT11-2 (used by Dan Gurney in 1964-5) fitted with a Repco 620 engine. The main drivers were Tony Jefferies and Dave Charlton. After the South African Grand Prix, BT24-2-Repco – the car mainly used by Hulme in his Championship season – went to Team Gunston for the use of Sam Tingle in what was then Rhodesia, now Zimbabwe. Also in Southern Africa, Team STP bought BT24-1 and it was driven by Basil van Rooyen. It later went to Gordon Henderson.

South African Grand Prix, Kyalami, 1.1.68
BT24-1	Brabham	5	rtd	valve spring
BT24-2	Rindt	4	3	
BT20-1	Love	17	9	
BT11-2	Charlton	14	rtd	crownwheel and pinion
BT11A-5	Pretorious	23	10	not running at the finish

Race of Champions, Brands Hatch, 17.3.68
BT20-2	Moser	11	rtd	oil pressure
BT21-33	Gethin	15	10	not running at the finish

International Trophy, Silverstone, 25.4.68
BT20-2	Moser	13	7	
BT23B-3	Lanfranchi	14	rtd	oil pressure*

*Coventry Climax FPF engine.

Spanish Grand Prix, Jarama, 12.5.68
BT26-1	Brabham	DNS		engine
BT24-3	Rindt	9	rtd	oil pressure

Monaco Grand Prix, Monte Carlo, 26.5.68
BT26-1	Brabham	12	rtd	radius arm
BT24-2	Rindt	5	rtd	crash
BT20-2	Moser	DNQ		

Belgian Grand Prix, Spa, 9.6.68
BT26-1	Brabham	18	rtd	throttle slide
BT26-2	Rindt	17	rtd	valve insert

Dutch Grand Prix, Zandvoort, 23.6.68

BT26-1	Brabham	4	rtd	spin and stall
BT26-2	Rindt	2	rtd	ignition
BT24-3	Gurney	12	rtd	throttle slide
BT20-2	Moser	17	5	

French Grand Prix, Rouen, 7.7.68

BT26-1	Brabham	13	rtd	fuel
BT26-2	Rindt	1	rtd	driver sickness

British Grand Prix, Brands Hatch, 20.7.68

BT26-1	Brabham	8	rtd	engine
BT26-2	Rindt	5	rtd	fire
BT20-2	Moser	19	11	not running at the finish

German Grand Prix, Nürburgring, 4.8.68

BT26-1	Brabham	15	5	
BT26-2	Rindt	3	3	
BT24-3	Ahrens	17	12	

International Gold Cup, Oulton Park, 17.8.68

BT26-1	Brabham	4	rtd	engine
BT26-2	Rindt	9	rtd	engine

Italian Grand Prix, Monza, 8.9.68

BT26-1	Brabham	16	rtd	oil pressure
BT26-2	Rindt	10	rtd	engine
BT20-2	Moser	DNQ		

Canadian Grand Prix, Mont Tremblant, 22.9.68

BT26-1	Brabham	10	rtd	wishbone
BT26-3	Rindt	1	rtd	overheating

United States Grand Prix, Watkins Glen, 6.10.68

BT26-1	Brabham	8	rtd	cam follower
BT26-3	Rindt	6	11	not running at the finish

Mexican Grand Prix, Mexico City, 3.11.68

BT26-1	Brabham	8	10	not running at the finish
BT26-3	Rindt	10	rtd	ignition

Drivers' World Championship:
  1 Graham Hill (Lotus)   48
  2 Jackie Stewart (Matra)   36
  3 Denny Hulme (McLaren)   33
  4 Jacky Ickx (Ferrari)   27
  5 Bruce McLaren (McLaren)   22
  6 Pedro Rodriguez (BRM)   18
 12 Jochen Rindt (Brabham)   6
 22 Jack Brabham (Brabham)   2

Constructors' Cup
1 Lotus-Cosworth Ford	64
2 McLaren-Cosworth Ford	48
3 Matra-Cosworth Ford	47
4 Ferrari	35
5 BRM	28
6 Honda	14
8 *Brabham-Repco*	10

Brabham Formula Two victories:
Jochen Rindt	Thruxton*
Jochen Rindt	Crystal Palace*
Jochen Rindt	Hockenheim
Jonathan Williams	Monza
Jochen Rindt	Tulln-Langeblebarn*
Jochen Rindt	Enna*

* Denotes round of the European Championship

European Formula Two Championship:
1 Jean-Pierre Beltoise	Matra MS7-FVA	48
2 Henri Pescarolo	Matra MS7-FVA	30 (+1)
3 Tino Brambilla	Ferrari Dino 166	26
4 Derek Bell	Ferrari Dino 166	15
5 Jackie Oliver	Lotus 48-FVA	14
6 Kurt Ahrens	Brabham BT23C-FVA	13
Piers Courage	Brabham BT23C-FVA	13
Clay Regazzoni	Tecno 68-FVA	13

British Formula Three Champion:	Tim Schenken
Australian Gold Star Championship	Kevin Bartlett
South African Drivers' Championship:	John Love

1969
The BT26 works cars were retained for Formula One, but were adapted to take Cosworth Ford DFV engines. Jack Brabham missed several races through injury in a testing accident and BT26-2 was written off. Jack's main 1968 car, BT26-1, was bought by Frank Williams for Piers Courage to drive, its conversion to a DFV unit being undertaken by John Thompson under the engineering supervision of Robin Herd. BT24-3 was also bought by Frank Williams for Piers Courage to drive in the Tasman series, in which he finished third. This car, which had undergone a similar engine conversion, was then sold to Silvio Moser.

Repco-powered BT20-1 was sold to J Holme in South Africa, who entered it for Piet de Klerk and Clive Puzey. John Cordts made his only WC appearance in the Canadian Grand Prix in an elderly Brabham fitted with a Coventry Climax FPF engine.

South African Grand Prix, Kyalami, 1.3.69

BT26-2	Brabham	1	rtd	wing breakage
BT26-3	Ickx	13	rtd	wing breakage
BT20-1	de Klerk	17		unclassified
BT24-2	Tingle	18	8	

Race of Champions, Brands Hatch, 16.3.69

BT26-2	Brabham	5	rtd	ignition, fuel leak
BT26-3	Ickx	10	rtd	sticking throttle

International Trophy, Silverstone, 30.3.69

BT26-2	Brabham	2	1
BT26-3	Ickx	4	4

Spanish Grand Prix, Montjuich. 4.5.69

BT26-2	Brabham	5	rtd	con-rod
BT26-3	Ickx	7	6	not running at finish

Monaco Grand Prix, Monte Carlo, 18.5.69

BT26-2	Brabham	8	rtd	accident
BT26-3	Ickx	7	rtd	broken rear upright
BT24-3	Moser	15	rtd	drive-shaft

Dutch Grand Prix, Zandvoort, 21.6.69

BT26-2	Brabham	8	6	
BT26-3	Ickx	4	5	
BT24-3	Moser	14	rtd	steering
BT26-1	Courage	9	rtd	clutch

French Grand Prix, Clermont-Ferrand, 6.7.69

BT26-3	Ickx	4	3	
BT26-1	Courage	11	rtd	loose bodywork
BT20-3	Moser	13	7	

British Grand Prix, Silverstone, 19.7.69

BT26-3	Ickx	4	2
BT26-1	Courage	10	5

German Grand Prix, Nürburgring, 2.8.69

BT26-3	Ickx	1	1	
BT26-1	Courage	7	rtd	accident

International Gold Cup, Oulton Park, 16.9.69

BT26-3	Ickx	2	1	
BT20-2	Moser	7	11	not running at the finish

Italian Grand Prix, Monza, 7.9.69

BT26-4	Brabham	7	rtd	fuel line
BT26-3	Ickx	15	10	not running at finish
BT26-1	Courage	4	5	
BT20-3	Moser	13	rtd	engine

Canadian Grand Prix, Mosport, 20.9.69

BT26-4	Brabham	6	2	
BT26-3	Ickx	1	1	
BT26-1	Courage	10	rtd	oil leak
BT20-3	Moser	20	rtd	accident
BT23B-3	Cordts	19	rtd	oil leak

United States Grand Prix, Watkins Glen, 5.10.69

BT26-4	Brabham	10	4	
BT26-3	Ickx	8	rtd	engine
BT26-1	Courage	9	2	
BT20-3	Moser	19	6	

Mexican Grand Prix, Mexico City, 19.10.69

BT26-4	Brabham	1	3	
BT26-3	Ickx	2	2	
BT26-1	Courage	9	10	
BT20-3	Moser	13	rtd	fuel leak

Drivers' World Championship:
 1 Stewart (Matra)   63
 2 Ickx (Brabham)   37
 3 McLaren (McLaren)   26
 4 Rindt (Lotus)   22
 5 Beltoise (Matra)   21
 6 Hulme (McLaren)   20
 8 Courage (Brabham)   16
10 Brabham (Brabham)   14
16 Moser (Brabham)   1

Constructors' Cup:
 1 Matra-Cosworth Ford   66
 2 Brabham-Cosworth Ford   49 (+2)
 3 Lotus-Cosworth Ford   47
 4 McLaren-Cosworth Ford   38 (+2)
 5 BRM   7
   Ferrari   7

Brabham Formula Two victories:
 Brian Hart   Hockenheim
 Piers Courage   Enna*
 Robin Widdows   Monza
 Robin Widdows   Neubiberg
* Denotes round of European Championship.

European Formula Two Championship:
1 Johnny Servoz-Gavin	Matra MS7-FVA	37
2 Hubert Hahne	BMW	28
3 Francois Cevert	Tecno-FVA	21
4 Henri Pescarolo	Matra MS7-FVA	13
5 Derek Bell	Brabham BT30-FVA	11
Peter Westbury	Brabham BT30-FVA	11

Brabham Tasman Cup victories:
  Piers Courage   Teretonga Park

New Zealand Gold Star Championship: Roly Levis

1970
Rolf Stommelen joined the works team alongside Jack Brabham. BT33-1 was damaged after Stommelen's accident during practice for the British Grand Prix, but was refettled for the first part of the 1971 season. Tom Wheatcroft bought BT26-4 and entered Derek Bell in it. In Southern Africa, Gordon Henderson drove BT24-1, Ivor Robertson drove BT11-2 and Piet de Klerk took over BT26-1.

South African Grand Prix, Kyalami, 7.3.70
BT33-2	Brabham	3	1	
BT33-1	Stommelen	15	rtd	valve spring
BT26-1	de Klerk	21	11	

Race of Champions, Brands Hatch, 22.3.70
BT33-2	Brabham	2	4	
BT26-4	Bell	DNS		accident

Spanish Grand Prix, Jarama, 19.4.70
BT33-2	Brabham	1	rtd	engine seized
BT33-1	Stommelen	17	rtd	broken valve springs

International Trophy, Silverstone, 26.4.70
BT33-2	Brabham	5	rtd	engine

Combined Formula One/Formula 5000 race.

Monaco Grand Prix, Monte Carlo, 10.5.70
BT33-2	Brabham	4	2
BT33-1	Stommelen	DNQ	

Belgian Grand Prix, Spa, 7.6.70
BT33	Brabham	5	rtd	loose clutch ring gear
BT33	Stommelen	7	5	
BT26-1	Bell	15	rtd	gear linkage

Dutch Grand Prix, Zandvoort, 21.6.70
BT33-2	Brabham	12	11
BT33-1	Stommelen	DNQ	

Appendix D

French Grand Prix, Clermont-Ferrand, 5.7.70
BT33-2	Brabham	5	3
BT33-1	Stommelen	14	7

British Grand Prix, Brands Hatch, 18.7.70
BT33-2	Brabham	2	2	
BT33-1	Stommelen	DNS		crash

German Grand Prix, Hockenheim, 2.8.70
BT33-2	Brabham 1	2	rtd	broken oil union
BT33-3	Stommelen	11	5	

Austrian Grand Prix, Österreichring, 16.8.70
BT33-2	Brabham	8	13
BT33-3	Stommelen	17	3

Italian Grand Prix, Monza, 6.9.70
BT33-2	Brabham	8	rtd	accident
BT33-3	Stommelen	17	5	

Canadian Grand Prix, St Jovite, 20.9.70
BT33-2	Brabham	19	rtd	oil leak
BT33-3	Stommelen	18	rtd	damaged steering

United States Grand Prix, Watkins Glen, 4.10.70
BT33-2	Brabham	16	10	
BT33-3	Stommelen	19	12	
BT26-3	Hutchinson	22	rtd	lost fuel tank

Mexican Grand Prix, Mexico City, 25.10.70
BT33-2	Brabham	4	rtd	engine
BT33-3	Stommelen	17	rtd	loss of fuel pressure

Drivers' World Championship:
1 Rindt (Lotus)	45
2 Ickx (Ferrari)	40
3 Regazzoni (Ferrari)	33
4 Hulme (McLaren)	27
5 Brabham (Brabham)	25
Stewart (March & Tyrrell)	25
11 Stommelen (Brabham)	10

Constructors' Cup:
1 Lotus-Cosworth Ford	59
2 Ferrari	52
3 March-Cosworth Ford	48
4 Brabham-Cosworth Ford	35
McLaren-Cosworth Ford	35
6 BRM	23
Matra	23

Brabham Formula Two victories:
Derek Bell   Montjuich*
Jackie Stewart   Crystal Palace
Alan Rollinson   Phoenix Park
* Denotes round of European Championship.

European Formula Two Championship:
1 Clay Regazzoni	Tecno-FVA	44
2 Derek Bell	Brabham BT30-FVA	35
3 Emerson Fittipaldi	Lotus 69-FVA	25
4 Ronnie Peterson	March 702-FVA	14
Dieter Quester	BMW	14
6 Francois Cevert	Brabham BT30-FVA	9
Tetsu Ikuzawa	Lotus 69-FVA	9
Robin Widdows	Brabham BT30-FVA	9

Swedish Formula Three Champion: Palm

1971
Graham Hill was joined in the works Formula One team by Tim Schenken after the first race of the World Championship. Alain de Cadenet bought BT33-2 and usually entered it for Chris Craft. Dave Charlton was entered by the works in the South African Grand Prix, although usually he drove a Lotus 49. Jackie Pretorious campaigned BT26-1 in Southern Africa.

Formula Three regulations changed in 1971; engine capacity rose to 1,600cc and the block and head had to be derived from a production car of which at least 5,000 had been made in a year. The same applied to the gearbox and differential casings, although these could be from a different car. There was a minimum weight of 440kg, minimum wheelbase and track requirements and a limit on tyre width.

South African Grand Prix, Kyalami, 6.3.71
BT33-4	Hill	19	9	
BT33-3	Charlton	12	rtd	broken valve spring
BT26-1	Pretorious	20	rtd	broken camshaft

Race of Champions, Brands Hatch, 21.3.71
BT34	Hill	4	rtd	engine
BT33-1	Schenken	9	4	

United States (West) Grand Prix, Ontario, 28.3.71
BT34	Hill	6	rtd
BT33-1	Schenken	14	5

Combined Formula One/Formula 5000 race.

Spanish Grand Prix, Montjuich, 18.4.71
BT34	Hill	16	rtd	steering damage
BT33-1	Schenken	22	9	

Appendix D

		International Trophy, Silverstone, 8.5.71			
BT34	Hill	7	1	aggregate of two heats	

		Monaco Grand Prix, Monte Carlo, 23.5.71			
BT34	Hill	9	rtd	accident
BT33-1	Schenken	18	10	

		Dutch Grand Prix, Zandvoort, 20.6.71			
BT34	Hill	16	10	
BT33-3	Schenken	19	rtd	accident damage

		French Grand Prix, Le Castellet, 4.7.71			
BT34	Hill	4	rtd	loss of oil
BT33-3	Schenken	14	12	

		British Grand Prix, Silverstone, 17.7.71			
BT34	Hill	16	rtd	start line collision
BT33-3	Schenken	7	12	not running at the finish

		German Grand Prix, Nürburgring, 1.8.71			
BT34	Hill	13	9	
BT33-3	Schenken	9	6	

		Austrian Grand Prix, Österreichring, 15.8.71			
BT34	Hill	8	5	
BT33-3	Schenken	7	3	

		Italian Grand Prix, Monza, 6.9.71			
BT34	Hill	14	11	not running at the finish
BT33-3	Schenken	9	rtd	shock absorber mounting

		Canadian Grand Prix, Mosport, 19.9.71			
BT34	Hill	15	rtd	accident damage
BT33-3	Schenken	17	rtd	ignition
BT33-2	Craft	DNS		engine

		United States Grand Prix, Watkins Glen, 3.10.71			
BT34	Hill	18	7	
BT33-3	Schenken	15	rtd	valve spring
BT33-2	Craft	27	rtd	rear cross-member

Drivers' World Championship:
  1 Stewart (Tyrrell)   62
  2 Peterson (March)   33
  3 Cevert (Tyrrell)   26
  4 Ickx (Ferrari)   19
    Siffert (BRM)   19
  6 Fittipaldi (Lotus)   16
  14= Schenken (Brabham)   5
  21 Hill (Brabham)   2

Constructors' Cup:
1 Tyrrell-Cosworth Ford	73
2 BRM	36
3 Ferrari	33
March-Cosworth Ford	33 (+1)
5 Lotus-Cosworth Ford	21
6 McLaren-Cosworth Ford	10
9 *Brabham-Cosworth Ford*	5

Brabham Formula Two victories:
Alan Rollinson	Bogotá
Graham Hill	Thruxton*
John Watson	Mondello Park
Rolf Stommelen	Mendig
Carlos Reutemann	Hockenheim
Carlos Reutemann	Porto Allegre
Tim Schenken	Cordoba

*Denotes round of European Championship.

European Formula Two Championship:
1 Ronnie Peterson	March 712-FVA	54
2 Carlos Reutemann	Brabham-FVA	40
3 Dieter Quester	March 712-BMW	27
4 Tim Schenken	Brabham-FVA	27
5 Francois Cevert	Tecno-FVA	22
6 Wilson Fittipaldi	March 712-FVA	16

Shell Super Oil (British) Formula Three Championship:
1 David Walker	Lotus 69-Ford	86
2 Roger Williamson	March 713-Ford	56
3 Bev Bond	Ensign LN1-Ford & March 713-Ford	48
4 Colin Vandervell	Brabham BT35-Ford	21
5 Barrie Maskell	Chevron B18-Ford	16
6 Jochen Mass	Brabham BT35-Ford	16

Lombard North Central (British) Formula Three Championship:
1 Roger Williamson	March 713-Ford	90
2 Colin Vandervell,	Brabham BT35-Ford	63
3 Jody Scheckter	EMC 606-Ford & Merlyn Mk 21-Ford	28
4 Alan Jones	Brabham BT28-Ford	21
5 David Purley	Ensign LN2-Ford	20
6 Bernard McInerney	Brabham BT35-Ford	13

New Zealand Gold Star Championship:	Graeme Lawrence
Swedish Formula Three Champion:	Torsten Palm

1972

Ron Tauranac left MRD at the beginning of 1972.

Works cars were fielded for Graham Hill and, variously, Carlos Reutemann and Wilson Fittipaldi. Willie Ferguson drove BT33-1 in Southern Africa where John Love drove BT33-4 for Team Gunston.

Rules governing Formula Two were changed. The upper capacity limit was raised to 2,000cc, but engines had to be derived from production units of which at least 1,000 had been made. Drive had to be through no more than five gears and two wheels. Four-cylinder cars had a minimum weight limit of 450kg, six-cylinder cars had a limit of 475kg and there was a limit of 500kg for cars with more than six cylinders. In practice, however, virtually everyone used an enlarged Ford BDA engine. Those who tried to stretch this iron-block unit to close to the 2-litre limit suffered unreliability and many were content to run the 1,800cc Cosworth version.

Argentine Grand Prix, Buenos Aires, 13.1.72

BT33-3	Hill	16	rtd	puncture, fuel pump
BT34	Reutemann	1	7	

South African Grand Prix, Kyalami, 4.3.72

BT33-3	Hill	14	6	
BT34	Reutemann	15	rtd	broken fuel line
BT33-1	Ferguson	DNS		engine

Brazilian Grand Prix, Interlagos, 30.3.72

BT34	Reutemann	1	1
BT33-3	Fittipaldi, W	3	3

Non-Championship event run prior to inclusion in World Championship in 1973.

Spanish Grand Prix, Jarama, 1.5.72

BT37-1	Hill	23	10
BT33-3	Fittipaldi, W 1	4	7

Monaco Grand Prix, Monte Carlo, 14.5.72

BT37-1	Hill	19	12
BT33-3	Fittipaldi, W	21	9

Belgian Grand Prix, Spa, 4.6.72

BT37-1	Hill	16	rtd	rear upright
BT34	Fittipaldi, W	18	rtd	gearbox
BT37-2	Reutemann	9	13	

French Grand Prix, Clermont-Ferrand, 2.7.72

BT37-1	Hill	20	10
BT34	Fittipaldi, W	14	8
BT37-2	Reutemann	17	12

		British Grand Prix, Brands Hatch, 15.7.72			
BT37-1	Hill	21		rtd	accident
BT34	Fittipaldi, W	22		12	
BT37-2	Reutemann	10		8	

		German Grand Prix, Nürburgring, 30.7.72			
BT37-1	Hill	15		6	
BT34	Fittipaldi, W	12		7	
BT37-2	Reutemann	6		rtd	transmission

		Austrian Grand Prix, Österreichring, 13.8.72			
BT37-1	Hill	14		rtd	fuel metering unit valve
BT34	Fittipaldi, W	15		rtd	fuel metering unit valve
BT37-2	Reutemann	5		rtd	fuel metering unit valve

		Italian Grand Prix, Monza, 10.9.72			
BT37-1	Hill 1	3		5	
BT34	Fittipaldi, W 1	5		rtd	suspension
BT37-2	Reutemann	11		rtd	accident

		Canadian Grand Prix, Ontario, 24.9.72			
BT37-1	Hill	17		8	
BT34	Fittipaldi, W 1	1		rtd	gearbox
BT37-2	Reutemann	9		4	

		United States Grand Prix, Watkins Glen, 8.10.72			
BT37-1	Hill	27		11	
BT34	Fittipaldi, W	13		rtd	engine
BT37-2	Reutemann	5		rtd	engine

Drivers' World Championship:
  1 Emerson Fittipaldi (Lotus)   61
  2 Jackie Stewart (Tyrrell)   45
  3 Denny Hulme (McLaren)   39
  4 Jacky Ickx (Ferrari)   27
  5 Peter Revson (McLaren)   23
  6 Clay Regazzoni (Ferrari)   16
  15 Graham Hill (Brabham)   4
  16= Carlos Reutemann (Brabham)   3

Constructors' Cup:
  1 Lotus-Cosworth Ford   61
  2 Tyrrell-Cosworth Ford   51
  3 McLaren-Cosworth Ford   49
  4 Ferrari   33
  5 Surtees-Cosworth Ford   18
  6 March-Cosworth Ford   15
  9 Brabham-Cosworth Ford   7

Appendix D

Brabham Formula Two victories:
Dave Morgan   Mallory Park*
Jean-Pierre Jaussaud   Hockenheim*
Graham Hill   Monza
Jean-Pierre Jaussaud   Albi*
Tim Schenken   Hockenheim
*Denotes round of European Championship.

European Formula Two Championship:
1 Mike Hailwood   Surtees TS10-FVA   55
2 Jean-Pierre Jaussaud   Brabham BT38-FVA   37
3 Patrick Depailler   March 722-FVA   27
4 Carlos Reutemann   Brabham BT38-FVA   26
5 Niki Lauda   March 722-FVA   24
6 David Morgan   Brabham BT38-FVA
                               & Tui BH2-FVA   23

Shell Super Oil (British) Formula Three Championship:
1 Roger Williamson   March 723 & GRD 372-Ford 78
2 Colin Vandervell   Ensign LNF3-Ford   44
3 Jacques Coloun   Martini 9-Ford   26
4 Mike Walker   Ensign LNF3-Ford   23
5 Rikki von Opel   Ensign LNF3-Ford   21
6 Tony Brise   Brabham BT38
                               & GRD 372-Ford   18

Lombard North Central (British) Formula Three Championship:
1 Rikki von Opel   Ensign LNF3-Ford   61
2 Tony Brise   Brabham BT38
                               & GRD 372-Ford   55
3 Andy Sutcliffe   GRD 373-Ford   53
4 Roger Williamson   March 723 & GRD 372-Ford 30
5 Damian Magee   Palliser WDF3
                               & Brabham BT35-Ford   24
6 Bob Evans   March 723-Ford   21

Forward Trust (British) Formula Three Championship:
1 Roger Williamson   GRD 372-Ford   50
2 Rikki von Opel   Ensign LNF3-Ford   48
3 Mike Walker   Ensign LNF3-Ford   46
4 Tony Brise   Brabham BT38
                               & GRD 372-Ford   18
5 Barrie Maskell   Lotus 69-Ford   13
6 Andy Sutcliffe   GRD 372-Ford   10

Swedish Formula Three Champion: Conny Andersson

APPENDIX E
Freelance Tauranac designs, 1973-78

Trojan
When Trojan ceased building McLaren customer cars it turned to Formula 5000 and employed Ron Tauranac as a consultant. Three single-seater designs resulted.

T101 (Produced 1973.)
This was a reworked McLaren Formula Two design which won Formula 5000 races in Europe and America, Jody Scheckter winning the American series and Keith Holland finishing a strong third in the European Championship.

T102 (Produced 1974.)
For the 1974 Formula 5000 season Ron designed the T102, which bore some similarity to his Brabham BT34 'lobster claw' Formula One car, but the planned season for Keith Holland fell through. Later Brian McGuire drove a T102 for a few races before switching to a Lola.

T103 (Produced 1974.)
This was a low-budget revision of the T102 design, turning it into a thoroughly conventional 'British Formula One Kit Car', with a Cosworth Ford DFV engine and Hewland gearbox installed behind a simple monocoque. The works car was driven by Tim Schenken, but Trojan decided to withdraw from racing before the end of the season.

Theodore
In 1977, Ron Tauranac responded to a request from Teddy Yip, a Macau-based businessman and racing enthusiast, to design a Formula One car for him. Two examples were produced, but Ron had little to do with them after they had been built, being fully engaged by this time in producing Ralts.

TR-1 (Produced 1977.)
This was another conventional 'British Formula One Kit Car', which Yip's driver, Eddie Cheever, tried unsuccessfully to qualify for two Grands Prix early in 1978.

TR-2 (Produced 1978.)
The second chassis was distinguishable from the first by its larger air intake. It was driven by Keke Rosberg, who won the 1978 International Trophy race at Silverstone with it, but subsequently he failed to qualify for four Grands Prix, at which point the car was withdrawn.

APPENDIX F

The later Ralts

RT1 (Produced 1975-9 – 165 made.)
A single aluminium alloy monocoque with rear tubular subframe served for Formula Three, Formula Two and Formula Atlantic, the three categories in which the RT1 initially ran. Additional deformable structures were added when demanded by a category (F2) and the fuel tanks were in side sponsons, right-hand only for F3, both sides for F2. A wider cockpit surround, always part of the original design, was held back until the car proved itself through fear of negative customer reaction. Front suspension was by outboard coil springs and double wishbones, rear suspension by a lower wishbone, a single upper link and twin radius rods. Track narrowed slightly on F3 cars in 1976.

Formula C and *Formule Libre* versions produced in 1977, Formula SuperVee in 1978, and in 1979 designations carried a suffix to identify racing category, eg: RT1/3 – Formula Three; RT1/4 – Formula Atlantic; RT1/5 – Formula SuperVee. In 1978 a Formula Atlantic RT1 was fitted with an enveloping ground-effect body by Tony Cicale and run in the CanAm Challenge, where most competitors used 5-litre engines.

RT2 (Produced 1979-80 – 5 made.)
Ground-effect Formula Two car made exclusively for use by the Toleman team, but very much on the same lines as the RT3/4. Toleman's designer, Rory Byrne, was consulted during the build phase. During the season the team incorporated its own modifications. For 1980 Toleman built its own version of the RT2, using aircraft-grade materials and finished 1-2 in the Formula Two Championship. In 1981 Lola built customer versions, which were sold as Toleman T850s. SPA Fabrications later acquired surplus monocoques and spares from Lola and these became the basis of the successful Rowan hillclimb cars. In 1980, a Hart-powered RT2 was given an enveloping single-seater body and run by Gary Gove in the CanAm Challenge.

RT3 (Produced 1980-4 – 160 made.)
Ground-effect car with aluminium monocoque with honeycomb bulkheads, inboard suspension all round (for the first time on a Tauranac car), a central fuel cell and a Hewland Mk 9 gearbox. In 1979 an RT3 was run unsuccessfully in Britain only by Eliseo Salazar. The car needed development of its aerodynamics. Sliding skirts were made of plastic sheet, for low friction, but at speed the skirts were sucked into the low-pressure area beneath the car, causing them to stick and vary both downforce and centre of pressure.

RT4 (Produced 1980-7 – 134 made.)
Another variation of the RT2/3 for Formula Atlantic which used the Ford BDA engine. Ray Mallock drove both an RT1 and an RT4 to win the British Atlantic series. One RT4 appeared occasionally in Formula Two events. The Championship was won by Toleman, using TG280Bs, a development of the Ralt RT2s the team had run in 1979.

RT5 (Produced 1980-8 – 117 made.)
SuperVee development of the RT2/3/4 series.

RH6 (Produced 1980-4 – 16 made.)
The designation indicates the association with Honda, whose 300bhp V6 Honda Formula Two engine was used as a stressed member. The first RH6 was run by the works late in 1980 with Nigel Mansell, who finished second at Hockenheim. Then he and Geoff Lees formed the two-car works team in 1981, when an engine power increase to 330bhp and a change from Goodyear crossply tyres to Pirelli radials necessitated suspension geometry changes. Pushrod front suspension was adopted for 1982, a revised designation of RH6/82 also identifying a revised aluminium honeycomb monocoque with the cockpit further forward than previously. Further suspension changes accompanied a wider rear track. In 1983 the RH6/83 incorporated further monocoque revisions, a wider front track, a change to Michelin tyres and a power increase to 340bhp with a wider rev-range. The RH6/84 was fitted with a Jabroc wear-resistant floor.

RB20 (Produced 1985 – 3 made.)
For the new 'flat bottom' 3-litre Formula 3000, which replaced Formula Two, Ralt continued the development of the RH6/83. The 'RB' designation of the new car referred to Bridgestone, which sponsored the team.

The major chassis difference was the use of pushrod suspension at the rear with the springs mounted on top of the gearbox, as on the RT30. The use of Cosworth DFV engines, rev-limited to 9,000rpm, meant a power increase of approximately 125bhp over the previous Formula Two engines.

RT20 (Produced 1986 – 8 made.)
Reverting to the traditional RT designation for the 1986 Formula 3000 car, Ralt also abandoned the honeycomb monocoque and returned to sheet aluminium with honeycomb bracing. There was also a new pushrod front suspension layout with the springs mounted horizontally above the driver's legs.

Works cars used a new Honda V8 engine, which was actually designed by John Judd and Neil Walker at Engine Developments. This was lighter than the Cosworth DFV, and the Hewland FT200 gearbox was lighter than the FGB transmission used in 1985. The car being under the weight limit, it could be ballasted to best effect. Customer cars used DFV engines.

RT21 (Produced 1987 – 7 made.)
Developed from the RT20, the monocoque was stiffened not only by more honeycomb, but by the judicious use of carbonfibre. There was new pushrod front suspension but the previous pushrod rear layout was retained. The works continued to use Judd/Honda engines whereas customers used Cosworth DFVs.

Appendix F

RT22 (Produced 1988 – 8 made.)
This combined an all-new carbonfibre monocoque with the proven suspension of the RT21. In testing, however, severe traction problems were experienced and the designated works drivers took their sponsorship elsewhere. Only a sixth and a fourth place were achieved before the works Ralts were withdrawn from the Formula 3000 season prior to the company being acquired by March Group plc in October 1988.

RT23 (Produced 1991 – 12 made.)
Formula 3000 car.

RT24 (Produced 1992 – 2 made.)
Simtek update of RT23.

RT30 (Produced 1985-6 – 104 made.)
New 'flat bottom' regulations and new rules concerning width demanded a new car for 1985. The monocoque RT30 was along the lines of the RT3, aluminium with a honeycomb front bulkhead and a tubular frame to support the engine, but the suspension was pushrod all round with the rear springs on top of the gearbox. In 1986 the springs were relocated vertically on each side of the gearbox.

The car's most surprising feature was its asymmetrical body, incorporating just a water radiator on the left-hand side, with a mandatory low-down side protection panel jutting out from the right-hand side. Glenn Waters' company, Intersport, offered a body kit to convert existing RT3s to comply with the new rules – 48 kits were sold.

RT31 (Produced 1987 – 43 made.)
Developed from the RT30 with a greater use of honeycomb, making the monocoque stiffer, and repositioned front spring units allowing a slimmer profile than before.

RT32 (Produced 1988 – 39 made.)
Engines were mounted 20mm lower and Hewland produced a new magnesium gearbox casing. The monocoque was new, with a honeycomb lower half riveted to a carbonfibre top. There was pushrod suspension all round.

RT33 (Produced 1989 – 37 made.)
Successor to the RT32 offering a cleaner body shape and detail revisions to the aerodynamics including new profiles for the sidepods.

RT34 (Produced 1990 – 81 made.)
Formula Three car.

RT35 (Produced 1991 – 56 made.)
Final expression of the line which began with the RT32 and Ron Tauranac's last Formula Three car for Ralt.

RT36 (Produced 1992 – 30 made.)
Formula Three car designed by Andy Thorby.

RT37 (Produced 1993 – 4 made.)
Formula Three car.

RT40 (Produced 1992-3 – 20 made.)
Tauranac-designed Formula Atlantic car.

RT41 (Produced 1994-8 – 32 made*.)
Formula Atlantic car.

* Provisional figure

This indicates a total of 1,083 Ralt cars, of which Ron Tauranac takes credit for 1,047.

Appendix F

RALT by model	1975	1976	1977	1978	1979	1980	1981	1982	1983	1984	1985	1986	1987	1988	1989	1990	1991	1992	1993	Total
RT1	10	28	51	55	21															165
RT2				4	1															5
RT3						10	26	25	52	47										160
RT4						6	37	38	10	2	14	15	12							134
RT5						13	13	15	18	19	17	6	13	3						117
RH6						3	3	4	3	3										16
RB20											3									3
RT20												8								8
RT21													7							7
RT22														8						8
RT23																	12			12
RT24																		2		2
RT30											55	49								104
RT31													43							43
RT32															39					39
RT33																37				37
RT34																	81			81
RT35																		56		56
RT36																		30		30
RT37																			4	4
RT40																		3	17	20
Total	10	28	51	55	25	33	79	82	83	71	89	78	75	50	37	81	68	35	21	1051

RALT by category	1975	1976	1977	1978	1979	1980	1981	1982	1983	1984	1985	1986	1987	1988	1989	1990	1991	1992	1993	Total
F3	4	20	30	22	6	10	26	25	52	47	55	49	43	39	37	81	56	30	4	636
F2	3	2	9	3	4	3	3	4	3	3										37
Atlantic	3	6	8	16	9	6	37	38	10	2	14	15	12					3	17	196
FC			1																	1
F Libre			3																	3
Super Vee				14	6	13	13	15	18	19	17	6	13	3						137
F300											3	8	7	8				12	2	40
CanAm					1															1
Total	10	28	51	55	25	33	79	82	83	71	89	78	75	50	37	81	68	35	21	1051

APPENDIX G

MRD/Ralt racing record, 1975-97

1975
BP (British) Formula Three Championship:
1 Gunnar Nilsson	March 753-Toyota	74
2 Alex Ribeiro	March 753-Toyota	59
3 Danny Sullivan	Modus M1-Toyota	59
4 Patrick Neve	Safir RJ-Ford	50
5 Larry Perkins	Ralt RT1-Ford	40
6 Ingo Hoffman	March 753-Toyota	34

European Formula Three Champion: Larry Perkins

1976
Ralt Formula Two victories:
Freddy Kottulinsky   Nürburgring

Shellsport (British) Formula Three Championship:
1 Bruno Giacomelli	March 763-Toyota	79
2 Rupert Keegan	March 743-Toyota & Chevron B34-Toyota	62
3 Geoff Lees	Chevron B34-Toyota	42
4 Mike Young	Modus M1-Toyota	36
5 Ian Flux	Ralt RT1-Toyota	29
6 Stephen South	March 763-Toyota	21

BP (British) Formula Three Championship:
1 Rupert Keegan	March 743-Toyota & Chevron B34-Toyota	74
2 Bruno Giacomelli	March 763-Toyota	71
3 Geoff Lees	Chevron B34-Toyota	31
4 Stephen South	March 763-Toyota	27
5 Mike Young	Modus M1-Toyota	21
6 Tiff Needell	Safir RJ03-Toyota	11

Appendix G

European Formula Three Championship:
1 Riccardo Patrese	Chevron B34-Toyota	52 (56)
2 Conny Andersson	March 763-Toyota	52 (54)
3 Bruno Giacomelli	March 763-Toyota	36
4 Marc Surer	March 763 & Chevron B34-BMW	13
5 Bertrand Shäfer	Ralt RT1-BMW	12
6 Piercarlo Ghinzani	March 763-Toyota	11

German Formula Three Champion: Bertram Schäfer

1977
Ralt Formula Two victories:
Eddie Cheever — Rouen

European Formula Two Championship:
1 René Arnoux	Martini Mk22-Renault	52
2 Eddie Cheever	Ralt RT1-BMW	40
3 Didier Pironi	Martini Mk22-Renault	38
4 Bruno Giacomelli	March 772-BMW	32
Riccardo Patrese	Chevron B35-BMW	32
6 Keijo Rosberg	Chevron B40-Hart	25

BP (British) Formula Three Championship:
1 Derek Daly	Chevron B38-Toyota	69
2 Stephen South	March 773-Toyota	56
Eje Elgh	Chevron B38-Toyota	56
4 Geoff Lees	Chevron B38-Toyota	41
5 Derek Warwick	Ralt RT1-Toyota	40
6 James King	March 773-Toyota	22

Vandervell (British) Formula Three Championship:
1 Stephen South	March 773—Toyota	75
2 Brett Riley	March 773-Toyota	58
3 Derek Warwick	Ralt RT1-Toyota	41
4 Geoff Brabham	Ralt RT1-Toyota	36
5 Eje Elgh	Chevron B38-Toyota	34
Derek Daly	Chevron B38-Toyota	34

The Vandervell Championship was run over fewer rounds than the BP series and had a different points system (20-15-12-10-8-6 plus points for pole and fastest lap). The BP Championship was regarded as the more important and its points system was: 8-6-4-3-2-1 plus points for pole and fastest lap.

European Formula Three Championship:
1 Piercarlo Ghinzani	March 773-Toyota	58 (+3)
2 Anders Olofsson	Ralt RT1-Toyota	46
3 Nelson Piquet	March 773 & Ralt RT1-Toyota	33
4 Beppe Gabbiani	Chevron B38-Toyota	26
5 Oscar Pedersoli	Ralt RT1-Toyota	24
6 Piero Necchi	Ralt RT1-Toyota	22

Italian Formula Three Champion: Elio de Angelis
Swedish Formula Three Champion: Anders Olofsson

1978
BP (British) Formula Three Championship:
1 Nelson Piquet	Ralt RT1-Toyota	101
2 Derek Warwick	Ralt RT1-Toyota	72
3 Chico Serra	March 783-Toyota	72
4 Philip Bullman	March 783-Toyota	22
5 Tiff Needell	March 783-Toytoa	22
6 Rob Wilson	Ralt RT1-Toyota	20

Vandervell (British) Formula Three Championship:
1 Derek Warwick	Ralt RT1-Toyota	162 (164)
2 Nelson Piquet	Ralt RT1-Toyota	124
3 Chico Serra	March 783-Toyota	78
4 Rob Wilson	Ralt RT1-Toyota	49
5 Brett Riley	March 783-Triumph	30
6 John Bright	March 783-Toyota	24
Tiff Needell	March 783-Triumph	24

European Formula Three Championship:
1 Jan Lammers	Ralt RT1-Toyota	71 (+1)
2 Anders Olofsson	Ralt RT1-Toyota	71
3 Patrick Gaillard	Chevron B43-Toyota	49
4 Teo Fabi	March 783-Toyota	45
5 Michael Bleekemolen	Chevron B43-Toyota	30
6 David Kennedy	Argo JM1-Toyota	24
Derek Warwick	Ralt RT1-Toyota	13

Lammers and Olofsson each scored 71 points from their best 12 results and each had four wins. The Championship was decided on second places, Lammers having five to the three of Olofsson.

German Formula Three Champion: Bertram Schäfer
Swedish Formula Three Champion: Anders Olofsson

1979
Ralt Formula Two victories:
Brian Henton Mugello
Brian Henton Misano

European Formula Two Championship:
1 Marc Surer	March 792-BMW	38
2 Brian Henton	Ralt RT2-Hart	36
3 Derek Daly	March 792-BMW	33
4 Eddie Cheever	Osella-BMW	32
5 Rad Dougall	March 792-Hart	19
Beppe Gabbiani	March 792-BMW	19
Stephen South	March 792-BMW	19

Appendix G

Vandervell (British) Formula Three Championship:
1 Chico Serra	March 793-Toyota	103
2 Andrea de Cesaris	March 793-Toyota	90
3 Mike Thackwell	March 793-Toyota	71
4 Stefan Johansson	March 793-Toyota	54
5 Brett Riley	March 793-Triumph	40
6 Kenny Acheson	March 793-Toyota	35

European Formula Three Championship:
1 Alain Prost	Martini Mk27-Renault	67
2 Michael Bleekemolen	Ralt RT1 & March 793-Toyota	28
3 Slim Borgudd	Ralt RT1-Toyota	23
4 Mauro Baldi	March 793-Toyota	22
5 Richard Dallest	Martini Mk 27-Toyota	21
6 Michele Alboreto	March 793-Toyota	21

All-Japan Formula Three Champion:	Toshio Suzuki
Swedish Formula Three Champion:	Slim Borgudd
British Formula Atlantic Champion:	Ray Mallock
North American SuperVee Champion:	Geoff Brabham
North American Atlantic Champion:	Tom Gloy

1980
Vandervell (British) Formula Three Championship:
1 Stefan Johansson	March 803 & Ralt RT3-Toyota	97
2 Kenny Acheson	March 803-Toyota	95
3 Roberto Guerrero	Argo JM6-Toyota	95
4 Thierry Tassin	Argo JM6-Toyota	40
5 Rob Wilson	Ralt RT3-Toyota	40
6 Mike White	March 803-Toyota	37

German Formula Three Champion:	Frank Jelinski
Swedish Formula Three Champion:	Thorbjorn Carlsson
British Formula Atlantic Champion:	David Leslie
North American SuperVee Champion:	Peter Kuhn
Pacific Formula Atlantic Champion:	Dave McMillan

1981
Ralt Formula Two victories:
Mike Thackwell	Silverstone
Geoff Lees	Pau
Geoff Lees	Spa
Geoff Lees	Donington

European Formula Two Championship:
1 Geoff Lees	Ralt RH6-Honda	51
2 Thierry Boutsen	March 812-BMW	37
3 Eje Elgh	Maurer MM81-BMW	35
4 Stefan Johansson	Toleman T850-Hart	30
5 Corrado Fabi	March 812-BMW	29
6 Mike Thackwell	Ralt RH6-Honda	22

Marlboro (British) Formula Three Championship:
1 Jonathan Palmer   Ralt RT3-Toyota   105
2 Thierry Tassin   Ralt RT3-Toyota   92
3 Raul Boesel   Ralt RT3-Toyota   81
4 Mike White   March 813-Alfa Romeo   38
5 David Leslie   Ralt RT3-Toyota   29
6 Dave Scott   Ralt RT3-Toyota   29

European Formula Three Championship:
1 Mauro Baldi   March-Alfa Romeo   94
2 Alain Ferté   Martini-Alfa Romeo   63
3 Philippe Alliot   Martini-Alfa Romeo   41
4 Philippe Streiff   Martini-Alfa Romeo   36
5 Oscar Larrauri   March-Toyota   32
6 Emanuele Pirro   Martini-Toyota   19

German Formula Three Champion: Frank Jelinski
British Formula Atlantic Champion: Ray Mallock
Australian Formula Atlantic Champion: Bruce Allison
Pacific Formula Atlantic Champion: Dave Oxton
European SuperVee Champion: John Nielsen

1982
European Formula Two Championship:
1 Corrado Fabi   March 822-BMW   57
2 Johnny Cecotto   March 822—BMW   56 (+1)
3 Thierry Boutsen   Spirit 201-Honda   50 (+1)
4 Stefan Bellof   Maurer MM82-BMW   33
5 Beppe Gabbiani   Maurer MM82-BMW   26
6 Philippe Streiff   AGS JH19-BMW   22
7 Kenny Acheson   Ralt RH6-Honda   12
9 Jonathan Palmer   Ralt RH6-Honda   10

Marlboro (British) Formula Three Championship:
1 Tommy Byrne   Ralt RT3-Toyota   101
2 Enrique Mansilla   Ralt RT3-Toyota   98 (+1)
3 Dave Scott   Ralt RT3-Toyota   74
4 Martin Brundle   Ralt RT3-VW   60
5 James Weaver   Ralt RT3-Toyota   53
6 Roberto Moreno   Ralt RT3-Toyota   42

European Formula Three Championship:
1 Oscar Larrauri   Euroracing 101-Alfa Romeo   91
2 Emanuele Pirro   Euroracing 101-Alfa Romeo   62
3 Alain Ferté   Martini Mk37-Alfa Romeo   42
4 James Weaver   Ralt RT3-Toyota   33
5 Didier Theys   Martini Mk37-Alfa Romeo   30
6 Philippe Alliot   Martini Mk37-Alfa Romeo   25

Appendix G

All-Japan Formula Three Champion: Kengo Nakamoto
French Formula Three Champion: Pierre Petit
German Formula Three Champion: John Nielsen
Italian Formula Three Champion: Enzo Coloni
Swedish Formula Three Champion: Torbjorn Carlsson
British Formula Atlantic Champion: Alo Lawler
Pacific Formula Atlantic Champion: Roberto Moreno
North American Atlantic Champion: Dave McMillen
North American SuperVee Champion: Michael Andretti

1983
Ralt Formula Two victories:
Jonathan Palmer	Hockenheim
Mike Thackwell	Jarama
Jonathan Palmer	Donington
Jonathan Palmer	Misano
Jonathan Palmer	Enna
Jonathan Palmer	Zolder
Jonathan Palmer	Mugello

European Formula Two Championship:
1 Jonathan Palmer	Ralt RH6-Honda	68 (+7)
2 Mike Thackwell	Ralt RH6-Honda	51
3 Beppe Gabbiani	March 832-BMW	39
4 Phillipe Streiff	AGS JH19B-BMW	25
5 Christian Danner	March 832-BMW	21
6 Jo Gartner	Spirit 201-BMW	14

Marlboro (British) Formula Three Championship:
1 Ayrton Senna	Ralt RT3-Toyota	132
2 Martin Brundle	Ralt RT3-Toyota	123 (+4)
3 Davy Jones	Ralt RT3-VW	77
4 Calvin Fish	Ralt RT3-VW	67
5 Allen Berg	Ralt RT3-Toyota	32
6 Mario Hytten	Ralt RT3-Toyota & Sparton SE420-VW	23

European Formula Three Championship:
1 Pierluigi Martini	Ralt RT3-Alfa Romeo	66
2 John Nielsen	Ralt RT3-VW	62
3 Emanuele Pirro	Ralt RT3-Alfa Romeo	52
4 Tommy Byrne	Ralt RT3-Toyota	35
5 Roberto Ravaglia	Ralt RT3-Toyota	32
6 Didier Theys	Ralt RT3-Alfa Romeo	25

All-Japan Formula Three Champion: Yoshimasa Fujiwara
Italian Formula Three Champion: Ivan Capelli
Swedish Formula Three Champion: Leo Anderson
British Formula Atlantic Champion: Alo Lawler
North American Atlantic Champion: Michael Andretti

North American SuperVee Champion: Ed Pimm
(who also won races in an Anson)
Pacific Formula Atlantic Champion: Allen Berg

1984

1984 saw the last year of the European Formula Three Championship which had begun in 1975. A total of 130 races were run and Ralts won 50 of them, more than any other marque.

Ralt Formula Two victories:

Mike Thackwell	Silverstone
Roberto Moreno	Hockenheim
Mike Thackwell	Thruxton
Mike Thackwell	Vallelunga
Mike Thackwell	Mugello
Mike Thackwell	Pau
Mike Thackwell	Misano
Mike Thackwell	Enna
Roberto Moreno	Donington

European Formula Two Championship:

1 Mike Thackwell	Ralt RH6-Honda	72
2 Roberto Moreno	Ralt RH6-Honda	44
3 Michel Ferté	Martini 002-BMW	29
4 Phillipe Streiff	AGS JH19C-BMW	27
5 Christian Danner	March 842-BMW	23
6 Thierry Tassin	March 842-BMW	18
Emanuele Pirro	March 842-BMW	18

Marlboro (British) Formula Three Championship:

1 Johnny Dumfries	Ralt RT3-VW	106
2 Allen Berg	Ralt RT3-Toyota	67
3 Russell Spence	Ralt RT3-VW	64
4 Mario Hytten	Ralt RT3-VW	45
5 Ross Cheever	Ralt RT3-VW	39
6 Carlos Abella	Ralt RT3-Toyota	26

Class B (year-old cars): Keith Fine

European Formula Three Championship:

1 Ivan Capelli	Martini Mk42-Alfa Romeo	60
2 Johnny Dumfries	Ralt RT3-VW	54
3 Gerhard Berger	Ralt RT3-Alfa Romeo	49
4 Claudio Langes	Ralt RT3-Toyota	36
5 John Nielsen	Ralt RT3-VW	35
6 Tommy Byrne	Anson SA4B-VW	14

Appendix G

German Formula Three Champion: Kurt Thiim
Italian Formula Three Champion: Alessandro Santin
Swedish Formula Three Champion: Leif Lindstrom
North American SuperVee Champion: Arie Luyendyk
Pacific Formula Atlantic Champion: Ken Smith
North American Formula Atlantic Champion: Dan Marvin

1985
Ralt Formula 3000 victories:
Mike Thackwell   Silverstone
John Nielsen   Estoril
Mike Thackwell   Spa
Mike Thackwell   Enna
John Nielsen   Curacao (non-Championship).

European Formula 3000 Championship:
1 Christian Danner   March 85B-Cosworth   51 (+1)
2 Mike Thackwell   Ralt RT20-Cosworth   45
3 Emanuele Pirro   March 85B-Cosworth   38
4 John Nielsen   Ralt RT20-Cosworth   34
5 Michel Ferté   March 85B-Cosworth   17
6 Gabriele Tarquini   March 85B-Cosworth   14

Marlboro (British) Formula Three Championship:
1 Mauricio Gugelmin   Ralt RT30-VW   84 (+2)
2 Andy Wallace   Reynard 853-VW   76
3 Russell Spence   Reynard 853-VW   64
4 Dave Scott   Ralt RT30-VW   52
5 Gerrit van Kouwen   Ralt RT30-VW   46
6 Tim Davies   Reynard 853-VW   39
Class B: Carlton Tingling

All-Japan Formula Three Champion: Kouji Sato
North American SuperVee Champion: Ken Johnson
Pacific Formula Atlantic Champion: Ross Cheever
North American Atlantic (Eastern) Champion: Michael Angus
North American Atlantic (Western) Champion: Jeff Wood

1986
Ralt Formula 3000 victories:
Mike Thackwell   Pau
Pierluigi Martini   Imola
Pierluigi Martini   Mugello
Luis Sala   Enna
Luis Sala   Birmingham

FIA Formula 3000 International Championship:
1 Ivan Capelli	March 86B-Cosworth	39
2 Emanuele Pirro	March 86B-Cosworth	32
3 Pierluigi Martini	Ralt RT20-Cosworth	27
4 Michel Ferté	March 86B-Cosworth	26
5 Luis Sala	Ralt RT20-Cosworth	24.5
6 John Nielsen	Ralt RT20-Honda	18
8 Mike Thackwell	Ralt RT20-Honda	10.5
10 Satoru Nakajima	Ralt RT20-Honda	7

Lucas (British) Formula Three Championship:
1 Andy Wallace	Reynard 863-VW	121
2 Maurizio Sandro Sala	Ralt RT30/86-VW	83
3 Martin Donnelly	Ralt RT30/86-VW	59
4 Gerrit van Kouwen	Ralt RT30/86-VW	24
5 Gary Brabham	Ralt RT30/86-VW	22
6 Julian Bailey	Ralt RT30/86-VW	21

Class B: Steve Kempton

All-Japan Formula Three Champion:	Akio Morimoto
German Formula Three Champion:	Kris Nissen
North American SuperVee Champion:	Steve Bren
Pacific Atlantic Champion:	Jeff MacPherson
South African Drivers' Championship:	Wayne Taylor
North American Atlantic (Eastern) Champion:	Scott Goodyear
North American Atlantic (Western) Champion:	Ted Prappas

1987
Ralt Formula 3000 victories:
Mauricio Gugelmin	Silverstone
Luis Perez Sala	Donington
Roberto Moreno	Enna
Luis Perez Sala	Le Mans

FIA Formula 3000 International Championship:
1 Stefano Modena	March 87B-Cosworth	40 (41)
2 Luis Perez Sala	Ralt RT21-Cosworth	33
3 Robert Moreno	Ralt RT21-Honda	30
4 Mauricio Gugelmin	Ralt RT21-Honda	29
5 Yannick Dalmas	March 87B-Cosworth	20
6 Michel Trollé	Lola T87/50-Cosworth	16.5

Lucas (British) Formula Three Championship:
1 Johnny Herbert	Reynard 873-VW	79
2 Betrand Gachot	Ralt RT31-Alfa Romeo	64
3 Martin Donnelly	Ralt RT31-Toyota	61
4 Thomas Danielsson	Reynard 873-Alfa Romeo	56
5 Damon Hill	Ralt RT31-Toyota	49
6 Gary Brabham	Ralt RT31-VW	37

Appendix G

EFDA Euroseries Championship:
1 Dave Coyne	Reynard 873-VW	67
2 Victor Rosso	Ralt RT31-VW	41
3 Johnny Herbert	Reynard 873-VW	40
4 Peter Zakowski	Ralt RT31-VW	36
5 Roland Ratzenberger	Ralt RT31-VW	35
6 Betrand Gachot	Ralt RT31-Alfa Romeo	30

Swedish Formula Three Champion: Mikael Johansson
Pacific Formula Atlantic Champion: Mike Thackwell
North American Atlantic (Eastern) Champion: Calvin Fish
North American Atlantic (Western) Champion: Johnny O'Connell
North American SuperVee Champion: Scott Atchison

1988
Lucas (British) Formula Three Championship:
1 JJ Lehto	Reynard 883-Toyota	113
2 Gary Brabham	Ralt RT32-VW	81
3 Damon Hill	Ralt RT32-Toyota	57
4 Martin Donnelly	Ralt RT31-Toyota	54
5 Eddie Irvine	Ralt RT32-Afa Romeo	53
6 Ross Hockenhull	Ralt RT32-VW	22

All-Japan Formula Three Champion: Akihiko Nakaya
Swedish Formula Three Champion: Mikael Johansson
Pacific Formula Atlantic Champion: Paul Radisich
North American SuperVee Champion: Ken Murillo

1989
Lucas (British) Formula Three Championship:
1 David Brabham	Ralt RT33-VW	80
2 Allan McNish	Ralt RT33-Mugen	70
3 Derek Higgins	Ralt RT33-Mugen	46
4 Rickard Rydell	Reynard 893-VW	35
5 Steve Robertson	Ralt RT33-VW	27
6 Philippe Adams	Ralt RT33-VW	23

All-Japan Formula Three Champion: Masahiko Kageyama
German Formula Three Champion: Karl Wendlinger
North American SuperVee Champion: Mark Smith

1990
British Formula Three Championship:
1 Mika Hakkinen	Ralt RT34-Mugen	121 (+5)
2 Miko Salo	Ralt RT34-Mugen	98 (+1)
3 Steve Robertson	Ralt RT33-VW	49
4 Christian Fittipaldi	Ralt RT34-Mugen	36
5 Peter Kox	Ralt RT33-VW	28
6 Phillipe Adams	Ralt RT33-VW	25

French Formula Three Championship:
1	Eric Hélary	Reynard 903-Mugen	101
2	Ludovic Faure	Dallara 390-VW	90
3	Olivier Beretta	Dallara 390-Alfa Romeo	76
4	Olivier Panis	Dallara 390-Alfa Romeo	70
5	Laurent Aïello	Ralt RT33-VW	68
6	Yvan Muller	Dallara 390-Alfa Romeo	65

German Formula Three Championship:
1	Michael Schumacher	Reynard 903-VW	148
2	Otto Rensing	Ralt RT34-VW	117
3	Wolfgang Kaufmann	Reynard 903-Opel	81
4	Klaus Panchyrz	Reynard 903-VW	73
5	Jörg Muller	Reynard 903-VW	65
6	Peter Zakowski	Reynard 903-VW	61

Italian Formula Three Championship:
1	Roberto Colciago	Reynard 903-Alfa Romeo	38
2	Alessandro Zanardi	Dallara 390-Alfa Romeo	25
3	Massimiliano Agnelelli	Dallara 390-Alfa Romeo	30
4	Mirko Savoldi	Dallara 390-Alfa Romeo	24
5	Andrea Gilardi	Dallara 390-Alfa Romeo	20
6	Giuseppe Bugatti	Reynard 903-Alfa Romeo	17
	Fabrizio Bettini	Reynard 903-Mugen	17

Swedish Formula Three Championship:
1	Niclas Jönsson	Reynard 903-Mugen	100
2	Fredrik Ekblom	Reynard 903-VW	80
3	Linus Lundberg	Reynard 903-Mugen	49
4	Micke Gustavson	Reynard 903-Mugen	47
5	Thomas Johansson	Ralt RT34-Alfa Romeo	42
6	Svend Hansen	Reynard 883-VW	32

All-Japan Formula Three Champion:	Naoki Hattori
Brazilian Formula Three Champion:	Osvaldo Negri
North American SuperVee Champion:	Stuart Crow

1991
Ralt Formula 3000 victories:
Jean-Marc Gounon   Pau

FIA International Formula 3000 Championship:
1	Christian Fittipaldi	Reynard 91D-Mugen	47
2	Alessandro Zanardi	Reynard 91D-Mugen	42
3	Emanuele Naspetti	Reynard 91D-Cosworth	37
4	Antonio Tamburini	Reynard 91D-Mugen	22
5	Marco Apicello	Lola T91/50-Mugen	18
6	Jean-Marc Gounon	Ralt RT23-Cosworth	13

Appendix G

British Formula Three Championship:
1 Rubens Barrichello	Ralt RT35-Mugen	74
2 David Coulthard	Ralt RT35-Mugen	66
3 Gil de Ferran	Reynard 913-Mugen	54
4 Jordi Gene	Ralt RT35-Mugen	50
5 Marcel Albers	Ralt RT35-Mugen	43
6 Rickard Rydell	TOM'S 031F-Toyota	41

French Formula Three Championship:
1 Christophe Bouchet	Ralt RT33-VW	120
2 Olivier Panis	Ralt RT35-Alfa Romeo	103
3 Eric Chéli	Reynard 913-Alfa Romeo	89
4 Franck Lagorce	Dallara 191-Opel	81
5 Ludovic Faure	Ralt RT35-VW	65
6 'Jules' Boullion	Bowman BC1-VW	59

German Formula Three Championship:
1 Tom Kristensen	Ralt RT35-VW	136
2 Marco Werner	Ralt RT35-Opel	101
3 Marc Hessel	Ralt RT35-Mugen	93
4 Jörg Müller	Reynard 913-VW	85
5 Frank Krämer	Reynard 913-Opel	83
6 Klaus Panchyrz	Ralt RT35-VW	68

Italian Formula Three Championship:
1 Giambattista Busi	Dallara 391-VW	44
2 Domenico Schiattarella	Ralt RT35-Alfa Romeo	38
3 Andrea Giardi	Dallara 391-VW	36
4 Luca Badoer	Dallara 391-Alfa Romeo	34
5 Mirko Savoldi	Dallara 391-Alfa Romeo	22
6 Jacques Villeneuve	Ralt RT35-Alfa Romeo	20

Sud-Am Formula Three Champion:	Alfonso Giaffone Neto
Brazilian Formula Three Champion:	Marco Gueiros

1992
British Formula Three Championship:
1 Gil de Ferran	Reynard 923-Mugen	102 (+7)
2 Philippe Adams	Ralt RT36-Mugen	56
3 Kelvin Burt	Reynard 923-Mugen	55
4 Oswaldi Negri	Reynard 923-Mugen	43
5 Mikke van Hool	Reynard 923-Mugen	29
6 Marc Goossens	Reynard 923-Mugen	28

Sud-Am Formula Three Champion:	Marco Gueiros
Brazilian Formula Three Champion:	Marco Gueiros
All-Japan Formula Three Champion:	Anthony Reid
Swedish Formula Three Champion:	Peter Aslund

Ralts won single races in the French and Italian Championships and won 14 of the 26 rounds of the German Championship.

1993
Sud-Am Formula Three Champion: Fernando Croceri
Brazilian Formula Three Champion: Fernando Croceri
Swedish Formula Three Champion: Magnus Wallinder
North American Atlantic Champion: David Empringham

1994 North American Atlantic Champion: David Empringham

1995 North American Atlantic Champion: Richard Hearn

1996 North American Atlantic Champion: Patrick Carpentier

1997 North American Atlantic Champion: Alex Barron

APPENDIX H

The post-Ralt Tauranac cars

Honda School Car
Commissioned by Honda for the Suzuka Racing School, in which Honda has a close interest, this was built along Formula Three car lines, but featured aluminium honeycomb construction for ease of manufacture and repair, and shorter sidepods than those required in Formula Three in order to reduce pitch-sensitivity.

It had a tuned 1.6-litre Honda Civic engine and a transverse gearbox designed by Yanagawa, a company set up by ex-Honda personnel. Location of the transmission ahead of the rear axle line was another departure from Formula Three requirements.

The cars were built at Honda's facility at Langley, Bucks., from components supplied by sub-contractors. Three prototypes were assessed by Honda and a batch of 12 production cars was completed by 1995. Four more were ordered at the end of 1996 and were delivered early in 1997.

Ronta
The Ronta FR1 of 1995 was a Formula Renault car designed in conjunction with Dave Wynne, more or less on a whim. It was supposed to be taken over by an outfit which would manufacture copies and run a team of cars, but the deal fell through and the car was returned to Ron Tauranac. It was later being offered under the Hawke name.

CPSIA information can be obtained
at www.ICGtesting.com
Printed in the USA
BVHW090115141120
593070BV00005B/276